LATIN
MADE SIMPLE

Revised Edition

BY
DOUG JULIUS

Made
Simple
BOOKS

A Made Simple Book
Broadway Books
New York

Produced by The Stonesong Press, LLC

LATIN MADE SIMPLE. Copyright © 1992, 2001, 2006 by Broadway Books, a division of Random House, Inc.

For information, address Broadway Books, a division of Random House, Inc.,

1745 Broadway, New York, NY 10019.

Printed in the United States of America.

Produced by The Stonesong Press, LLC

Typesetting: Publications Development Company

Visit our website at www.broadwaybooks.com

First Broadway Books trade paperback edition published 2006.

The Library of Congress Cataloging-in-Publication Data:

CIP data is on file with the Library of Congress

ISBN 0-7679-1861-4

CONTENTS

PREFACE
About This Book

Although a "classical" language, Latin is far from dead—linguists use that term merely to define a language that has no native speakers. Latin is very much vital and living. It is a pillar of our own language, our culture, and our civilization. Latin is a thread that connects us with our own history; if it were to snap, we would lose our relationship to the past.

Fortunately, more and more people are discovering the importance and rewards of learning Latin. We are witnessing a major revival—one that seems likely to continue. As Latin is no longer a spoken language, today's students are interested primarily in being able to *read* Latin, for pleasure and profit, with reasonable facility and comprehension. *Latin Made Simple* was conceived, organized, and written to help achieve this objective.

The book presents Latin grammar with economy and clarity, and this alone makes it valuable to the reader and student. Of even greater value is the book's focus on the practical reading requirements of non-specialists. We have tried to anticipate your questions, divine your needs, and respond to your most likely interests and concerns.

This newest edition adds a number of reference features that make *Latin Made Simple* not only an excellent self-guided tutorial, which it has always been, but a useful tool for review and for expanding one's command of the language beyond the beginning stages.

Each chapter introduces a number of new grammatical concepts that should be mastered before proceeding to the next chapter—learning a language is a cumulative experience. These sections are numbered, in this edition, in order to facilitate use of the index to which they are keyed. Each chapter is organized to introduce (1) new reading vocabulary, (2) new morphology (the shapes of the words), (3) new syntax (rules for constructing sentences), and (4) exercises to work through (with an answer key in the back) to ensure command of the new material covered. Each chapter, lastly, ends with a review of the material covered in the chapter and a reading, in Latin, to test your progress before moving on.

Latin Made Simple is for the readers and students who want to read the rich treasury of Latin literature, history, law, and religion in the original—since all translations have their failings. The rewards are many and include understanding of innumerable ways in which Latin has nourished and enriched English and become woven into contemporary life. Our coins and bills, the legend on school diplomas, language on medical prescriptions, and scores of words and phrases we use unconsciously every day all reflect the continuing vitality of Latin. *Latin Made Simple* is intended for the lively minded and curious, in school or no longer in school, who want to know more about a language and a culture that have done much to shape our own.

INTRODUCTION

Brief History of Latin

Latin was one of the many languages spoken in Italy before 200 B.C. Over the next century, it became the common dialect of the peninsula and developed into a literary language as well as a spoken one. This we call Classical Latin.

As the Roman Empire expanded, dialects of Latin developed, some giving rise to the Romance languages—Romanian, Italian, Spanish, French, and Portuguese.

One dialect, known as Medieval Latin, was used in the Middle Ages both as a spoken trade language and as a written language. Though extremely similar to Classical Latin, Medieval Latin dispensed with some of the more complex constructions of Classical Latin. Thus, if you learn Classical Latin, you can read Medieval Latin as well.

Until quite recently, the Catholic liturgy used spoken Latin, and today, many churches are attempting to revive its use.

It is unfortunate that Latin is often referred to as a "dead" language. It is true that no one speaks Latin as his or her first language, but not that Latin is not used, spoken, or useful in today's world. Written Latin never died. Renaissance scholars used it, and today scientists draw new words from it—many of the chemical elements have Latin names. Lawyers and doctors also draw on Latin, and in this book you will learn some of the phrases that they have borrowed.

I. Latin and English

English is not derived from Latin in the same way as the Romance languages named above. Rather, English comes from Anglo-Saxon, a Germanic language. Germanic is a cognate language, containing words derived from both languages. Germanic and Latin stem from the same parent language, a reconstructed language known as Indo-European.

Nevertheless, Latin has greatly influenced English. When the Normans invaded Britain in A.D. 1066, they brought with them the French language, derived from a Latin dialect. French had an indirect influence on the development of English during the Middle Ages, the period when Chaucer wrote *The Canterbury Tales* and other works.

The Normans also brought Latin to Britain. Latin was Europe's trade language and was also used in church and in official documents. Needed new words were often taken from Latin. Thus, Latin directly influenced the development of English; as borrowing still occurs, Latin continues to influence the development of English.

2. Word Derivation

A. MANY OF OUR ENGLISH WORDS COME DIRECTLY FROM LATIN, WITH LITTLE OR NO CHANGE IN SPELLING.

animal	labor	captivus	fortuna	multitudo	natio
animal	labor	captive	fortune	multitude	nation

B. OTHER WORDS DERIVED FROM LATIN ARE FAMILIAR TO US BECAUSE OF THEIR FREQUENT USE IN THE ROMANCE (ROMAN-BASED) LANGUAGES.

Latin	Italian	French	Spanish	Portuguese	English
filia	la figlia	la fille	la hija	a filha	daughter
vos	voi	vous	vosotros	vos	you
bonus	buono	bon	bueno	bom	good
terra	la terra	la terre	la tierra	a terra	earth

C. A THIRD GROUP OF ENGLISH WORDS COMES FROM LATIN IN THE FORM OF DERIVATIVES.

Latin	English	English Derivative
agricola	farmer	agriculture
stella	star	constellation
terra	earth	terrace
filia	daughter	filial

You will find that you are familiar with more Latin than you realized. Watch for Latin words that have come directly or indirectly into English, for English derivatives, and for Latin phrases and expressions in everyday use. These will be brought to your attention throughout the book.

3. The Parts of Speech

Latin has the same parts of speech as English, and a clear understanding of them will make it much easier to learn Latin. However, Latin has no articles (*the, a, an*), and we must supply them when translating into English.

Noun—the name of a person, place, or thing, e.g., *Caesar, Rome, town, book*

Pronoun—a word used instead of a noun, e.g., *he, it*. In the sentence *Caesar wrote a book about the victories he won*, the word *he* is used instead of repeating the word *Caesar; he* replaces *Caesar.*

Adjective—a word that describes a noun or a pronoun, e.g., *good*. In the sentence *I read a good book*, the word *good* describes, or modifies, the noun *book*. An article is a kind of adjective. As mentioned above, Latin does not have articles. A strictly literal translation of **Habeo librum** is *I have book*. For grammatically correct English, you would translate **Habeo librum** as *I have a* *book*, or as *I have the book*, depending on the context.

Verb—a word that shows action or state of being, e.g., *run, is*. Verbs can be one of three types: transitive (requiring a direct object to complete their meaning), intransitive (complete without a direct object), or linking (requiring either a noun or an adjective as a subject complement).

Adverb—a word that modifies, or describes, a verb, adjective, or adverb, e.g., *quickly, very*. In the sentence *I ran quickly*, the word *quickly* modifies the verb *ran*. In the sentence *The book is very good*, the word *very* modifies the adjective *good*. In the sentence *I ran very quickly*, the word *very* modifies the adverb *quickly*.

Preposition—a word that shows relationship between a noun or pronoun and another word or words, e.g., *in, by, with*. In the sentence *The shirt is in the closet*, the word *in* shows the relationship between the words *shirt* and *closet*. In Latin, each preposition is followed by a noun or pronoun in a particular case (a concept which will be explained in greater detail below).

Conjunction—a word that joins words, phrases, clauses, or sentences, e.g., *and*. In the sentence *He bought milk and bread*, the word *and* joins the words *milk* and *bread*.

Interjection—an exclamation showing emotion, e.g., *oh!*

4. Inflection

The biggest single difference between English and Latin is that Latin is a highly inflected language. In English, the order of the words in a sentence indicates the meaning of the sentence; in Latin, on the other hand, the spelling of the words (not their order) indicates the meaning. The changes in spelling are known as *inflections*. Inflections in nouns, adjectives, and pronouns are considered *declensions*; inflections in verbs are called *conjugations*.

A. DECLENSION

As stated above, in English the order of the words in a sentence indicates the meaning of the sentence. Notice the following two sentences:

The man bites the dog. (subject—verb—object)

The dog bites the man. (subject—verb—object)

In both sentences, the word order makes it clear who is doing the biting (the subject) and who is being bitten (the object).

In Latin, it is the spelling of the words that indicates their meaning. Thus, the six sentences following all mean: *The man bites the dog.*

Homo canem mordet.	**Mordet canem homo.**	**Canem mordet homo.**
Canem homo mordet.	**Mordet homo canem.**	**Homo mordet canem.**

The spelling of the words in the six sentences given below indicates a different meaning: *The dog bites the man.*

Hominem canis mordet.   **Mordet canis hominem**   **Canis mordet hominem.**
Canis hominem mordet.   **Mordet hominem canis.**   **Hominem mordet canis.**

Homo and **hominem** both mean *man.* **Canis** and **canem** both mean *dog.* The difference in spelling indicates the use of the word as subject or object. Thus:

Homo is used if *man* is the subject of the sentence; **hominem** if *man* is the object. Similarly, **canis** is used if *dog* is the subject and **canem** if *dog* is the object of the sentence.

The terms *subject* and *object* define nouns in relation to verbs. The verb in this sentence is **mordet,** meaning *bites.* Clearly, the subject is the person or animal doing the biting, and the object is the person or animal being bitten.

In English, the subject usually comes before the verb, and the object usually comes after it. The word order *The man bites the dog* indicates that *man* is the subject and *dog* is the object. The man is doing the biting; the dog is being bitten.

However, in Latin, the word order *The man bites the dog* could mean either that the man is biting the dog or that the dog is biting the man. The spelling (inflection) confirms the meaning. If the sentence reads: **Homo mordet canem,** then the man is biting the dog; if it reads: **Hominem mordet canis,** then the dog is biting the man.

Furthermore, Latin can use word orders not allowed in English. In English, you would never write: *The man the dog bites* or *Bites the dog the man* as these sentences are meaningless; they give no clear indication of who is biting whom. In Latin, this is not a problem. You could write: *Bites the dog the man* with one of two different spellings:

Mordet canis hominem.   This means: *The dog bites the man.*
Mordet canem homo.   This means: *The man bites the dog.*

The change in the spelling of **canis** to **canem** changes the dog from subject to object, and changing **hominem** to **homo** changes man from object to subject, changing the meaning of the sentences. This process of change is called *inflection.* Inflection occurs in English as well as in Latin:

singular: boy   subject: I   present: does
plural: boys   object: me   past: did

Declension, the inflectional change in the form or ending of a noun, pronoun, or adjective, shows case, number, and gender.

Case indicates whether a word is used as a subject **(homo, canis)**, object **(hominem, canem)**, or in a different way. The cases have names; e.g., if a noun is used as the subject, it is said to be in the nominative case. Case names will be explained later, in greater detail.

Number shows whether a word is singular (*man*) or plural (*men*). **Homo** and **canis** are both singular.

Gender can be masculine, feminine, or neuter. In Latin, gender can be natural (male or female) or grammatical (based not on sex, but on classification of the word or the spelling of the nominative case). **Homo** is masculine; **femina,** a feminine noun, means *woman;* **canis** may be either masculine or feminine, depending on the sex of the dog.

B. CONJUGATION

The inflectional change in a verb is called conjugation and shows person, number, tense, voice, and mood. Person refers to the subject (I, you, he, etc.); number to one or more than one (singular or plural); tense refers to time of an action (past, present, or future) as well as whether the action is considered complete or ongoing; voice to whether the subject is acting or being acted upon (active or passive); and mood to the manner in which a sentence is expressed (statement, question, command).

In **Homo canem mordet,** *The man bites the dog,* the verb is **mordet** or *bites.* The subject is in the third person; therefore, the verb is also in the third person. Since there is only one man, the verb must be singular. It is in the present tense, because the man is biting the dog now. The man is acting (doing the biting), so the verb is in the active voice. If the sentence was: *The man is bitten by the dog, man* would still be the subject, but the verb, *is bitten,* would be in the passive voice. Finally, the sentence is a statement, not a command or a question, so is in the indicative mood. **Mordet** is identified, therefore, as a verb in the third person singular present active indicative. Later, all of these terms will be more fully described and explained.

Latin is a highly inflected language, so the ending of a word is of primary importance and must be considered as carefully as the base of the word, which shows only the basic vocabulary meaning. Inflection will be clearly explained throughout this book and ample practice will be given.

5. The Alphabet

The Latin and English alphabets are identical, except for lack of **j** and **w** in Latin. Latin uses **i** for both **i** and **j,** and **v** for both **v** and **w.** The letter **k** is used, but rarely and only at the beginning of a word, and **y** and **z** were introduced later, appearing almost exclusively in words taken from Greek.

6. Pronunciation

Pronunciation is not necessary for reading Latin, but it is helpful in comparing Latin words with those of English and other languages. The consonants are pronounced as they are in English, except:

c and **ch** are always like *k,* as in *coop.*
t is always like *t,* as in *tie,* not like *sh.*
g is always hard, as in *go.*
v is always like *w,* as in *woman.*

i-consonant is like *y,* as in *you.*
x is like *x,* as in *axe.*
s is always *s,* as in *so,* not like *z.*
gu, qu are like *gw, qw,* as in *queen.*

Vowels are either long or short, with a long vowel taking longer to pronounce than a short vowel. There are no fixed rules for the length of vowels, and the proper pronunciation can be learned best by paying close attention to the phonetic pronunciation given in the practice below and by listening to a practiced Latin speaker. Some Latin texts indicate the length of long vowels by using a long dash or *macron* over the vowel as an aid to learning. Because the Romans themselves did not use macrons, neither does this text.

The diphthongs (two vowels pronounced as one) are as follows:

ae, pronounced like *ai,* as in *aisle.*

oe, pronounced like *oi,* as in *soil.*

au, pronounced like *ou,* as in *ouch.*

ui, pronounced like *we.*

ei, pronounced like *ei,* as in *eight.*

7. Syllables

A Latin word contains as many syllables as it has vowels and diphthongs. When dividing a word into syllables:

1. A single consonant (t) is placed with the following vowel: **pa - ter.**
2. Double consonants (tt) are separated: **di - mit - te.**
3. If there are two or more consonants, the first is generally placed with the preceding vowel: **nos - trum.**

8. Accent

Latin words are accented as follows:

1. On the next-to-last syllable (the penultimate syllable), if it is long: **di - mit´ - te.**
2. On the third-to-last syllable (the antepenult), if the next-to-last is short: **ad - ve´ - ni - at.**
3. On the first syllable of a two-syllable word: **nos´ - ter.**

In general, the accent goes as far back as possible. Because the accent is generally determined by the length of the next-to-last syllable, this is known as the *penultimate rule.*

9. Using the Dictionary

Latin dictionaries, including the dictionary included in *Latin Made Simple,* follow certain conventions in listing vocabulary items. Each of the inflected forms (nouns, pronouns, adjectives, and verbs) is listed according to the following conventions:

Nouns are listed by the nominative singular form, the genitive singular form (some dictionaries list only the genitive ending if the stem is the same), the gender (indicated by m. for masculine, f. for feminine and n. for neuter). The gender of a noun should be memorized when learning vocabulary—e.g., **aqua, aquae,** f. water.

Pronouns take the gender of the noun that they replace (their antecedent) and are therefore listed by the nominative singular forms of the masculine, feminine, and neuter (in that order)—e.g. **hic, haec, hoc** this; he, she, it.

Adjectives are like pronouns, taking the gender of the noun that they modify, and are listed in the dictionary by the nominative singular forms of the masculine, feminine, and neuter (in that order)—e.g., **certus, certa, certum** certain, sure. Some dictionaries list only the gender ending if the stem persists, e.g., **certus, -a, -um.** Third declension adjectives will often list only one or two forms, as will be explained later.

Verbs normally have four principal parts, from which all forms of the verb can be generated. It is essential to learn these principal parts when you learn a verb—e.g., **mitto, mittere, misi, missus** send. Generally the principal parts of a verb follow recognizable patterns, but some forms cannot be predicted. Some verbs have fewer principal parts due to the nature of the verb. Principal parts and their importance will be explained in greater detail throughout the course of the book.

Prepositions are listed with their root meaning(s) and, in most dictionaries, the case or cases that are associated with the given preposition.—e.g., **ad,** to, towards (+ acc.)

The other noninflected forms (adverbs, conjunctions, and interjections) are simply listed in the dictionary as single items. Some dictionaries will list the part of speech, although *Latin Made Simple* does not, since the part of speech is normally evident from the meaning of the word.

10. Practice In Pronunciation

Practice reading this passage aloud, following the English sound guide, until you can read it clearly and without hesitation. Remember that in Latin every consonant and vowel is pronounced.

Pater noster qui es in caelis	Our father who art in heaven,
(**Pah**-*tehr* **naws**-*tehr quee ehs in* **kai**-*lees*)	
sanctificetur nomen tuum.	hallowed be thy name.
(**sahnk**-*tih-fih*-**kay**-*toor* **noh**-*mehn* **too**-*uhm*)	
Adveniat regnum tuum.	Thy kingdom come.
(*Ahd*-**weh**-*nee-aht* **reg**-*nuhm* **too**-*uhm*)	
Fiat voluntas tua	Thy will be done
(**Fee**-*aht woh*-**luhn**-*tahs* **too**- *ah*)	
sicut in caelo et in terra.	on earth as it is in heaven.
(**seek**-*uht in* **kai**-*loh eht in* **tehr**-*rah*)	
Panem nostrum cotidianum [our daily bread]	
(**Pah**-*nehm* **nohs** -*trum* **koh**-*tee-dee*-**ah**-*num*)	
da nobis hodie.	Give us this day [our daily bread].
(*dah* **noh**-*bees* **hoh**-*dee-ay*)	
Et dimitte nobis debita nostra	And forgive us our debts
(*Eht dee*-**miht**-*eh* **noh**-*bees* **deh**-*biht-ah* **naws**-*trah*)	
sicut et nos dimittimus	as we forgive
(**seek**-*uht eht nohs dee*-**miht**-*tih-muhs*)	
debitoribus nostris. Et	our debtors. And
(*deh-bih*-**taw**-*rih-buhs* **naws**-*trees. Eht*)	
nos ne inducas in tentationem	lead us not into temptation,
(*nohs nay in*-**doo**-*kahs in* **ten**-*tah-tee*-**oh**-*nehm*)	
sed libera nos a malo.	but deliver us from evil.
(*sehd* **lee**-*beh-rah nohs ah* **mah**-*loh*)	
Amen.	Amen.
(**ah**-*mehn*)	

DECLENSIONS AND CONJUGATIONS

Some Women's Names of Latin Origin and Their Meanings

Rosa	rose	**Regina**	queen	**Flora**	flowers
Victoria	victory	**Gloria**	glory	**Augusta**	majestic
Barbara	foreign	**Viola, Violet**	violet	**Alma**	cherishing
Amabel	lovable	**Clara**	bright	**Letitia**	happiness
Amy	beloved	**Laura**	laurel	**Sylvia**	of the forest
Amanda	worthy of love	**Stella, Estelle**	star	**Gratia, Grace**	grace,
Beatrice	making happiness	**Celestine**	heavenly	**Miranda**	gratitude worthy of admiration

---

As you study the reading grammar in this section, you will see that most of these names end in **-a** because they are feminine and come from the first declension, or **a-declension**.

11. New Reading Vocabulary

CONJUNCTIONS

et (eht), and

et . . . et (eht . . . eht), both . . . and

Listed below are some verbs that you can start to incorporate into your Latin vocabulary. For each verb, the first person singular (I) present tense (ending in **-o**) and the infinitive (ending in **-are**) are given. For example, **amo** (ah-*moh*) is I love, I like; **amare** (ah-**mah**-reh) is to love, to like. This is explained in greater detail later in this chapter.

VERBS

amo (ah-*moh*), **amare** (*ah*-**mah**-reh), like, love (amateur)

laboro (*lah*-bor-*oh*), **laborare** (*lah*-bor-**ah**-reh), work (laboratory)

laudo (lou-*doh*), **laudare** (*lou*-**dah**-reh), praise (laudable)

porto (por-*toh*), **portare** (*por*-**tah**-reh), carry (portage, deportment)

voco (woh-*koh*), **vocare** (*woh*-**kah**-reh), call (vocation, vocative)

The Signs of the Zodiac

The names of the signs of the zodiac are all Latin words and we can easily remember them by associating their meanings with their pictorial representations.

Aries: the Ram   **Leo:** the Lion   **Sagittarius:** the Archer

Taurus: the Bull   **Virgo:** the Maiden   **Capricorn[us]:** the Goat

Gemini: the Twins   **Libra:** the Scales   **Aquarius:** the Water Bearer

Cancer: the Crab   **Scorpio:** the Scorpion **Pisces:** the Fishes

The Planets

Many of the planets are named for the Roman deities, such as:

Jupiter from **Iuppiter**   King of the gods   **Mars**   god of War

Saturn from **Saturnus**   god of Sowing   **Neptune** from **Neptunus**   god of the Sea

Mercury from **Mercurius** the Messenger god   **Pluto**   god of the Lower World

Venus   goddess of Love

Remember that the names of the signs of the zodiac and the names of the planets are nouns and are declined according to their use in a sentence.

In the vocabulary below, two forms of each noun are given, followed by its grammatical gender—feminine (f), masculine (m), or neuter (n). This is how nouns are listed in most Latin dictionaries. The first form is the subject case, called the nominative case. The second form is the possessive case, called the genitive case. According to certain rules, which will be explained later in this book, the genitive case furnishes the stem, or base, to which the rest of the case endings are added, forming all of the other forms of the noun.

NOUNS

agricola (*ah-grih-koh-lah*), **agricolae** (*ah-grih-koh-lai*), **m.,** farmer (agriculture)
aqua (*ah-kwah*), **aquae** (*ah-quai*), **f.,** water (aquarium)
casa (*kah-sah*), **casae** (*kah-sai*), **f.,** cottage, house
femina (*fay-mih-nah*), **feminae** (*fay-mih-nai*), **f.,** woman (feminine)
puella (*poo-eh-lah*), **puellae** (*poo-eh-lai*), **f.,** girl
stella (*steh-lah*), **stellae** (*steh-lai*), **f.,** star (stellar, constellation)
terra (*tehr-rah*), **terrae** (*tehr-rai*), **f.,** land, earth (terrace, territory)

In the nouns listed above, the stems, or bases, are **agricol-, aqu-, cas-, femin-, puell-, stell-,** and **terr-.** These stems are obtained by dropping the genitive singular ending **-ae.**

12. New Morphology—Noun Declensions

Latin nouns are identified by listing their case, number, and gender. The different forms of a noun, which are indicated by the endings, are known as cases. The cases include nominative (subject), genitive (possession), dative (indirect object), accusative (object), ablative (prepositional phrase), and vocative (direct address). Nouns can also be either singular or plural in number. The gender of a noun is part of its meaning and should be memorized when learning new vocabulary.

The most important case to know while learning Latin is the genitive singular. As stated before, this is the case that supplies the stem, or base, of the noun. All other cases, except for the nominative singular, are formed by adding case-specific endings to the base. The nominative singular may also be formed that way, as it is in the nouns you have seen so far, but it may also be formed differently. A Latin dictionary will supply the genitive singular, along with the nominative singular. This will give you enough information to form the other cases of the noun in ways that will be explained later on.

Nouns fall into predictable patterns—five of them—known as declensions. More information about these different declensions and how to form different cases in each will follow.

13. First Declension Nouns

When you list the different cases of a noun, you are declining that noun. Latin has five different declensions, and each noun belongs to one of these five declensional patterns. In this chapter, you are learning the first declension, also known as the **a-declension.** Nouns with a genitive singular ending in **-ae,** as those above, are known as first declension nouns, and are typically, although not always, feminine in gender. It should be noted that some Latin dictionaries will list only the genitive singular ending, rather than the entire genitive form, for words which use the same base in the genitive as in the nominative form (for example, **stella, -ae**). All first declension nouns use the same base in both the nominative and genitive singular forms. First declension nouns have -a- in most of the case endings.

First declension nouns are all feminine, unless the word indicates a male, as in the case of **agricola,** which means *farmer.* Most masculine first declension nouns are words that have been borrowed from Greek.

Consider the declension of the **first declension** noun **stella:**

Case Name	Use	Singular	Plural	Example
Nominative	subject	**stella** the star	**stellae** the stars	The star shines brightly.
Genitive	possession	**stellae** of the star	**stellarum** of the stars	The light of the star is bright.
Dative	indirect object	**stellae** to, for the star	**stellis** to, for the stars	The rocket flies to the stars.
Accusative	direct object	**stellam** the star	**stellas** the stars	I like the stars.
Ablative	prepositional phrases	**stella** from, by, with, in the star	**stellis** from, by, with, in the stars	The light came from the stars.
Vocative	direct address	**stella** O star	**stellae** O stars	O stars, shine brightly!

The base, or root, of **stella, stellae** is **stell-**. This is obtained by dropping the genitive singular ending, **-ae.** The other endings can be added directly onto the base. The endings are:

Case	Singular	Plural
Nominative	-a	-ae
Genitive	-ae	-arum
Dative	-ae	-is
Accusative	-am	-as
Ablative	-a	-is
Vocative	-a	-ae

This is true of all **first declension** nouns.

You will notice that some cases have the same endings. For example, the genitive and dative singular, as well as the nominative and vocative plural, all end in -ae. However, when you encounter the word **stellae,** you will be able to figure out which case it is in from the words around it. The -a of the ablative singular form is long and is pronounced differently from the nominative and vocative singular forms. For the purpose of clarity, the vocative will not be used in the exercises, except where specifically indicated.

Later lessons will explore the use and meanings of the various cases in greater detail. For now, all you have to do is practice what you have learned so far.

14. Grammar Practice No. 1

Decline **puella, terra, aqua, casa, femina,** and **agricola** in the same way **stella** is declined, giving the Latin form and its English meaning, and then check your answers in the Answer Chapter. Do this until you can give all the forms, including the vocative, easily and quickly.

Example: puella, the girl; **puellae,** of the girl; **puellae,** to, for the girl; **puellam,** the girl; etc.

15. New Morphology—Verb Conjugations

Verbs are identified by listing their person, number, tense, voice and mood. *Person* can be first, second or third, depending on whether the subject includes the speaker (I or we), is being addressed directly (you or you all) or is referred to (he, she, it, they or an expressed subject like "the king"). *Number,* as with nouns, is either singular or plural. Latin has six *tenses* (present, imperfect, future, perfect, pluperfect or past perfect, and future perfect). *Voice* refers to whether an action is active (the subject performs the action) or passive (action is performed upon the subject). The most important *moods* are indicative, subjunctive and imperative, but others include the infinitive, participle, gerund, and supine.

The first form of each verb listed in the vocabulary section is the first person singular of the present active indicative tense. For example, **amo,** I like, I am liking, I do like (all three possible translations indicate present time, but also indicate simple, progressive, or emphatic aspect). The second form is the present active infinitive. For example, **amare,** to like. This infinitive furnishes the base or stem on which the present tenses are formed. Bases of the verbs previously listed are: **ama-, porta-, lauda-, labora-, voca-.**

In a Latin dictionary, verbs are usually listed under the first person singular of the present tense. This form is followed by the present infinitive (as above) and then by one, or more often, two other forms. These forms are called the principal parts of the verb.

The principal parts are those forms of the verb from which all other forms are derived. In other words, if you know the principal parts of a verb in Latin, you can figure out all the other forms of that verb from them. Each verb, fortunately, belongs to one of four patterns known as **conjugations** (described in greater detail later) which greatly facilitates learning.

Verbs with infinitives ending in **-are,** as those listed above, are known as first conjugation verbs. The appendices include a listing of the principal parts for all of the verbs used in this text. To keep things simple in the earlier portions of *Latin Made Simple,* only the first two principal parts are listed for now.

16. First Conjugation Verbs

The ending of a verb changes to show person (the subject of the verb), number (singular or plural), and tense (time). These endings are added to one of the four principal parts, depending on the tense. You already know the first two principal parts of the verbs listed in the vocabulary for this chapter: the first person singular of the present active indicative and the present active infinitive.

When you list the different forms of a verb, you are conjugating that verb. Latin has four different conjugations. Each verb belongs to one of the four conjugations and is conjugated in only one way. A few verbs are irregular and do not belong to any of the four conjugations. The first of these irregular verbs will be examined later in this chapter. At this point, you are learning the first or **a-conjugation.**

Verbs that end in **-are** in the present active infinitive (the second principal part) are **first conjugation verbs,** also known as **a-conjugation verbs.** This infinitive supplies the base onto which the endings for the present active indicative are added. **First conjugation verbs** have -a- in most of the forms.

A verb must be in the same person and number as its subject. This is known as subject-verb agreement. For example:

agricola laborat, the farmer works (third person singular)

agricolae laborant, the farmers work (third person plural)

17. Present Active Indicative Tense of First Conjugation Verbs

You will notice that verbs in this tense can be translated in three ways. Although all three translations are listed only for the first person singular, they are understood to be present for all three persons, singular and plural, in this tense. These different translations represent progressive, simple, or emphatic aspect within present time.

Person	Singular	Plural	Example
1st	**amo** I like, am liking, do like	**amamus** we like	**Amamus aquam.** We like water.
2nd	**amas** you like	**amatis** you like	**Amas aquam.** You like water.
3rd	**amat** he, she, it likes	**amant** they like	**Amant aquam.** They like water.

These are the present active indicative forms of **amo.** Present because the action is taking place in the present; active because the subject of the verb is doing, not receiving, the action. Consider the following sentences:

The girl likes the farmer.   The girl is liked by the farmer.

The subject of both sentences is *The girl.* However, the verb is active in the first sentence, in which *The girl* is doing the liking, and passive in the second, in which she is receiving the liking. *The farmer* is doing the liking, but is not the subject of the sentence. Later chapters will explain the use of the passive in greater detail. For now, unless otherwise indicated, you will be dealing with the active voice.

The forms of **amo** given above are also indicative. The indicative mood is used when dealing with concrete situations. There are several other moods in Latin; the two most important are the imperative, for giving orders, and the subjunctive, used to express hoped-for or possible actions. These will be considered much later. For now, unless otherwise indicated, you will be dealing only with the indicative mood.

There is one other form of **amo** that you already know. This is **amare,** the present active infinitive. **Amare** means *to love.* Infinitives, by definition, are not limited (in + finis) by person and number like the finite (limited) forms of the verb, and therefore are identified by tense, voice, and mood only.

Amare supplies the base for the present active indicative forms. Most present active infinitives end in **-vowel + re.** The vowel provides a good indication of which conjugation the verb belongs to. In this case, the second -a- shows that **amare** is a first conjugation or **a-conjugation verb.** The letters before the vowel provide the base for the present active indicative. In the **first conjugation,** the -a- is also part of the base. The endings of the present tense are added to the base. The one exception to this is the first person of the present tense. As you can see, **amo** does not have the -a- before the tense ending. This is true of the first person singular of all **a-conjugation** verbs.

The endings for the present active indicative are as follows:

	Singular		*Plural*	
1st person	I	-o	we	-mus
2nd person	you	-s	you	-tis
3rd person	he, she, it	-t	they	-nt

Remember:

1. If the subject of the verb is a pronoun (I, you, he, she, it, we, they), you do not need to use a separate word to express the pronoun. The verb itself will tell you what the subject is. For example, **amo** means *I like*. You do not need a separate word for *I* because *I* is part of the verb (although such a word does exist in Latin).
2. Latin distinguishes between the singular and plural *you*. This distinction is lost in English, except in some literary and biblical expressions that use *ye* or *thou*.
3. The first person ending of the **a-conjugation** does not have -a- before it. All other endings in the present tense do have -a-.
4. The present active infinitive of **a-conjugation** verbs ends in -are.

18. Grammar Practice No. 2

Conjugate the present tense of **porto, laudo, laboro,** and **voco** in the same way as **amo,** giving the Latin form and its English meaning, and then check your answers in the Answer Chapter. Do this until you can give all the forms easily and quickly. The ability to read Latin depends on the rapid recognition of the meanings of the endings and of the vocabulary, so it is essential that you master these.

Example: **porto,** I carry, I do carry, I am carrying
portas, you carry
portat, he, she, it carries, etc.

19. Practice Exercises 1–5

No. 1. For each of these singular forms, give the corresponding plural.

Example: **stellam,** the star **stellas,** the stars
vocas, you call **vocatis,** you call

1. **aquam,** the water
2. **puellae,** of the girl
3. **terra,** the land
4. **agricolae,** for the farmer
5. **stella,** by the star
6. **vocat,** he calls
7. **laboras,** you work
8. **porto,** I carry

No. 2. Supply the English to complete the translation.

Example: **puellarum,** _____ girls   *of the* girls

1. **agricolarum,** _____ farmers
2. **puellam,** _____ girl
3. **casae,** _____ cottages
4. **feminae,** for the _____
5. **terris,** by the _____

6. **laudat,** _____ praising
7. **vocatis,** _____ call
8. **laborant,** _____ working
9. **amamus,** _____ like

No. 3. What is the English pronoun shown by each of the following?

1. **-mus**
2. **-t**
3. **-o**

4. **-tis**
5. **-nt**

No. 4. What case uses each pair of endings? How is this case used in a sentence?

1. **am, as**
2. **a, is**
3. **a, ae**

4. **ae, is**
5. **ae, arum**

No. 5. Change the following to the singular or plural.

Example: **portat**   **portant**

1. **porto**
2. **amant**
3. **portamus**
4. **laudo**
5. **vocat**

6. **laboras**
7. **portant**
8. **vocatis**
9. **amo**
10. **laudas**

Introduction to Adjectives

20. New Reading Vocabulary

NOUNS

filia (fee-*lee-ah*), filiae (fee-*lee-ai*), f., daughter (filial)
nauta (nou-*tah*), nautae (nou-tai), m., sailor (nautical)

ADJECTIVES

bona (**boh**-*nah*), good (bonanza)
magna (**mahg**-*nah*), large, great
(magnanimous)
mala (**mah**-*lah*), bad, evil (malice)
mea (**may**-*ah*), my, mine

parva (**pahr**-*wah*), small
pulchra (**puhl**- *krah*), pretty, beautiful
Romana (*roh*-**mah**-*nah*), Roman
tua (**too**-*ah*), your, yours

VERBS

nato (**nah**-*toh*), **natare** (*nah*-**tah**-*reh*), swim

sum (*suhm*), **esse** (**ehs**-*seh*), be

ADVERBS

non (*nohn*), not (nonstop)
male (**mah**-*leh*), badly (malformed)

bene (**beh**-*neh*), well (benefactor)

SIGN OF A QUESTION

-ne (*neh*) (attached to the end of the first word of the sentence)

21. New Reading Grammar—Adjectives

A. AN ADJECTIVE DESCRIBES OR TELLS SOMETHING ABOUT A NOUN.

filia	**filia pulchra**	**filia bona**
daughter	pretty daughter	good daughter

You will notice that although the adjective generally comes before the noun it describes in English, in Latin it can come after the noun it describes.

B. AN ADJECTIVE MUST BE IN THE SAME GENDER (MASCULINE, FEMININE, OR NEUTER) AND NUMBER (SINGULAR OR PLURAL) AND HAVE THE SAME CASE (THE SAME USE IN THE SENTENCE) AS THE NOUN IT MODIFIES.

This is known as noun-adjective agreement. As you will learn later, the inflectional endings need not be the same, however; what matters is the agreement between the adjective and the noun that it modifies in case, number, and gender.

Case	Singular	Plural
Nominative	**casa magna** large cottage	**casae magnae** large cottages
Genitive	**casae magnae** of the large cottage	**casarum magnarum** of the large cottages
Dative	**casae magnae** to, for the large cottage	**casis magnis** to, for the large cottages
Accusative	**casam magnam** the large cottage	**casas magnas** the large cottages
Ablative	**casa magna** from, with, by, in the large cottage	**casis magnis** from, with, by, in the large cottages
Vocative	**casa magna** O large cottage	**casae magnae** O large cottages

Adjectives have masculine and neuter forms as well as feminine forms. These will be introduced later.

22. Adverbs

An adverb tells something about the verb, and usually precedes it.

Agricola non natat.	The farmer does not swim.
Agricola bene natat.	The farmer swims well.
Agricola male natat.	The farmer swims badly.

The adverbs **bene, male,** and **non** all tell something about the verb **natat.** They answer the question: *How does the farmer swim?* In the first sentence, the answer is *not:* The farmer does not swim at all. In the second sentence, the answer is *well,* while in the third sentence, the answer is *badly.*

23. Questions

-**ne** on the end of the first word of a sentence is one common way to indicate that the sentence is a question.

Natatne agricola?	Does the farmer swim?

24. The Verb *sum,* To Be

As mentioned earlier, Latin has a few irregular verbs. Their conjugations must be learned separately. The first irregular verb you are going to learn is the verb **sum,** meaning *to be.*

Its present tense is as follows:

Singular	Plural
sum I am	**sumus** we are
es you are	**estis** you are
est he, she, it is; there is	**sunt** they are; there are

Present Active Infinitive: **esse,** to be

Familiar Phrases

Many Latin phrases are in everyday use and can be recognized and used easily, with a little practice.

nota bene, note well, is used in writing and speaking to draw attention to something that should be noticed especially. It is often abbreviated: **N.B.**

bona fide, with good faith or honesty. For example: It is a **bona fide** certificate. The opposite is **mala fide,** in bad faith.

adsum, I am present, is used often in answering a roll call.

meum et tuum, mine and thine, is used frequently in place of the English phrase.

terra firma, firm land. For example: They were glad to step on **terra firma.**

aqua occurs frequently in English. Examples include: **aqua pura,** pure water; **aqua vitae,** water of life (brandy or alcohol); **aqua fortis** (literally, strong water), nitric acid; and **aqueous humor,** the watery fluid between the cornea and lens of the eye.

As you can see, although the endings are the same as the regular present tense endings (other than the first person singular ending in **-m** which, as we will discover later, is a normal ending for other tenses in the indicative), the base is not always derived from the infinitive **esse**. In addition, the infinitive form **esse** is itself irregular. As the term irregular suggests, there is no set pattern to describe the conjugation of **esse** and the other irregular verbs. You will have to memorize the way these verbs are conjugated.

Notice that in the third person of **esse**—**est** or **sunt**—the verb **est** (singular) can mean not only *he, she, it is* but also *there is*. Similarly the verb **sunt** (plural) means not only *they are* but also *there are*. For example:

Est aqua means: *There is water.*
Sunt nautae means: *There are sailors.*

This is the impersonal use of **sum,** because the subject is not a person.

25. Practice Exercises 6–9

No. 6. Supply the correct ending for each adjective.

Example: aquam mal _____ , bad water

1. **casam parv** _____ , small cottage
2. **me** _____ **filiarum,** of my daughters
3. **pulchr** _____ **stellas,** pretty stars
4. **tu** _____ **terra,** your land
5. **filiae mal** _____ to the bad girl
6. **casis Roman** _____ , for Roman cottages
7. **puellas parv** _____ , small girls
8. **aquam bon** _____ , good water
9. **feminae parv** _____ , to the small woman
10. **casarum pulchr** _____ , of pretty cottages

No. 7. What is the English for each of the following?

1. estis
2. est
3. sunt

4. sum
5. es
6. sumus

No. 8. Make questions of the following and then translate the questions.

Example: natat natatne?   Does he (she, it) swim?

1. natant
2. portas
3. amamus
4. laborat
5. vocatis
6. sunt
7. natamus
8. portat

9. estis
10. laudas
11. laudat
12. vocant
13. est
14. natas
15. amant

No. 9. Give three translations for each of the following:

1. amas
2. laudamus
3. vocas
4. laboro
5. amant

6. vocatis
7. natat
8. portamus
9. laboras
10. laudat

26. Roman Numerals

The basic Roman numerals and the corresponding Arabic numerals are:

I, 1	**L,** 50	**M,** 1000
V, 5	**C,** 100	
X, 10	**D,** 500	

A fun mnemonic, or memory device, for remembering the order of the values of the Roman numerals is to take the first letter of each of the words in the phrase: "If Victor's X-Ray Looks Clear, Don't Medicate." These Roman numerals are used in various combinations to express any desired number.

1. A smaller numeral placed in front subtracts from the larger.

For example,

IV, 4
IX, 9
XC, 90
CM, 900.

Note that this is actually a modern rule, created for convenience. The Romans would have written the above numbers as follows:

IIII, 4
VIIII, 9
LXXXX, 90
DCCCC, 900.

2. A smaller numeral placed after adds to the larger.

For example,

VI, 6
XI, 11
CX, 110
MC, 1100.

3. Repeated numerals double, triple a number, and so on.

For example,

XX, 20
XXX, 30
CC, 200
CCC, 300.

4. When a line is drawn over a numeral, it multiplies that numeral by 1,000.

For example,

$\overline{V}$, 5000
$\overline{X}$, 10,000
$\overline{C}$, 100,000
$\overline{D}$, 500,000.

27. A Guide to Roman Numerals

For the sake of simplicity, only the later shorter forms of large numbers are given here.

I 1	XIII 13	XLI 41	CI 101	DCCI 701
II 2	XIV 14	L 50	CC 200	CCM 800
III 3	XV 15	LI 51	CCI 201	CCMI 801
IV 4	XVI 16	LX 60	CCC 300	CM 900
V 5	XVII 17	LXI 61	CCCI 301	CMI 901
VI 6	XVIII 18	LXX 70	CD 400	M 1000
VII 7	XIX 19	LXXI 71	CDI 401	MI 1001
VIII 8	XX 20	XXC 80	D 500	MM 2000
IX 9	XXI 21	XXCI 81	DI 501	MMI 2001
X 10	XXX 30	XC 90	DC 600	
XI 11	XXXI 31	XCI 91	DCI 601	
XII 12	XL 40	C 100	DCC 700	

28. Roman Numeral Practice

1. Give the corresponding Arabic numerals for the following. Note that the later forms of the Roman numerals are used (IV instead of IIII, CCM instead of DCCC).

XIII	MC	XLIII	DII	CXX
CCC	XXV	DCX	CDXX	XCCC
IX	CM	XXXVI	XCV	LXXIV

2. Give the corresponding Roman numerals for the following. You may use the later forms of the Roman numerals (IX instead of VIIII, XIX instead of XVIIII).

59	42	65	2222	818
304	5040	1066	26	271
85	1492	753	960	101

29. New Reading Vocabulary

NOUNS

insula (**een**-*soo-lah*), **insulae** (**een**-*soo-lai*), f., island (insular, insulate)
patria (**pah**-*tree-ah*), **patriae** (**pah**-*tree-ai*), f., native country (patriot)
paeninsula (*pai*-**neen**-*soo-lah*), **paeninsulae** (*pai*-**neen**-*soo-lai*), f., peninsula
copia (**koh**-*pee-ah*), **copiae** (**koh**-*pee-ai*), f., supply, abundance (copious, cornucopia)
copiae (plural), forces, troops
silva (**sihl**-*wah*), **silvae** (**sihl**-*wai*) f., forest, woods (sylvan)
Germania (*gehr*-**mah**-*nee-ah*), **Germaniae** (*gehr*-**mah**-*nee-ai*), f., Germany

Britannia (*brih-***tah***-nee-ah*), **Britanniae** (*brih-***tah***-nee-ai*), **f.,** Britain
Italia (*ih-***tah***-lee-ah*), **Italiae** (*ih-***tah***-lee-ai*), **f.,** Italy
Iulia (**yoo**-*lee-ah*), **Iuliae** (**yoo**-*lee-ai*), **f.,** Julia

ADJECTIVES

multa (**muhl**-*tah*), much. In the plural, **multae** means many
    (multicolored)
clara (**klah**-*rah*), clear, famous, bright (clarity)
antiqua (*ahn-***tee***-kwah*), ancient, old (antique)

VERBS

pugno (**puhg**-*noh*), **pugnare** (*puhg-***nah***-reh*), fight (pugnacious)
oppugno (*ohp-***puhg**-*noh*), **oppugnare** (*ohp-puhg-***nah***-reh*), attack
iuvo (**yoo**-*woh*), **iuvare** (*yoo-***wah***-reh*), help, aid

ADVERBS

cur (*kuhr*), why

CONJUNCTIONS

quod (*kwohd*), because

30. New Reading Grammar—Noun Cases

A. THE NOMINATIVE CASE SHOWS:

1. The subject of the verb.

The subject is the person or thing that the sentence is primarily about. If the verb is in the active voice, the subject initiates the action of the verb. If the verb is in the passive voice, the subject receives the action of the verb. These are active voice examples.

Nauta pugnat.	*The sailor* fights.
Nautae pugnant.	*The sailors* fight.

Nauta is the singular subject of **pugnat; nautae** is the plural subject of **pugnant.** Both are in the nominative case.

2. The predicate noun.

This is also known as the predicate nominative.

Britannia insula est.   Britain is *an island.*

Insula is a noun in the predicate and tells something about the subject, **Britannia.** The predicate is usually used with the verb **esse,** *to be.*

You will notice that there is no action in this sentence. Instead, a state of being is described. Consider the following sentences:

I call the doctor.   *I am a doctor.*

The first sentence describes an action. Thus, *doctor* is the direct object. However, in the second sentence, there is no action. The verb, *to be,* functions somewhat like an equals sign (=) in math. The subject on one side of the verb is equal to the predicate on the other side:

I am a doctor.   I = a doctor.   Britain is an island.   Britain = an island.

If you can replace the verb with an equals sign, you are dealing with the predicate noun. You cannot do this with the sentence *I call the doctor.*

This is true of Latin as well. However, you will recall that word order is not as important to the meaning of a sentence in Latin as it is in English. Thus, you could say **Britannia insula est** or **Britannia est insula.** Both mean *Britain is an island.* In both sentences, **Britannia** is the subject and **insula** is the predicate nominative.

3. The predicate adjective.

This is another kind of predicate nominative; however, the predicate is an adjective in this case.

Britannia est pulchra.   Britain is *pretty.*

Pulchra is an adjective in the predicate and describes the subject, **Britannia.** Predicate adjectives, like predicate nouns, can precede or follow the verb. Thus, **Britannia pulchra est** also means *Britain is pretty.* Note, however, that you would be unlikely to find the sentence **Pulchra Britannia est,** and that the sentence **Insula Britannia est** means something slightly different from **Britannia est insula.** The first sentence means *The island is Britain.* The second sentence means *Britain is an island.* In the first sentence, **Insula** is the subject and **Britannia** is the predicate. In the second sentence, this is reversed. Thus, while word order is less important in Latin than in English, it is not by any means unimportant. Later lessons will cover the rules for traditional word order in Latin in greater detail.

4. *The first declension (or a-declension) nouns and adjectives end in -a (ah) in the nominative singular and -ae (ai) in the nominative plural.*

B. THE GENITIVE CASE SHOWS POSSESSION.

terra agricolae, the land *of the farmer— the farmer's* land

terra agricolarum, the land *of the farmers— the farmers'* land

Agricolae (of the farmer) and **agricolarum** (of the farmers) tell something about **terra.** Compare this to the use of an adjective:

terra pulchra, *the pretty land*

Pulchra, *pretty,* tells something about **terra.** However, an adjective must have the same case, number, and gender as the noun it modifies. This is not true of the genitive; **agricolarum** is a masculine genitive plural, whereas **terra** is a feminine nominative singular. As we learned earlier, the a-declension nouns and adjectives end in **-ae** (*ai*) in the genitive singular and **-arum** (*ah-ruhm*) in the genitive plural.

31. Practice Exercises 10–13

No. 10. Give the English for each of the following:

Example: *filiae nautarum, the daughters of the sailors*

1. casa puellae
2. copia aquae
3. terra agricolarum
4. casae feminarum
5. patria nautae
6. insula nautae
7. filia agricolae
8. casae nautarum
9. copia stellarum

No. 11. Pick out and translate the subjects:

Example: Femina laborat. Femina, the woman

1. Feminae laborant.
2. Puella portat.
3. Agricolae amant.
4. Nauta oppugnat.
5. Agricola amat.
6. Filiae laudant.
7. Patria est.
8. Insulae sunt.
9. Filia laborat.

No. 12. Pick out and translate the predicate adjectives:

Example: Insula est pulchra. pulchra, pretty

1. Insula est magna.
2. Silvae sunt pulchrae.
3. Filiae sunt bonae.
4. Copiae sunt Romanae.
5. Terra est mala.
6. Paeninsula est tua.
7. Casae sunt parvae.
8. Silva est pulchra.
9. Femina est bona.

No. 13. Pick out and translate the predicate nouns:

Example: Sunt agricolae. agricolae, farmers

1. Est agricola.
2. Sunt nautae.
3. Germania est patria mea.
4. Sunt casae.
5. Sum nauta.
6. Estis feminae.
7. Es puella.
8. Sumus agricolae.
9. Non est silva.

Familiar Quotations

Many quotations from Latin authors are in use today, either in Latin or in translation. If you become so familiar with these quotations and their meanings that you know them by heart, you will have acquired some of the real flavor of the Latin language and thought.

Roma aeterna, Eternal Rome. (Tibullus)
Errare humanum est, To err is human. (Seneca)
Dira necessitas, Dire necessity. (Horace)
Aurea mediocritas, The golden mean. (Horace)
Rara avis, A rare bird. (Horace)
Ars longa, vita brevis, Art is long, life is short. (Seneca)
Fortuna caeca est, Fortune is blind. (Cicero)
Laborare est orare, To labor is to pray. (Motto of the Benedictine Order)

---

32. New Reading Vocabulary

NOUNS

fabula (fah-*buh-lah*), **fabulae** (fah-*buh-lai*), **f.,** story (fable, fabulous)
via (wee-*ah*), **viae** (wee-*ai*), **f.,** road, way, street (via, viaduct)
incola (ihn-*koh-lah*), **incolae** (ihn-*koh-lai*) **m.** or **f.,** inhabitant
fama (fah-*mah*), **famae** (fah-*mai*) **f.,** rumor, renown, report (fame)
Europa (*yoo*-roh-*pah*), **Europae** (*yoo*-roh-*pai*) **f.,** Europe

ADJECTIVES

longa (lawn-*gah*), long (longitude)   lata (lah-*tah*), wide (latitude)

VERBS

do (*doh*), **dare** (dah-*reh*), give (dative)
ambulo (ahm-*buh-loh*), **ambulare** (*ahm-buh*-lah-*reh*), walk (ambulance, perambulator)
narro (nah-*roh*), **narrare** (*nah*-rah-*reh*), tell, relate (narrate)
monstro (mawn-*stroh*), **monstrare** (*mawn*-strah-*reh*), point out, show (monstrance, demonstrate)
habito (hah-*bih-toh*), **habitare** (*hah-bih*-tah-*reh*), dwell, live (habitat)
navigo (nah-*wih-goh*), **navigare** (*nah-wih*-gah-*reh*), sail, cruise (navigate)

PREPOSITIONS

ad (*ahd*), to, toward (administer)   cum (*kuhm*), with
a (*ah*) or **ab** (*ahb*), from, away from (abdicate)   in (*ihn*), in, on, into, onto (inhabit, induce)
e (*ay*) or **ex** (*ehks*), from, out from (emit, exceed)

33. New Reading Grammar—Additional Case Uses

A. THE ACCUSATIVE CASE SHOWS THE DIRECT OBJECT OF THE VERB.

1. The direct object shows the person or thing that receives the action of the verb.

Fabulam narro.	I tell *a story.*
Fabulas narro.	I tell *stories.*

Fabulam, *story,* and **fabulas,** *stories,* are the direct objects of **narro,** *I tell.* Both are in the accusative case.

2. All first declension nouns and adjectives end in -am (ahm) in the accusative singular and -as (ahs) in the accusative plural.

B. THE DATIVE CASE SHOWS THE INDIRECT OBJECT OF THE VERB.

1. The indirect object shows to whom or what something is given, said, or directed.

Puellae aquam do.	I give the water *to the girl.*
Puellis aquam do.	I give the water *to the girls.*

Puella, *to the girl* and **puellis,** *to the girls,* are the indirect objects of **do,** *I give.* Both are in the dative case. *Water,* the direct object, is in the accusative case.

In English, if a word is being used as the direct object, it usually comes immediately after the verb, with no words in between. The indirect object will often, although not always, have prepositions such as *to* or *for* between it and the verb. Hence, in the sentence, *I give the water to the girls,* water is the direct object. You would not say *I give to the water* in this case (although you could say *I give the girls water. The girls* would still be the indirect object). In Latin, the case endings of a word will make it immediately obvious whether you are dealing with a direct or an indirect object.

2. The a-declension nouns and adjectives end in -ae (ai) in the dative singular and -is (ees) in the dative plural.

C. THE ABLATIVE CASE IS USED WITH PREPOSITIONAL PHRASES.

In this chapter, you will begin to learn how to use this case. (See E. below.)

The **a-declension** nouns and adjectives end in **-a** *(ah)* in the ablative singular and **-is** *(ees)* in the ablative plural.

D. THE VOCATIVE CASE IS USED WHEN ADDRESSING SOMEONE, OR SOMETHING, DIRECTLY.

There may be no obvious relation between the word in the vocative case and the verb.

Navigo, femina.	I am sailing, *O woman.*
Navigo, feminae.	I am sailing, *O women.*

Femina, *woman,* and **feminae,** *women,* are being spoken to directly, although they have no obvious connection with the verb, **Navigo,** *I am sailing.* Both are in the vocative case.

The a-declension nouns and adjectives end in **-a** (*ah*) in the vocative singular and **-ae** (*ai*) in the vocative plural.

E. PREPOSITIONAL PHRASES IN LATIN GENERALLY ARE IN EITHER THE ACCUSATIVE OR ABLATIVE CASE.

A prepositional phrase is merely one in which a preposition is used. Some prepositions are used only with one case; others may be used with either case. If a preposition can be used with both the accusative and the ablative case, you will be able to tell which case is being used, or which case you should use, from the context of the preposition.

1. Accusative prepositional phrases are used with these prepositions:

ad, to, toward	**in,** into, onto
Ad casam ambulo. I walk *toward the cottage.*	**In casam ambulo.** I walk *into the cottage.*
Ad casas ambulo. I walk *toward the cottages.*	**In casas ambulo.** I walk *into the cottages.*

2. Ablative prepositional phrases are used with these prepositions.

cum, with
Cum puella ambulo. I walk *with the girl.*
Cum puellis ambulo. I walk *with the girls.*

Cum is used only with nouns or pronouns indicating people.

in, in, on

In casa sum. I am *in the cottage.*	**In terra sum.** I am *on land.*
In casis sunt. They are *in the cottages.*	**In viis sunt.** They are *on the streets.*

e or **ex,** from, out from

ex via *out of the street*	**ex viis** *out of the streets*

a or **ab,** from, away from

a silva *away from* the forest	**a silvis** *away from* the forests

a or **e** are not used before a vowel or before **h**; **ab** or **ex** are substituted.

34. Reading

See how much of the Latin you can translate on your own. Cover the English below, translate, then uncover to see the answers.

Italia

1. **Italia est paeninsula in Europa.**
2. **Paeninsula longa est et non lata.**
3. **Incolae multae sunt agricolae et nautae.**
4. **Italia est clara et antiqua.**
5. **Magna est fama Italiae.**
6. **In Italia sunt viae multae et pulchrae et longae.**
7. **Sicilia et Sardinia et Corsica sunt magnae et pulchrae insulae.**
8. **Incolae patriam amant et bene laborant.**

Italy

1. Italy is a peninsula in Europe.
2. The peninsula is long and not wide.
3. Many inhabitants are farmers and sailors.
4. Italy is famous and old.
5. The fame of Italy is great.
6. In Italy, there are many beautiful and long roads.
7. Sicily and Sardinia and Corsica are large and pretty islands.
8. The inhabitants love their country and work hard.

Word Derivation

Derivatives are words that come from the same origin or source. Thus, many English words have the same basic meaning as their Latin sources, even though there may have been some changes in spelling and general meaning during the course of time. For example, **terra**, *earth, land.* From this Latin word are derived: 1) *terrestrial,* having to do with the earth or land; 2) *territory,* a tract of land or earth; 3) *terrace,* a flat raised area of earth or land.

Remember that similarity of sound and appearance alone are not enough to make a derivative; they must be combined with similarity of meaning. Continue to notice the English derivatives given in the Reading Vocabularies and see if you can add to them.

---

35. Practice Exercises 14–17

No. 14. Give the English for the following:

Example: in vias, into the roads

1. **ad viam**
2. **in casa**
3. **cum femina**
4. **in silvam**
5. **ex casis**
6. **ab terra**
7. **a casis**
8. **e silvis**
9. **in insulas**
10. **ad vias**
11. **in silvas**
12. **cum puella**
13. **in aqua**
14. **ad aquam**
15. **ab puellis**
16. **ad insulam**
17. **ex terra**
18. **cum agricola**
19. **in patria**
20. **cum puellis**

No. 15. Pick out and translate the direct objects in the following:

Example: **Puellam amat. Puellam,** the girl

1. **Puellis aquam do.**
2. **Puellae fabulam narro.**
3. **Puellae aquam do.**
4. **Nautam monstro.**
5. **Agricolas iuvat.**

6. **Nautis fabulam narrat.**
7. **Nautae viam monstro.**
8. **Terram amant.**
9. **Nautae terram amant.**

No. 16. Pick out and translate the indirect objects in the following:

Example: **Nautis aquam do. Nautis,** to the sailors

1. **Feminae silvas monstramus.**
2. **Nautae aquam do.**
3. **Nautis fabulas narrant.**
4. **Puellae viam monstrat.**
5. **Puellis fabulam narrat.**

6. **Feminis casas monstratis.**
7. **Agricolis terram dant.**
8. **Feminae casam das.**
9. **Puellis silvas monstrat.**

No. 17. Give three English meanings for each of the following, except 13 and 14, which have one English meaning each:

1. ambulatis
2. narrat
3. ambulant
4. habito
5. navigamus
6. das
7. dat
8. vocant
9. laboras
10. portamus

11. laudatis
12. amant
13. estis
14. sumus
15. natant
16. natas
17. pugnat
18. pugnamus
19. oppugno
20. oppugnant

Translate each of the words below into English. Then check your answers in the Answer Chapter.

36. Vocabulary Review

NOUNS

1. agricola
2. aqua
3. Britannia
4. casa
5. copia
6. copiae
7. Europa
8. fabula
9. fama
10. femina
11. filia
12. Germania
13. incola
14. insula
15. Italia
16. Iulia
17. nauta
18. paeninsula
19. patria
20. puella
21. silva
22. stella
23. terra
24. via

ADJECTIVES

1. antiqua
2. bona
3. clara
4. lata
5. longa
6. magna
7. mala
8. mea
9. multa
10. multae
11. parva
12. pulchra
13. Romana
14. tua

VERBS

1. ambulo
2. amo
3. do
4. habito
5. iuvo
6. laboro
7. laudo
8. monstro
9. narro
10. nato
11. navigo
12. oppugno
13. porto
14. pugno
15. sum
16. voco

ADVERBS

1. bene   2. cur   3. male   4. non

PREPOSITIONS

1. a, ab   3. cum   5. in
2. ad   4. e, ex

CONJUNCTIONS

1. et   2. quod

37. Practice Exercises 18–21

No. 18. Give the correct form of these adjectives, with their nouns:

Example: aquam (pulchra), aquam pulchram

1. Europam (antiqua)
2. aquae (pulchra)
3. silvis (parva)
4. stellas (clara)
5. insularum (multa)
6. terra (Romana)
7. filias (bona)
8. famam (mala)
9. puellarum (pulchra)
10. incolis (multa)

No. 19. Give the genitive and gender of these nouns:

Example: casa, casae, f.

1. casa
2. femina
3. stella
4. aqua
5. fabula
6. insula
7. puella
8. copia
9. filia
10. nauta
11. terra
12. Britannia
13. fama
14. Italia
15. silva
16. patria
17. incola
18. Europa
19. agricola
20. via

No. 20. Give the infinitive for each of these verbs:

Example: amo, amare

1. amo
2. laudo
3. navigo
4. sum
5. voco
6. oppugno
7. monstro
8. do
9. habito
10. porto
11. narro
12. laboro
13. nato
14. pugno
15. ambulo

No. 21

1. *Make a list of all six Latin cases and give the use of each.*
2. *Give the complete declension of these phrases, with the English meaning of each form, including the vocative case:*

insula lata, the wide island
insulae latae, of the wide island

via longa, the long road
viae longae, of the long road

3. *Give the complete present tense of these verbs, with the English meaning of each form.*

laboro, I work; I am working; I do work
laudo, I praise; I am praising; I do praise
sum, I am

38. Reading

The author of this hymn is unknown, but it was composed in the seventeenth century and translated by Frederick Oakley in the nineteenth century.

Adeste, Fideles
Adeste, fideles, laeti triumphantes,
Venite, venite in Bethlehem;
Natum videte regem Angelorum;

Venite adoremus Dominum.
Deum de Deo, Lumen de Lumine,
Gestant puellae viscera;
Deum verum, genitum non factum;
Venite adoremus Dominum.
Cantet nunc hymnos, Chorus Angelorum;
Cantet nunc aula caelestium,
Gloria in excelsis Deo!
Venite adoremus Dominum.
Ergo, Qui natus die hodierna,

Iesu, tibi sit gloria;
Patris aeterni verbum caro factum;
Venite adoremus Dominum.

Oh Come All Ye Faithful
Oh come, all ye faithful, joyful and triumphant,
Oh come ye, oh come ye to Bethlehem;
Come and behold him, born the King of Angels;
Oh come, let us adore him, Christ the Lord.
God of God, Light of Light,
Lo! he abhors not the Virgin's womb;
Very God, begotten, not created;
Oh come, let us adore him, Christ the Lord.
Sing, choirs of angels, sing in exultation,
Sing, all ye citizens of heaven above:
"Glory to God in the highest!"
Oh come, let us adore him, Christ the King.
Yea, Lord, we greet thee, born in this happy morning,
Jesu, to thee be glory given,
Word of the Father, now in flesh appearing;
Oh come, let us adore him, Christ the Lord.

MAKING LATIN SENTENCES

Familiar Quotations

Many of the nouns in these quotations belong to the **a-declension**.

Sed non culpa mea est. But the blame is not mine. (Ovid)

Licentia poetica. Poetic license. (Seneca)

Summa summarum. The total of totals. (Plautus)

Periculum in mora. Peril in delay. (Livy)

Si qua via est. If there is any way. (Virgil)

Tanta potentia formae est. So great is the power of beauty. (Ovid)

Sollicitae tu causa, pecunia, vitae. You, money, are the cause of an anxious life. (Propertius)

---

39. New Reading Vocabulary

NOUNS

provincia, provinciae, f., province (provincial)
victoria, victoriae, f., victory (victorious)
Hispania, Hispaniae, f., Spain (Hispanic)
praeda, praedae, f., booty, plunder (predatory)

gloria, gloriae, f., glory (glorious)
Graecia, Graeciae, f., Greece (Grecian)
fossa, fossae, f., ditch (foss)

ADJECTIVES

alta, high, deep (alto, altitude)

VERBS

supero, superare, surpass, overcome, conquer (superable)
aedifico, aedificare, build (edify)
exspecto, exspectare, to await, expect, wait for (expectant)
sto, stare, stand (station)

ADVERBS

saepe, often
ibi, there, in that place (alibi)

ubi, where, when (ubiquitous)
hic, here, in this place

PREPOSITIONS

ante, before, in front of (antedate, antecedent). With the accusative case.
post, behind, in back of (postdate, postpone). With the accusative case.

40. New Reading Grammar—Latin Word Order

A. REVIEW OF LATIN SENTENCE CONSTRUCTION

In an English sentence, the meaning is shown by the position of the words, and any changes in position change the meaning. For example, *The farmer calls the girl* means something completely different from *The girl calls the farmer.* In Latin, the inflection or form of the endings of words shows their use in the sentence, and a change in the position of the words does not change the meaning of the sentence. For example, **Agricola puellam vocat** and **Puellam agricola vocat** both mean the same thing: *The farmer calls the girl.* You can tell by the endings that **agricola** is in the nominative case (i.e., the subject of the sentence) and **puellam** is in the accusative case (i.e., the direct object) in both sentences.

B. LATIN WORD ORDER

1. Even though word order does not change the meaning of a sentence, there is a normal word order in a Latin sentence.

a. The subject or question word stands first.

Puella fabulas narrat.	The girl (subject) tells stories.
Narratne puella fabulas?	Does (question) the girl tell stories?

b. Adjectives and genitives stand next to their nouns.

filia pulchra -or- **pulchra filia**	pretty daughter
filia agricolae -or- **agricolae filia**	the farmer's daughter

c. Adverbs precede the word they modify.

non narrat	she does not tell
non multae puellae	not many girls
non saepe	not often

d. An indirect object usually precedes the direct object.

Puella agricolae fabulas narrat.	The girl tells stories to the farmer.

e. Verbs stand at the end of their clauses. The verb *to be,* however, usually has the same position as in English.

Puella fabulas narrat.	The girl tells stories.
Puella est pulchra.	The girl is pretty.

2. Any change in the normal word order of a Latin sentence is usually for emphasis or a special effect.

Puellam femina amat quod bona est.   The woman likes the girl because she is good.

C. THE WORD *there.* BE CAREFUL TO DISTINGUISH BETWEEN THE TWO USES OF THE WORD *there.*

1. With the third person of the verb "to be," there is or there are.

Est femina in casa.   There is a woman in the cottage.
Sunt feminae in casa.   There are women in the cottage.

2. The adverb ibi, there or in that place.

Ibi pugnant.   They are fighting there.
Ibi sunt feminae.   There are the women.

41. Reading

Proserpina

1. Dea agricolarum est Ceres.
2. Filia sua est Proserpina et Ceres filiam pulchram amat.
3. Ceres et Proserpina terram et silvas amant et agricolas iuvant.
4. Proserpina est clara et incolae terrarum multarum Proserpinam bene amant et laudant.
5. Pluto Proserpinam ad terram infernam[1] portat quod puellam amat.
6. Dea Ceres filiam vocat quod misera est et agricolae non laborant et terra non bona est.
7. Pluto agricolis Proserpinam dat et terra est pulchra et bona quod bene laborant.
8. Aestate[2] Proserpina est hic cum agricolis et hieme[3] est ibi in terra inferna et non cum agricolis.

Proserpina

1. The goddess of the farmers is Ceres.
2. Her daughter is Proserpina and Ceres loves her beautiful daughter.
3. Ceres and Proserpina love the land and woods and help the farmers.
4. Proserpina is famous and the inhabitants of many lands love Proserpina well and praise her.
5. Pluto carries Proserpina to the lower world because he loves the girl.
6. The goddess, Ceres, calls her daughter because she is unhappy and the farmers do not work and the land is not good.
7. Pluto gives Proserpina to the farmers and the earth is pretty and good because they work well.
8. In summer Proserpina is here with the farmers and in winter she is there in the lower world and not with the farmers.

NOTES: (1) **infernam,** lower. (2) **aestate,** in summer. (3) **hieme,** in winter.

42. Practice Exercises

No. 22. Give the English meanings for these forms:

1. sumus
2. superant
3. stat
4. est
5. exspectatis
6. aedificat
7. sunt
8. natamus
9. superat
10. navigant
11. datis
12. vocas
13. aedificamus
14. ambulant
15. statis

No. 23. Translate these prepositional phrases:

1. in Italia
2. ad Britanniam
3. cum feminis
4. ad Italiam
5. in provincia
6. cum copiis
7. in paeninsula
8. ante casas
9. post casas
10. cum puella
11. in silvis
12. ad viam

No. 24. Give the English translations for the following:

1. incolae
2. Cur laborant?
3. Patriam tuam iuvas.
4. Praedam portat.
5. Bene pugnat.
6. Sunt pulchrae.
7. multarum victoriarum
8. patria clara
9. fabulam longam
10. ex casa
11. ab via
12. Ubi est?
13. Hic sum.
14. ante insulam
15. post victoriam
16. cum copiis
17. ex provinciis
18. Sunt copiae hic.
19. ad vias
20. Ibi est provincia.
21. Ibi sunt feminae.
22. Est gloria.
23. Sunt multae puellae.
24. Ubi sunt?
25. Hic sunt.

Second Declension Nouns

43. New Reading Vocabulary

NOUNS

amicus, amici, m., friend (amicable)
inimicus, inimici, m., (personal) enemy (inimical)
arma, armorum, n. pl., arms, weapons (armory)
auxilium, auxilii or auxili, n., help, aid (auxiliary)
socius, socii or soci, m., ally, comrade (social)
gladius, gladii or gladi, m., sword (gladiatorial)
nuntius, nuntii or nunti, m., messenger,
message (nuncio, announcement)

puer, pueri, m., boy (puerile)
vir, viri, m., man (virile)
ager, agri, m., field (agriculture)
proelium, proelii or proeli, n., battle
periculum, periculi, n., danger (peril)
oppidum, oppidi, n., town (oppidan)
bellum, belli, n., war (bellicose)
castra, castrorum, n. pl., camp (castle)

Note: **castra, castrorum** is actually a neuter plural noun (introduced later in the chapter), but is translated as a singular, **camp.**

ADJECTIVES

angusta, narrow (anguish)

VERBS

aro, arare, plow (arable)
nuntio, nuntiare, announce, report (pronounce)
occupo, occupare, seize, take possession of (occupy)

neco, necare, kill
armo, armare, arm (army)

PREPOSITIONS

per, through (persevere, permeate). With the accusative case.
de, about, concerning, down from (descend). With the ablative case.

ADVERBS

etiam, even, also

CONJUNCTIONS

sed, but

Some Men's Names of Latin Origin and Their Meanings

Rex, king, ruler

Claude, lame

Constant, firm, true

Patrick, patrician

Octavius, the eighth child

Dexter, on the right, fortunate

Pius, devoted, faithful

Leo, Leon, lion

Sylvester, of the woods

Augustus, majestic, august

Valentine, healthy, strong

Dominic, of the Lord

Martin, of Mars

Vincent, conquering

Rufus, red

Clarence, Clare, bright

Victor, conqueror

Lucius, light

Felix, happy, lucky

Septimus, the seventh child

Aurelius, golden

Benedict, blessed

Clement, kind, mild

Paul, small

OVID

VERGIL

SUETONIUS

44. New Reading Grammar—Second Declension Nouns

A. INTRODUCTION TO SECOND DECLENSION NOUNS (ALSO KNOWN AS o-declension NOUNS).

1. *Nouns that have -i as the ending of the second, or genitive singular form, are considered to be o-declension or second declension nouns.*

2. *o-declension nouns that end in -us or -er or -ir in the nominative singular case, or first form, are masculine gender.*

3. *o-declension nouns that end in -um in the nominative singular case are neuter (literally, neither) gender.*

4. *although there are a few feminine second declension nouns, (e.g., alvus, =i, f., belly) they are extremely rare.*

45. Masculine Second Declension Nouns

Although the nominative singular and the vocative singular and plural sometimes vary, there is one basic pattern for all masculine **o-declension** nouns:

Case	Singular	Plural
Nominative	**-us**	**-i**
Genitive	**-i**	**-orum**
Dative	**-o**	**-is**
Accusative	**-um**	**-os**
Ablative	**-o**	**-is**
Vocative	**-e**	**-i**

Consider **amicus,** a typical masculine second declension noun:

Case	Singular		Plural	
Nom.	**amicus**	the friend	**amici**	the friends
Gen.	**amici**	of the friend	**amicorum**	of the friends
Dat.	**amico**	to, for the friend	**amicis**	to, for the friends
Acc.	**amicum**	the friend	**amicos**	the friends
Abl.	**amico**	from/with/by/in the friend	**amicis**	from/with/by/in the friends
Voc.	**amice**	O friend	**amici**	O friends

The endings of the **o-declension** nouns are added on to the base, or stem, just as the endings of **a-declension** nouns are. In both cases, the base is identified by dropping the genitive singular ending, in this declension, **-i.** Thus, the stem of **amicus** is **amic-.**

Prefixes

Prefixes are syllables that occur at the beginning of a word. In both Latin and English, they are used to modify the basic meaning of a word. For example, if you add the prefix "im-" to the word "moral" in English, you have the word "immoral," which means "not moral." If you add "re-" to the word "do," you have "redo," which means "do again."

In Latin, the prefixes are usually prepositions. An understanding of the meaning of the prefix makes the meaning of the Latin or English compound word clearer. Prefixes occur most frequently in verb forms. These are some of the most common Latin prepositions and their meanings as prefixes:

a, ab, abs, away   **absum,** be away, be absent
ante, before, in front   **antecedo,** go before
post, after, behind   **postpono,** put after, put behind
de, down, from, away   **depono,** put down, put away
ad, to, toward   **advoco,** call to

---

46. SECOND DECLENSION I-STEM NOUNS

Some masculine **o-declension** nouns are spelled with an -i- in the stem. Compare **socius** with **amicus:**

Case	Singular		Plural	
Nom.	**socius**	the ally	**socii**	the allies
Gen.	**socii** or **soci**	of the ally	**sociorum**	of the allies
Dat.	**socio**	to, for the ally	**sociis**	to, for the allies
Acc.	**socium**	the ally	**socios**	the allies
Abl.	**socio**	from/with/by/in the ally	**sociis**	from/with/by/in the allies
Voc.	**soci**	O ally	**socii**	O allies

Note that the vocative singular of **filius** is **fili**. The vocative singular of a proper noun (a name), if an i-stem, also ends in **-i**. Thus, the vocative singular of Mercury is **Mercuri**.

47. Second Declension Nouns in -er

Some masculine **o-declension** nouns end in **-er**. Of these, some keep the **-e-** in all forms and others drop the **-e-** after the nominative singular. As always, the stem of the noun is given by the genitive form (minus the -i ending); the genitive form should always be noted when learning new vocabulary. Notice the declension of the nouns **puer** and **ager** and compare them with **amicus** and **socius** above.

a. Nouns that keep the -e.

Case	Singular		Plural	
Nom.	**puer**	the boy	**pueri**	the boys
Gen.	**pueri**	of the boy	**puerorum**	of the boys
Dat.	**puero**	to, for the boy	**pueris**	to, for the boys
Acc.	**puerum**	the boy	**pueros**	the boys
Abl.	**puero**	from/with/by/in the boy	**pueris**	from/with/by/in the boys
Voc.	**puer**	O boy	**pueri**	O boys

b. Nouns that drop the -e.

Case	Singular		Plural	
Nom.	**ager**	the field	**agri**	the fields
Gen.	**agri**	of the field	**agrorum**	of the fields
Dat.	**agro**	to, for the field	**agris**	to, for the fields
Acc.	**agrum**	the field	**agros**	the fields
Abl.	**agro**	from/with/by/in the field	**agris**	from/with/by/in the fields
Voc.	**ager**	O field	**agri**	O fields

48. Second Declension Neuter Nouns

Case	Singular		Plural	
Nom.	**bellum**	the war	**bella**	the wars
Gen.	**belli**	of the war	**bellorum**	of the wars
Dat.	**bello**	to, for the war	**bellis**	to, for the wars
Acc.	**bellum**	the war	**bella**	the wars
Abl.	**bello**	from, with, by, in the war	**bellis**	from/with/by/in the wars
Voc.	**bellum**	O war	**bella**	O wars

Some neuter **o-declension** nouns are spelled with an **-i-** in the stem. Compare **proelium** with **bellum**:

Case	Singular		Plural	
Nom.	**proelium**	the battle	**proelia**	the battles
Gen.	**proelii/proeli**	of the battle	**proeliorum**	of the battles
Dat.	**proelio**	to, for the battle	**proeliis**	to, for the battles
Acc.	**proelium**	the battle	**proelia**	the battles
Abl.	**proelio**	from/with/by/in the battle	**proeliis**	from/with/by/in the battles
Voc.	**proelium**	O battle	**proelia**	O battles

Regardless of the peculiarities of individual nouns, the case endings for **o-declension** neuter nouns are:

Case	Singular	Plural
Nom.	**-um**	**-a**
Gen.	**-i**	**-orum**
Dat.	**-o**	**-is**
Acc.	**-um**	**-a**
Abl.	**-o**	**-is**
Voc.	**-um**	**-a**

Note that neuter nouns, of whatever declension, always have the same ending in the nominative, accusative, and vocative singular (-um for second declension), and in the nominative, accusative, and vocative plural (-a for second declension). In fact, the nominative, accusative, and vocative plurals of all neuter nouns, regardless of the declensional pattern to which they belong, end in -a.

49. Practice Exercises

No. 25. Give the English for these forms:

1. **agro**
2. **bellis**
3. **proeliorum**
4. **pueri**
5. **socium**
6. **amicos**
7. **castra**
8. **gladios**
9. **auxilium**
10. **nuntio**
11. **pericula**
12. **armorum**
13. **oppidi**
14. **virum**
15. **inimicos**

No. 26. Change each of these singular forms to the plural, and give the English:

1. **amicus**
2. **pueri**
3. **agro**
4. **belli**
5. **oppidum**
6. **vir**
7. **periculum**
8. **gladi**
9. **nuntium**
10. **auxilio**
11. **nuntio**
12. **viro**
13. **periculo**
14. **ager**
15. **bellum**

No. 27. Fill in the blanks with the correct English:

1. **castrorum,** _____ camps
2. **socius,** _____ ally
3. **gladium,** _____ sword
4. **de bello,** _____ the war
5. **per periculum,** _____ danger
6. **oppidi,** _____ town
7. **viri,** _____ the man
8. **inimici,** _____ enemies
9. **agros,** _____ fields
10. **pueri,** _____ the boy

No. 28. Give the English translation for the following:

1. ex agro
2. Armantne?
3. angusta via
4. amicos
5. cum puero
6. Ibi arat.
7. post castra
8. amicorum
9. cum viro
10. Bellum pugnant.
11. Oppida monstrant.
12. Viro arma dant.
13. Fabulas de bello narramus.
14. Pericula amat.
15. Castra sunt in agro.

First and Second Declension Adjectives

50. New Reading Vocabulary

NOUNS

equus, equi, m., horse (equestrian)
servus, servi, m., slave, servant (servitude)
dominus, domini, m., master (dominion)
frumentum, frumenti, n., grain
(frumentaceous)

domina, dominae, f., mistress
filius, filii or fili, m., son (filial)
cura, curae, f., care (curate)

ADJECTIVES

miser, misera, miserum, wretched, unhappy
(miser)
laetus, laeta, laetum, happy

liber, libera, liberum, free (liberal)
aeger, aegra, aegrum, sick, ill

VERBS

libero, liberare, free, set free (liberate)
curo, curare, care for, cure (curator)

erat, he, she, it was; there was
erant, they were; there were

ADVERBS

hodie, today

51. New Reading Grammar—First and Second Declension Adjectives

Adjectives in Latin follow two basic patterns. One type of adjective, which is described below, uses either first or second declensional endings depending on whether the adjective is modifying a feminine (1st declension), masculine (2nd declension), or neuter (2nd declension neuter) noun. The other type uses 3rd declensional endings for all three genders; this type of adjective will be learned in a subsequent chapter.

A. YOU HAVE ALREADY STUDIED a-declension ADJECTIVES.

These same adjectives also belong to the **o-declension**. The **a-declension** and **o-declension** adjectives are known as first and second declension adjectives. An adjective must agree with (or match) the noun it modifies in gender, as well as in case and number. Therefore, an adjective has different endings when it modifies a feminine noun, masculine noun, or neuter noun. The adjectives have the same cases as the nouns of these declensions.

The basic endings for **a-declension** and **o-declension** adjectives are:

	Singular				*Plural*		
Case	*Masculine*	*Feminine*	*Neuter*	*Case*	*Masculine*	*Feminine*	*Neuter*
Nominative	-us	-a	-um	Nominative	-i	-ae	-a
Genitive	-i	-ae	-i	Genitive	-orum	-arum	-orum
Dative	-o	-ae	-o	Dative	-is	-is	-is
Accusative	-um	-am	-um	Accusative	-os	-as	-a
Ablative	-o	-a	-o	Ablative	-is	-is	-is
Vocative	-e	-a	-um	Vocative	-i	-ae	-a

Consider the declension of **bonus**, a typical first and second declension adjective:

	Singular				*Plural*		
Case	*Masculine*	*Feminine*	*Neuter*	*Case*	*Masculine*	*Feminine*	*Neuter*
Nominative	**bonus**	**bona**	**bonum**	Nominative	**boni**	**bonae**	**bona**
Genitive	**boni**	**bonae**	**boni**	Genitive	**bonorum**	**bonarum**	**bonorum**
Dative	**bono**	**bonae**	**bono**	Dative	**bonis**	**bonis**	**bonis**
Accusative	**bonum**	**bonam**	**bonum**	Accusative	**bonos**	**bonas**	**bona**
Ablative	**bono**	**bona**	**bono**	Ablative	**bonis**	**bonis**	**bonis**
Vocative	**bone**	**bona**	**bonum**	Vocative	**boni**	**bonae**	**bona**

B. ADJECTIVES THAT END IN -er IN THE MASCULINE NOMINATIVE SINGULAR MAY EITHER KEEP OR DROP THE -e- IN ALL OTHER FORMS.

1. Adjectives that keep the -e-.

Case	Masculine	Feminine	Neuter
Nominative	**miser**	**misera**	**miserum**
Genitive	**miseri**	**miserae**	**miseri**
Dative	**misero,** etc.	**miserae,** etc.	**misero,** etc.

2. Adjectives that drop the -e-.

Case	Masculine	Feminine	Neuter
Nominative	**pulcher**	**pulchra**	**pulchrum**
Genitive	**pulchri**	**pulchrae**	**pulchri**
Dative	**pulchro,** etc.	**pulchrae,** etc.	**pulchro,** etc.

Note that first and second declension adjectives are normally listed with the masculine nominative singular form first, followed by the feminine and then by the neuter. Thus, **bonus** would be listed as **bonus, bona, bonum.** Most Latin dictionaries, however, will list first and second declension adjectives under the masculine nominative singular form, followed by the feminine and neuter endings only. Thus, **bonus** would be listed as **bonus, -a, -um.** If the adjective ends in **-er** in the masculine nominative singular, the dictionary will indicate whether the adjective keeps or drops the **-e-.** Thus, **miser** would be listed as **miser, -ra, -rum,** but **pulcher** would be listed as **pulcher, -chra, -chrum.**

The vocabulary at the back of this book gives the complete forms (rather than just the endings) of the feminine and neuter nominative singular nouns for first and second declension adjectives.

52. Agreement of Adjectives

Adjectives must agree with the nouns they modify in case, number, and gender. Note that they do not necessarily agree in declension or spelling. For example, **nauta bonus** below is a masculine **a-declension** noun modified by a masculine **o-declension** adjective. Although the declensional patterns differ, the noun and its adjective **agree** in case, number and gender (in this example, nominative, singular, and masculine).

cura bona, good care (f.)
nauta bonus, good sailor (m.)
equus bonus, good horse (m.)
puer bonus, good boy (m.)
servus miser, wretched slave (m.)

equus pulcher, pretty horse (m.)
frumentum bonum, good grain (n.)
bellum miserum, wretched war (n.)
oppidum pulchrum, pretty town (n.)

53a. Adjectives Used Substantively

The masculine nominative and accusative plural of adjectives are commonly used to mean *men* (or *people*). The neuter nominative and accusative plural of adjectives are commonly used to mean *things*. Because the gender makes it clear, the noun may be omitted. When adjectives are used in this way, they act as nouns or substantives.

boni, good people (subject)

bonos, good people, (direct object)

bona, good things or goods (subject, direct object)

multi, many people (subject)

multos, many people, (direct object)

multa, many things (subject, direct object)

Sometimes the noun is omitted with other cases in the plural.

multorum, of many people; of many things (possession)

multis, to, for many people; to, for many things (indirect object)

53. New Grammar—Second Conjugation Verbs

e-conjugation or second conjugation verbs have an -e- in the present infinitive (although *Latin Made Simple* does not indicate the quantity of vowels with macrons, this is a long -e, which distinguishes it from the short -e of third conjugations, which will be learned in a later chapter).

hab-e-re, to have   **tim-e-re,** to fear   **vid-e-re,** to see

e-conjugation verbs form the present tense in the same way as the **a-conjugation** verbs, but there is an -e- in each form, not an -a-.

Singular:

		Plural:	
habeo	I have, do have, am having	**habemus**	we have
habes	having	**habetis**	you have
habet	you have	**habent**	they have
	he, she, it has		

You will notice that in **e-conjugation** verbs, even the first person singular has an -e-.

54. New Reading Grammar—Imperfect Tense

All of the verbs you have encountered so far have been in the present tense. This tense is used to show action which occurs in the present time. Another tense, the imperfect tense, is used to show action going on in the past over a period of time, as in the sentence *He was walking*. Thus, it deals with continuous action in the past, rather than with an action done once and completed.

1. IN THE INDICATIVE MOOD (THE ONLY MOOD YOU HAVE LEARNED SO FAR), THE IMPERFECT TENSE OF A REGULAR VERB IS FORMED BY ADDING -ba- BETWEEN THE BASE AND THE ENDING, WHICH INDICATES PERSON, OR WHO IS PERFORMING THE ACTION.

Thus, in the present active tense, the imperfect endings are:

Singular:		Plural:	
	-bam		-bamus
	-bas		-batis
	-bat		-bant

The -ba- in the verb may be translated as *was, used to,* or *did.*

You will notice that the first person singular ends in -m, not -o. -m is actually the normal ending for the first person singular in the active voice. The present active tense uses the -o, as do a couple of other tenses, but this is the exception, not the rule.

2. IMPERFECT TENSE OF first conjugation (a-conjugation) VERBS.

Singular:		Plural:	
amabam	I was loving/used to love/did love/loved	amabamus	we were loving
		amabatis	you were loving
amabas	you were loving	amabant	they were loving
amabat	he, she, it was loving		

Note that in the first person singular, the -a-, which indicates a first conjugation verb, does appear.

Thus, **amabam** is made up of four separate elements: **am-** is the base of the verb; -a- shows which conjugation the verb is from; -ba- shows that the verb is in the imperfect tense; and -m shows that the verb is both active and in the first person singular. The other forms of the imperfect can also be broken down in this way.

3. IMPERFECT TENSE OF second conjugation (e-conjugation) VERBS.

Singular:		Plural:	
habebam	I was having/used to have/did have/had	habebamus	we were having
		habebatis	you were having
habebas	you were having	habebant	they were having
habebat	he, she, it was having		

These forms can be broken down in the same way as the forms for **a-conjugation** verbs. Thus, in **habebam, hab-** is the root; -e- shows that the verb is from the second, or **e-conjugation**; -ba- shows that it is imperfect; -m shows that it is active and first person singular.

55. The Imperfect Tense of *sum, esse* (to be)

The imperfect tense of **sum** may be recognized easily by the stem, **era-**. All the endings of the imperfect are added on to this stem.

Singular:		Plural:	
eram	I was/used to be	eramus	we were
eras	you were	eratis	you were
erat	he, she, it was; there was	erant	they were; there was

56. Reading

Servi

1. Romani servos multos in bello occupant.
2. Ex oppidis Graeciae ad Italiam servos portant.
3. Servi erant boni, sed in Italia saepe non erant laeti.
4. Servi erant praeda belli et multi servos bene curant, sed multi servos male curant.
5. Servi in agris et in casis et in viis laborant.
6. Saepe aegri erant, sed multi servos aegros bene curant.
7. Romani servis multa dant et curam bonam dant.
8. Servi dominos bonos et dominas bonas amant.
9. Multi servi erant clari et filios dominorum bene iuvant.
10. Multi domini servos liberant et multi servi liberi erant viri clari.

Slaves

1. The Romans seize many slaves in war.
2. They carry the slaves to Italy from the towns of Greece.
3. The slaves were good, but in Italy they were often not happy.
4. Slaves were the booty of war and many people care for their slaves well, but many care for them badly.
5. The slaves work in the fields and in the houses and on the roads.
6. They were often sick, but many people took good care of the sick slaves.
7. The Romans give many things to the slaves and give them good care.
8. The slaves like good masters and good mistresses.
9. Many slaves were famous and aided the sons of their masters well.
10. Many masters free their slaves and many free slaves were famous men.

Latin on Tombstones and Monuments

Latin often appears on tombstones and monuments. The following are some of the abbreviations and phrases frequently used.

c., standing for **circa** or **circum**, about, is used with dates.

in aeternum, forever

in perpetuum, forever

ae., aet., aetat., stands for **aetatis**, of age

anno aetatis suae, in the year of his (her) age

ob., standing for **obiit**, he (she) died

hic iacet, here lies

R.I.P., standing for **requiescat in pace**, may he (she) rest in peace

in memoriam, in memory, to the memory of

A.D., standing for **Anno Domini**, in the year of (our) Lord

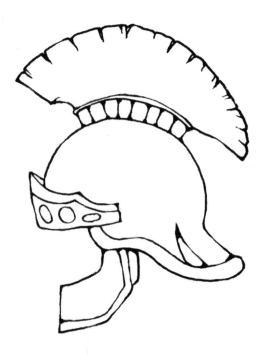

57. Practice Exercises

No. 29. Give the English for the following:

1. Amicus meus ibi est.
2. ad casas tuas
3. ex fossis altis
4. cum viris claris
5. ante castra Romana

6. post agros meos
7. de aqua bona
8. per silvam magnam
9. mali amici

No. 30. Add the correct ending to the adjectives:

1. virorum mult _____
2. filiae me _____
3. frumento bon _____
4. me _____ filiis
5. pueros aegr _____

6. puellae miser _____
7. soci liber _____
8. feminam miser _____
9. agris pulchr _____

No. 31. Match the English adjective in Column I (e.g., many, sick, pretty) with the Latin adjective in Column II:

Column I
1. many **viros**
2. sick **pueri**
3. pretty **oppidum**
4. many **servorum**
5. happy **puellam**
6. good **fili**
7. bad **famam**
8. wretched **equis**
9. Roman **terrae**
10. happy **agricola**

Column II
1. **pulchrum**
2. **multorum**
3. **multos**
4. **laetam**
5. **aegri**
6. **boni**
7. **laetus**
8. **malam**
9. **miseris**
10. **Romanae**

No. 32. Complete the verbs with the correct endings:

1. **cura** _____ (we)
2. **libera** _____ (you s.)
3. **labora** _____ (you pl.)
4. **porta** _____ (he)
5. **ar** _____ (I)

6. **neca** _____ (they)
7. **nuntia** _____ (she)
8. **occupa** _____ (we)
9. **sta** _____ (you pl.)

No. 33. Give the English for the following:

1. Sunt liberi.
2. dominarum laetarum
3. in aquam altam
4. de curis magnis
5. in agris latis

6. de dominis bonis
7. Cur estis laeti?
8. Sunt multi.
9. Sumus aegri.
10. cum amicis bonis

11. in terris liberis
12. Est pulchra.
13. Suntne pulchrae?
14. Est miser.
15. multa

58. New Reading Vocabulary

NOUNS

deus, dei, m., god (deity)
oceanus, oceani, m., ocean (oceanic)
sapientia, sapientiae, f., wisdom (sapience)
templum, templi, n., temple (templar)
fortuna, fortunae, f., fortune, fate, luck (fortunate)

dea, deae, f., goddess
caelum, caeli, n., sky, heaven (celestial)
regina, reginae, f., queen
luna, lunae, f., moon (lunar)

NOTE: The dative and ablative plural of **dea** is **deabus,** to distinguish it from **deis.**

ADJECTIVES

suus, sua, suum, his, her, its, their (own)
noster, nostra, nostrum, our, ours (nostrum)

vester, vestra, vestrum, your, yours (pl.)

VERBS

adoro, adorare, worship, adore (adorable)
timeo, timere, fear, be afraid of (timid)
regno, regnare, rule (regnant)

habeo, habere, have, hold (habit)
video, videre, see (vision, video)

PREPOSITIONS

trans, across. With the accusative case (trans-Atlantic).

59. New Reading Grammar—Possessive Adjectives

Possessive adjectives are used when the subject of the verb is the possessor, as in the sentence *I lost my book*. Thus, the word *own* may always be added for clarity.

The possessive adjectives are listed below. For each person, the masculine, feminine, and neuter Latin forms are given. Remember that adjectives, including possessive adjectives, must agree with the nouns they modify in case, number, and gender.

Singular:		Plural:	
1st person	**meus, mea, meum,** my (own), mine	1st person	**noster, nostra, nostrum,** our (own), her (own), its (own)
2nd person	**tuus, tua, tuum,** your (own), yours	2nd person	**vester, vestra, vestrum,** your (own), yours
3rd person	**suus, sua, suum,** his (own), her (own), its (own)	3rd person	**suus, sua, suum,** their (own), theirs

These adjectives are declined just like other adjectives of the first and second declension, except for the masculine vocative singular of **meus,** which is **mi.** Thus,

mea puella, O my girl   **meae puellae,** O my girls
mi puer, O my boy   **mei pueri,** O my boys

Remember that the possessive adjectives are indeed adjectives. Therefore, they must agree with the nouns they modify in case, number, and gender. For example, you would say **suam casam** regardless of whether the owner of the house is male or female; **suam** must be feminine because **casam** is feminine. The context will tell you whether a man or a woman owns the house.

Similarly, you would say **Amas tuas filias,** you love your daughters; **filias** is plural, so **tuas** must also be plural, even though it refers to a single person. **tuas** is also accusative, because **filias** is accusative. This is true even though *you* (*singular*) is the subject of the sentence. The ending of an adjective is determined by the noun it modifies, not by the subject of the sentence, unless the two are the same.

60. Reading

Dei Antiqui

1. **Romani deos multos et deas multas adorant et fabulas antiquas de deis suis narrant.**
2. **Iuppiter in caelo habitat et erat bonus et magnus.**
3. **Mercurius erat nuntius deorum et trans terram et aquam viris et deis famas portat.**
4. **Nautae Neptunum adorant quod deus oceani est.**
5. **In aqua habitat et amicus nautarum erat.**
6. **Mars viros in proeliis et in bellis curat.**
7. **Vulcanus est deus et deis arma dat.**
8. **In patria nostra et in vestra deas et deos non adoramus, sed in Italia antiqua deae et dei erant amici virorum et feminarum.**
9. **Hodie in Italia deos multos non adorant.**

Deae Antiquae

1. **Multas fabulas de deabus Romanis narrant.**
2. **Feminae Romanae deas in templis et in casis suis saepe adorant.**
3. **Iuno regina dearum erat.**
4. **Clara et bona est et deas regnat.**
5. **Vesta curam casarum habet.**
6. **Diana puellas curat et nautae non timent quod nautis in oceano fortunam bonam et auxilium dat.**
7. **Dea lunae etiam est et silvas amat.**
8. **Venus pulchra erat et erant feminae multae in templo.**
9. **Agricolae bene arant quod Ceres agricolas iuvat et frumentum curat.**
10. **Etiam hodie magna est fama dearum Romanarum.**

The Ancient Gods

1. The Romans worship many gods and many goddesses and tell old stories about their gods.
2. Jupiter lives in the sky and was good and great.
3. Mercury was the messenger of the gods and carries reports to men and gods across land and water.
4. The sailors worship Neptune because he is the god of the ocean.
5. He lives in the water and was the sailors' friend.
6. Mars takes care of men in battles and in wars.
7. Vulcan is a god and he gives weapons to the gods.
8. In our native country and in yours, we do not worship goddesses and gods, but in ancient Italy, goddesses and gods were the friends of the men and women.
9. Today in Italy, they do not worship many gods.

The Ancient Goddesses

1. They tell many stories about the Roman goddesses.
2. Roman women often worship the goddesses in the temples and in their homes.
3. Juno was the queen of the goddesses.
4. She is famous and good and she rules the goddesses.
5. Vesta has the care of houses.
6. Diana cares for girls, and sailors are not afraid because she gives good fortune and help to sailors on the ocean.
7. She is also the goddess of the moon and loves the forests.
8. Venus was beautiful and there were many women in her temple.
9. Farmers plow well because Ceres helps farmers and cares for the grain.
10. Even today the fame of the Roman goddesses is great.

61. Practice Exercises

No. 34. Fill in the correct possessive adjective:

1. our **reginam**
2. your (sing.) **deas**
3. his own **fortuna**
4. their own **templa**
5. your (pl.) **reginae**

6. our own **patriam**
7. its own **oceani**
8. their own **filiarum**
9. my **sapientiam**

No. 35. Give the English for the following:

1. timeo
2. videt
3. timetis
4. adorat
5. regnant
6. vides
7. timent
8. habemus

9. regnamus
10. habent
11. timet
12. videtis
13. habeo
14. regnas
15. adoratis

No. 36. Give the English for the following:

1. antiquos deos
2. deae Romanae
3. meorum amicorum
4. tuam praedam
5. filias nostras

6. suus dominus
7. suum filium
8. sua sapientia
9. gloriam nostram

No. 37. Translate the following sentences into English:

1. Gloria vestra non est magna.
2. Cur inimicum tuum necas?
3. Nuntiusne multa narrat?
4. Viri trans agros suos ambulant.
5. Feminae in casis suis sunt.
6. Filiae tuae hodie sunt aegrae.
7. Multi trans oceanum navigant.
8. Sunt deae nostrae.
9. Sunt dei nostri.
10. Femina suas filias curat.

11. Ante casas sto.
12. Non multa habet.
13. De luna narramus.
14. Fortuna vestra est bona.
15. Servi dominos timent.
16. Cur non timetis?
17. Templa pulchra videmus.
18. Castra ibi habet.
19. Pueros post fossam videmus.
20. Sapientiam magnam habetis.

REVIEW

62. Vocabulary Review

NOUNS

1. ager	10. deus	19. gloria	28. praeda
2. amicus	11. domina	20. Graecia	29. proelium
3. arma	12. dominus	21. Hispania	30. provincia
4. auxilium	13. equus	22. inimicus	31. puer
5. bellum	14. filius	23. luna	32. regina
6. caelum	15. fortuna	24. nuntius	33. sapientia
7. castra	16. fossa	25. oceanus	34. servus
8. cura	17. frumentum	26. oppidum	35. socius
9. dea	18. gladius	27. periculum	

ADJECTIVES

1. aeger	6. miser
2. altus	7. noster
3. angustus	8. suus
4. laetus	9. vester
5. liber	

VERBS

1. adoro	6. exspecto	11. occupo
2. aedifico	7. habeo	12. regno
3. armo	8. libero	13. sto
4. aro	9. neco	14. supero
5. curo	10. nuntio	15. timeo

ADVERBS

1. etiam	3. hodie	5. saepe
2. hic	4. ibi	6. ubi

PREPOSITIONS

1. ante	3. per	5. trans
2. de	4. post	

CONJUNCTIONS

1. sed

63. Practice Exercises

No. 38. Give the infinitive of each of these verbs:

1. aedifico	6. libero	11. neco
2. nuncio	7. regno	12. adoro
3. exspecto	8. aro	13. timeo
4. supero	9. sto	14. habeo
5. video	10. curo	15. occupo

No. 39. Give the genitive and gender of these nouns:

1. dea	6. socius	11. puer	16. vir
2. proelium	7. fortuna	12. ager	17. gladius
3. provincia	8. amicus	13. castra	18. cura
4. bellum	9. inimicus	14. periculum	19. praeda
5. oceanus	10. regina	15. victoria	20. equus

No. 40.

1. Rearrange these sentences in the usual Latin order:

   a. **Frumentum cur datis non viris?**

   b. **Curam dat insularum bonamne incolis?**

2. Give the present tense with English meanings of **sto** and **timeo**.

No. 41. Put into English:

1. agricolas nostros	6. suos filios	11. multi
2. filiarum laetarum	7. miseros	12. parvus puer
3. caelum altum	8. vias angustas	13. agrorum latorum
4. patriae liberae	9. tuus nuntius	14. cura bona
5. vester servus	10. fortuna mea	15. gladi longi

No. 42. Translate these vocatives:

1. amici	6. domina	11. bone vir
2. bella	7. fili	12. bona puella
3. deae	8. gloria	13. multi amici
4. deus	9. nuntii	14. bone agricola
5. domine	10. mi serve	15. amici noster

64. Reading

GAIUS VALERIUS CATULLUS

Catullus was born about 84 B.C. at Verona, in northeastern Italy, but spent most of his life in Rome. He was a master of lyric poetry, especially love poems, and made use of many of the best features of Greek verse. Catullus died in 54 B.C. (From now on, the translations of the Chapter Review Readings will be found in the Answers section. Check the Latin-English Vocabulary and a good Latin dictionary for words not yet studied.)

Da mi basia mille, deinde centum,
dein mille altera, dein secunda centum,
deinde usque altera mille, deinde centum.
Dein, cum milia multa fecerimus,
conturbabimus illa, ne sciamus,
aut ne quis malus invidere possit,
cum tantum sciat esse basiorum.

Catullus V

Odi et amo. Quare id faciam, fortasse requiris.
Nescio, sed fieri sentio et excrucior.

Catullus LXXXV

THE VULGATE BIBLE

Toward the end of the fourth century, the Bible was translated into Latin by St. Jerome and others. This Latin version is called the Vulgate, meaning the Bible for the common people.

In principio erat Verbum et
Verbum erat apud Deum, et Deus erat
Verbum. Hoc erat in principio
apud Deum. Omnia, per ipsum facta
sunt, et sine ipso factum est nihil,
quod factum est; in ipso vita erat,
et vita erat lux hominum; et lux in
tenebris lucet, et tenebrae eam non
comprehenderunt. Fuit homo missus
a Deo, cui nomen erat Ioannes. Hic
venit in testimonium, ut testimonium
perhiberet de lumine, ut omnes crederent
per illum. Non erat ille lux, sed ut
testimonium perhiberet de lumine. Erat lux
vera, quae illuminat omnem hominem
venientem in hunc mundum: in mundo
erat, et mundus per ipsum factus
est et mundus eum non cognovit.

Evangelium Secundum Ioannem, I, i-x

VERBS AND TENSES: *POSSUM AND EO*

Familiar Phrases

persona grata, an acceptable (or welcome) person.

persona non grata, an unacceptable (or unwelcome) person.

verbatim ac litteratim, word for word and letter for letter.

pro bono publico, for the public good.

ad infinitum, to infinity; with no limit.

sine dubio, without doubt.

vice versa, changed and turned; turned about.

addenda et corrigenda, things added and corrected; a supplement, especially to a book.

---

65. New Reading Vocabulary

NOUNS

populus, populi, m., people (popular)
lingua, linguae, f., language (linguist)
aedificium, aedificii or **aedifici, n.,** building (edifice)

Troia, Troiae, f., Troy
Latium, Latii or **Lati, n.,** Latin

ADJECTIVES

latinus, latina, latinum, Latin

VERBS

paro, parare, prepare, get ready (preparation)
maneo, manere, remain, stay (manor, mansion)
debeo, debere, owe, ought (debit)

possum, posse, be able, can
eo, ire, go
propero, properare, hurry, hasten

ADVERBS

nonne, expects the answer "yes"
minime, by no means, not at all (minimum)
certe, certainly, surely, indeed (certes)

num, expects the answer "no"
ita, yes; thus, so
vero, truly, in truth (verity)

When **populus** is a collective noun (when it represents a group), it is in the singular and its verb, in Latin, is also singular (although in English it usually sounds better to use a plural verb, as below). In the plural, it means *peoples*.

populus est, the people are

populi terrae sunt, the peoples of the earth are

66. New Reading Grammar—*Possum*, Present Tense

A. THE VERB possum, posse, MEANING *can, be able*, IS IRREGULAR. IT IS CONJUGATED IN THE PRESENT TENSE LIKE sum, esse:

Singular:		Plural:		Present Infinitive:	
possum	I am able, can	**possumus**	we are able, can	**posse**	to be able
potes	you are able, can	**potestis**	you are able, can		
potest	he, she, it is able, can	**possunt**	they are able, can		

The endings for the present tense of **possum** are the various forms of the verb **sum**. When the form begins with s-, it is attached to the prefix **pos-**. When the form begins with e-, it is attached to the prefix **pot-**. The change from **pos-** to **pot-** before the vowel **e** is made so that it will be easier to pronounce the word clearly.

67. New Reading Grammar—*Possum*, Imperfect Tense

To make the imperfect tense of **possum**, add the forms of the imperfect tense of **sum** to the base. Since all forms of **sum** begin with the vowel **e** in this tense, the stem is always **pot-**.

Singular:		Plural:	
poteram	I was able/used to be able/could	**poteramus**	we were able
		poteratis	you were able
poteras	you were able		
poterat	he, she, it was able	**poterant**	they were able

68. New Reading Grammar—*Eo*, Present Tense

The verb **eo, ire,** meaning *go*, is irregular. In the present tense, it is conjugated as follows:

Singular:		Plural:		Present Infinitive:	
eo	I go, am going, do go	**imus**	we go, are going, do go	**ire**	to go
is	you go, are going, do go	**itis**	you go, are going, do go		
it	he, she, it goes, is going, does go	**eunt**	they go, are going, do go		

69. New Reading Grammar—*Eo*, Imperfect Tense

The imperfect tense of **eo** is formed by adding the imperfect endings on to the stem, **i-**. (**i-** is usually used as the stem of this verb; however, since **eo** is irregular, **e-** is sometimes used instead.)

Singular:		Plural:	
ibam	I was going/used to go/did go/went	**ibamus**	we were going
		ibatis	you were going
ibas	you were going	**ibant**	they were going
ibat	he, she, it was going		

70. New Grammar—Questions and Answers

1. QUESTIONS

Although many Latin books today have modern punctuation added for clarity, Latin had no question mark. Thus, certain words had to be used in sentences to show that a question was being asked.

a. A question word like cur (why?) *asks a direct question.*

Cur manes	Why do you stay?

b. A simple question is indicated by -ne *on the end of the first word.*

Suntne boni	Are they good?

c. Nonne *at the beginning of a sentence asks a question expecting the answer* yes.

Nonne sunt boni	They are good, aren't they?

d. Num *at the beginning of a sentence asks a question expecting the answer* no.

Num sunt boni   They are not good, are they?

2. ANSWERS

Answers to questions may be expressed in various ways.

a. By a statement, either positive or negative.

Sunt boni   They are good.   **Non sunt boni**   They are not good.

b. By a positive or affirmative word.

Ita   Yes.   **Vero**   Yes, truly.   **Certe**   Certainly.

c. By a negative word.

Non   No.   **Minime**   By no means. Not at all.

71. New Reading Grammar—Complementary Infinitives

Some verbs, such as **paro** (*prepare*), **debeo** (*ought*), **propero** (*hasten*), or **possum** (*be able, can*), *are not* complete unless another verb is used with them to complete their meaning. The completing verb is always an infinitive, and is called a complementary infinitive (from the Latin **compleo,** to complete). This is often true of the corresponding verbs in English as well.

Manere debeo   I ought to stay.   **Manere parat**   He prepares to stay.
Navigare properas   You hasten to sail.   **Navigare possumus**   We are able to (can) sail.

72. Reading

Populus Romanus

1. **Populus Romanus certe clarus est.**
2. **Nonne populum Romanum amas? Ita.**
3. **Populos terrarum multarum superabant et viri Romani in provinciis Romanis habitabant.**
4. **Multae copiae in provinciis manent et incolas bene regnant.**
5. **Vias bonas et aedificia magna et templa pulchra ibi aedeficabant.**
6. **Incolis fortunam bonam portabant.**
7. **Incolae provinciarum saepe erant socii et populus Romanus erat dominus bonus.**
8. **Socii populo Romano auxilium vero dant.**

The Roman People

1. The Roman people are indeed famous.
2. You like the Roman people, don't you? Yes.
3. They conquered the peoples of many lands and the Roman men lived in the Roman provinces.
4. Many troops stay in the provinces and rule the inhabitants well.
5. They built good roads and large buildings and beautiful temples there.
6. They brought good fortune to the inhabitants.
7. The inhabitants of the provinces often were allies and the Roman people were good masters.
8. The allies truly give aid to the Roman people.

Alba Longa

1. **Alba Longa erat oppidum in Italia antiqua.**
2. **In Latio erat et agros latos et bonos habebat.**
3. **Vergilius de Alba Longa in fabula sua narrabat.**
4. **Quod populus Graeciae Troiam superabat, multi viri erant clari.**
5. **Aeneas est vero clarus.**
6. **In Troia non manet, sed ad Latium navigat.**
7. **Latinus in Latio regnabat.**
8. **Aeneas Latinum oppugnare parabat et castra ibi aedificabat.**
9. **Castra erant Alba Longa.**
10. **Aeneas Latinum superat et Latium occupat.**
11. **Populus Lati erat Latinus et lingua erat Latina**

Alba Longa

1. Alba Longa was a town in ancient Italy.
2. It was in Latium and had wide and good fields.
3. Virgil told about Alba Longa in his story.
4. Because the people of Greece conquered Troy, many men were famous.
5. Aeneas is truly famous.
6. He does not stay in Troy, but sails to Latium.
7. Latinus ruled in Latium.
8. Aeneas prepared to attack Latinus and built a camp there.
9. The camp was Alba Longa.
10. Aeneas conquers Latinus and seizes Latium.
11. The people of Latium were Latin and the language was Latin.

73. Practice Exercises

No. 43. Give the English for these questions and answers:

1. **Nonne amicos habetis? Certe.**
2. **Aedificantne casas? Ita. Casas aedificant.**
3. **Nonne vero times? Vero timeo.**
4. **Num populus pugnat? Populus non pugnat.**
5. **Num viae sunt longae? Viae minime sunt longae.**
6. **Cur ad oppidum ambulant?**
7. **Manetne vir in aedificio? Vir in aedificio manet.**
8. **Estne provincia libera? Provincia vero est libera.**
9. **Num in oceano navigat? In oceano non navigat.**

No. 44. Complete these verbs by filling in the correct vowel:

1. vid _____ tis
2. pot _____ st
3. hab _____ o
4. ador _____ s
5. vid _____ o
6. e _____ nt
7. iuv _____ t
8. man _____ nt
9. hab _____ s
10. st _____ tis
11. par _____ nt
12. deb _____ mus
13. poss _____ nt
14. aedific _____ s
15. oppugn _____ nt
16. ambul _____ tis
17. tim _____ t
18. proper _____ t

No. 45. Fill in the correct completing infinitive:

1. (To walk) **debeo.**
2. (To fight) **parat.**
3. (To kill) **non debent.**
4. (To conquer) **paratis.**
5. (To call) **debemus.**
6. (To swim) **non parant.**

7. (To help) **properatis.**
8. (To work) **non debetis.**
9. (To attack) **parat.**
10. (To stay) **debes.**
11. (To sail) **possum.**
12. (To go) **non potest.**

No. 46. Translate these into English:

1. **Cur frumentum ibi parat?**
2. **Nonne linguam latinam amatis?**
3. **Ubi aedificia vestra stant?**
4. **Pueris gladios dare non debetis.**
5. **Dei arma sua etiam habent.**

6. **De bello longo Troiae fabulam narrant.**
7. **Aeneas cum viris suis ad Italiam navigat.**
8. **Deus populum Graeciae iuvat.**
9. **Cur Romani socios suos timent?**
10. **In caelo lunam claram videt.**

74. New Reading Vocabulary

NOUNS

avunculus, avunculi, m., uncle (avuncular)
ripa, ripae, f., bank (of a river) (riparious)
ludus, ludi, m., game or school (ludicrous)
forum, fori, n., forum, market place (forensic)
Sabini, Sabinorum, m. pl., the Sabines
praemium, praemii or **praemi, n.,** reward (premium)

arca, arcae, f., chest, box (ark)
vita, vitae, f., life (vital)
lupa, lupae, f., she-wolf (lupine)
Roma, Romae, f., Rome
Romanus, Romani, m., a Roman

VERBS

servo, servare, save, preserve (preservation)

loco, locare, place, put

ADVERBS

nunc, now

tum, then

PREPOSITIONS

sine, without. With the ablative case (sinecure).

CONJUNCTIONS

cum, when, while

State Mottoes

Ditat Deus, God enriches. (Arizona)

Regnant populi, The people rule. (Arkansas)

Esto perpetua, May it be everlasting. (Idaho)

> **Ad astra per aspera,** To the stars through hardships. (Kansas)
>
> **Dirigo,** I direct. (Maine)
>
> **Virtute et armis,** By courage and weapons. (Mississippi)
>
> **Excelsior,** Loftier. (New York)
>
> **Imperium in imperio,** An empire in an empire. (Ohio)
>
> **Montani semper liberi,** Mountaineers are always free. (West Virginia)
>
> **Cedant arma togae,** Let weapons yield to the toga. (Wyoming)

75. *Cum* (Preposition and Conjunction)

Cum is used as both a conjunction and a preposition.

1. **Cum, AS A CONJUNCTION WITH THE INDICATIVE MOOD, MEANS** *when* **OR** *while* **AND INTRODUCES A CLAUSE SHOWING TIME.**

Cum puerum videbat, ambulabat.	When he saw the boy, he was walking.
Cum ambulabat, puerum videbat.	While he was walking, he saw the boy.

2. **Cum, AS A PREPOSITION, MEANS** *with* **AND IS USED WITH THE ABLATIVE CASE.**

Cum puero ambulabat.	He was walking with the boy.
Cum pueris ambulabat.	He was walking with the boys.

Cum is also used with the subjunctive mood. You will learn about this use of **cum** in later lessons.

76. Reading

Romulus et Remus

1. **Quod Romulus et Remus filii erant dei armorum et belli, populus Romanus proelia amabat.**
2. **Erant etiam filii Rheae Silviae.**
3. **Amulius erat avunculus Rheae Silviae et Albam Longam regnabat, sed pueros non amabat.**
4. **Pueros amare debet.**
5. **Amulius filios Rheae Silviae necare parabat, sed servus in aqua in arca pueros locabat et vitas puerorum servabat.**
6. **Mars filios suos ad ripam Tiberis portabat.**
7. **Lupa pueros ibi curabat et agricola bonus ad casam suam Romulum et Remum portabat.**

Romulus and Remus

1. Because Romulus and Remus were the sons of the god of weapons and of war, the Roman people liked battles.
2. They were also the sons of Rhea Silvia.
3. Amulius was the uncle of Rhea Silvia and ruled Alba Longa, but he did not love the boys.
4. He ought to love the boys.
5. Amulius prepared to kill the sons of Rhea Silvia, but a slave placed the boys in a chest and saved the lives of the boys.
6. Mars carried his sons to the banks of the Tiber.
7. A wolf took care of the boys there and a good farmer carried Romulus and Remus to his cottage.

Sabini

1. **Romulus et Remus cum amicis suis Romam aedificabant, sed oppidum erat parvum et viri erant miseri quod sine feminis tum ibi erant.**
2. **Romulus ad ludos magnos Sabinos vocat et Sabini ad ludos feminas et filias suas portant.**
3. **Viri Romani ad casas suas puellas portant et Sabini pugnare properant.**
4. **In Foro Romano tum pugnabant, sed feminae erant miserae quod Sabini multos necabant.**
5. **Sabini vitas virorum suorum servabant, sed Romani praemium victoriae habebant.**
6. **Feminae et filiae Sabinorum cum Romanis nunc habitabant.**

The Sabines

1. Romulus and Remus were building Rome with their friends, but the town was small and the men were unhappy because then they were there without women.
2. Romulus calls the Sabines to great games and the Sabines bring their women and daughters to the games.
3. The Roman men carry the girls to their cottages and the Sabines hasten to fight.
4. They fought then in the Roman Forum, but the women were unhappy because the Sabines were killing many people.
5. The Sabines saved the lives of their men, but the Romans had the reward of victory.
6. The women and daughters of the Sabines now lived with the Romans.

Legal Terms

ius civile, civil law, referring to the laws of legal systems modeled after Roman law.

ius gentium, the law of nations, referring to International Law.

lex scripta, written law. Written laws are those passed and put into effect by a legislative body or corporation.

lex non scripta, unwritten law. Unwritten law develops out of common practice, custom, and usage. It is sometimes called common law.

sub iudice, before the judge, referring to a case under consideration by the judge, or court, but not yet decided.

corpus iuris, the body of law, comprised of all the laws of a sovereign power or legislative body collectively.

subpoena, under penalty or punishment. A **subpoena** is a writ naming a person and ordering him or her to appear in court, under penalty for failure to do so.

corpus delicti, the body of the crime or offense. The **corpus delicti** refers to the circumstances necessary to a crime. In murder, the **corpus delicti** is the fact of a criminal agent or of the death of the victim. It does not refer to the victim's body.

onus probandi, the burden of proof. The burden of proving its case rests with the side that makes the affirmation in a suit.

prima facie, on or at first appearance. **Prima facie** evidence is evidence that, at first presentation, is adequate enough to establish a fact.

77. Practice Exercises

No. 47. Fill in the blanks with the correct letters to complete the imperfect tense:

1. deb _____ mus
2. par _____ m
3. proper _____ nt
4. man _____ nt
5. tim _____ t
6. vid _____ s
7. cur _____ m
8. ador _____ mus
9. loc _____ s
10. d _____ tis

11. hab _____ tis
12. st _____ t
13. laud _____ m
14. man _____ s
15. vid _____ mus
16. hab _____ s
17. port _____ tis
18. iuv _____ t
19. voc _____ t
20. tim _____ mus

No. 48. Give the English for the following:

1. monstrabat
2. voco
3. paramus
4. regnabatis
5. debebas
6. timetis
7. erat
8. pugnatis
9. properabam
10. videbant
11. laudabatis
12. portatis

13. ibamus
14. poteram
15. manemus
16. servabat
17. locabam
18. oppugnabas
19. habebatis
20. eratis
21. poterat
22. ibant
23. superabatis
24. narrant

No. 49. Translate these phrases and clauses:

1. cum stabat
2. cum filia
3. cum laboramus
4. cum exspecto
5. cum amicis
6. cum superat
7. cum lupa
8. cum videtis

9. cum erat
10. cum pugnabatis
11. cum puella
12. cum erant
13. cum avunculo meo
14. cum Romanis
15. cum feminis multis

No. 50. Translate the following into English:

1. **Num viros in castris habet?**
2. **Ibi esse hodie parabamus.**
3. **Amicus tuus in oppido nostro famam bonam habet.**
4. **Cum puellis manere parabam.**
5. **Nonne in silvis multas lupas saepe necat?**
6. **Romani gladios Sabinorum timere non debent.**
7. **Cum oppidum aedificant, templa et aedificia ibi locant.**
8. **Cur servis suis praemia dant?**
9. **Agricola cum amico suo in agro erat.**
10. **Nonne sine aqua estis?**

78. New Reading Vocabulary

NOUNS

barbarus, barbari, m., barbarian (barbarous)

finitimus, finitimi, m., neighbor

ADJECTIVES

finitimus, finitima, finitimum, neighboring
amicus, amica, amicum, friendly (amicable)
inimicus, inimica, inimicum, unfriendly (inimical)
barbarus, barbara, barbarum, savage, uncivilized, barbarian (barbarous)

idoneus, idonea, idoneum, fit, suitable
gratus, grata, gratum, pleasing (grateful)
propinquus, propinqua, propinquum, near (propinquity)

VERBS

moneo, monere, warn, advise (admonition, monitor)
incito, incitare, arouse, stir up, incite (incitement)

ADVERBS

cras, tomorrow (procrastinate)

PREPOSITIONS

ob, on account of, because of. With the accusative case.

CONJUNCTIONS

atque or **ac,** and also, also. **ac** is used only before consonants.

79. New Reading Grammar—Adjectives with the Dative

Some adjectives are followed by the dative case. They translate into English with the preposition *to* or *for*. They include **propinquus** (*near*), **idoneus** (*fit*), **amicus** (*friendly*), **inimicus** (*unfriendly*), **gratus** (*pleasing*), and **finitimus** (*neighboring*).

Est propinquus agro.	He is near to the field.
Est idoneus bello.	He is fit for war.
Est amicus puero.	He is friendly to the boy.
Est inimicus populo.	He is unfriendly to the people.
Est gratus viris.	He is pleasing to the men.
Est finitimum oppido.	It is neighboring to the town.

80. New Reading Grammar—Future Tense

The future tense shows action going on in the future, as in the sentence *We will go.* It is translated with either *shall* or *will*.

1. IN first AND second conjugation VERBS, ALL BUT THE FIRST PERSON SINGULAR AND THIRD PERSON PLURAL ADD -bi- BEFORE THE BASIC ENDINGS TO SHOW THE FUTURE TENSE.

These add **-bo** and **-bu-** respectively for the future tense. Thus, the basic endings are:

Singular:	Plural:
-bo	**-bimus**
-bis	**-bitis**
-bit	**-bunt**

Remember, these are the endings only for the first and second conjugation verbs. The third and fourth conjugation verbs, which you will learn about in later chapters, form the future tense differently.

2. FUTURE TENSE OF a-conjugation VERBS.

Singular:		Plural:	
amabo	I shall love/like	**amabimus**	we shall love
amabis	you will love	**amabitis**	you will love
amabit	he, she, it will love	**amabunt**	they will love

These forms can be broken down, just like the forms of the imperfect. Thus, when you see the word **amabitis**, am- is the stem; -a- shows that the verb is of the **a-conjugation**; -bi- shows that it is in the future tense; and -tis shows that it is the active second person plural.

3. FUTURE TENSE OF e-conjugation VERBS.

Singular:		Plural:	
habebo	I shall have/hold	**habebimus**	we shall have
habebis	you will have	**habebitis**	you will have
habebit	he, she, it will have	**habebunt**	they will have

These forms can be broken down like the **a-declension** forms above. Of course, they will have an -e- instead of an -a- before the endings.

81. Future Tense of the Irregular Verbs *sum*, *possum*, and *eo*

a. The future tense of sum is recognized by the stem, eri-, to which the basic endings are added. Note that the first person singular is ero and the third person plural is erunt.

Singular:		Plural:	
ero	I shall be	**erimus**	we shall be
eris	you will be	**eritis**	you will be
erit	he/she/it will be; there will be	**erunt**	they will be/there will be

b. The future tense of possum is formed by adding the future tense of sum to the stem pot-. pot- is used because all the forms of sum in the future tense begin with the letter e.

Singular:		Plural:	
potero	I shall be able	**poterimus**	we shall be able
poteris	you will be able	**poteritis**	you will be able
poterit	he, she, it will be able	**poterunt**	they will be able

c. The future tense of eo is formed by adding the normal future tense endings of the first and second conjugation verbs to the stem of eo, i-.

Singular:		Plural:	
ibo	I shall go	**ibimus**	we shall go
ibis	you will go	**ibitis**	you will go
ibit	he, she, it will go	**ibunt**	they will go

82. Reading

Graecia

1. Gloria Graeciae et fama incolarum suarum sunt clarae.
2. Graecia est paeninsula et agri et silvae populo bonam fortunam et vitam laetam dabant.
3. Nautae trans oceanum ad terras multas navigabant et multa ad fora oppidorum Graeciae portabant.
4. Graecia est propinqua Italiae, sed non est finitima.
5. Proelia et bella non erant grata incolis, sed cum populis finitimis pugnare saepe parabant.
6. Populus multis amicis erat et bellum populo non idoneum erat.
7. Italia erat inimica Graeciae et terram occupabat.
8. Tum populus Graeciae erat socius populi Italiae, sed populus Romanus linguam et templa aedificia Graeciae laudabat.

Greece

1. The glory of Greece and the fame of her inhabitants are well-known.
2. Greece is a peninsula and the fields and forests gave good fortune and a happy life to the people.
3. The sailors sailed across the ocean to many lands and brought many things to the market places of the towns of Greece.
4. Greece is near to Italy, but it is not neighboring.
5. Battles and wars were not pleasing to the inhabitants, but they often got ready to fight with the neighboring peoples.
6. The people were friendly to many and war was not suitable for the people.
7. Italy was unfriendly to Greece and seized the land.
8. Then the people of Greece were allies of the people of Italy, but the Roman people praised the language and temples and buildings of Greece.

Barbari

1. Romani multos finitimos barbaros habebant.
2. Barbari ob praedam bella et proelia saepe incitabant.
3. Nonne nuntii de periculo monebant?
4. Cum nuntium portabant, socii auxilium portare atque copias suas armare debebant.
5. Romani non timebant, sed in terris barbaris pugnabant.
6. Oppida multa ibi oppugnabant et superabant.
7. Populus Germanus non erat amicus Romanis.
8. Erat barbarus et patriae Romanorum finitimus.
9. Victoriae copiarum Romanarum erant clarae et magnae.
10. Copiis praemia dabant, cum nuntii famas bonas de gloria in provinciis narrabant.

The Barbarians

1. The Romans had many uncivilized neighbors.
2. The barbarians often stirred up wars and battles on account of booty.
3. The messengers warned about the danger, didn't they?
4. When they brought the message, the allies had to bring aid and arm their troops.
5. The Romans were not afraid, but they fought in barbarian lands.
6. They used to attack many towns there and conquer them.
7. The German people were not friendly to the Romans.
8. They were uncivilized and neighboring to the native country of the Romans.
9. The victories of the Roman troops were famous and great.
10. They gave the troops rewards, when the messengers related good reports about their glory in the provinces.

83. Practice Exercises

No. 51. Give the English for these verb forms:

1. oppugnat
2. liberabant
3. videbo
4. manebit
5. erant
6. sunt
7. debent
8. amare
9. habebitis
10. pugnabas
11. dabant
12. erit
13. incitabunt
14. monebit
15. portare
16. timebit
17. pugnabis
18. superabimus
19. parabamus
20. erunt
21. narrabunt
22. incitabat
23. monebatis
24. sumus
25. oppugnabamus
26. incitabit
27. natabant
28. locabatis
29. servabis
30. iuvabitis
31. ibitis
32. potero

No. 52. Give the English for these phrases:

1. de caelo claro
2. finitimus patriae meae
3. propinquum insulis
4. cum amico nostro
5. ad aedificia alta
6. in fossis latis
7. gratus socio suo
8. ante agros
9. amicus servis
10. post bellum
11. inimici reginae
12. de victoria tua
13. per proelia multa
14. idoneus viro
15. sine praeda

No. 53. Give the tense of the following verbs:

1. sum
2. monebunt
3. manebat
4. debet
5. erat
6. dabat
7. narrabit
8. oppugnant
9. pugnabis
10. erit
11. iuvabis
12. natabas
13. amabunt
14. timebat
15. incitabis
16. liberabam
17. debebit
18. narrabant
19. pugnabamus
20. erunt

No. 54. Translate the following into English:

1. Ad vias angustas ambulabit.
2. Ante templa stabant.
3. Ex oceano natabatis.
4. In aqua pugnabunt.
5. Femina grata erat.
6. Patriam liberam habere debebunt.
7. Puellae natabunt.
8. Finitimos suos amabat.
9. Avunculos tuos servabis.
10. Reginam laudabunt.

11. Ubi esse debetis?
12. Puerum vocabas.
13. Erit inimicus nuntio.
14. Non est provinciae propinquum.
15. Gladios tuos non timebimus.
16. Servi vestri iuvant.
17. Vir ibi manebit.
18. Fossam altam parabamus.
19. Dominus fabulam narrabit.
20. Agrum arabimus.

84. New Reading Vocabulary

NOUNS

memoria, memoriae, f., memory (memorial)
Germanus, Germani, m., a German (person)
(Germanic)

legatus, legati, m., lieutenant, legate (legion)
Gallia, Galliae, f., Gaul (the country) (Gallic)
Gallus, Galli, m., a Gaul (person)

VERBS

teneo, tenere, hold, keep, have (tenable)
memoria tenere, to remember. Literally, to keep by memory

PREPOSITIONS

contra, against. With the accusative case (contradict).
pro, for, in behalf of, on behalf of (procurator)

85. New Reading Grammar—Nouns in Apposition

In the sentence *John, the doctor, is going home,* the word *doctor* is in apposition to the word *John.* In *The doctor, John, is going home,* the word *John* is in apposition to the word *doctor.* The two nouns are used in the same way, as the subject of the sentence; one could replace the other. In Latin, a noun in apposition to another noun must be in the same case, number, and, if possible, gender as well.

Puer amat puellam, filiam legati. The boy likes the girl, the daughter of the lieutenant.

Filiam is in apposition to **puellam.** Therefore, **filiam,** like **puellam,** is in the accusative case (showing that it acts as the direct object) and is singular. **Filiam** is also of the same gender as **puellam,** feminine. This will usually be the case with nouns in apposition, but not always.

Familiar Quotations

Virginibus puerisque. For boys and girls. (Horace)

Non scholae sed vitae discimus. We learn not for school, but for life. (Seneca)

Parvum parva decent. Small things become the small. (Horace)

Eheu fugaces anni. Alas, the fleeting years. (Horace)

Vera amicitia est inter bonos. There is true friendship only among good men. (Cicero)

Ave atque vale. Hail and farewell. (Catullus)

Da dextram misero. Give your right hand to the wretched. (Virgil)

86. New Reading Grammar—Imperatives

To give direct commands, such as *Put that down!*, Latin uses the imperative mood of a verb. This mood uses only the second person singular and plural (the word *you,* whether singular or plural, is not expressed).

1. THE IMPERATIVE OF a-conjugation VERBS.

The imperative singular is formed by dropping the **-re** from the infinitive. What remains is the stem of the verb plus **-a**. The imperative plural is formed by adding **-te** to the imperative singular.

Singular: **ama** love! like! Plural: **amate** love! like!

2. THE IMPERATIVE OF e-conjugation VERBS.

This is formed in the same way as the imperative of **a-conjugation** verbs, except that there is an **-e-** instead of an **-a-**.

Singular: **habe** have! hold! Plural: **habete** have! hold!

3. IMPERATIVE OF THE IRREGULAR VERBS sum, possum, AND eo.

a. sum forms the imperative as follows:

Singular: **es** be! Plural: **este** be!

b. possum does not have the imperative mood.

c. eo forms the imperative as follows:

Singular: **i** go! Plural: **ite** go!

4. THERE ARE FOUR VERBS IN LATIN THAT FORM THEIR IMPERATIVES IRREGULARLY: (1) *dic, dicite,* SAY, (2) *duc, ducite,* LEAD, (3) *fac, facite,* MAKE OR DO, AND (4) *fer, ferte,* CARRY OR BRING.

5. LATIN ALSO HAS A FUTURE IMPERATIVE THAT EXISTS IN BOTH SECOND AND THIRD PERSON, SINGULAR AND PLURAL, AND IN BOTH THE ACTIVE AND PASSIVE VOICE (PASSIVE VOICE HAS NO SECOND PERSON PLURAL FORM).

Because these forms are extremely rare, existing primarily in legal documents, they are not covered in this text.

87. Reading

Gallia

1. Patria Gallorum erat Germaniae et Hispaniae finitima.
2. Galli proelia et bella non amabant, sed bellum non timebant.
3. Romani contra Gallos saepe pugnabant et Galli pro patria sua tum bene pugnabant.

4. Romani in Gallia legatos habebant quod Galli Romanis amici non erant.

5. Legati bellum cum Gallia pugnare saepe parabant.
6. Caesar ob victorias suas in Gallia gloriam magnam habebat.
7. Oppida in Gallia erant clara.
8. Ibi erant oppida multa et pulchra ac silvae multae et agri boni.
9. Ob periculum belli Romani in multis terris finitimis legatos habebat.

10. Romani pro patria etiam sine praemiis magnis et praeda pugnabant.
11. Erant in Gallia multi agri lati atque agricolis idonea erat.
12. Cum in Gallia habitabant, Romani linguam Latinam tenebant.

Gaul

1. The native country of the Gauls was neighboring to Germany and Spain.
2. The Gauls did not like battles and wars, but they did not fear war.
3. The Romans often fought against the Gauls, and the Gauls then fought hard for their native country.
4. The Romans had lieutenants in Gaul because the Gauls were not friendly to the Romans.
5. The lieutenants often got ready to fight with the Gauls.
6. Caesar had great glory because of his victories in Gaul.
7. The towns in Gaul were famous.
8. There were many and beautiful towns there, and also many forests and good fields.
9. On account of the danger of war, the Romans had legates in many neighboring lands.
10. The Romans fought for their country even without large rewards and booty.
11. There were many wide fields in Gaul, and it was suitable for farmers.
12. When they were living in Gaul, the Romans kept the Latin language.

88. Practice Exercises

No. 55. Translate these imperatives and indicate whether they are singular or plural:

1. ambula
2. amate
3. natate
4. pugna
5. laudate
6. navigate
7. date
8. habita
9. timete
10. vide
11. state
12. habete
13. tene
14. regna
15. tenete
16. superate
17. sta
18. iuvate
19. monete
20. mane

No. 56. Translate the nouns, which are in apposition:

1. vir, agricola
2. viri, nautae
3. patria, Britannia
4. regina, puella
5. Galli, socii nostri
6. nuntius, puer
7. Gallos, inimicos
8. dominum, amicum
9. filiorum, puerorum

No. 57. Translate the following into English. Note: the vocative case is used in some of the sentences:

1. Puer aeger, filius tuus, in oppido manebit.
2. In proelio, amice, socios habere debes.
3. Contra bellum, popule Romane, viros tuos incita.
4. Incolas Galliae, nuntii, monete.
5. Sabinos, finitimos nostros, ad ludos vocabo.
6. Templa, puellae, aedificia pulchra, videte.
7. Roma, oppidum in Italia, clara erit.
8. Galliam, fili mi, memoria tene.
9. Habebimusne, amici, forum magnum?
10. Avunculos meos, nuntios, exspectabo.

Roman busts were remarkably realistic.

Trajan's column commemorates the victory of Emperor Trajan over enemies on Rome's borders.

89. Vocabulary Review

NOUNS

1. aedificium
2. arca
3. avunculus
4. barbarus
5. finitimus
6. forum
7. Gallia
8. Gallus
9. Germanus
10. Latinus
11. Latium
12. legatus
13. lingua
14. ludus
15. lupa
16. memoria
17. populus
18. praemium
19. ripa
20. Roma
21. Romanus
22. Sabini
23. Troia
24. vita

ADJECTIVES

1. amicus
2. barbarus
3. finitimus
4. gratus
5. idoneus
6. inimicus
7. latinus
8. propinquus

VERBS

1. debeo
2. incito
3. loco
4. maneo
5. moneo
6. paro
7. propero
8. servo
9. teneo
10. memoria tenere
11. eo
12. possum

ADVERBS

1. certe
2. cras
3. ita
4. minime
5. nonne
6. num
7. nunc
8. tum
9. vero

PREPOSITIONS

1. contra
2. ob
3. pro
4. sine

CONJUNCTIONS

1. atque, ac

90. Practice Exercises

No. 58. Tell whether each of the following is a simple question, expects the answer "yes," or expects the answer "no."

1. Estne aeger?
2. Ubi est puer?
3. Cur times?
4. Num manebat?
5. Nonne amici sunt?
6. Num manetis?
7. Properatne?
8. Cur debent?
9. Ubi arcam locat?

No. 59. Change these verbs to the imperfect tense:

1. debeo
2. locas
3. incitat
4. paratis
5. tenemus
6. servas
7. teneo
8. manemus
9. monet

No. 60. Change these verbs to the future tense:

1. videbam
2. stabant
3. timebas
4. necabatis
5. habebamus
6. aedificabam
7. superabas
8. curabamus
9. nuntiabant

No. 61. Give both the singular and plural imperatives of these infinitives:

1. servare
2. monere
3. incitare
4. navigare
5. parare
6. tenere
7. properare
8. necare
9. pugnare

No. 62. Give both the singular and plural vocative of these nouns:

1. populus
2. memoria
3. legatus
4. amicus
5. femina
6. bellum
7. avunculus
8. vir
9. filius
10. agricola

91. Reading

Check the Latin-English Vocabulary and a good Latin dictionary for words not yet studied.

GAIUS IULIUS CAESAR

Caesar was born of a noble family, in Rome, in 100 B.C. He was educated as an orator and lawyer, but soon turned to politics and became consul in 59 B.C. For the next seven years, he was proconsul in Gaul, where he was successful in subduing and conquering the Gallic tribes. His **Commentaries on the Gallic War** are a military history of this period. Caesar's refusal to surrender the command of his army led to civil war, with his long dictatorship and political turmoil resulting in his assassination in 44 B.C.

Natio est omnis Gallorum admodum dedita religionibus . . . Deum maxime Mercurium colunt. Huius sunt plurima simulacra; hunc omnium inventorem artium ferunt, hunc viarum atque itinerum ducem, hunc ad quaestus pecuniae mercaturasque habere vim maximam arbitrantur.

Post hunc Apollinem et Martem et Iovem et Minervam. De his eandum fere, quam reliquae gentes, habent opinionem: Apollinem morbos depellere, Minervam operum atque artificiorum initia tradere, Iovem imperium caelestium tenere, Martem bella regere.

Commentarii de Bello Gallico, VI, xvi, xvii

THE BIBLE

In principio creavit Deus caelum et terram. Terra autem erat inanis et vacua, et tenebrae erant super faciem abyssi, et spiritus Dei ferebatur super aquas.

Dixitque Deus: Fiat lux. Et facta est lux. Et vidit Deus lucem quod esset bona et divisit lucem a tenebris. Appellavitque lucem diem et tenebras noctem. Factumque est vespere et mane, dies unus.

Dixit quoque Deus: Fiat firmamentum in medio aquarum et dividit aquas ab aquis. Et fecit Deus firmamentum divisitque aquas, quae erant sub firmamento, ab his quae erant super firmamentum. Et factum est ita. Vocavitque Deus firmamentum caelum. Et factum est vespere et mane, dies secundus.

Dixit vero Deus: Congregentur aquae, quae sub caelo sunt, in locum unum, et appareat arida. Et factum est ita. Et vocavit Deus aridam terram congregationesque aquarum appellavit maria. Et vidit Deus quod esset bonum. Et ait: Germinet terra herbam virentem et facientem semen et lignum pomiferum faciens fructum iuxta genus suum, cuius semen in semetipso sit super terram. Et factum est its. Et protulit terra herbam virentem et facientem semen iuxta genus suum lignumque faciens fructum et habens unumquoque sementem secundum speciem suam. Et vidit Deus quod esset bonum. Et factum est vespere et mane, dies tertius.

Liber Genesis I, i–xiii

PASSIVE VOICE • THIRD DECLENSION

Familiar Phrases

vi et armis, by force and arms.

pax vobiscum, peace be with you.

tempus fugit, time flies.

agenda, things that have to be done.

sic passim, thus everywhere.

multum in parvo, much in little.

senatus populusque Romanus, the Senate and the Roman people. Abbr. to S.P.Q.R.

res gestae, things done; acts or deeds.

alter idem, another self, referring to a close friend.

apparatus criticus, critical apparatus or material; reference material used in the critical study of a piece of literature.

---

92. New Reading Vocabulary

NOUNS

sagittarius, sagittarii or **sagittari, m.,** archer (Sagittarius)

pecunia, pecuniae, f., money (pecuniary)

littera, litterae, f., letter (of the alphabet). In the plural, a letter or epistle (literal, literature)

sagitta, sagittae, f., arrow (sagittal)

donum, doni, n., gift, present (donation)

Vandalii, Vandaliorum, m. pl., Vandals, a German tribe known for fierceness in battle (vandalism)

ADJECTIVES

robustus, robusta, robustum, strong, robust

VERBS

castra movere, to break (move) camp

terreo, terrere, frighten, scare, terrify (terrorize)

moveo, movere, move (movable)

doleo, dolere, grieve, be sorry (dolorous)

ADVERBS

mox, soon, presently

PREPOSITIONS

a or **ab,** by, away from, from (absent). With the ablative case.
inter, between, among (interlinear). With the accusative case.

CONJUNCTIONS

aut, or

93. New Reading Grammar—Passive Voice

The passive voice of a verb shows the subject as the receiver of the action.
Puer amatur, The boy is loved.

A. THE PASSIVE VOICE OF THE PRESENT, IMPERFECT, AND FUTURE TENSES OF FIRST AND SECOND CONJUGATION VERBS IS FORMED IN THE SAME WAY AS THE ACTIVE VOICE, EXCEPT THAT THE PERSONAL ENDINGS ARE PASSIVE INSTEAD OF ACTIVE.

These endings are:

Singular:			Plural:	
	1st person	**-r**		**-mur**
	2nd person	**-ris**		**-mini**
	3rd person	**-tur**		**-ntur**

First and second conjugation verbs add passive endings directly to the stem plus the **-a** or **-e-**, or, in the case of the first person singular, on to the stem plus **-o-** or **-eo-**. In the imperfect, the endings are added after **-ba-**, which indicates the use of that tense. Similarly, in the future tense, the endings are added on to **-bo-**, **-be-**, **-bi-**, or **-bu-**. The only irregularity is that **-be-** is used for the second person singular (i.e., **-beris**).

1. Present Passive Tense

A-Conjugation

		E-Conjugation	
amor	I am loved/being loved	**habeor**	I am held/being held
amaris	you are loved	**haberis**	you are held
amatur	he, she, it is loved	**habetur**	he, she, it is held
amamur	we are loved	**habemur**	we are held
amamini	you are loved	**habemini**	you are held
amantur	they are loved	**habentur**	they are held

2. Imperfect Passive Tense

A-Conjugation		E-Conjugation	
amabar	I was loved/being loved	habebar	I was held/being held
amabaris	you were loved	habebaris	you were held
amabatur	he, she, it was loved	habebatur	he, she, it was held
amabamur	we were loved	habebamur	we were held
amabamini	you were loved	habebamini	you were held
amabantur	they were loved	habebantur	they were held

3. Future Passive Tense

A-Conjugation		E-Conjugation	
amabor	I shall be loved	habebor	I shall be held
amaberis	you will be loved	habeberis	you will be held
amabitur	he, she, it will be loved	habebitur	he, she, it will be held
		habebimur	we shall be held
amabimur	we shall be loved	habebimini	you will be held
amabimini	you will be loved	habebuntur	they will be held
amabuntur	they will be loved		

Remember the irregularity in the second person singular: **amaberis, habeberis.**

4. *VIDEO often means SEEM when it is in the passive voice, rather than TO BE SEEN.*

5. *SUM and POSSUM do not have passive forms. EO does not generally use the passive voice either.*

B. IN THE PASSIVE VOICE, THE SUBJECT RECEIVES THE ACTION OF THE VERB. HOWEVER, SOMEONE OR SOMETHING IS DOING THE ACTION.

1. *If the doer is a person, he or she is called the agent of the action.*

The agent of a passive verb, when it is a personal agent, is expressed in the ablative case, with the preposition **a** (or **ab** when a vowel follows).

Puer ab agricola amatur.   The boy is loved by the farmer.

Puer, *The boy* is the subject of the verb, **amatur,** *is loved.* *The boy* does not do the loving but receives it; therefore, the verb is in the passive voice. **Agricola,** *the farmer* does the loving; therefore, he is the agent. **Puer,** the subject of the sentence, is in the nominative case, and **agricola** follows **ab,** and as agent is in the ablative case.

2. *If the doer is a thing, it is called the instrument by means of which the action is performed, and it is expressed in the ablative case, without any preposition.*

This is known as the *instrumental ablative* or *ablative of instrument.*

Puer sagitta necatur.   The boy is killed by an arrow.

Both active and passive verbs can have instruments. If an active verb has an instrument, the ablative case it uses is often referred to as an *ablative of means.*

Puer sagitta lupam necat.   The boy kills the wolf with an arrow.

Puer, *the boy,* is the subject in both sentences. However, in the first example, the verb, **necatur,** *is killed,* is passive. *The boy* receives the action of *an arrow.* In the second example, **necat,** *kills,* is active. *The boy* is doing the killing. He kills *the wolf,* **lupam,** which is the direct object. In both sentences, **sagitta,** *an arrow,* is the instrument by means of which the killing is done.

94. Reading

Germani
1. **Germania Galliae finitima erat et Italiae propinqua.**
2. **Incolae Germaniae, terrae magnae, non in oppidis magnis et pulchris, sed in silvis aut in casis parvis habitabant, quod barbari erant.**
3. **Inter Germanos erant multi sagittarii boni et in silvis lupae multae sagittis Germanorum necebantur.**
4. **Multae terrae et patriae a Vandaliis oppugnabantur atque superabantur.**
5. **Germani populis Galliae et Italiae non erant amici.**
6. **Vandalii robusti Italiam opugnabant et populus certe terrebatur quod pro vita sua timebat.**
7. **Ubi Vandalii populum superabant, multi vero erant miseri.**

The Germans
1. Germany was neighboring to Gaul and near Italy.
2. The inhabitants of Germany, a big country, did not live in large and beautiful towns, but in forests or in small cottages, because they were uncivilized.
3. Among the Germans, there were many good archers, and in the forest, many wolves were killed by the arrows of the Germans.
4. Many lands and native countries were attacked by the Vandals and conquered.
5. The Germans were not friendly to the peoples of Gaul and Italy.
6. The strong Vandals attacked Italy and the people were indeed frightened, because they feared for their lives.
7. When the Vandals conquered the people, many were truly wretched.

95. Practice Exercises

No. 63. Give the English for the following:

1. timeberis
2. laudabam
3. curor
4. laudantur
5. narrabuntur
6. stabo
7. armabatur
8. aras
9. occupabitur
10. stabitis
11. necabat
12. aedificabuntur
13. superabo
14. navigabit
15. habitabam
16. monstrabar
17. ambulabant
18. dabitur
19. iuvamini
20. vocabor

No. 64. Change these verbs to the passive voice:

1. exspectabam
2. tenent
3. monebit
4. videbat
5. amabit
6. habet
7. videbatis
8. portabit
9. movebitis
10. parant
11. laudabant
12. locatis
13. properabunt
14. timemus
15. incito
16. monebas
17. servas
18. debebat
19. vident
20. monebant

No. 65. Give the English for these phrases in the ablative case:

1. cum legato
2. gladio
3. a pueris
4. fossis
5. ab amicis
6. a nuntio
7. cum avunculis
8. bellis
9. ab dominis
10. cum socio
11. equis
12. sagittis
13. a sagittario
14. a dea
15. cum servo
16. sapientia
17. a populo
18. cum inimicis
19. aqua
20. ab viro

No. 66. Translate the following into English:

1. Pecunia viro atque puellae dabitur quod puer aeger est.
2. Memoria tenebar cum ad oppidum finitimum movebam.
3. Dolere videntur sed donum portabitur.
4. Ob pericula viri litteras timebant.
5. Pro Britannia, patria vestra, bene pugnate.
6. Multi ad templa deorum ambulabant.
7. Ubi ludus ab amico vestro dabitur?
8. In casa ubi puellas videtis habitabamus.
9. Num vir gladio oppugnabitur?
10. Nonne populus castra movere parabat?

Suffixes

Latin adds suffixes to nouns and adjectives to modify their basic meaning; they may also be used to form one part of speech from another. For example, if you add the suffix *-able* to the noun *miser,* the adjective *miserable* is formed. Some of the common suffixes in Latin and their effects are given below.

-tor (m.), **-trix** (f.) denote the doer or agent. In English, these suffixes become -er or -or.

victor, conqueror   **genitor,** father   **genetrix,** mother

-**or** denotes an action or state. In English, this remains -or.

terror, fear, terror	**pallor**, pallor	**horror**, horror

-**tio** (**gen.** -tionis) denotes status or activity. In English, this becomes -tion.

natio, nation	**oratio**, oration	**statio**, station

-**ia**, -**tia**, -**tudo**, -**tas** denote quality or state.

-**ia** becomes -y in English

miseria, misery	**iniuria**, injury	**victoria**, victory

-**tia** becomes -ce, -ship, or -ness in English.

influentia, influence	**amicitia**, friendship	**laetitia**, happiness

-**tudo** becomes -tude in English.

longitudo, longitude	**latitido**, latitude	**altitudo**, altitude

-**tas** becomes -ty in English.

gravitas, gravity	**dignitas**, dignity	**suavitas**, suavity

96. New Reading Vocabulary

NOUNS

dictator, dictatoris, m., dictator (dictatorial)
Cincinnatus, Cincinnati, m., Cincinnatus
pars, partis, f., part (**partium**) (partake, particle)
caedes, caedis, f., slaughter, murder (**caedium**)
hostis, hostis, m., enemy (**hostium**) (hostile); in the singular, an individual enemy in war; in the plural, a collective noun, "the enemy," taking a plural verb.

homo, hominis, m., man (homicide)
urbs, urbis, f., city (**urbium**) (suburb)
Horatius, Horati, m., Horatius
pons, pontis, m., bridge (**pontium**)
mare, maris, n. sea (**marium**) (marine)
miles, militis, m., soldier (military)
pax, pacis, f., peace (pacific)
caput, capitis, n., head, leader (capital)

Many of the nouns listed above include the genitive plural form, ending in -**ium** in parentheses, e.g., *pars, partis . . . partium.* This class of nouns is known as third declension i-stem nouns, and will be explained more fully below.

ADVERBS

semper, always, ever (sempiternal)

97. New Reading Grammar—Introduction to Third Declension Nouns

More nouns belong to the **third declension,** or **i-declension,** than to any other declension. Thus, in learning Latin, it is important to master this declension. These **third declension (i-declension)** nouns may be of any gender—masculine, feminine, or neuter.

a. The masculine and feminine nouns have the same basic endings.

Case	Singular	Plural
Nom.	(endings vary)	-es
Gen.	-is	-ium or -um
Dat.	-i	-ibus
Acc.	-em	-es
Abl.	-i or -e	-ibus
Voc.	same as nominative	-es

b. The endings for neuter third declension nouns are as follows:

Case	Singular	Plural
Nom.	(endings vary)	-ia or -a
Gen.	-is	-ium or -um
Dat.	-i	-ibus
Acc.	same as nominative	-ia or -a
Abl.	-i or -e	-ibus
Voc.	same as nominative	-ia or -a

c. As indicated in the tables above, i-declension nouns have a variety of spellings in the nominative singular case, which often have little similarity to the way the stem of the noun is spelled in the rest of the cases.

Thus, you will have to look at the genitive singular case to determine the noun stem. When you drop the genitive case ending -**is,** you will have the stem for the rest of the cases. This is why a Latin dictionary always gives you the genitive singular case after the nominative singular case. The genitive ending determines the declensional pattern to which the noun belongs; so far we have learned first declension genitive singular ending in –**ae** (e.g., **puella, -ae**), second declension genitive singular ending in -**i** (e.g., **servus, -i**), and, now, third declension genitive singular ending in –**is** (e.g., **urbs, urbis**).

For neuter nouns, all case endings except the nominative singular, vocative singular, and accusative singular are added onto the stem as determined from the genitive singular.

d. The first two cases give no clues as to whether a noun is masculine, feminine, or neuter.

Thus, a Latin dictionary always gives the gender of a noun, which you will have to memorize along with the meaning of the noun. Make it a habit to think of the gender as part of the definition of the word when learning new vocabulary.

98. New Reading Grammar—Third Declension i-stem Nouns

Third declension (**i-declension**) nouns are divided into two groups—those that have -**ium** for the genitive plural ending and those that have -**um.** The former are known as **i-stems,** because the -**i** is actually part of the stem. The vocabulary in this book indicates the genitive plural in -**ium** for those nouns that have this form. Masculine and feminine nouns of this type may have -**i** as an alternative ending to the more usual -**e** in the ablative singular. Neuter nouns of this type almost always end in -**i** in the ablative singular. However, a very few neuter nouns, such as **mare,** may also end in -**e** in that case. Neuter nouns with -**ium** in the genitive singular end in -**ia** in the nominative, accusative, and vocative plural.

There are guidelines that can help you determine whether a particular word is likely to be an **i-stem** or not, based on whether it can be classified as increasing (i.e., the genitive singular form has more syllables than the nominative singular form) or non-increasing (i.e., nominative singular and genitive singular have the same number of syllables). But there are so many exceptions to the general rules that it is usually much simpler to learn that a particular third-declension noun is or is not an **i-stem** when first encountering it as a vocabulary item, just as one would learn the gender.

1. Third declension NOUNS WITH -ium IN THE GENITIVE PLURAL DECLINE AS FOLLOWS:

Masculine and Feminine Nouns

Case	Singular		Plural	
Nom.	**urbs**	the city	**urbes**	the cities
Gen.	**urbis**	of the city	**urbium**	of the cities
Dat.	**urbi**	to, for the city	**urbibus**	to, for the cities
Acc.	**urbem**	the city	**urbes**	the cities
Abl.	**urbe, urbi**	from/with/by/in the city	**urbibus**	from/with/by/in the cities
Voc.	**urbs**	O city	**urbes**	O cities

Neuter

Case	Singular		Plural	
Nom.	**mare**	the sea	**maria**	the seas
Gen.	**maris**	of the sea	**marium**	of the seas
Dat.	**mari**	to, for the sea	**maribus**	to, for the seas
Acc.	**mare**	the sea	**maria**	the seas
Abl.	**mari, mare**	from/with/by/in the sea	**maribus**	from/with/by/in the seas
Voc.	**mare**	O sea	**maria**	O seas

The stem of **urbs** is **urb-** and the stem of **mare** is **mar-**. Both are derived by dropping the -**is** from the genitive singular.

2. Third declension NOUNS WITH -um IN THE GENITIVE PLURAL DECLINE AS FOLLOWS:

Masculine and Feminine

Case	Singular		Plural	
Nom.	**homo**	the man	**homines**	the men
Gen.	**hominis**	of the man	**hominum**	of the men
Dat.	**homini**	to, for the man	**hominibus**	to, for the men
Acc.	**hominem**	the man	**homines**	the men
Abl.	**homine**	from/with/by/in the man	**hominibus**	from/with/by/in the men
Voc.	**homo**	O man	**homines**	O men

Neuter

Case	Singular		Plural	
Nom.	**caput**	the head	**capita**	the heads
Gen.	**capitis**	of the head	**capitum**	of the heads
Dat.	**capiti**	to, for the head	**capitibus**	to, for the heads
Acc.	**caput**	the head	**capita**	the heads
Abl.	**capite**	from/with/by/in the head	**capitibus**	from/with/by/in the heads
Voc.	**caput**	O head	**capita**	O heads

The stem of **homo** is **homin-** and the stem of **caput** is **capit-** (as evident from the genitive singular forms).

A note on adjectives: You have already encountered adjectives of the first and second declension type (Section 51). There is another group of adjectives that use third declensional endings. You will learn about these **third declension (i-declension)** adjectives in a later lesson. It is important to remember that adjectives will not always be of the same declension as the nouns they modify, but they must always agree in case, number, and gender.

ponti longo	to, for the long bridge	**maris inimicis**	of the unfriendly sea
pontibus longis	to, for the long bridges	**urbs bona**	the good city
marium inimicorum	of the unfriendly seas	**urbes bonae**	the good cities

99. Reading

Cincinnatus

1. **Roma pacem saepe non habebat, sed in periculo erat et contra finitimos suos pugnabat.**

2. **Roma copias bonas atque arma habebat, sed oppugnabatur et populus caput habere debebat quod terrebatur.**

3. **Nuntii ad Cincinnatum properant et ubi Cincinnatum, agricolam Romanum, in agro vident, de bello et magno periculo narrant.**

4. **Cincinnatus agros suos bene amabat et bellum gratum non erat, sed Romam bene amabat et ab nuntiis movebatur.**

5. **Populo Romano magnum auxilium portabat quod dictator erat et Romam servabat.**

6. **Copiae Romanae a periculo patriam suam liberabant et Cincinnatus a Romanis semper memoria tenebatur.**

Cincinnatus

1. Often, Rome did not have peace, but was in danger and fought against her neighbors.

2. Rome had good troops and weapons, but she was being attacked and the people needed to have a leader because they were frightened.

3. Messengers hurried to Cincinnatus and when they see Cincinnatus, a Roman farmer, in the field, they tell him about the war and great danger.

4. Cincinnatus loved his fields well and war was not pleasing, but he loved Rome very much and was moved by the messengers.

5. He brought great help to the Roman people because he was dictator and he saved Rome.

6. The Roman troops freed their country from danger and Cincinnatus was always remembered by the Romans.

Horatius

1. Magnae copiae hostium Romam oppugnabant.
2. Pars urbis Romae erat in periculo quod hostes pontem ibi occupare parabant.

3. Homines Romae ab Horatio, milite bono, contra hostes incitabantur, sed pontem non tenbant.
4. Tum Horatius in ponte sine auxilio stat. Pro vita sua non timet.
5. Gladio suo multos milites hostium mox necat et hostes ab ponte tenet. Magna erat caedes.
6. Post Horatium milites Romani laborabant et mox pons non stabat.

7. Romani victoriam habent et Roma servatur quod aqua inter Romam et hostes stat.

8. Horatius trans aquam ad ripam ubi erant socii natat.
9. Horatius inter Romanos laudabatur et multi agri Horatio dabantur.

Horatius

1. Large forces of the enemy were attacking Rome.
2. Part of the city of Rome was in danger because the enemy was preparing to seize the bridge there.
3. The men of Rome were being stirred up against the enemy by Horatius, a good soldier, but they did not hold the bridge.
4. Then Horatius stood on the bridge without aid. He did not fear for his life.
5. Soon he killed many of the enemy's soldiers with his sword and held the enemy away from the bridge. The slaughter was great.
6. In back of Horatius, the Roman soldiers were working and soon the bridge was not standing.
7. The Romans had the victory and Rome was saved because the water stood between Rome and the enemy.
8. Horatius swam across the water to the river bank where his comrades were.
9. Horatius was praised among the Romans and many fields were given to Horatius.

100. Practice Exercises

No. 67. Give the English for the following phrases:

1. pacis longae
2. pro milite
3. milites clari
4. pax Romana
5. capita vestra
6. dictatoribus suis
7. caput tuum
8. ab hominibus laetis
9. pars idonea
10. in urbe antiqua
11. maris nostri
12. milites robustos
13. homines boni
14. pacem longam
15. in capitibus suis
16. contra dictatores
17. cum hominibus
18. sine militibus tuis
19. de pace grata
20. homo amicus

No. 68. Fill in the blanks with the correct English:

1. **militum,** _____ the soldiers
2. **pacis,** _____ peace
3. **caput,** _____ head
4. **partem,** _____ part
5. **in urbibus,** _____ the cities

6. **maria,** _____ seas
7. **cum milite,** _____ the soldier
8. **pontium,** _____ the bridges
9. **hostes,** _____ enemy
10. **de caede,** _____ slaughter

No. 69. Change each of the following to the plural, and give the English:

1. **pax**
2. **milite**
3. **capiti**
4. **partem**
5. **hosti**
6. **urbis**
7. **caedem**
8. **pons**
9. **homo**
10. **caput**

11. **militis**
12. **partis**
13. **hominem**
14. **pacis**
15. **dictatorem**
16. **ponti**
17. **maris**
18. **pontis**
19. **hostem**
20. **urbe**

No. 70. Translate the following into English. Note that the vocative is used in some of the sentences:

1. **Cincinnatus ex agro suo vocabatur et aux ilium dabat.**
2. **Homines in terra regnant sed dei caelum atque terram regnant.**
3. **Praemia homini magno ab populo Ro mano dabuntur.**
4. **Lingua Latina semper servabitur.**
5. **Cras non arabit sed patriam nostram mox servabit.**
6. **Ad ripam natabat quod pons non stabat.**
7. **Gladio pro patria tua, Horati, bene pugna.**
8. **Milites, filii mei, gladiis armabuntur.**
9. **Ob pericula tuam aquam servare debes.**
10. **Natua mare amat sed agricola agros suos amat.**

101. New Reading Vocabulary

NOUNS

labor, laboris, m., work, toil, labor (laboratory)

magnitudo, magnitudinis, f., size, great size (magnitude)

celeritas, celeritatis, f., speed, swiftness (celerity, accelerator)

virtus, virtutis, f., courage, valor (virtue)

natio, nationis, f., nation (national)

consilium, consilii or **consili, n.,** plan, advice (council)

vis, vis, f., force; in the plural, strength

sol, solis, m., sun (solar)

cera, cerae, f., wax

ala, alae, f., wing

pater, patris, m., father (paternal)

Daedalus, Daedali, m., Daedalus

Creta, Cretae, f., Crete

Icarus, Icari, m., Icarus

ADJECTIVES

medius, media, medium, middle, middle of (medium)
summus, summa, summum, greatest, highest, top of (summit, sum)

Please note: the *of* in *in the middle of* (**medius, media, medium**) or *top of* (**summus, summa, summum**) is part of the adjective and, therefore, does not affect the case of the noun it modifies. The noun has the case that its use in the sentence requires, and the adjective simply agrees with it in case, number, and gender.

in caelo	in the sky	**medio in caelo**	in the middle of the sky
in terra	on land	**in summa terra**	on top of the land

VERBS

volo, volare, fly (volatile)

ADVERBS

diu, long, for a long time

CONJUNCTIONS

-que, and   **et . . . et,** both . . . and

PREPOSITIONS

circum, around, about (circumnavigate)

102. New Reading Grammar—Irregular Noun *vis*

Vis, a third declension noun meaning *force* in the singular and *strength* in the plural, is one of the very few irregular nouns in the Latin language. It is declined as follows:

Case	Singular		Plural	
Nom.	**vis**	the force	**vires**	the strength
Gen.	**vis**	of the force (rarely used)	**virium**	of the strength
Dat.	**vi**	to, for the force (rarely used)	**viribus**	to, for the strength
Acc.	**vim**	the force from/with/by/in	**vires**	the strength
Abl.	**vi**	the force	**viribus**	from/with/by/in the strength
Voc.	**vis**	O force	**vires**	O strength

You will notice that the irregularities are in the singular forms. The plural forms of **vis** are regular.

Chemical Elements

The following are common chemical elements, with their Latin derivations.

Calcium, Ca, from **calx, calcis,** lime.

Carbon, C, from **carbo,** coal.

Copper, Cu, from **cuprum,** derived from the island Cyprus, anciently renowned for its copper mines.

Gold, Au, from **aurum,** gold.

Iron, Fe, from **ferum,** iron.

Lead, Pb, from **plumbum,** lead.

Radium, Ra, from **radius,** ray, because of alpha, beta, and gamma rays.

Silicon, Si, from **silex, silicis,** flint.

Silver, Ag, from **argentum,** silver.

Tellurium, Te, from **tellus, telluris,** earth.

---

103. New Reading Grammar: Adjective + Preposition + Noun

As you will notice in the reading below, the preposition **in** (*in, on*) may stand after the adjective and before the noun.

parva in insula	on a small island	**medio in caelo**	in the middle of the sky

This is a very common word order with some prepositions (despite the fact that the word **preposition** means *placed before*), especially with the prepositions **in** (in, on) and **cum** (with) as in the phrase **summa cum laude.**

104. The Conjunction -*que*

The conjunction -**que** (and) never stands alone, but is added to the second of two similarly used words or phrases (one popular phrasing of this rule that covers all cases is: "-**que** goes on the back end of the first word of the second part of a naturally occurring series"). When the conjunction -**que** occurs at the end of a word or phrase it has the same meaning as **et** preceding that word or phrase.

vir feminaque	the man and the woman	**pueris puellisque**	to the boys and girls
vir et femina	the man and the woman	**pueris et puellis**	to the boys and girls

105. New Reading Grammar—Determining Gender of Third Declension Nouns

The following guidelines are helpful for remembering the gender of some **i-declension** nouns.

1. Nouns ending in **-or** are usually masculine, e.g., **labor**
2. Nouns ending in **-io** (genitive singular **-ionis**) are usually feminine, e.g., **natio**
3. Nouns ending in -**tudo, -tus,** or -**tas** are feminine, e.g., **magnitudo, virtus, celeritas**

106. Reading

Daedalus et Icarus

1. **Daedalus hominem necat et cum filio suo, Icaro, ex Graecia ad Cretam, insulam in mari, properat.**
2. **Parva in insula diu manebant et tum pater filiusque ad Graeciam volare parant.**
3. **Bene laborant et alas parant.**
4. **Pater puerum monet: "Per caelum, sed non ad solem volabimus."**
5. **Sol erat clarus et Icarus ob alas suas erat laetus.**
6. **Consilium patris sui non diu memoria tenebat.**
7. **Cum patre suo non manebat, sed summo in caelo ante solem volebat.**
8. **Cera in alis pueri non manebat.**
9. **Pater filium suum medio in mari mox videt.**
10. **Icarus non servatur et Daedalus vero dolebat quod puer consilio patris non bene monebatur.**

Daedalus and Icarus

1. Daedalus killed a man and with his son, Icarus, hurried from Greece to Crete, an island in the sea.
2. They stayed for a long time on the small island and then the father and son prepared to fly toward Greece.
3. They work hard and get wings ready.
4. The father warns the boy: "We shall fly through the sky, but not toward the sun."
5. The sun was bright and Icarus was happy because of his wings.
6. He did not remember the advice of his father for long.
7. He did not stay with his father, but flew very high in the sky in front of the sun.
8. The wax did not stay on the boy's wings.
9. The father soon sees his son in the middle of the sea.
10. Icarus was not saved and Daedalus was truly grieved because the boy was not well warned by his father's advice.

107. Practice Exercises

No. 71. *Give the English for the following:*

1. **dei et deae**
2. **deus deaque**
3. **tenemus et damus**
4. **tenebat dabatque**
5. **hominem et feminas**
6. **hominum feminarumque**
7. **ad solem et lunam**
8. **ad solem lunamque**
9. **ex mare et terra**
10. **ex terra mareque**
11. **cum vi et armibus**
12. **cum vi armibusque**

No. 72. Translate these phrases:

1. in mediis viis
2. multis in oppidis
3. bello in magno
4. in summis aedificiis
5. bona in parte

6. in oceanis latis
7. multis in terries
8. medio in caelo
9. summo in mare

No. 73. Translate these phrases:

1. ad mare
2. ex urbibus
3. cum patribus suis
4. ante forum
5. post templum
6. de arca
7. sine consilio
8. trans oceanum
9. per maria
10. ob alas

11. pro regina tua
12. contra populum
13. inter hostes
14. ab viris
15. ab oppidis
16. ante castra
17. per pericula
18. ad dominum
19. trans agrum
20. de pace

No. 74. Give the English for these verbs:

1. erit
2. terrebitur
3. volabat
4. natabit
5. dolent
6. portamur
7. tenebatur
8. amabimur
9. movebo
10. laudabantur

11. pugnabat
12. locabis
13. vocabor
14. monebamur
15. laborabunt
16. incitantur
17. debebit
18. parant
19. curabantur
20. liberaberis

No. 75. Translate these vocatives and appositives:

1. Homo, avunculus meus
2. Amici boni
3. Fili bone
4. Nationum, Italiae Germaniaeque
5. Ob pecuniam, praemium

6. Feminarum, reginarum
7. Vir clare
8. Puer, servus
9. Puellis, filiis meis
10. Pater noster

108. Reading Vocabulary

NOUNS

Pluto, Plutonis, m., Pluto (plutonium)
captivus, captivi, m., captive (captivity)
gladiator, gladiatoris, m., gladiator (gladitorial)
Colosseum, Colossei, n., the Colosseum (colossal)
amphitheatrum, amphitheatri, n., amphitheater (amphitheatrical)
Inferi, Inferorum, m. pl., Those Below, the shades or ghosts of Hades

animal, animalis, n., animal (animalium)
annus, anni, m., year (annual)
Ceres, Cereris, f., Ceres (cereal)
Proserpina, Proserpinae, f., Proserpina
mater, matris, f., mother (maternal)
Iuppiter, Iovis, m., Jupiter (jovial)
Mercurius, Mercuri, m., Mercury

VERBS

specto, spectare, spectavi, spectatus, look at, watch (spectacle)
obtineo, obtinere, obtinui, obtentus, secure, obtain (obtainable)

PREPOSITIONS

sub, under, below, at the foot of (subordinate)

1. With the accusative case after verbs showing motion (transitive verbs), as in the sentence *I walk under the stars.*
2. With the ablative case after verbs showing rest (intransitive verbs), as in the sentence *I sit under the tree.*

109. New Reading Grammar—Introduction to the Principal Parts of Verbs

When you look up a verb in a Latin dictionary, the entry includes what are known as the verb's **Principal Parts** (usually four, sometimes two or three, depending on the verb). Learning these principal parts is essential to mastering the Latin language, since all of the possible tenses and forms of a verb can be generated from one of the principal parts. English verbs also have principal parts that perform the same function (e.g., *sing, sang, sung; carry, carried, carried*). If you know all four principal parts of a Latin verb, you can derive all of the different forms of that verb. Conversely, not knowing the principal parts of a verb can add unnecessary difficulties to the learning process and can severely limit your ultimate understanding of the Latin language. Fortunately, principal parts do tend to follow certain patterns, which are included in the appendices to *Latin Made Simple*.

A. YOU HAVE ALREADY STUDIED TWO OF THE PRINCIPAL PARTS OF VERBS:

1. **amo, habeo**   First Person Singular Present Active Indicative
2. **amare, habere**   Present Active Infinitive

B. THE FIRST TWO PRINCIPAL PARTS ARE USED TO FORM THE TENSES YOU HAVE LEARNED SO FAR:

1. Present Tense, Active and Passive
2. Imperfect Tense, Active and Passive
3. Future Tense, Active and Passive

C. THE FIRST TWO PRINCIPAL PARTS ALSO SHOW THE CONJUGATION TO WHICH THE VERB BELONGS:

1. **amo, amare** (First or a-conjugation)
2. **habeo, habere** (Second or e-conjugation)

It is sometimes possible to determine a verb's conjugation from only one of these parts, but often you will need both of them. This is especially true of second, third and fourth conjugation verbs. (These last two will be introduced in later lessons.)

D. THE THIRD PRINCIPAL PART IS THE FIRST PERSON SINGULAR, PERFECT ACTIVE INDICATIVE (THE PERFECT TENSES, WHICH SHOW COMPLETED ACTION, WILL BE COVERED IN LATER CHAPTERS).

1. **amavi** (a-conjugation)   I have loved; I have liked
2. **habui** (e-conjugation)   I have had; I have held

The third principal part for most of the **a-conjugation** verbs is formed by adding **-avi** to the stem. The exact spelling of this principal part will vary for the other conjugations. Thus, you will have to memorize this part for each individual verb. However, it will always end in **–i,** since this is the first person singular ending for the perfect active indicative tense.

Additional Prefixes

These Latin prepositions are commonly used as prefixes:

e, ex, out. **exspecto,** look out for, wait for, expect.

per, through; thorough, very. **perduco,** lead through. **pervenio,** arrive.

inter, between. **interpono,** put between.

in, in, on; into; not. **invenio,** discover (come on). **infirmus,** weak (not strong).

trans, across. **transmitto,** send across.

sub, under. **subligo,** drive under.

From the third principal part, the following tenses can be formed:

1. Perfect Active Tense   e.g., I have loved.
2. Pluperfect Active Tense   e.g., I had loved.
3. Future Perfect Active Tense   e.g., I shall have loved.

These tenses will be introduced in the next chapter.

E. THE FOURTH PRINCIPAL PART IS THE MASCULINE NOMINATIVE SINGULAR OF THE PERFECT PASSIVE PARTICIPLE (PARTICIPLES WILL BE EXPLAINED IN A LATER CHAPTER).

Some texts list this principal part in the neuter accusative singular, e.g., **amatum, habitum,** in which case it is referred to as the supine stem. It should be noted that only transitive verbs (verbs which take a direct object) can have passive forms, and therefore only transitive verbs will have the perfect passive participle listed as their fourth principal part.

1. **amatus** (a-conjugation)   having been loved; having been liked.
2. **habitus** (e-conjugation)   having been had; having been held.

From the fourth principal part, the following tenses can be formed:

1. Perfect Passive Tense   e.g., I have been or was loved.
2. Pluperfect Passive Tense   e.g., I had been loved.
3. Future Perfect Passive Tense   e.g., I shall have been loved.

F. MOST OF THE a-conjugation VERBS FORM THEIR PRINCIPAL PARTS LIKE AMO:

amo, amare, amavi, amatus

Those that do not are:

do, dare, dedi, datus   give
iuvo, iuvare, iuvi, iutus   help, aid
sto, stare, steti, status   stand

G. MANY OF THE e-conjugation VERBS FORM THEIR PRINCIPAL PARTS LIKE habeo.

habeo, habere, habui, habitus

Of those you have met so far, these do not:

maneo, manere, mansi, mansus   remain, stay
moveo, movere, movi, motus   move
video, videre, vidi, visus   see

H. THE PRINCIPAL PARTS OF sum, possum, AND eo:

1. sum: sum, esse, fui, futurus

Note that **futurus** is the future active participle, *about to be.* **Sum** does not have a perfect passive participle, since it is a linking verb, not a transitive verb. As noted above, only transitive verbs can have passive forms, and therefore only transitive verbs will have a perfect passive participle listed as their fourth principal part. Verbs that list future active participles as their fourth principal part (like **sum**) can be readily identified, since the fourth principal part will always end in **-urus.**

2. possum: possum, posse, potui

possum does not have either the fourth principal part or the perfect passive participle. All forms of **possum** can be derived from the three principal parts that it does have.

3. eo: eo, ire, ii or ivi, itus

110. Reading

Proserpina

1. **Ceres, dea frumenti, filiam Proserpinam, habebat.**
2. **Pluto, deus Inferorum, Proserpinam in agro videt et ad Inferos Proserpinam portat.**
3. **Quod filiam suam non videbat, Ceres, mater, dolebat.**
4. **Quod Ceres misera erat, frumentum in agris agricolarum non erat.**
5. **Tum Iuppiter vitas populi in terra servat quod Mercurium vocat et Mercurius pro Iove ad Plutonem nuntiam portat.**
6. **Iuppiter movebatur et agricolis auxilium dabat.**
7. **Tum Proserpina cum Iove non semper manebat, sed in terra partem anni habebat.**
8. **Cum Proserpina in terra erat, Ceres laeta erat et agricolis copiam magnam frumenti dabat, sed cum Proserpina sub terra erat Ceres misera erat et frumentum non erat.**

Proserpina

1. Ceres, the goddess of grain, had a daughter, Proserpina.
2. Pluto, god of Those Below, saw Proserpina in a field and carried Proserpina to Those Below.
3. Because she did not see her daughter, Ceres, the mother, grieved.
4. Because Ceres was unhappy, there was not grain in the farmers' fields.
5. Then Jupiter saved the lives of the people on earth because he called Mercury and Mercury carried a message for Jupiter to Pluto.
6. Jupiter was moved and gave help to the farmers.
7. Then Proserpina did not always stay with Jupiter, but had part of the year on earth.
8. When Proserpina was on earth, Ceres was happy and gave a great plenty of grain to the farmers, but when Proserpina was under the earth, Ceres was unhappy and there was not grain.

Colosseum

1. **Romani in urbe sua aedificia multa habebant.**
2. **Colosseum bene amabant quod ludos ibi spectabant.**
3. **Colosseum erat magnum amphitheatrum et etiam nunc stat.**
4. **Milites Romani bello servos captivosque obtinebant.**
5. **Captivi, gladitores, gladiis suis contra homines aut contra animalia ibi pugnabant.**
6. **Multi captivi virtutem magnam habebant et liberabantur quod bene pugnabant.**

The Colosseum

1. The Romans had many buildings in their city.
2. They liked the Colosseum very much because they watched the games there.
3. The Colosseum was a large amphitheatre and is standing even now.
4. The Roman soldiers secured slaves and captives in war.
5. The captives, as gladiators, fought there with their swords against men or against animals.
6. Many captives had great courage and were freed because they fought well.

III. Practice Exercises

No. 76. Give the second principal part (the present active infinitive) of these verbs and the English translation:

1. voco	6. moneo	11. nuntio	16. paro
2. debeo	7. timeo	12. volo	17. servo
3. ambulo	8. narro	13. terreo	18. laudo
4. eo	9. curo	14. adoro	19. do
5. sum	10. doleo	15. moveo	20. video

No. 77. Give the third principal part (the first person singular perfect active indicative) of these verbs and the translation:

1. paro	6. eo	11. propero	16. monstro
2. incito	7. terreo	12. habeo	17. timeo
3. aro	8. aedifico	13. do	18. nato
4. debeo	9. habito	14. teneo	19. moveo
5. libero	10. moneo	15. servo	20. maneo

No. 78. Give the fourth principal part (the perfect passive participle) of these verbs and the translation:

1. amo	6. exspecto	11. do	16. adoro
2. habeo	7. narro	12. moneo	17. moveo
3. libero	8. terreo	13. servo	18. specto
4. neco	9. occupo	14. iuvo	19. obtineo
5. moneo	10. porto	15. video	20. loco

No. 79. Translate the following into English:
1. Et mater tua et pater tuus de virtute consilium dabant.
2. Medio in oppido erant aedificia multa.
3. Fama de natione mea ab nuntiis portabitur.
4. Puella puerque sub aqua natant.
5. Circum urbem ambulare et multa videre debemus.
6. Nonne multa mala memoria tenes?
7. Sol summa in aqua esse videbatur.
8. Nationes Europae non semper pugnabunt.
9. Nautae in maribus oceanisque navigant.
10. Milites Romani virtutem magnam habent.

112. Vocabulary Review

NOUNS

1. ala
2. amphitheatrum
3. animal
4. annus
5. caedes
6. captivus
7. caput
8. celeritas
9. cera
10. Ceres
11. Cincinnatus
12. Colosseum
13. consilium
14. Creta
15. Daedalus
16. dictator
17. donum
18. gladiator
19. homo
20. Horatius
21. hostis
22. Icarus
23. Inferi
24. Iuppiter
25. labor
26. littera
27. magnitudo
28. mare
29. mater
30. Mercurius
31. miles
32. natio
33. pars
34. pater
35. pax
36. pecunia
37. Pluto
38. pons
39. Proserpina
40. sagitta
41. sagittarius
42. sol
43. Stella
44. urbs
45. virtus

ADJECTIVES

1. medius
2. robustus
3. summus

VERBS

1. doleo
2. moveo
3. obtineo
4. specto
5. terreo

ADVERBS

1. diu
2. mox
3. semper

PREPOSITIONS

1. a, ab
2. circum
3. inter
4. sub

CONJUNCTIONS

1. aut
2. et . . . et
3. -que

113. Practice Exercises

No. 80. Complete these infinitives by filling in the correct vowel:

1. dol _____ re
2. terr _____ re
3. mov _____ re
4. voc _____ re
5. obtin _____ re

6. d _____ re
7. spect _____ re
8. vol _____ re
9. laud _____ re
10. man _____ re

11. deb _____ re
12. tim _____ re
13. hab _____ re
14. vid _____ re
15. nec _____ re

16. par _____ re
17. occup _____ re
18. st _____ re
19. iuv _____ re
20. mon _____ re

No. 81. Fill in the missing principal part:

1. specto, spectare, _____ , spectatus
2. curo, _____ , curavi, curatus
3. _____ , monere, monui, monitus
4. do, dare, _____ , datus
5. moveo, movere, movi, _____

6. paro, parare, _____ paratus
7. servo, servare, servavi, _____
8. terreo, terrere, terrui, _____
9. _____ , habitare, habitavi, habita-tus
10. laudo, _____ , laudavi, laudatus

No. 82. Translate these phrases:

1. animalium hominumque
2. a patre
3. a matribus
4. mare stellamque
5. patres matresque

6. celeritatis magnitudinisque
7. a Mercurio
8. a militibus
9. a Plutone
10. bellum paxque

No. 83. Translate these verb forms:

1. laudabatur
2. dolebant
3. monebamur
4. necantur
5. vocamini
6. erunt

7. obtinebimus
8. videris
9. iuvabatis
10. habebo
11. moveberis
12. potes

13. occupantur
14. timebantur
15. parabitur
16. dabis
17. servaris
18. ibant

19. parabamur
20. debebitur
21. curabaris
22. spectabamur
23. terrebunt
24. eram

114. Reading

Check the Latin-English Vocabulary and a good Latin dictionary for words not yet studied.

EUTROPIUS

Very little is known about Eutropius, except that he held official positions in Rome and in the provinces, and that he may have been a secretary to the Emperor Constantine. Of his works, the only one extant is the **Brevarium,** a brief history of Rome from the founding of the city in 753 B.C. to A.D. 364.

Hic quoque ingens bellum civile commovit cogente uxore Cleopatra, regina Aegypti, dum cupiditate muliebri optat etiam in urbe regnare. Victus est ab Augusto navali pugna clara et inlustri apud Actium, qui locus in Epiro est, ex qua fugit in Aegyptum et desperatis rebus, cum omnes ad Augustum transirent, ipse se interemit. Cleopatra sibi aspidem admisit et veneno eius exstincta est. Aegyptus per Octavianum Augustum imperio Romano adiecta est praepositusque ei C. Cornelius Gallus. Hunc primum Aegyptus Romanum iudicem habuit.

Breviarii, Liber VII, vii

THE BIBLE

Psalmus David, cum fugeret a facie Absalom filii sui
Domine, quid multiplicati sunt qui tribulant me!
Multi insurgunt adversum me;
multi dicunt animae meae:
Non est salus ipsi in Deo eius.
Tu autem, Domine, susceptor meus es,
gloria mea et exaltans caput meum.
Voce mea ad Dominum clamavi,
et exaudivit me de monte sancto suo.
Ergo dormivi et soporatus sum
et exsurrexi, quia Dominus suscepit me.
Non timebo milia populi circumdantis me.
Exsurge, Domine, salvum me fac, Deus meus;
quoniam tu percussisti omnes adversantes mihi sine causa,
dentes peccatorum contrivisti.
Domini est salus, et super populum tuum benedictio tua.

Liber Psalmorum iii

Familiar Abbreviations

fl. or **flor., floruit,** he (she) flourished. Used with the date at which artists produced their work.

I.H.S., In hoc signo, In this sign. Or, **Iesus Hominum Salvator,** Jesus Savior of Men.

I.N.R.I., Iesus Nazarenus, Rex Iudaeorum, Jesus of Nazareth, King of the Jews.

pinx., pinxit, he (she) painted it.

sculp., sculpsit, he (she) carved it.

op. cit., opere citato, in the work cited. Used in footnotes instead of repeating the title of a book already referred to.

ibid, or **ib., ibidem,** in the same place. Used in footnotes, if the reference is the same as one made just previously.

---

115. New Reading Vocabulary

NOUNS

ignis, ignis, m., fire (**ignium**) (ignite)
audacia, audaciae, f., boldness, bravery, daring (audacity)

pretium, pretii or preti, n., price (precious)
Tarquinius, Tarquini, m., Tarquinius
liber, liberi, m., book (library)

ADJECTIVES

Sibyllinus, Sibyllina, Sibyllinum, Sibylline
superbus, superba, superbum, proud (superb)

novem, nine (November)
sex, six (sextet)

VERBS

rogo, rogare, rogavi, rogatus, ask, ask for (interrogate)

CONJUNCTIONS

postquam, after, when

116. New Reading Grammar—Introduction to the Perfect Active Tenses

A. THE THIRD PRINCIPAL PART OF THE VERB IS USED TO FORM THE ACTIVE VOICE
perfect, pluperfect, AND future perfect tenses.

These are known collectively as the perfect tenses. The third principal part is the first person singular of the perfect active indicative tense.

B. IN LATIN, AS IN ENGLISH, THE perfect TENSES DIFFER FROM THE simple TENSES (PRESENT, IMPERFECT, AND FUTURE).

Latin verbs are concerned not only with the time that an action occurs, but also its aspect, that is, whether the action is seen as simple and possibly ongoing, or whether it is seen as completed at some point in time. The pefect tenses (from **perfectus,** the fourth principal part of **perficio,** *to complete or accomplish*) are used to express actions that have this completed aspect. Some texts refer to present, imperfect, and future tenses collectively as the **imperfective** tenses, to stress their incomplete or ongoing aspect.

C. THE BASIC ENDINGS FOR THE THREE PERFECT ACTIVE TENSES ARE AS FOLLOWS:

		Perfect	*Pluperfect*	*Future Perfect*
Singular:	1st person	-i	-eram	-ero
	2nd person	-isti	-eras	-eris
	3rd person	-it	-erat	-erit
Plural:	1st person	-imus	-eramus	-erimus
	2nd person	-istis	-eratis	-eritis
	3rd person	-erunt	-erant	-erint

These endings are added on to the perfect stem, which is derived by omitting the **-i** of the third principal part. Thus, the perfect stem of **amo** is **amav-.** The set of endings used for perfect active tense is unique. The endings for pluperfect and future perfect are nearly identical to the imperfect and future forms of the verb **sum, esse,** with the exception of the third person plural ending of the future perfect.

117. New Reading Grammar—Perfect Active Indicative

The perfect tense functions as both a true perfect tense and as a simple past tense. The true perfect shows action completed in the past but still relevant to the present ("in the present and enduring state of having been completed" is one explanation)—*I have closed the window* carries the implication that the window remains closed in the present. The perfect may also be used as a simple past—*I closed the window*—which carries no such implication. The third principal part is the first person singular of this tense. The endings, unique to this tense, are added directly to the stem.

A-Conjugation		*E-Conjugation*	
amavi	I have loved; I loved	**habui**	I have had; I had
amavisti	you have loved	**habuisti**	you have had
amavit	he, she, it has loved	**habuit**	he, she, it has had
amavimus	we have loved	**habuimus**	we have had
amavistis	you have loved	**habuistis**	you have had
amaverunt	they have loved	**habuerunt**	they have had

The perfect tense used as a simple past tense should be clearly distinguished from the imperfect as a past tense. The action of the perfect tense, when used as a simple past, happens once at a definite point in time and is finished, while the action of the imperfect tense takes place over a longer period of time and is often repeated. Thus, the first person singular of **pugno** in the perfect, **pugnavi,** means *I fought.* The fighting took place at one time in the past and was finished. However, the first person imperfect, **pugnabam,** means *I used to fight/did fight/was fighting.* The fighting still took place in the past, but it happened repeatedly. It is not made clear when the fighting stopped.

118. New Reading Grammar—Pluperfect Active Indicative

The pluperfect active tense is formed by adding the imperfect forms of **sum** to the perfect stem. It shows action completed at a definite point of time in the past—*I had loved.* The word *pluperfect* means *more perfect.* Thus, since the perfect tense describes action taking place in the past, the pluperfect describes action taking place even more in the past, or before the action of the perfect tense. Thus, the pluperfect is occasionally called the *past perfect.*

A-Conjugation

amaveram	I had loved
amaveras	you had loved
amaverat	he, she, it had loved
amaveramus	we had loved
amaveratis	you had loved
amaverant	they had loved

E-Conjugation

habueram	I had had
habueras	you had had
habuerat	he, she, it had had
habueramus	we had had
habueratis	you had had
habuerant	they had had

119. New Reading Grammar—Future Perfect Active Indicative

The **future perfect** active tense is formed by adding the future forms of **sum** to the perfect stem. The one exception is the third person plural of the future perfect active tense. This is formed by adding **-erint** to the perfect stem, to avoid confusion with the third person plural of the perfect active tense, which is formed by adding **-erunt** to the perfect stem.

The **future perfect** tense shows action to be completed before a definite point of time in the future—*I shall have loved.* Thus, it differs from the **future tense** in the same way that the **perfect** and **pluperfect** tenses differ from the **imperfect** tense.

A-Conjugation

amavero	I shall have loved
amaveris	you will have loved
amaverit	he/she/it will have loved
amaverimus	we shall have loved
amaveritis	you will have loved
amaverint	they will have loved

E-Conjugation

habuero	I shall have had
habueris	you will have had
habuerit	he/she/it will have had
habuerimus	we shall have had
habueritis	you will have had
habuerint	they will have had

120. New Reading Grammar—Perfect Active of *sum, possum,* and *eo*

The verbs **sum, possum,** and **eo** are regular in the perfect tenses. Indeed, one of the nice things about the perfect tenses is that the rules apply to all verbs. There is no such thing as irregular verbs when it comes to the perfect tenses.

1. THE FORMS OF sum ARE AS FOLLOWS:

Perfect Tense

		Pluperfect Tense	
fui	I have been	**fueram**	I had been
fuisti	you have been	**fueras**	you had been
fuit	he/she/it has been	**fuerat**	he/she/it had been
fuimus	we have been	**fueramus**	we had been
fuistis	you have been	**fueratis**	you had been
fuerunt	they have been	**fuerant**	they had been

Future Perfect Tense

fuero	I shall have been
fueris	you will have been
fuerit	he/she/it will have been
fuerimus	we shall have been
fueritis	you will have been
fuerint	they will have been

2. THE THIRD PRINCIPAL PART OF possum IS potui, AND THE PERFECT STEM IS potu-.

Thus:

Perfect Tense

		Pluperfect Tense	
potui	I have been able	**potueram**	I had been able
potuisti	you have been able	**potueras**	you had been able
potuit	he/she/it has been able	**potuerat**	he/she/it had been able
potuimus	we have been able	**potueramus**	we had been able
potuistis	you have been able	**potueratis**	you had been able
potuerunt	they have been able	**potuerant**	they had been able

Future Perfect Tense

potuero	I shall have been able
potueris	you will have been able
potuerit	he/she/it will have been able
potuerimus	we will have been able
potueritis	you will have been able
potuerint	they will have been able

3. THE THIRD PRINCIPAL PART OF eo IS ii OR ivi. THE PERFECT STEM IS i-.

Thus:

Perfect Tense		*Pluperfect Tense*	
ii, ivi	I have gone	**ieram**	I had gone
iisti, isti	you have gone	**ieras**	you had gone
iit, it	he/she/it has gone	**ierat**	he/she/it had gone
iimus	we have gone	**ieramus**	we had gone
iistis, istis	you have gone	**ieratis**	you had gone
ierunt	they have gone	**ierant**	they had gone

Future Perfect Tense	
iero	I shall have gone
ieris	you will have gone
ierit	he/she/it will have gone
ierimus	we shall have gone
ieritis	you will have gone
ierint	they will have gone

As you can see, some forms of the perfect active for **eo, ire** have alternatives. The **ii-** stem may be changed to **i-** if there is no other form of **eo** with which it can be confused. Thus, the first person plural, **iimus** would not be written as **imus**; it might be confused with the first person plural of the present active.

120. Reading

Libri Sibyllini

1. **Inter antiquos erat fabula de libris Sibyllinis.**
2. **Tarquinius Superbus urbem Romam regnabat.**
3. **Femina ad Tarquinium libros novem portavit et pro libris pecuniam rogavit.**
4. **Tarquinius feminae pecuniam non dedit.**
5. **Femina in igni libros tres turn locavit.**
6. **Pro sex libris pretium librorem novem rogavit.**
7. **Tarquinius feminae pecuniam non dedit.**
8. **Postquam femina in igni libros sex locaverit Tarquinius feminae pro libris pecuniam dedit quod audacia feminae movebatur.**
9. **Libri erant libri Sibyllini.**
10. **Cum populus Romanus periculo incitabatur aut cum Roma oppugnabatur ad libros properabant.**
11. **Libri Romanis auxilium multum semper dabant.**
12. **Erantne libri deorum?**

The Sibylline Books

1. Among the ancients, there was a story about the Sibylline books.
2. Tarquinius the Proud was ruling the city of Rome.
3. A woman brought nine books to Tarquinius and asked for money for the books.
4. Tarquinius did not give the money to the woman.
5. The woman then put three books in the fire.
6. For the six books, she asked the price of the nine books.
7. Tarquinius did not give the money to the woman.
8. After the woman had placed six books in the fire, Tarquinius gave the money to the woman for the books because he was moved by the woman's boldness.
9. The books were the Sibylline books.
10. When the Roman people were aroused by danger, or when Rome was being attacked, they hurried to the books.
11. The books always gave much help to the Romans.
12. Were they the books of the gods?

121. Practice Exercises

No. 84. Complete these principal parts:

1. ambulo, ambulare, _____ , ambu-latus
2. laudo, laudare, _____ , laudatus
3. moneo, monere, _____ , monitus
4. debeo, debere, _____ , debitus
5. porto, portare, _____ , portatus
6. servo, servare, _____ , servatus
7. voco, vocare, _____ , vocatus
8. moveo, movere, _____ , motus
9. do, dare, _____ , datus
10. rogo, rogare, _____ , rogatus

No. 85. Translate these perfect tenses:

1. rogavit
2. spectaverunt
3. monuimus
4. iuvi
5. fuisti
6. necavisti
7. narravistis
8. habitavi
9. vidi
10. timuerunt
11. doluisti
12. habuistis
13. debuimus
14. laboraverunt
15. superavisti
16. monstravit
17. narraverunt
18. occupavistis
19. paravimus
20. volavit

No. 86. Translate these pluperfect tenses:

1. ambulaveram
2. adoraverant
3. araverat
4. moverant
5. manseramus
6. videratis
7. paraveras
8. dederas
9. tenueratis
10. steteram
11. paraverat
12. locaverant
13. incitaveras
14. curaveratis
15. nataveram
16. dolueramus
17. rogaverat
18. spectaverant
19. viderat
20. vocaveratis

No. 87. Translate these future perfect tenses:

1. amaveris
2. curaverit
3. laudavero
4. locaverimus
5. habuerint
6. terruerit
7. moverit
8. dederint
9. steteris
10. tenuerit
11. vocaverimus
12. servavero
13. portaverit
14. paraverint
15. nuntiaveris
16. narraverimus
17. habueritis
18. debuerit
19. adoraverint
20. ambulaveris

122. New Reading Vocabulary

NOUNS

rex, regis, m., king (regal)
nomen, nominis, n., name (nomenclature)
mulier, mulieris, f., woman
mons, montis, m., mountain, mount **(montium)**
finis, finis, m., end, border **(finium).** In the plural, boundaries (finish)

lex, legis, f., law (legal)
pugna, pugnae, f., fight
murus, muri, m., wall (mural)
flumen, fluminis, n., river, stream (flume)
collis, collis, m., hill **(collium)**

ADJECTIVES

proximus, proxima, proximum, next, nearest (approximate)

ultimus, ultima, ultimum, last, farthest (ultimate)
septem, seven (September)

VERBS

augeo, augere, auxi, auctus, increase, enlarge (augment)

ADVERBS

postea, afterwards

123. New Reading Grammar—Introduction to the Perfect Passive Tenses

The perfect tenses are generated quite differently when they are in the passive voice. These tenses are formed as a compound of the fourth principal part and the verb *to be* in the appropriate tense. The fourth principal part of the verb is called the perfect passive participle. Like all participles, which will be covered in greater detail in a later chapter, the perfect passive participle is a *verbal adjective*, that is, an adjective that retains some of its verbal characteristics. Since it is an adjective, it must agree with the word it modifies in case, number, and gender. Thus, **amatus,** *loved,* is really the adjective **amatus, amata, amatum,** and it is declined like any other first and second declension adjective. However, since it is a *verbal* adjective, it also has some of the qualities of a verb, such as voice and tense. The perfect passive tenses are formed by combining the perfect passive participle with the verb **sum.** When it is used with **sum** to form the perfect passive tenses, the participle is always in the nominative case, since it is modifying the subject of the sentence, and it must *agree* with the subject in gender and number. For example:

mulier amata est, the woman has been loved.

mulieres amatae sunt, the women have been loved.

vir amatus est, the man has been loved.

viri amati sunt, the men have been loved.

nomen vocatum est, the name has been called.

nomina vocata sunt, the names have been called.

Familiar Phrases

carpe diem, seize the day. Often used to mean "seize the opportunity" or "seize the chance."

cave canem, beware of the dog. Literally, beware the dog.

ex libris, from the library of. Used often on bookplates.

ex officio, because of an office (held previously).

in toto, in the whole; completely.

per capita, by heads; per person or individual.

post mortem, after death.

exeunt omnes, all go out. Used as a stage direction in plays.

ultimatum, the last thing; the farthest thing. Used for the final terms offered by one party to another.

---

124. New Reading Grammar—Pluperfect Passive Indicative

The perfect passive tense is formed by using the fourth principal part together with the present tense of **sum.**

First Conjugation

amatus, -a, -um sum	I have been loved
amatus, -a, -um es	you have been loved
amatus, -a, -um est	he/she/it has been loved
amati, -ae, -a sumus	we have been loved
amati, -ae, -a estis	you have been loved
amati, -ae, -a sunt	they have been loved

Second Conjugation

habitus, -a, -um sum	I have been held
habitus, -a, -um es	you have been held
habitus, -a, -um est	he/she/it has been held
habiti, -ae, -a sumus	we have been held
habiti, -ae, -a estis	you have been held
habiti, -ae, -a sunt	they have been held

125. New Reading Grammar—Pluperfect Passive Indicative

The pluperfect passive tense is formed by using the fourth principal part with **eram**, the imperfect tense of **sum**.

First Conjugation

amatus, -a, -um eram	I had been loved
amatus, -a, -um eras	you had been loved
amatus, -a, -um erat	he/she/it had been loved
amati, -ae, -a eramus	we had been loved
amati, -ae, -a eratis	you had been loved
amati, -ae, -a erant	they had been loved

Second Conjugation

habitus, -a, -um eram	I had been held
habitus, -a, -um eras	you had been held
habitus, -a, -um erat	he/she/it had been held
habiti, -ae, -a eramus	we had been held
habiti, -ae, -a eratis	you had been held
habiti, -ae, -a erant	they had been held

126. New Reading Grammar—Future Perfect Passive Indicative

The future perfect passive tense is formed by using the fourth principal part with **ero**, the future tense of **sum**.

First Conjugation

amatus, -a, -um ero	I shall have been loved
amatus, -a, -um eris	you will have been loved
amatus, -a, -um erit	he/she/it will have been loved
amati, -ae, -a erimus	we shall have been loved
amati, -ae, -a eritis	you will have been loved
amati, -ae, -a erunt	they will have been loved

Second Conjugation

habitus, -a, -um ero	I shall have been held
habitus, -a, -um eris	you will have been held
habitus, -a, -um erit	he/she/it will have been held
habiti, -ae, -a erimus	we shall have been held
habiti, -ae, -a eritis	you will have been held
habiti, -ae, -a erunt	they will have been held

127. New Reading Grammar—Perfect Passives and Irregular Verbs

The verbs **sum** and **possum** do not have perfect passive tenses, since only transitive verbs can have passive forms. **Possum** only has **three principal parts**, while in **sum**, the fourth principal part, **futurus**, is actually the future active participle. The fourth principal part of **eo** is **itus**. **Eo** does have perfect passive forms, but these are rarely used.

128. Reading

Reges Romae

1. **Urbs Roma septem reges habuit. Romulus urbem parvam in monte Palatino aedificavit.**
2. **Urbi nomen Romam dedit. Romulus ob sapientam suam urbem bene regnabat.**
3. **Populo consilium bonum dedit.**
4. **Quod in urbe non erant mulieres Romani finitimos suos ad ludos vocaverunt.**
5. **Tum feminas puellasque pugna obtinuerunt.**
6. **Et Sabini et socii sui contra Romanos bella multa pugnaverunt, sed copiae Romanae hostes superaverunt.**
7. **Postea Numa Pompilius erat rex Romanorum.**
8. **Pacem amavit et populo erat gratus quod Romanis leges multas bonasque dedit.**
9. **Aedificia templaque etiam aedificavit.**
10. **Tum Romani ab Anco Marcio regnabantur.**
11. **Multos bello superavit et murum circum montem Caelium aedificavit.**
12. **Postea Roma a Prisco Tarquinio regnabatur.**
13. **Circum Maximum, ubi Romani ludos habebant, aedificavit.**
14. **Contra Sabinos bellum pugnavit et agris finitimis et monte Capitolio fines urbis auxit.**
15. **Proximus rex, Servius Tullius, Sabinos superavit.**
16. **Colles Romae ad septem auxit. Circum colles murum et circum murum fossas aedificavit.**
17. **Multi in urbe habitaverunt et multi erant agricolae in agris et post colles et post flumen.**
18. **Tarquinius Superbus erat ultimus rex Romae, sed bene diuque regnavit.**
19. **Copiae Tarquini Superbi bella multa pugnaverunt et nationes proximas Romae superaverunt.**

The Kings of Rome

1. The city of Rome had seven kings. Romulus built a small city on the Palatine mount.
2. To the city he gave the name Rome. Romulus ruled the city well because of his wisdom.
3. He gave good advice to the people.
4. Because there were not women in the city, the Romans called their neighbors to games.
5. Then they got women and girls by a fight.
6. Both the Sabines and their allies fought many wars against the Romans, but the Roman forces conquered the enemy.
7. Afterward, Numa Pompilius was king of the Romans.
8. He liked peace and he was pleasing to the people because he gave many and good laws to the Romans.
9. He also built buildings and temples.
10. Then the Romans were ruled by Ancus Marcius.
11. He defeated many people in war and he built a wall around the Caelian mount.
12. Afterwards, Rome was ruled by Tarquinius Priscus.
13. He built the Circus Maximus, where the Romans held their games.
14. He fought a war against the Sabines and increased the territory of the city by neighboring fields and the Capitoline mount.
15. The next king, Servius Tullius, overcame the Sabines.
16. He increased the hills of Rome to seven. Around the hills, he built a wall, and around the wall, ditches.
17. Many people lived in the city and many were farmers in the fields both in back of the hills and in back of the river.
18. Tarquinius the Proud was the last king of Rome, but he ruled well and for a long time.
19. The troops of Tarquinius the Proud fought many wars and defeated the nations next to Rome.

129. Practice Exercises

No. 88. Give the English for these perfect tenses:

1. fuerunt
2. ambulavit
3. portatus est
4. amati sunt
5. curata es
6. laudatae sunt
7. monitus sum
8. debuimus
9. stetistis
10. narratum est
11. vocati sumus
12. natavi
13. servatae estis
14. nuntiatum est
15. moti sunt
16. timuisti
17. paratus est
18. locata sunt
19. laudaverunt
20. movistis

No. 89. Give the English for these pluperfect tenses:

1. dederant
2. moverat
3. territus erat
4. manseratis
5. tenueras
6. pugnaverat
7. laudata eram
8. curati erant
9. amata eras
10. incitati eratis
11. parati erant
12. occupaveras
13. liberati eratis
14. necatus erat
15. servati eramus
16. monuerat
17. habueratis
18. tenueras
19. iuti eramus
20. adoraverant

No. 90. Give the English for these future perfect tenses:

1. monuero
2. fuerit
3. portatum erit
4. moniti erunt
5. habuerint
6. terrueris
7. moverimus
8. visi eritis
9. timuerit
10. mota erit
11. dederimus
12. steterint
13. fuerimus
14. necati eritis
15. laudatae erimus
16. armatus eris
17. curati erunt
18. locatum erit
19. fuerint
20. servata erit

No. 91. Translate these verb forms:

1. habitum erat
2. videro
3. oppugnata erunt
4. laudata eris
5. portata eras
6. debitum erit
7. debuerant
8. exspectavisti
9. vidistis
10. monstratum est

11. moniti sunt
12. rogatae sumus
13. spectaverunt
14. moti sumus
15. paraveramus
16. monitus est
17. steterat
18. dati erant
19. narraverunt
20. tenuero

130. New Reading Vocabulary

NOUNS

Hesperides, Hesperidum, f., the Hesperides
Hercules, Herculis, m., Hercules
hortus, horti, m., garden (horticulture)
serpens, serpentis, f., snake, serpent
(serpentium) (serpentine)
mille passus, a mile. Literally, a thousand paces.
Pl.: milia passuum, miles
locus, loci, m., place, position. Sometimes
neuter in the plural (location, local)

Atlas, Atlantis, m., Atlas
Pythia, Pythiae, f., Pythia
corpus, corporis, n., body (corporeal)
hora, horae, f., hour (horology)
amor, amoris, m., love (amorous)
Apollo, Apollinis, m., Apollo
Eurystheus, Eurysthei, m., Eurystheus
Iuno, Iunonis, f., Juno

ADJECTIVES

aureus, aurea, aureum, golden, of gold (aureate)   duodecim, twelve (duodecimal)

VERBS

volo, velle, volui, wish, want, be willing (volition)
nolo, nolle, nolui, not to wish, be unwilling
malo, malle, malui, prefer
doceo, docere, docui, doctus, teach, show (docile)
iubeo, iubere, iussi, iussus, order, command (jussive)
demonstro, demonstrare, demonstravi, demonstratus, point out, show (demonstrate)

ADVERBS

domi, at home (domicile)
ruri, in the country (rural)

quam diu, how long

PREPOSITIONS

in, into, onto (inhale). With the accusative case.

131. New Reading Grammar—Time and Place Cues

A. BOTH THE ACCUSATIVE AND ABLATIVE CASES ARE USED TO SHOW TIME.

1. The accusative case is used to show how long something goes on (duration).

multos annos	for many years	**duodecim horas**	for twelve hours

2. The ablative case is used to show when something happens (position).

anno	in (during) a year	**sex annis**	in (during) six years
hora	in (during) an hour		

B. BOTH THE ACCUSATIVE AND ABLATIVE CASES ARE USED TO SHOW PLACE.

1. The accusative case with a preposition shows to or into what place motion is directed, or how far.

ad urbem	to the city	**in oppidum**	into the town
multa milia passuum	many miles, for many miles		

2. The ablative case with a preposition shows where the place is, or from where the motion is directed.

in oppido	in the town	**in mare**	on the sea
ab oppido	away from the town	**ex urbe**	out of the city
de muro	down from the wall		

C. WITH THE NAMES OF CITIES, TOWNS, AND SMALL ISLANDS, AND WITH THE WORDS
    ruri (IN THE COUNTRY) AND domi (AT HOME), NO PREPOSITION IS USED.

Romam	to Rome	**Roma**	from Rome

132. New Reading Grammar—Cardinal and Ordinal Numbers

Numbers are adjectives. There are two kinds of numbers. One, two, five, ten, etc. are called **cardinal** numbers. First, second, fifth, tenth, etc. are called **ordinal numbers.** You will learn more about numbers in a later chapter. For now, all you need to remember is that most **cardinal** numbers are not declined. **Ordinal** numbers typically use first and second declension adjectival endings.

duodecim puellae	twelve girls	duodecim puellarum	of twelve girls
duodecim horti	twelve gardens	duodecim hortorum	of twelve gardens
duodecim corpora	twelve bodies	duodecim corporum	of twelve bodies

133. New Reading Grammar—Irregular Verbs *volo*, *nolo*, and *malo*

1. THESE THREE VERBS ARE CONJUGATED SIMILARLY, AND ARE CLOSELY RELATED IN MEANING.

a. *Volo means to wish for something, to want something, or to be willing to do something.*

b. *Nolo means to wish not to have or to do something, or to be unwilling to do something. Nolo comes from an assimilation of non and volo, to not want. Some of the forms remain uncontracted.*

c. *Malo means to prefer something. Malo comes from an assimilation of magis and volo, to want more, to prefer.*

2. THESE VERBS ARE ALMOST ALWAYS USED WITH THE COMPLEMENTARY INFINITIVE OF ANOTHER VERB:

| **volo ire** | I want to go | **nolo pugnare** | I do not want to fight | **malo manere** | I prefer to stay |

3. THESE VERBS ONLY HAVE THE FIRST THREE PRINCIPAL PARTS:

| volo, velle, volui | nolo, nolle, nolui | malo, malle, malui |

4. NONE OF THESE VERBS HAVE PASSIVE FORMS, SINCE THEY ARE NOT TRANSITIVE IN MEANING.

5. PRESENT TENSE:

volo	I want/am willing	**nolo**	I do not want/am not willing	**malo**	I prefer
vis	you want			**mavis**	you prefer
vult	he, she, it wants	**non vis**	you do not want	**mavult**	he, she, it prefers
volumus	we want	**non vult**	he, she, it does not want	**malumus**	we prefer
vultis	you want			**mavultis**	you prefer
volunt	they want	**nolumus**	we do not want	**malunt**	they prefer
		non vultis	you do not want		
		nolunt	they do not want		

Note that **malo** was originally **mavolo, malumus** was originally **mavolumus,** and **malunt** was originally **mavolunt.** The first of these forms (first person singular) does appear occasionally, but usually the contracted form **malo** is used. The remaining forms of the present tense (**mavis, mavult** and **mavultis**) are not contracted.

Present active infinitives:

velle	to want, to be willing	malle	to prefer	nolle	not to want, to be unwilling

6. volo USES THE STEM vol- FOR THE IMPERFECT AND FUTURE TENSES; nolo USES nol- AND malo USES mal-.

a. Imperfect:

volebam	I used to want/was wanting	nolebam	I did not want/was unwilling	malebam	I used to prefer/was preferring
volebas	you used to want	nolebas	you did not want	malebas	you used to prefer
volebat	he, she, it used to want	nolebat	he, she, it did not want	malebat	he, she it used to prefer
etc.		etc.		etc.	

b. Future:

volam	I shall want/be willing	nolam	I shall not want/be unwilling	malam	I shall prefer
voles	you will want			males	you will prefer
volet	he, she, it will want	noles	you will not want	malet	he, she, it will prefer
volemus	we shall want	nolet	he, she, it will not want	malemus	we shall prefer
voletis	you will want	nolemus	we shall not want	maletis	you will prefer
volent	they will want	noletis	you will not want	malent	they will prefer
		nolent	they will not want		

You will notice that the future endings for these verbs are different from those you have previously encountered. These are the normal future endings for third and fourth conjugation verbs. These conjugations will be introduced later in this chapter.

7. IN THE PERFECT TENSES, volo, nolo, AND malo ARE CONJUGATED NORMALLY, AS ARE ALL VERBS. THE PERFECT STEMS ARE volu-, nolu-, AND malu-.

134. New Reading Grammar—Negative Imperatives

Volo and **malo** do not have imperative forms. The imperative forms for **nolo** are:

Singular: **noli**   do not want! be unwilling!

Plural: **nolite**   do not want! be unwilling!

These forms are generally used together with complementary infinitives as negative imperatives; that is, to command someone *not* to do something.

noli ire   do not go! (literally, do not want to go, be unwilling to go!)

nolite pugnare   do not fight! (literally, do not want to fight, be unwilling to fight!)

135. Reading

Labores Herculis

1. **Pythia ab Apolline docebatur et populo consilium dei dedit.**
2. **Hercules a femina amorem suum Apollinis demonstrare iussus est.**
3. **Hercules ad urbem regis, Eurysthei, properavit. Ibi Eurystheus Herculi labores duodecim dedit.**
4. **Sunt multae fabulae de laboribus Herculis.**
5. **Duodecim annos laborabat quod erat servus regis, sed Hercules de laboribus suis minime dolebat.**
6. **Corpus robustum habebat et regem laboremque non timebat.**
7. **A rege diu tenebatur, sed post duodecim annos liberatus est quod regem bene iuverat.**
8. **Deo Apollini amorem suum demonstraverat.**

The Labors of Hercules

1. Pythia was taught by Apollo and gave the advice of the god to the people.
2. Hercules was ordered by the woman to show his love for Apollo.
3. Hercules hurried to the city of the king, Eurystheus. There, Eurystheus gave Hercules twelve labors.
4. There are many stories about the labors of Hercules.
5. He labored for twelve years because he was the servant of the king, but Hercules grieved very little about his labors.
6. He had a strong body and did not fear the king and the work.
7. He was held for a long time by the king, but after twelve years, he was freed because he had helped the king well.
8. He had shown the god, Apollo, his love.

Poma Aurea Hesperidum

1. **Hercules pro rege, Eurystheo, bene laboravit, sed etiam turn non erat liber et domi non mansit.**
2. **Rex Herculem poma aurea ex horto Hesperidum obtinere iussit.**
3. **Hesperides erant filiae pulchrae Atlantis et in loco ultimo in fini terrae ruri habitabant.**
4. **Pro Iunone poma aurea ibi curabant.**
5. **Multi praemio pomorum moti erant, sed Hesperides poma semper bene servabant.**
6. **Erat murus magnus altusque circum hortum ubi erant poma, atque ante horum erat serpens.**
7. **Serpens capita multa habuit.**
8. **Hercules multa milia passuum ambulavit. Post annum ad hortum venit.**
9. **Erat in fini ultimo terrae et proximus Oceano.**
10. **Hercules Atlantem, virum robustum et amicum, ibi vidit.**
11. **Auxilium rogavit.**

The Golden Apples of the Hesperides

1. Hercules worked well for the king, Eurytheus, but even then he was not free and did not stay at home.
2. The king ordered Hercules to get the apples from the garden of the Hesperides.
3. The Hesperides were the beautiful daughters of Atlas and lived in the country in the farthest place on the end of the earth.
4. They took care of the golden apples there for Juno.
5. Many people had been moved by the reward of the apples, but the Hesperides always preserved the apples well.
6. There was a large and high wall around the garden where the apples were, and in front of the garden was a serpent.
7. The serpent had many heads.
8. Hercules walked many miles. After a year, he came to the garden.
9. It was on the farthest end of the earth and next to the Ocean.
10. Hercules saw Atlas there, a strong and friendly man.
11. He asked for help.

Academic Degrees and Terms

We use many Latin words and phrases in academic degrees and terms, as shown below. **Cum laude,** with praise, is given with a diploma that has been earned with a grade of work higher than ordinary.

magna cum laude, with great praise.
summa cum laude, with highest praise.
alumnus, pl. **alumni,** male graduate or graduates.
alumna, pl. **alumnae,** female graduate or graduates.
alma mater, foster mother. Refers to one's school or college.
M.A. or A.M., **Artium Magister,** Master of Arts.
B.A. or A.B., Baccalaureus Artium, Bachelor of Arts.
B.S., Baccalaureus Scientiae, Bachelor of Science.
D.D., Divinitatis Doctor, Doctor of Divinity.
D.Litt. or Litt.D., Doctor Litterarum, Doctor of Literature or Letters.
M.D., Medicinae Doctor, Doctor of Medicine.
Ph.D., Philosophiae Doctor, Doctor of Philosophy.
LL.D., Legum Doctor, Doctor of Laws.
D.M.D., Dentariae Medicinae Doctor, Doctor of Dental Medicine.

Assimilation

Some prefixes take on the first letter of the word to which they are attached. This process is called assimilation and often smooths out pronunciation. Assimilation occurs with these prefixes:

ad   **ad** and **pono** (put, place) become **appono,** put to, put near
con   **con** and **mitto** (send) become **committo,** send together
in   **in** and **mortalis** become **immortalis,** immortal

Sometimes there is a change to a different letter:

in and **porto** become **importo,** carry in, bring in
con and **pono** become **compono,** put together

136. Practice Exercises

No. 92. Give the English for these expressions of time:

1. **multos annos**
2. **proximo anno**
3. **multas horas**
4. **proxima hora**
5. **septem horas**
6. **medio anno**
7. **sex horis**
8. **annos longos**
9. **hora**
10. **duodecim horas**

No. 93. Give the English for these expressions of place:

1. **ad urbes**
2. **ex oppidis**
3. **Roma**
4. **Romam**
5. **in castra**
6. **ante forum**
7. **post hortum**
8. **in agro**
9. **in agros**
10. **de collibus**
11. **e casa**
12. **ruri**
13. **domi**
14. **a flumine**
15. **sub maribus**
16. **sub muris**
17. **in fossam**
18. **a templo**
19. **e viis**
20. **de sole**

No. 94. Translate these verbs:

1. **videbo**
2. **pugnaverat**
3. **stabatis**
4. **laborabimus**
5. **fuerat**
6. **obtinebunt**
7. **natabamus**
8. **erit**
9. **videmus**
10. **spectatum est**
11. **movebitur**
12. **aedificata erant**
13. **fuisti**
14. **oppugnabamur**
15. **manserunt**
16. **vult**
17. **non vis**
18. **malo habere**
19. **malebam**
20. **noles**

No. 95. Translate these sentences:

1. Proximo anno Romam movebimus.
2. Sex horas in urbe manserunt.
3. Medio in colle oppugnati erant.
4. Multas horas in Italia manebam.
5. Ibi erit horam.
6. Nonne multos annos laborabunt?
7. Ad oppidum multas horas longas ambulabat.
8. A rege non liberatus est.
9. Suntne in horto cum pueris?
10. Septem milia passuum ab urbe movi.
11. Nolite ad urbem ire.
12. Malo in oppidum manere.

137. New Reading Vocabulary

NOUNS

causa, causae, f., cause, reason (causeless)
signum, signi, n., signal, standard (signify)
Hippomenes, Hippomenis, m., Hippomenes
iter, itineris, n., journey, march, way, route (itinerary)

mora, morae, f., delay (moratorium)
umerus, umeri, m., shoulder (humerus)
pes, pedis, m., foot (pedal)
nox, noctis, f., night (**noctium**) (nocturnal)
Atalanta, Atalantae, f., Atalanta

PRONOUN AND ADJECTIVE

is, ea, id, he, she, it; this, that. Can be used either as a pronoun or as an adjective.

VERBS

duco, ducere, duxi, ductum, lead (conduct, aqueduct)
mitto, mittere, misi, missus, send (mission, manumit)
peto, petere, petivi, petitus, seek, ask (petition)

curro, currere, cucurri, cursus, run (current)
dico, dicere, dixi, dictus, say, speak (diction)

ADVERBS

paene, almost, nearly (peninsula)

138. New Reading Grammar—Third Conjugation Verbs

e/i-conjugation or third conjugation verbs follow the same rules as the regular verbs you have met so far, except in the future tense. The predominant vowels are **e** and **i**.

Consider the verb **pono.**

1. PRINCIPAL PARTS: pono, ponere, posui, positus, PUT OR PLACE

The first two principal parts show that **pono** is a third conjugation verb. The infinitive ends in -**ere**, like a second conjugation verb, although this –**e** (the first –e) is short, whereas the –**e** of second conjugations is long. Third conjugation also has no -e- in the first person singular of the present active tense, which distinguishes it from second conjugation. The stem for the present, imperfect, and future forms is **pon-**. The stem for the perfect active forms is **posu-**, while the perfect passive forms are derived from **positus**.

2. PRESENT TENSE

Active
(I put, place; am putting, placing; do put, place)

Singular	*Plural*
pono	ponimus
ponis	ponitis
ponit	ponunt

Passive
(I am being put, placed; am put, placed)

Singular	*Plural*
ponor	ponimur
poneris	ponimini
ponitur	ponuntur

As you can see, the vowel connecting the stem to the ending varies, depending on the form. You will have to memorize which forms use which vowels.

Imperatives: Singular: **pone**   Plural: **ponite**

For the imperative singular, -e is added to the stem. In the plural, the basic ending **-te** is added on to the present stem plus the vowel -i-.

3. IMPERFECT TENSE

Active (I put, place; was putting, placing)

Singular	*Plural*
ponebam	ponebamus
ponebas	ponebatis
ponebat	ponebant

Passive (I was being put, placed; was put, placed)

Singular	*Plural*
ponebar	ponebamur
ponebaris	ponebamini
ponebatur	ponebantur

The vowel used between the stem and the imperfect endings is -e-.

4. FUTURE TENSES

The active future tense endings of third conjugation verbs are:

Singular	*Plural*
-am	-emus
-es	-etis
-et	-ent

These are the same as the basic endings of the present tense added to the vowel -e-, with the exception of the first person singular. The basic ending for this form is -m, and it is added to the vowel -a-. The future passive endings are the basic passive endings added to the vowel used for the active future tense:

Singular	Plural
-ar	-emur
-eris	-emini
-etur	-entur

Thus, the future tense of **pono** is:

Active (I shall put, place)

Singular	Plural
ponam	ponemus
pones	ponetis
ponet	ponent

Passive (I shall be put, placed)

Singular	Plural
ponar	ponemur
poneris	ponemini
ponetur	ponentur

5. PERFECT TENSE

Active (I put, place; have put, placed)

Singular	Plural
posui	posuimus
posuisti	posuistis
posuit	posuerunt

Passive (I have been put, placed)

Singular	Plural
positus, -a, -um sum	positi, -ae, -a sumus
positus, -a, -um es	positi, -ae, a estis
positus, -a, -um est	positi, -ae, -a sunt

6. PLUPERFECT TENSE

Active (I had put, placed)

Singular	Plural
posueram	posueramus
posueras	posueratis
posuerat	posuerant

Passive (I had been put, placed)

Singular	Plural
positus, -a, -um eram	positi, -ae, -a eramus
positus, -a, -um eras	positi, -ae, -a eratis
positus, -a, -um erat	positi, -ae, -a erant

7. FUTURE PERFECT TENSE

Active (I shall have put, placed)

Singular	Plural
posuero	posuerimus
posueris	posueritis
posuerit	posuerint

Passive (I shall have been put, placed)

Singular	Plural
positus, -a, -um ero	positi, -ae, -a erimus
positus, -a, -um eris	positi, -ae, -a eritis
positus, -a, -um erit	positi, -ae, -a erunt

139. New Reading Grammar: *is, ea, id*

is, ea, id can be used as either a pronoun (*he, she, it*; plural: *they*) or an adjective (*this, that*; plural: *these, those*). As a pronoun, **is, ea, id** may be considered either a third person **personal pronoun,** or as a weak **demonstrative pronoun.** The declension is given below.

1. AS A *pronoun*, IT HAS THE SAME GENDER AND NUMBER AS ITS ANTECEDENT (I.E., THE NOUN IT REPLACES OR REFERS BACK TO), BUT ITS CASE IS DETERMINED BY ITS FUNCTION WITHIN ITS OWN CLAUSE OR SENTENCE AND MAY NOT ALWAYS AGREE WITH THE CASE OF ITS ANTECEDENT.

Puerum video, I see the boy. **Eum video,** I see him. Same case (accusative), number (singular), and gender (masculine) as **puerum. Is in casa est,** He is in the house. Same number and gender as **puerum.** However, the case is different. It is nominative, not accusative, because **is** is the subject of the verb **est,** and the subject is put in the nominative case.

Singular

Case	Masculine	Feminine	Neuter
Nom.	**is** he	**ea** her	**id** it
Gen.	**eius** his	**eius** hers	**eius** its
Dat.	**ei** to, for him	**ei** to, for her	**ei,** to, for it
Acc.	**eum** him	**eam** her	**id** it
Abl.	**eo** from/with/by/in him	**ea** from/with/by/in her	**eo** from/with/by/in it

Plural

Case	Masculine	Feminine	Neuter	
Nom.	**ei** or **ii**	**eae**	**ea**	they
Gen.	**eorum**	**earum**	**eorum**	their
Dat.	**eis** or **iis**	**eis** or **iis**	**eis** or **iis**	to, for them
Acc.	**eos**	**eas**	**a**	them
Abl.	**eis** or **iis**	**eis** or **iis**	**eis** or **iis**	from/with/by/in them

Note that most pronouns are not used in the vocative case.

2. AS AN *adjective*, is, ea, or id MUST HAVE THE SAME GENDER, NUMBER, AND CASE AS THE NOUN IT MODIFIES. IT IS DECLINED IN THE SAME WAY AS THE PRONOUN.

is puer, this boy, that boy   **ea puella,** this girl, that girl   **id bellum,** this war, that war

As an **adjective,** the singular means *this* or *that,* and the plural means *these* or *those.*

Case	Singular	Plural
Nom.	this, that	these, those
Gen.	of this, of that	of these, of those
Dat.	to, for this; to, for that	to, for these; to, for those
Acc.	this, that	these, those
Abl.	from/with/by/in this; from/with/by/in that	from/with/by/in these; from/with/by/in those

3. THE USE OF eius.

a. The possessive form of the pronoun is, ea, id is eius; plural, eorum. It does not refer to the subject.

Pomum eius videmus.	We see his (her) apple.
Pomum eius videt.	He (she) sees someone else's apple.

Note that **eius** might still be translated as *his* or *her,* but the person it refers to is somone other than the subject of **videt.**

b. When the possessor is the same as the subject, the reflexive adjective suus, -a, -um is used.

Pomum suum habet.	He has his (own) apple.

140. Reading

Poma Aurea Hesperidum (concl'd)

1. Postquam Hercules auxilium petiverat, causam itineris sui ad finem terrae Atlantem docuit.
2. Atlas erat pater Hesperidum et Herculi de loco ubi erant poma aurea narravit, sed Atlas caelum in umeris suis tenebat.
3. Atlas Herculi caelum dedit et Herculum in umeris caelum tenere iussit.
4. Atlas ad hortum Hesperidum properavit.
5. Diu Hercules in umeris suis caelum tenebat. Diu Atlantem non viderat.
6. Hercules famam de Atlante non habuerat. Et timebat et dolebat.
7. Pretium pomorum erat certe magnum.
8. Post multas noctes Atlantem vidit et laetus erat.
9. Mox poma aurea habuit. Turn Atlas caelum in umeris suis locavit et Hercules erat liber.
10. Ad Graecam cum pomis properavit.

The Golden Apples of the Hesperides (concl'd)

1. After Hercules had sought help, he showed Atlas the cause of his journey to the end of the earth.
2. Atlas was the father of the Hesperides and he told Hercules about the place where the golden apples were, but Atlas was holding the sky on his shoulders.
3. Atlas gave the sky to Hercules and he ordered Hercules to hold the sky on his shoulders.
4. Atlas hurried to the garden of the Hesperides.
5. For a long time Hercules held the sky on his shoulders. He had not seen Atlas for a long time.
6. Hercules had not had a report about Atlas. He was both afraid and grieving.
7. The price of the apples was certainly great.
8. After many nights, he saw Atlas and he was happy.
9. Soon he had the golden apples. Then Atlas placed the sky on his own shoulders and Hercules was free.
10. He hurried to Greece with the apples.

Atalanta

1. **Atalanta erat puella Graeciae et vero pulchra.**
2. **Multi viri contra eam cucurrerant, sed magnam celeritatem habebat et non superata erat.**
3. **Venus consilium habebat. Puella erat praemium victoriae et pedibus eos currere iussit.**
4. **Hippomenes contra eam currere paratus est.**
5. **Multi spectabant et eum incitabant.**
6. **Signum datum est.**
7. **Atalanta celeritatem suam demonstrabat. Paene volabat.**
8. **Quam longe ante eum currit!**
9. **Sed Venus Hippomeni viam ad victoriam docuerat. Ei poma aurea dederat.**
10. **Hippomenes pomum ad terram misit.**
11. **Atalanta ad moram movebatur.**
12. **Hippomenes celeritatem suam auxit.**
13. **Finis erat propinquus.**
14. **Venus, dea amoris, eum bene iuverat.**
15. **Hippomenes consilio donoque deae puellam superaverat.**

Atalanta

1. Atalanta was a girl of Greece and truly beautiful.
2. Many men had raced against her, but she had great speed and had not been surpassed.
3. Venus had a plan. The girl was the reward of victory and she ordered them to run on foot.
4. Hippomenes was prepared to run against her.
5. Many were watching and urging him on.
6. The signal is given.
7. Atalanta was showing her speed. She was almost flying.
8. How far in front of him she runs!
9. But Venus had shown Hippomenes the way to victory. She had given him golden apples.
10. Hippomenes threw an apple to the ground.
11. Atalanta was moved toward delay.
12. Hippomenes increased his speed.
13. The end was near.
14. Venus, goddess of love, had helped him well.
15. Hippomenes had overtaken the girl by the plan and gift of the goddess.

141. Practice Exercises

No. 96. Translate these verb forms:

1. mittunt
2. doctus sum
3. petimur
4. debet
5. moniti eratis
6. parati erunt
7. duxit
8. liberavisti
9. adorabam
10. miserit
11. iubebit
12. spectabamur
13. demonstratis
14. rogabunt
15. ducebas
16. mittet
17. servavi
18. timueras
19. petiveratis
20. mansuerunt

No. 97. *Translate these phrases:*

1. ob iniuriam
2. e proeliis
3. sex horas
4. in itinere
5. e finibus

6. ad Galliam
7. a colle
8. in litteris
9. a hominibus
10. in ripam

No. 98. *Translate the following:*

1. Eas peto.
2. eorum librorum
3. hortus eius
4. Ea eis dedi.
5. Is pugnabat.
6. Eum vidistis.
7. in eis locis
8. patri eius
9. Ab eo mittuntur.
10. Eos misisti.

11. ea hora
12. sua signa
13. ex eis urbibus
14. eam mulierem
15. Ab eis ducimur.
16. eorum poma
17. suos reges
18. cum eis
19. id iter
20. eam causam

No. 99. *Change these verb forms to the active (if they are passive) or to the passive (if they active):*

1. ducit
2. duxi
3. ducebar
4. ducti sunt
5. ducam
6. misisti
7. mittebantur
8. mittemini
9. missus es
10. miserat

11. petiverunt
12. petiti erimus
13. petet
14. petitur
15. petebaris
16. current
17. cucurrit
18. curritur
19. currebant
20. cursum erat

REVIEW

142. Vocabulary Review

NOUNS

1. amor
2. Apollo
3. Atalanta
4. Atlas
5. audacia
6. causa
7. collis
8. corpus
9. Eurystheus
10. fines
11. finis
12. flumen
13. Hercules
14. Hesperides
15. Hippomenes
16. hora
17. hortus
18. ignis
19. iter
20. Iuno
21. lex
22. liber
23. locus
24. milia passuum
25. mille passus
26. mons
27. mora
28. mulier
29. murus
30. nomen
31. nox
32. pes
33. pomum
34. pretium
35. pugna
36. Pythia
37. rex
38. serpens
39. signum
40. Tarquinius

PRONOUNS

1. is
2. ea
3. id

ADJECTIVES

1. aureus
2. duodecim
3. novem
4. proximus
5. septem
6. sex
7. Sibyllinus
8. superbus
9. ultimus
10. is, ea, id

VERBS

1. augeo
2. curro
3. demonstro
4. dico
5. doceo
6. duco
7. iubeo
8. malo
9. mitto
10. nolo
11. peto
12. rogo

ADVERBS

1. domi
2. paene
3. postea
4. quam diu
5. ruri

PREPOSITIONS
1. in

CONJUNCTIONS
1. postquam

143. Practice Exercises

No. 100. Give the English for these phrases:

1. in pedibus	4. ex agris	7. de corpore	10. Romam
2. a colli	5. in ignem	8. ruri	11. domi
3. ad flumina	6. in muris	9. Roma	12. e nocte

No. 101. Translate these perfect tenses:

1. fuerat	7. data sunt	13. incitati erant	19. laudati erimus
2. regnavimus	8. misistis	14. properaveratis	20. habuerat
3. rogatus est	9. petitum erit	15. fuerint	21. maluit
4. portaveris	10. auctum erat	16. rogatus sum	22. voluerunt
5. dederunt	11. movimus	17. stetit	23. malueram
6. locaverunt	12. fuimus	18. vocavisti	24. nolueritis

No. 102. Give the English for these phrases:

1. proximo anno	5. sex annos	9. eo anno
2. horas septem	6. ea nocte	10. ea hora
3. proximis horis	7. eas noctes	
4. multo anno	8. eos annos	

No. 103. Give the English for these pronouns:

1. eius	4. ei	7. ea	10. eum
2. eos	5. id	8. eorum	11. ii
3. eae	6. eas	9. eis	12. eo

No. 104. Translate these adjective phrases:

1. eum amorem	4. eas causas	7. ea poma	10. eius loci
2. eius audaciae	5. eis finibus	8. ei mulieri	11. ei regi
3. ea nomina	6. eorum itinerum	9. id corpus	12. eam noctem

144. Reading

MARCUS VALERIUS MARTIALIS

Martialis was born in Spain about A.D. 40 and went to Rome as a young man. He was a master of the epigram, and his poems, depicting scenes of everyday life, are full of wit, freshness, and satire. Martialis died about A.D. 103, after returning to Spain.

Non amo te, Sabidi, nec possum dicere quare;
hoc tantum possum dicere: non amo te.

Epigrammaton Liber I, xxxii

Cras te victurum, cras dicis, Postume, semper.
Dic mihi, cras istud, Postume, quando venit?
Quam longe cras istud, ubi est? aut unde petendum?
Numquid apud Parthos Armeniosque latet?
Iam cras istud habet Priami vel Nestoris annos.
Cras istud quanti, dic mihi, posset emi?
Cras vives? Hodie iam vivere, Postume, serum est;
ille sapit, quisquis, Postume, vixit heri.

Epigrammaton Liber V, lviii

The Bible

Omnia tempus habent,
et suis spatiis transeunt universa sub caelo.
Tempus nascendi et tempus moriendi,
tempus plantandi et tempus evellendi quod plantatum est,
tempus occidenti et tempus sanandi,
tempus destruendi et tempus aedificandi,
tempus flendi et tempus ridendi,
tempus plangendi et tempus saltandi,
tempus spargendi lapides et tempus colligendi,
tempus amplexandi et tempus longe fieri ab amplexibus,
tempus adquirendi et tempus perdendi,
tempus custodiendi et tempus abiciendi,
tempus scindendi et tempus consuendi,
tempus tacendi et tempus loquendi,
tempus dilectonis et tempus odii,
tempus belli et tempus pacis.
Quid habet amplius homo de labore suo?

Liber Ecclesiastes III, i-ix

DEMONSTRATIVE PRONOUNS

Latin Phrases Used in the Constitution of the United States

In Section 3, dealing with Officers of the Senate:

"The Senate shall choose their officers, and also a president **pro tempore,** in the absence of the Vice-President, or when he shall exercise the office of President of the United States." **pro tempore** means *for the time.*

In Section 9, dealing with Powers Forbidden to the United States:

"The privilege of the writ of **habeas corpus** shall not be suspended, unless when in cases of rebellion or invasion the public safety may require it." **habeas corpus** means *thou shall have the body.* A writ of habeas corpus is a legal document making it mandatory that an accused person be brought to court to be told the reason for his or her detention.

"No bill of attainder or **ex-post-facto** law shall be passed." **ex post facto** means *from what is done afterwards.* An ex-post-facto law is passed after a crime has been committed. Thus, a person who has committed a crime must be tried under the laws as they existed at the time of the commission of the crime.

---

145. New Reading Vocabulary

NOUNS

timor, timoris, m., fear, dread (timorous)
poena, poenae, f., punishment, fine (penal)
Bacchus, Bacchi, m., Bacchus (bacchanalian)
mors, mortis, f., death (**mortium**) (mortality)
diligentia, diligentiae, f., diligence, care (diligent)
studium, studii or studi, n., zeal, eagerness (studio)
tempus, temporis, n., time (temporary, ex tempore)

aurum, auri, n., gold (auriferous)
arena, arenae, f., sand (arena)
Silenus, Sileni, m., Silenus
Midas, Midae, m., Midas
cibus, cibi, m., food
arbor, arboris, f., tree (arboretum)

VERBS

capio, capere, cepi, captus, take, seize, capture (caption)
pono, ponere, posui, positus, put, place (position, postpone)

fero, ferre, tuli, latum, carry, bear
facio, facere, feci, factus, make, do (factory)
verto, vertere, verti, versus, turn (vertical)

PREPOSITIONS

propter, because of, on account of

146. New Reading Grammar—Third Conjugation i-stem Verbs

Some **third conjugation (e/i-conjugation)** verbs have **-io** in the first principal part. These also have an **-i-** in most forms of the present, imperfect, and future tenses. These verbs are known as third conjugation i-stems. As the name implies, the **-i-** is part of the present tense stem of the verb. Compare **duco** (a regular third conjugation) with **capio** (an i-stem).

1. PRESENT TENSE

Active		*Passive*	
duco, *I lead*	**capio,** *I seize*	**ducor,** *I am led*	**capior,** *I am seized*
ducis	**capis**	**duceris**	**caperis**
ducit	**capit**	**ducitur**	**capitur**
ducimus	**capimus**	**ducimur**	**capimur**
ducitis	**capitis**	**ducimini**	**capimini**
ducunt	**capiunt**	**ducuntur**	**capiuntur**

capio has an **-i-** in all forms of the present tense, except for the second person singular in the passive voice.

Imperatives:

	lead!	seize!
Singular:	**duc**	**cape**
Plural:	**ducite**	**capite**

You will notice that although the imperative plurals are formed the same way, the imperative singular of **capio** ends in **-e.** This is true, in fact, of most third conjugation verbs, of either type. Recall that **duco** is one of four verbs in Latin that have irregular imperatives. The others are **dico (dic, dicite),** **facio (fac, facite)** and **fero (fer, ferte).** Note in particular the absence of **-i-** in the plural of **fero.**

2. IMPERFECT TENSE

Active		Passive	
ducebam, *I was leading*	capiebam, *I was seizing*	ducebar, *I was led*	capiebar, *I was seized*
ducebas	capiebas	ducebaris	capiebaris
ducebat	capiebat	ducebatur	capiebatur
ducebamus	capiebamus	ducebamur	capiebamur
ducebatis	capiebatis	ducebamini	capiebamini
ducebant	capiebant	ducebantur	capiebantur

Where the forms of **duco** have -**e**-, the forms of **capio** have -**ie**-.

3. FUTURE TENSE

Active		Passive	
ducam, *I shall lead*	capiam, *I shall seize*	ducar, *I shall be led*	capiar, *I shall be seized*
duces	capies	duceris	capieris
ducet	capiet	ducetur	capietur
ducemus	capiemus	ducemur	capiemur
ducetis	capietis	ducemini	capiemini
ducent	capient	ducentur	capientur

The future forms of **capio** have -**ie**- and -**ia**- instead of -**e**- and -**a**-.

4. THE PERFECT TENSES ARE ALL REGULAR.

The active endings are added on to the perfect stem, just as with all other verbs. The perfect stem of **capio** is **cep**-, derived from the third principal part, **cepi**. The passive endings are formed with the fourth principal part, **captus**, and the verb **sum**.

147. New Reading Grammar—the irregular verb *fero*

1. THE PRINCIPAL PARTS OF THIS VERB ARE fero, ferre, tuli, latus.

2. MOST OF THE IRREGULARITIES ARE FOUND IN THE PRESENT FORMS:

Active	Passive
fero, *I carry, am carrying, do carry*	**feror,** *I am being carried, am carried*
fers	ferris
fert	fertur
ferimus	ferimur
fertis	ferimini
ferunt	feruntur

Some of these forms are quite strange, so you will have to memorize them.

Present Infinitive: **ferre**

Imperative:	Singular:	**fer**
	Plural:	**ferte**

2. THE IMPERFECT AND FUTURE FORMS OF fero ADD THE BASIC ENDINGS FOR THIRD CONJUGATION VERBS TO THE PRESENT STEM, fer-.

Imperfect Tense

Active	*Passive*
ferebam, *I was carrying, carried*	**ferebar**, *I was being carried, was carried*
ferebas	**ferebaris**
ferebat	**ferebatur**
ferebamus	**ferebamur**
ferebatis	**ferebamini**
ferebant	**ferebantur**

Future Tense

Active	*Passive*
feram, *I shall carry*	**ferar**, *I shall be carried*
feres	**fereris**
feret	**feretur**
feremus	**feremur**
feretis	**feremini**
ferent	**ferentur**

3. THE PERFECT TENSES ARE REGULAR.

However, you must remember the principal parts of the verb! The third principal part is **tuli** and the perfect active stem is **tul-**. The fourth principal part is **latus**. Thus:

Perfect Tense

Active	*Passive*
tuli, *I have carried, carried*	**latus, -a, -um sum**, *I have been carried*
tulisti	**latus, -a, -um es**
tulit	**latus, -a, -um est**
tulimus	**lati, -ae, -a sumus**
tulistis	**lati, -ae, -a estis**
tulerunt	**lati, -ae, -a sunt**

Pluperfect Tense

Active	*Passive*
tuleram, *I had carried*	**latus, -a, -um eram**, *I had been carried*
tuleras	**latus, -a, -um eras**
tulerat	**latus, -a, -um erat**
tuleramus	**lati, -ae, -a eramus**
tuleratis	**lati, -ae, -a eratis**
tulerant	**lati, -ae, -a erant**

Future Perfect Tense

Active	*Passive*
tulero, *I shall have carried*	**latus, -a, -um ero**, *I shall have been carried*
tuleris	**latus, -a, -um eris**
tulerit	**latus, -a, -um erit**
tulerimus	**lati, -ae, -a erimus**
tuleritis	**lati, -ae, -a eritis**
tulerint	**lati, -ae, -a erunt**

148. New Reading Grammar—Prepositional Usage (*cum, ob, propter*)

A. WHEN cum IS USED TO SHOW HOW SOMETHING WAS DONE, IT OFTEN FOLLOWS THE ADJECTIVE.

Cum diligentia laborat.	He works with diligence.
Laborat magna cum diligentia.	He works with great diligence.

B. THE CAUSE OF AN ACTION MAY BE SHOWN BY EITHER THE ABLATIVE CASE ALONE (ABLATIVE OF MEANS), OR BY ob OR propter FOLLOWED BY THE ACCUSATIVE CASE.

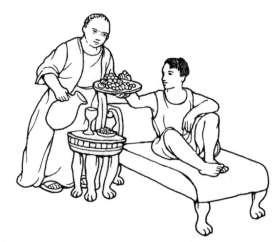

timore	because of (on account of) fear
ob timorem	because of (on account of) fear
propter timorem	because of (on account of) fear

149. Reading

Midas et Aurum

1. Temporibus antiquis erat rex, Midas.
2. Nomen eius regis erat clarum quod amicus Bacchi erat.
3. Silenus Bacchum docebat, sed ab hostibus captus erat.
4. A Mida liberatus erat. Bacchus vero fuit laetus.
5. Bacchus ei nuntiavit: "Donum dabo."
6. Midas bonam fortunam, sed non multam sapientam habebat.
7. Rex id donum accepit: Postea ea proxima ei in aurum vertebantur.
8. Rex donum dei bene amabat.
9. Midas aurum facere properavit.
10. In aurum arbores altas atque terram aquamque in eis locis ubi stabat aut ambulabat vertit.
11. Ob donum suum deum laudavit.
12. Rex superbus auro suo factus erat.
13. Nunc Midas domi est. Magno cum studio multa in aurum vertit.
14. Tum cibus aquaque ante eum a servo suo ponebantur.

Midas and the Gold

1. In ancient times, there was a king, Midas.
2. The name of this king was famous because he was a friend of Bacchus.
3. Silenus taught Bacchus, but he had been captured by the enemy.
4. He had been freed by Midas. Bacchus was indeed happy.
5. Bacchus told him: "I shall give a gift."
6. Midas had good fortune, but not much wisdom.
7. The king received this gift: Afterwards, those things nearest to him were turned into gold.
8. The king liked the gift of the god very much.
9. Midas hurried to make gold.
10. He turns into gold the high trees and also the land and water in those places where he was standing or walking.
11. He praised the god because of his gift.
12. The king had been made proud by his gold.
13. Now Midas is at home. With great eagerness, he turns many things into gold.
14. Then food and water were placed in front of him by his servants.

15. Ea petivit, sed sine mora in aurum versa sunt.
16. Tum Midas timore magno capiebatur. Suam mortem vero timebat.
17. In locis ultimis proximisque aurum videbat.
18. Ad Bacchus vocavit: "Id donum rogavi, sed non est donum bonum. Est poena magna malaque. Nunc auxilium peto."
19. Deus ei auxilium mox dedit.
20. Corpus caputque in flumine ponere eum iussit.
21. Midas magna cum diligentia id fecit. Mox liberatus est, sed flumini suum donum dederat.
22. Post id tempus arenae fluminis erant aureae.
23. Bacchus laetus erat quod nunc liber erat et arena ab eo tempore erat pulchra.

15. He sought these things, but without delay, they were turned into gold.
16. Then Midas was seized with great fear. He indeed feared his death.
17. He saw gold in the farthest and nearest places.
18. He called on Bacchus: "I asked for this gift, but it is not a good gift. It is a great and evil punishment. Now I seek help."
19. The god soon gave him help.
20. He ordered him to place his body and head in a river.
21. Midas did this with great care. Soon he was free, but he had given his own gift to the river.
22. After that time, the sands of the river were golden.
23. Bacchus was happy because now he was free and the sand was beautiful from that time on.

150. Practice Exercises

No. 105. Translate these phrases, showing cause or reason:

1. ob moram
2. cura mea
3. propter pericula
4. propter timorem
5. ob mortem
6. diligentia
7. celeritate
8. ob audaciam
9. propter moras
10. tempore

No. 106. Translate these phrases, showing manner:

1. cum studio
2. magna cura
3. magna cum diligentia
4. magno cum timore
5. cum celeritate
6. studio multo
7. magno cum studio
8. cum mora
9. magna celeritate
10. magna cum mora

No. 107. Complete these principal parts:

1. pono, ponere, _____ , positus
2. supero, _____ , superavi, superatus
3. do, dare, _____ , datus
4. capio, _____ , cepi, captus
5. servo, servare, servavi, _____

6. _____ , facere, feci, factus
7. verto, vertere, _____ , versus
8. terreo, terrere, _____ , territus
9. _____ , ducere, duxi, ductus
10. fero, ferre, _____ , latus

No. 108. Translate these verb forms:

1. iussit
2. duxisti
3. demonstraverunt
4. rogabam
5. fecimus
6. docetur
7. mitteris
8. capimini
9. spectabit
10. augebimus
11. petent
12. ferebant
13. obtinebas
14. vertebatur
15. terruerat
16. petiveratis
17. ceperant
18. moti erunt
19. ducti eramus
20. capiebat

No. 109. Translate these prepositional phrases:

1. ob horam
2. propter telum
3. ante castra
4. a timore
5. de arbore
6. a rege
7. ex arboribus
8. in eum locum
9. cum patre
10. cum cura
11. in aqua
12. sub oceano
13. circum muros
14. contra eum
15. inter oppida
16. per agrum
17. post castra
18. sine eis
19. trans mare
20. de viris

The Pronunciation of Church Latin

The pronunciation of Church Latin may follow either classical Latin pronunciation or the general patterns of Italian pronunciation. The rules are by no means fixed and standardized, but, with widened oral communication, the Italian pronunciation of liturgical Latin increased in the Roman Catholic Church and also in the singing of all Church Latin.

1. Vowels
The vowels have the same pronunciation, except that **u** is voiced as **ou**. meus, me**ous**

2. Consonants
The most noticeable difference is that **c** before **e** or **i** is not **k**, but **ch**. cibus, **chibous**

If **c** before **e** or **i** is preceded by an **s**, the **s** is dropped. scio, **chio**

ti between two vowels is **tsi**. nationem, **natsionem**

ti after a consonant (except **s**, **t**, or **x**) is **ci**. amanti, amanci

g before **e** or **i** is soft, like **j**. gens, jens

All double consonants are pronounced definitely, with equal stress on each. anno, an-no

151. New Reading Vocabulary

NOUNS

classis, classis, f., a fleet (**classium**) (class)
animus, animi, m., mind, spirit (animosity)
iniuria, iniuriae, f., injury, harm (injurious)
Minotaurus, Minotauri, m., the Minotaur
eques, equitis, m., horseman, knight (equestrian)
labyrinthus, labyrinthi, m., labyrinth (labyrinthine)
impedimentum, impedimenti, n., hindrance. In the plural, baggage (impediment)

Hannibal, Hannibalis, m., Hannibal
navis, navis, f., ship (**navium**) (navy)
pedes, peditis, m., foot soldier
Minos, Minois, m., Minos
Africa, Africae, f., Africa
adulescens, adulescentis, m., youth (**adulescentium**) (adolescent)
imperator, imperatoris, m., general, commander, emperor (imperative)

ADJECTIVES

hic, haec, hoc, this, the latter
idem, eadem, idem, the same

ille, illa, illud, that, the former
ipse, ipsa, ipsum, himself, herself, itself; very (This last use is somewhat archaic.)

PRONOUNS

idem, eadem, idem, he, she, it
ipse, ipsa, ipsum, he (himself), she (herself), it (itself)

ille, illa, illud, he, she, it
hic, haec, hoc, he, she, it

VERBS

interficio, interficere, interfeci, interfectus, kill
fio, fieri, factus sum, be made, become, be done
contendo, contendere, contendi, contentus, hasten, arrive, contend (contender)

gero, gerere, gessi, gestus, carry on, wage
vinco, vincere, vici, victus, conquer

CONJUNCTIONS

itaque, and so, therefore

152. New Reading Grammar—*hic, ille, ipse* and *idem*

A. THE WORDS hic, ille, ipse, AND idem ARE USED AS BOTH PRONOUNS AND ADJECTIVES, IN THE SAME WAY AS is, ea, id.

Pronoun

hic, haec, hoc	he, she, it (here)	this
ille, illa, illud	he, she, it (there)	that
idem, eadem,	he, she, it (the same)	
idem	he, she, it (-self)	
ipse, ipsa, ipsum		

Adjective

hic vir, this man	**hic,** he
ille homo, that man	**ille,** he
idem homo, the same man	**idem,** he
vir ipse, the man himself	**ipse,** he

The declension of these words is very much the same as the declension of **is, ea, id.**

1. hic, haec, hoc:

Singular

Case	Masculine	Feminine	Neuter
Nom.	**hic** he	**haec** she	**hoc** it; this
Gen.	**huius** his	**huius** her	**huius** its; of this
Dat.	**huic** to/for him	**huic** to/for her	**huic** to/for it; to/for this
Acc.	**hunc** him	**hanc** her	**hoc** it; this
Abl.	**hoc** from/with/by/in him	**hac** from/with/by/in her	**hoc** from/with/by/in it; from/with/by/in this

Plural

Case	Masculine	Feminine	Neuter
Nom.	**hi**	**hae**	**haec** they; these
Gen.	**horum**	**harum**	**horum** their; of these
Dat.	**his**	**his**	**his** to/for them; to/for these
Acc.	**hos**	**has**	**haec** them; these
Abl.	**his**	**his**	**his** from/with/by/in them; from/with/by/in these

As a demonstrative pronoun, **hic, haec, hoc** means *he, she, it.* As a demonstrative adjective, it means *this.* It can also mean the *latter* of two things. Plural means *they, them, these.*

2. ille, illa, illud:

Case	Singular			Plural		
	Masc.	*Fem.*	*Neut.*	*Masc.*	*Fem.*	*Neut.*
Nom.	**ille**	**illa**	**illud**	**illi**	**illae**	**illa**
Gen.	**illius**	**illius**	**illius**	**illorum**	**illarum**	**illorum**
Dat.	**illi**	**illi**	**illi**	**illis**	**illis**	**illis**
Acc.	**illum**	**illam**	**illud**	**illos**	**illas**	**illa**
Abl.	**illo**	**illa**	**illo**	**illis**	**illis**	**illis**

Ille, illa, illud has the same meanings (he, she, it) as **is, ea, id** or **hic, haec, hoc** when used as a demonstrative pronoun. When used as a demonstrative adjective, **ille, illa, illud** means *that*. It can also mean the *former* of two things. Plural means *they, them, those*.

3. *ipse, ipsa, ipsum is declined just like **is, ea, id** or **ille, illa, illud** after the first few forms:*

Case	Singular			Plural		
	Masc.	*Fem.*	*Neut.*	*Masc.*	*Fem.*	*Neut.*
Nom.	ipse	ipsa	ipsum	ipsi	ipsae	ipsa
Gen.	ipsius	ipsius	ipsius	ipsorum	ipsarum	ipsorum
Dat.	ipsi	ipsi	ipsi	ipsis	ipsis	ipsis
Acc.	ipsum	ipsam	ipsum	ipsos	ipsas	ipsa
Abl.	ipso	ipsa	ipso	ipsis	ipsis	ipsis

As an intensive pronoun, **ipse, ipsa, ipsum** means *he* (himself), *she* (herself), *it* (itself). As an intensive adjective, it means *himself, herself, itself, very*. Plural means *themselves, they themselves*.

4. *idem, eadem, idem is based on **is, ea, id** and declined in much the same way:*

Case	Singular			Plural		
Masc.		*Fem.*	*Neut.*	*Masc.*	*Fem.*	*Neut.*
Nom.	idem	eadem	idem	eidem, iidem	eaedem	eadem
Gen.	eiusdem	eiusdem	eiusdem	eorundem	earundem	eorundem
Dat.	eidem	eidem	eidem	eisdem, iisdem [in all genders]		[in all genders]
Acc.	eundem	eandem	idem	eosdem	easdem	eadem
Abl.	eodem	eadem	eodem	eisdem, iisdem [in all genders]		[in all genders]

As you can see, **isdem, eadem, idem** are made up of **is, ea, id** and the suffix **-dem**. Only the first part of the word is declined; **-dem** remains unchanged throughout. Any changes in the first part from the normal declension of **is, ea, id** are made for ease of pronunciation (the combination **-mdem** becomes **-ndem**, for example, in each case).

As a demonstrative pronoun, **idem, eadem, idem** means (the same) *he*, (the same) *she*, (the same) *it*. As a demonstrative adjective, it means *same*.

5. *Remember that when **hic, ille, idem,** and **ipse** are used as pronouns, they must agree with their antecedent nouns in number and gender, but not necessarily in case, since their case will be determined by their use in their own clause. When they are used as adjectives, they must agree with the nouns they modify in case, number, and gender.*

153. New Reading Grammar—*Possum* with Complementary Infinitive

The verb **possum, posse, potui** must always have a complementary infinitive.

ducere potest, he is able to lead, he can lead

vincere posse debet, he ought to be able to conquer

154. New Reading Grammar—The Irregular Verb *fio, fieri*

The verb **facio, facere, feci, factus,** does not have a real passive voice, even though it has all four principal parts. Instead, the verb **fio, fieri, factus sum** is used to express the passive voice of **facio.** In the simple tenses, **fio** conjugates in the active voice, but its meanings are all passive. It only needs three principal parts, because the active meanings of the perfect tense of **fio** are expressed by the verb **facio.** Note that the second principal part, the infinitive, is given in the passive form.

1. PRESENT TENSE

Singular:		Plural:
fio	I am made; I become	___
fis	you are made; you become	___
fit	he, she, it is made; he, she, it becomes; it is done	**fiunt** they are made; they become

You will note that **fio** does not have the first or second person plural in the present tense. It is said to be *defective* in those forms. The forms do exist, but only in passages of later Latin that are considered by scholars to be poor prose.

Present Passive Infinitive: **fieri,** to be done, to become, to be made

Since **fio** exists only in the passive, there is no present active infinitive, only a present passive infinitive.

Imperative:

Singular:	**fi**	be made! become! be done!
Plural:	**fite**	be made! become! be done!

2. THE IMPERFECT AND FUTURE TENSES ARE CONJUGATED THE SAME WAY AS THOSE OF A REGULAR e/i-conjugation VERB. THE STEM USED IS fi-.

Imperfect		*Future*	
Singular	*Plural*	*Singular*	*Plural*
fiebam, *I was made; I was becoming*	**fiebamus**	**fiam,** *I shall be made; I shall become*	**fiemus**
fiebas	**fiebatis**	**fies**	**fietis**
fiebat	**fiebant**	**fiet**	**fient**

3. SINCE fio HAS ONLY A PASSIVE VOICE, THE THIRD PRINCIPAL PART IS THE FIRST
   PERSON SINGULAR OF THE PERFECT PASSIVE, factus sum. IT IS MADE BY USING THE
   FOURTH PRINCIPAL PART OF facio AND THE VERB sum.

Perfect Tense	*Pluperfect Tense:*	*Future Perfect Tense*
I have been made/become	I had been made/become	I shall have been made/become
factus, -a, -um sum	factus, -a, -um eram	factus, -a, -um ero
factus, -a, -um es	factus, -a, -um eras	factus, -a, -um eris
factus, -a, -um est	factus, -a, -um erat	factus, -a, -um erit
facti, -ae, -a sumus	facti, -ae, -a eramus	facti, -ae, -a erimus
facti, -ae, -a estis	facti, -ae, -a eratis	facti, -ae, -a eritis
facti, -ae, -a sunt	facti, -ae, -a erant	facti, -ae, -a erunt

155. Reading

Hannibal

1. Adulescens, Hannibal, erat inimicus Romanis quod a patre suo ductus est.
2. In Africa habitaverunt, sed mox Hannibal cum suis trans aquam in navibus multis ad Hispaniam navigavit.
3. Ipse multas copias et classem bonam habuit.
4. In Hispania multa oppida oppugnavit et praedam captivosque cepit.
5. Tum ad Italiam viros suos duxit, sed inter Hispaniam Italiamque erant montes.
6. Eidem montes pedites equitusque eius minime iuverunt.
7. Multa impedimenta portabantur. Ad imperatorem Romanorum is nuntius portatus est.
8. Romani ad hostes iter facere properaverunt.
9. Romani proelio hostes non vicerunt, sed bellum ad Africam mox portatum est et Romani ad victoriam ab imperatore suo ibi ducti sunt.

Hannibal

1. The youth, Hannibal, was unfriendly to the Romans because he had been led by his father.
2. They lived in Africa, but soon Hannibal, with his men, sailed across the water in many ships to Spain.
3. He himself had many troops and a good fleet.
4. In Spain, he attacked many towns and took booty and captives.
5. Then he led his men to Italy, but between Spain and Italy, there were mountains.
6. These same mountains did not help his foot soldiers and horsemen at all.
7. They were carrying much baggage. This message was carried to the general of the Romans.
8. The Romans hurried to travel toward the enemy.
9. The Romans did not conquer the enemy in battle, but soon the war was carried to Africa and the Romans were led to victory there by their general.

Theseus et Minotaurus

1. **Populus Graeciae contra populum insulae Cretae multos annos bellum gesserat.**
2. **Graeci magno cum animo diu contendebant, sed ab copiis Minois, regis Cretae, victi erant.**
3. **Haec fuerat causa belli: Filius Minois a Graecis interfectus erat. Itaque rex ob iniuriam illam ab his poenam petebat.**

4. **Septem puellas et septem pueros rogavit.**
5. **Graeci erant miseri, sed illos miserunt.**
6. **Minos, rex, labyrinthum habebat. In labyrintho animal barbarum, Minotaurum, tenebat.**
7. **In labyrinthum puellas puerosque duxit.**
8. **In illo loco terrbantur quod contra eum sine armis pugnare non poterant et mortem acceperunt.**

Theseus and the Minotaur

1. The people of Greece had waged war against the people of the island of Crete for many years.
2. The Greeks fought for a long time with great spirit, but they had been conquered by the forces of Minos, the king of Crete.
3. This was the cause of the war: the son of Minos had been killed by the Greeks. And so, the king sought punishment from them because of that injury.
4. He asked for seven boys and seven girls.
5. The Greeks were unhappy, but they sent them.
6. Minos, the king, had a labyrinth. In the labyrinth, he kept a savage animal, the Minotaur.
7. He led the girls and boys into the labyrinth.
8. In that place, they were terrified because they were not able to fight against him without weapons, and they received death.

156. Practice Exercises

No. 110. Translate these phrases that use hic and ille:

1. hic murus
2. illam urbem
3. in illo loco
4. hi duces
5. illis militibus
6. illi legato
7. hos imperatores
8. illa consilia
9. illius oceani
10. horum hominum
11. in illo horto
12. illa dea
13. illius peditis
14. de hoc domino
15. ex illa arbore
16. hunc impedimentum
17. his patribus
18. has naves
19. ille liber
20. illi puellae
21. haec arma
22. harum partium
23. de illa pace
24. illarum arenarum
25. his annis
26. illam horam
27. illud signum
28. huius equi

No. 111. Translate these pronouns:

1. huius
2. ille
3. illi
4. hos
5. illis
6. harum
7. hoc
8. huic
9. illa
10. hi
11. haec
12. hanc
13. has
14. illum
15. illos

No. 112. Translate these phrases that use idem and ipse:

1. dea ipsa
2. e templis ipsis
3. urbem eandem
4. homines ipsos
5. ab eodem adulescenti
6. idem nomen
7. eiusdem nationis
8. nocte ipsa
9. eadem itinera
10. iisdem viris
11. ex agro ipso
12. annis ipsis
13. pueri ipsi
14. legati ipsius
15. eadem hora
16. lex ipsa
17. mons ipse
18. puellae ipsae
19. idem iter
20. a mulieribus ipsis
21. eodem tempore
22. pax ipsa
23. eadem oppida
24. in urbibus ipsis
25. eiusdem populi
26. iidem homines
27. ex iisdem locis
28. iisdem annis

No. 113. Translate these pronouns:

1. ipsi
2. eiusdem
3. idem
4. ipsa
5. ipsos
6. eadem
7. eundem
8. eorundem
9. ex iisdem
10. ipsius

No. 114. Give the English for these verb forms:

1. ducere poterant
2. manere potes
3. adorare non potuit
4. liberare poterit
5. curare possunt
6. necare non potuimus
7. iubere potueram
8. docere potes
9. rogare poteramus
10. augere non potui
11. iuvare poterimus
12. pugnare poteris
13. vocare non potuerunt
14. laborare non possum
15. manere potuistis
16. fiunt
17. factus est
18. fies
19. factae erant
20. fiebam
21. facimus
22. facietis
23. faciunt
24. faciebant

Suffixes

Some of the more common suffixes used to form adjectives are:

-eus, denoting the material. English, *of.* **aureus,** of gold
-osus, denoting fullness. English, *full of.* **periculosus,** full of danger
-bilis, denoting possibility. English, *able.* **amabilis,** able to be loved, lovable
-anus, -icus, -alis, -inus, denoting connection.
-anus becomes *-ane* or *an* in English. **Romanus,** Roman
-icus becomes *-ic* in English. **publicus,** public
-alis becomes *-al* in English. **mortalis,** mortal
-inus becomes *-in* or *-ine* in English. **Latinus,** Latin

157. New Reading Vocabulary

NOUNS

civis, civis, m. or f., citizen (civium) (civic)
Polyphemus, Polyphemi, m., Polyphemus
Ariadne, Ariadnes, f., Ariadne (a Greek noun)
Cyclops, Cyclopis, m., Cyclops
tempestas, tempestatis, f., storm, bad weather (tempest)

Theseus, Thesei, m., Theseus
poeta, poetae, m., poet (poetical)
opus, operis, n., work (opera)
Homerus, Homeri, m., Homer
Ulixes, Ulixis, m., Ulysses

ADJECTIVES

celer, celeris, celere, quick, swift (celerity)
acer, acris, acre, sharp, active, keen (acid)
brevis, breve, short, brief (brevity)
alter, altera, alterum, the one, the other (alternate)
solus, sola, solum, alone, only (solitude)
alius, alia, aliud, other, another (alien)
audax, audacis, gen. audacis, bold (audacious)

ullus, ulla, ullum, any
neuter, neutra, neutrum, neither
unus, una, unum, one (unite)
omnis, omne, all, every
uter, utra, utrum, which (of two)
totus, tota, totum, all, whole (total)
nullus, nulla, nullum, no, none (null)

VERBS

fugio, fugere, fugi, fugitus, flee, run away, escape
scribo, scribere, scripsi, scriptus, write (scribe)

ADVERBS

interea, meanwhile

PREPOSITIONS

apud, in the presence of. With the accusative case.
pro, in front of; for; instead. With the ablative case.

158. New Reading Grammar—Adjectives with Genitive in *-ius*

Some adjectives that belong to the **first and second declension** (a- and o-declension) have the genitive singular ending in -ius and the dative singular ending in -i for all genders (not unlike **hic, ille, is, ipse,** and **idem**). Otherwise, these adjectives decline regularly according to first and second declension patterns. For example, consider the declension of **totus, tota, totum,** *whole, all:*

Case	Masculine	Feminine	Neuter
Singular			
Nom.	totus	tota	totum
Gen.	totius	totius	totius
Dat.	toti	toti	toti
Acc.	totum	totam	totum
Abl.	toto	tota	toto
Plural			
Nom.	toti	totae	tota
Gen.	totorum	totarum	totorum
Dat.	totis	totis	totis
Acc.	totos	totas	tota
Abl.	totis	totis	totis

All forms other than the genitive and dative singular are regular. All forms in the plural for these kinds of adjectives are also regular. The following adjectives are declined like **totus.** (Note, however, that **unus,** since it is the number *one,* has only singular forms.)

alius, alia, aliud, other, another
alter, altera, alterum, the one, the other
neuter, neutra, neutrum, neither
nullus, nulla, nullum, no, none

solus, sola, solum, alone, only
ullus, ulla, ullum, any
unus, una, unum, one
uter, utra, utrum, which (of two)

B. SOMETIMES alius OR alter MAY BE USED IN PAIRS. WHEN THIS HAPPENS, THEIR MEANING IS SLIGHTLY DIFFERENT:

alius . . . alius, one . . . another
alter . . . alter, the one . . . the other (of two)

alii . . . alii, some . . . others

Alterum iter longum est, alterum non est.
Alii sunt boni, alii sunt mali.

One road is long, the other is not.
Some are good, some are bad.

159. New Reading Grammar—Third Declension Adjectives

It was noted when adjectives were first introduced that there are two basic types. One type, which we have already met, uses first and second declension endings. Those adjectives that do not belong to the second type are known as **third** or **i- declension** adjectives. Third declension adjectives are generally subdivided into three kinds, according to the number of spellings in the nominative singular, but all have the **i-declension** endings, and *all of them are i-stem declensions.* The masculine and feminine genders, therefore, are declined like **urbs;** the neuter like **mare.** See sections 97 and 98 in Chapter Four if you need to review these endings.

The three kinds of adjectives are:

1. **ONE TERMINATION ADJECTIVES—THOSE THAT HAVE ONE SPELLING FOR THE NOMINATIVE SINGULAR FOR ALL GENDERS:**

Case	Masculine	Feminine	Neuter
Singular			
Nom.	audax	audax	audax
Gen.	audacis	audacis	audacis
Dat.	audaci	audaci	audaci
Acc.	audacem	audacem	audax
Abl.	audaci	audaci	audaci
Voc.	audax	audax	audax

Case	Masculine	Feminine	Neuter
Plural			
Nom.	audaces	audaces	audacia
Gen.	audacium	audacium	audacium
Dat.	audacibus	audacibus	audacibus
Acc.	audaces (-is)	audaces (-is)	audacia
Abl.	audacibus	audacibus	audacibus
Voc.	audaces	audaces	audacia

Note the alternatives, **-es** and **-is,** for the masculine and feminine accusative plural.

2. **TWO TERMINATION ADJECTIVES—THOSE THAT HAVE TWO SPELLINGS FOR THE NOMINATIVE SINGULAR, ONE FOR THE MASCULINE AND FEMININE, AND ONE FOR THE NEUTER:**

Case	Masculine	Feminine	Neuter
Singular			
Nom.	omnis	omnis	omne
Gen.	omnis	omnis	omnis
Dat.	omni	omni	omni
Acc.	omnem	omnem	omne
Abl.	omni	omni	omni
Plural			
Nom.	omnes	omnes	omnia
Gen.	omnium	omnium	omnium
Dat.	omnibus	omnibus	omnibus
Acc.	omnes	omnes	omnia
Abl.	omnibus	omnibus	omnibus

3. THREE TERMINATION ADJECTIVES—THOSE THAT HAVE THREE SPELLINGS FOR THE NOMINATIVE SINGULAR, ONE FOR EACH GENDER:

Case	Masculine	Feminine	Neuter
Singular			
Nom.	celer	celeris	celere
Gen.	celeris	celeris	celeris
Dat.	celeri	celeri	celeri
Acc.	celerem	celerem	celere
Abl.	celeri	celeri	celeri
Plural			
Nom.	celeres	celeres	celeria
Gen.	celerium	celerium	celerium
Dat.	celeribus	celeribus	celeribus
Acc.	celeres	celeres	celeria
Abl.	celeribus	celeribus	celeribus

Remember that an adjective, regardless of its declension, must agree with the word it modifies in case, number, and gender. The declensional pattern of endings which an adjective uses, however, is part of the vocabulary item—third declension adjectives will use third declensional endings no matter what the declension of the noun being modified. It is not the shape of the endings which need to agree, but the case, number, and gender.

The vocabulary in this book gives an adjective's nominative singular case. If the adjective has more than one spelling for this case, all spellings will be given, as is usual in most Latin dictionaries.

160. Reading

Theseus et Minotaurus (concl'd)

1. Interea in Graecia Theseus fortuna misera puerorum puellarumque Graecorum incitatus est.
2. Rogavit: "Estne nullum auxilium pro his filiis civium nostrorum?"
3. Itaque ad Cretam cum sociis suis navi contendit.
4. Ariadne, filia regis, eum vidit et ob virtutem eius illum amavit.
5. Sine mora ille de labyrintho eum docuit.
6. Tum Theseus solus ad labyrinthum properavit. Arma portabat et bonum consilium Ariadnes memoria tenebat.

Theseus and the Minotaur (concl'd)

1. Meanwhile, in Greece, Theseus was aroused by the unhappy fortune of the Greek boys and girls.
2. He asked: "Is there no help for these children of our citizens?"
3. And so he hurried to Crete by ship with his comrades.
4. Ariadne, the daughter of the king, saw him and loved him because of his courage.
5. Without delay, she showed him about the labyrinth.
6. Then Theseus alone hurried to the labyrinth. He carried weapons and he remembered the good advice of Ariadne.

7. Mox Minotaurum spectabat. Cum illo animali diu contendebat, sed id interficere potuit.
8. Minotaurus necatus erat. Pueri puellaeque liberati erant.
9. Totos annos postea populus Graeciae laetus erat quod regi malo Cretae nullas poenas dabat.

Ulixes et Cyclops
1. Homerus, poeta antiquus, de bello inter viros Graeciae Troiaeque in suo magno opere scripsit.
2. Post multos annos longos Troia ab Graecis capta erat.
3. Graeci ab illo loco navigabant. Apud eos erat Ulixes, homo audax, sed brevi tempore navis eius tempestate ad aliam partem maris portata est.
4. Ex navi ad terram cum sociis suis Ulixes contendit.
5. Non longe ab illo loco ubi stabant corpus magnum Polyphemi, Cyclopis, mox viderunt. Ille in colli habitabat.
6. Graeci iniuriam timebant.
7. Polyphemus eos a mari celeribus pedibus duxit.
8. Viri cibum exspectabant, sed Cyclops pro cibo suo unum hominem, tum alterum, et alium cepit.
9. Alii pro sociis suis dolebant.
10. Illine ab Polyphemo fugere poterunt?

7. Soon he saw the Minotaur. He struggled with that animal for a long time, but was able to kill it.
8. The Minotaur had been killed. The boys and girls had been freed.
9. For all the years afterwards, the people of Greece were happy because they paid no penalties to the evil king of Crete.

Ulysses and the Cyclops
1. Homer, an ancient poet, wrote in his great work about the war between the men of Greece and Troy.
2. After many long years, Troy had been captured by the Greeks.
3. The Greeks were sailing away from that place. Among them was Ulysses, a bold man, but in a short time, his ship was carried by a storm to another part of the sea.
4. Ulysses hurried from his ship to the land with his comrades.
5. Not far from that place where they were standing, they soon saw the large body of Polyphemus, the Cyclops. He lived on a hill.
6. The Greeks feared injury.
7. Polyphemus led them away from the sea at a swift pace.
8. The men waited for food, but the Cyclops, for his own food, took one man, then another, and another.
9. The others grieved for their comrades.
10. Will they be able to flee from Polyphemus?

161. Practice Exercises

No. 115. Give the English for these phrases:

1. uno anno
2. nullam curam
3. utrius doni
4. ulli navi
5. totos annos
6. cum patre solo
7. nullarum mortium
8. neutri nationi
9. in altera via
10. alio nomine
11. ad utrum flumen
12. ullius collis
13. uni libro
14. ob nullas causas
15. a neutro homine

No. 116. Translate these verb forms:

1. timuerant
2. fuistis
3. mittent
4. cepit
5. timebit
6. spectabant
7. tenebuntur
8. mittar
9. laudati sunt
10. factum erat
11. navigabas
12. dabantur
13. gerit
14. fuerant
15. habuerunt

No. 117. Give the English for the following:

1. alter puer est, alter non est.
2. nullo tempore
3. ullius belli
4. ad utra castra
5. mulieres ipsae solae
6. neutrius adulescentis
7. alias urbes
8. unam partem
9. de neutra puella
10. aliud inter

No. 118. Give the English for these phrases:

1. hora breve
2. servi audacis
3. eques celer
4. in flumine celeri
5. a viris audacibus
6. tempora omnia
7. a legato acri
8. vita brevis
9. omnibus horis
10. in navi celeri
11. opus audax
12. brevi tempore
13. copiae acres
14. equi celeris
15. acres feminae
16. mortem celerem
17. itinera brevia
18. audaci homini
19. brevem annum
20. omni in loco

162. New Reading Vocabulary

NOUNS

oculus, oculi, m., eye (oculist)
saxum, saxi, n., stone, rock (saxatile)
porta, portae, f., gate, door, entrance (portal)

telum, teli, n., weapon
fuga, fugae, f., flight, escape

PRONOUNS

quis, quid, who?, what?

ADJECTIVES

fortis, forte, brave, strong (fort)
uterque, utraque, utrumque, each, every
gravis, grave, heavy, severe, serious (grave, gravity)

facilis, facile, easy (facility)
novus, nova, novum, new (novel)

VERBS

clamo, clamare, clamavi, clamatus, shout
(clamor)
cognosco, cognoscere, cognovi, cognitus,
learn, recognize, know (cognizance)

iacio, iacere, ieci, iactus, throw (project)
simulo, simulare, simulavi, simulatus,
pretend (simulate)

ADVERBS

noctu, at night (noctambular)

Familiar Quotations

Nil homini certum est, Nothing is certain to
man. (Ovid)
Virtus praemium est optimum, Virtue is the
best reward. (Plautus)
Omnia praeclara rara, All the best things
are rare. (Cicero)
Possunt quia posse videntur, They can be-
cause they think they can. (Virgil)
Alea iacta est, The die is cast. (Caesar)
Mens sana in copore sano, A sound mind
in a sound body. (Juvenal)
Carmina morte carent, Songs do not die.
(Ovid)

Wall paintings, like this one discovered in the ruins of
Pompeii, were popular among the Romans. Many
depicted mythological scenes and stories.

163. New Reading Grammar—The Adjective *uterque, utraque, utrumque*

uterque, utraque, utrumque, is declined by adding **-que** to the forms of **uter, utra, utrum** (see
162 above)

uterque vir, each man
utrique viro, to, for each man

utriusque viri, of each man
utrumque virum, each man

etc.

164. New Reading Grammar—Interrogative Pronoun

The declension of the interrogative pronoun, **quis, quid,** *who?, what?,* is similar to that of **is, ea, id.**

Singular

Case	Masc.	Fem.	Neut.	
Nom.	**quis**	**quis**	**quid**	who?, what?
Gen.	**cuius**	**cuius**	**cuius**	of whom?, whose?, of what?
Dat.	**cui**	**cui**	**cui**	to, for whom?; to, for what?
Acc.	**quem**	**quem**	**quid**	whom?, what?
Abl.	**quo**	**quo**	**quo**	from, with, by, in whom?, from, with, by, in what?

Plural

Case	Masc.	Fem.	Neut.	
Nom.	**qui**	**quae**	**quae**	who?, what?
Gen.	**quorum**	**quarum**	**quorum**	of whom?, whose?, of what?
Dat.	**quibus**	**quibus**	**quibus**	to, for whom?; to, for what?
Acc.	**quos**	**quas**	**quae**	whom?, what?
Abl.	**quibus**	**quibus**	**quibus**	from, with, by, in whom?; from, with, by, in what?

Quis, quid is called an interrogative pronoun because it is used in questions.

Quis est? Who is it? **Qui sunt?** Who are they?
Cuius est? Whose is it? **Quorum est?** Whose is it?
Quem vides? Whom do you see? **Quid vides?** What do you see?

Note that the neuter nominative and accusative plurals do not end in **-a,** the normal ending for neuter plurals. This is true, also, of **hic, haec, hoc** and of the relative pronoun **qui, quae, quod** (to be introduced later).

165. New Reading Grammar—Syntax with the Preposition *cum*

When **cum** is used with the ablative case, it is generally added to the end of the word.

quocum, with whom **quibuscum,** with whom

166. New Reading Grammar—Present Passive Infinitive

With rare exceptions, verbs have both active and passive present tense infinitives. The present active infinitive, of course, is the second principal part of most verbs. The present passive infinitives are formed according to the following rules:

1. THE PRESENT PASSIVE INFINITIVE OF first conjugation AND second conjugation VERBS IS THE SAME AS THE PRESENT ACTIVE INFINITIVE, EXCEPT THAT IT ENDS IN -i INSTEAD OF -e.

   amare, to love   **amari,** to be loved
   habere, to have   **haberi,** to be had

2. IN THE third conjugation, THE -i OF THE PRESENT PASSIVE INFINITIVE IS ADDED DIRECTLY ON TO THE STEM.

   ducere, to lead   **duci,** to be led
   capere, to take   **capi,** to be taken

3. THE VERBS sum, possum, eo, volo, nolo, AND malo HAVE NO PRESENT PASSIVE INFINITIVES, SINCE THEY ARE NOT TRANSITIVE IN MEANING.

   The present passive infinitive of **fero** is **ferri,** *to be carried.*

4. AS NOTED EARLIER, THE VERB fio DOES HAVE A PRESENT PASSIVE INFINITIVE, **fieri,** *to be made,* BUT NOT A PRESENT ACTIVE INFINITIVE.

167. Reading

Ulixes et Cyclops (concl'd)

1. Postquam Cyclops haec fecerat, Graeci fortes mortem exspectabant, sed Ulixes Polyphemum interficere in animo habebat.
2. Ob magnitudinem viri non erat ullum iter facile ex periculo eorum, sed consilium parabant et suos animos bonos tenebant.
3. Ante hoc tempus alia pericula gravia superaverant et hoc periculum novum superare in animo habuerunt.
4. Uterque Cyclopem timebat, sed Polyphemus inimicus omnibus erat.
5. Eum incitare non debebant. Itaque Ulixes suum consilium eis demonstravit.
6. Partem arboris in igni posuerunt. Post breve tempus finis arboris erat acer.

Ulysses and the Cyclops (concl'd)

1. After the Cyclops had done these things, the brave Greeks waited for death, but Ulysses had in mind to kill Polyphemus.
2. Because of the great size of the man, there was not any easy way out of their danger, but they prepared a plan and kept their good spirits.
3. Before this time, they had overcome other serious dangers and they had in mind to overcome this new danger.
4. Each feared the Cyclops, but Polyphemus was unfriendly to all.
5. They ought not to arouse him. And so, Ulysses showed them his plan.
6. They placed part of a tree in the fire. After a short time, the end of the tree was sharp.

Ulixes et Cyclops (concl'd)

7. Hoc erat telum eorum contra Cyclopem. Id magna cum diligentia paraverant.
8. Hoc telo Cyclops poenas dabit.

9. Polyphemus unum oculum solum habuit. Magna cum audacia Ulixes et socii sui in oculo eius finem arboris posuerunt.
10. Iniuria erat gravis et Cyclops postea videre non poterat.
11. Polyphemus etiam multa animalia habebat.
12. Ante portam ille saxum grave et magnam posuerat.
13. Id a Graecis moveri non potuit, sed Cyclops ab porta saxum movebat, cum animalia cibus petebant.
14. Hoc erat consilium: Ulixes et sui amici fugam suam noctu paraverunt.
15. Cyclops eos videre non potuit.
16. Saxum a porta movit.
17. Animalia per portam cucurrerunt. Sub animalibus erant Graeci.
18. Graeci simulabant et Polyphemus eos non cognovit.
19. Tum Ulixes clamavit. Itaque Cyclops fugam eorum cognovit.
20. Cyclops ad mare properavit. Saxum magnum ad Graecos iecit.
21. Polyphemus dixit: "Quis es?"
22. Ulixes clamavit: "Nullus homo sum," sed Graeci in navi erant et laeti erant quod a Polyphemo fugerant et ad Graeciam navigabant.
23. Postea de oculo suo Polyphemus dicebat: "Nullus id fecit."

Ulysses and the Cyclops (concl'd)

7. This was their weapon against the Cyclops. They had prepared it with great care.
8. With this weapon, the Cyclops will pay the penalty.

9. Polyphemus had only one eye. With great boldness, Ulysses and his companions put the end of the tree in his eye.
10. The injury was serious, and the Cyclops was not able to see after that.
11. Polyphemus also had many animals.
12. He put a heavy and large stone in front of the door.
13. This could not be moved by the Greeks, but the Cyclops moved the stone away from the door when the animals sought food.
14. This was the plan: Ulysses and his friends prepared their flight at night.
15. The Cyclops was not able to see them.
16. He moved the stone away from the door.
17. The animals ran through the door. Under the animals were the Greeks.
18. The Greeks pretended and Polyphemus did not recognize them.
19. Then Ulysses shouted. And so, the Cyclops learned of their flight.
20. The Cyclops hurried to the sea. He threw a large stone toward the Greeks.
21. Polyphemus said: "Who are you?"
22. Ulysses shouted: "I am no man," but the Greeks were on the ship and were happy because they had escaped from Polyphemus and were sailing to Greece.
23. Afterwards, Polyphemus said about his eye: "No one did it."

168. Practice Exercises

No. 119. Translate these adjectival phrases:

1. solis aurei
2. e neutro loco
3. summo in monte
4. itineris facilis
5. ullae horae
6. poenas graves
7. nationum proximarum
8. civem audacem
9. corpus robustem
10. fluminum celerium
11. libros latinos
12. homines alii
13. navis vestra
14. patrum multorum
15. utriusque regis

No. 120. Give the English for these interrogative phrases and clauses:

1. Qui estis?
2. Cui ea dedit?
3. Quos videbo?
4. Cuius oculi?
5. Quae cognoscit?
6. Quocum ambulabat?
7. A quo captus est?
8. Quis clamat?
9. Quis pugnat?
10. Quorum tela?
11. Quid habes?
12. Quem necavit?
13. Quibus id dabo?
14. Quid rogatum est?
15. Cui donum misisti?
16. Quem amas?
17. Quis fugit?
18. Quid facile est?
19. Cuius est?
20. Quibuscum?
21. Quos mittet?
22. Quid facit?
23. Qui contendunt?
24. A quo gestum est?

No. 121. Give the active form of these present passive infinitives:

1. pugnari
2. mitti
3. regi
4. dari
5. laudari
6. rogari
7. scribi
8. videri
9. cognosci
10. necari
11. capi
12. timeri
13. haberi
14. moveri
15. parari
16. duci
17. augeri
18. servari
19. vinci
20. terreri

No. 122. Give the passive forms of these present active infinitives:

1. demonstrare
2. ducere
3. movere
4. iubere
5. vertere
6. armare
7. amare
8. ferre
9. docere
10. occupare
11. mittere
12. gerere
13. accipere
14. timere
15. vocare
16. interficere
17. iuvare
18. tenere
19. cognoscere
20. simulare

REVIEW

169. Vocabulary Review

NOUNS

1. adulescens	9. cibus	17. Homerus	25. mors	33. porta
2. Africa	10. civis	18. impedimentum	26. navis	34. saxum
3. animus	11. classis	19. imperator	27. oculus	35. Silenus
4. arbor	12. Cyclops	20. iniuria	28. opus	36. studium
5. arena	13. diligentia	21. labyrinthus	29. pedes	37. telum
6. Ariadne	14. eques	22. Midas	30. poena	38. tempestas
7. aurum	15. fuga	23. Minos	31. poeta	39. tempus
8. Bacchus	16. Hannibal	24. Minotaurus	32. Polyphemus	40. Theseus

PRONOUNS

1. hic, haec, hoc   2. idem, eadem, idem   3. ille, illa, illud   4. ipse, ipsa, ipsum

ADJECTIVES

1. acer	6. celer	11. idem	16. nullus
2. alius	7. facilis	12. ille	17. omnis
3. alter	8. fortis	13. ipse	18. solus
4. audax	9. gravis	14. neuter	19. totus
5. brevis	10. hic	15. novus	20. ullus

VERBS

1. capio	5. facio	9. gero	13. scribo
2. clamo	6. fero	10. iacio	14. simulo
3. cognosco	7. fio	11. interficio	15. verto
4. contendo	8. fugio	12. pono	

ADVERBS
1. interea
2. noctu

PREPOSITIONS
1. apud
2. pro
3. propter

CONJUNCTIONS
1. itaque

170. Practice Exercises

No. 123. Translate these verbs:

1. capiunt	5. interficiebamus	9. ponetur	13. contendent
2. cognitum erat	6. fecerunt	10. gesserint	14. positi sunt
3. victi sunt	7. ceperas	11. scribit	15. gestum est
4. vertent	8. fugiebat	12. iacis	16. fis

No. 124. Translate these phrases:

1. propter mortem	5. propter cibum	9. ob impedimentum
2. ob iniuriam	6. ob classes	10. propter arenam
3. diligentia magna	7. parva cum poena	
4. ob imperatorem	8. magno cum studio	

No. 125. Translate these pronouns:

1. hunc	5. ipse	9. hic	13. cuius
2. huius	6. illorum	10. ipsorum	14. cui
3. illos	7. eadem	11. quem	15. quocum
4. illud	8. eiusdem	12. quid	

No. 126. Translate these verb forms:

1. clamare potuit	5. vincere potuistis	9. vertere potes
2. capere poterant	6. contendere poterit	10. gerere possunt
3. facere potes	7. scribere potuerunt	
4. ponere possumus	8. cognoscere poteramus	

No. 127. Translate these adjective phrases:

1. unius operis	5. brevi tempore	9. audaces equites
2. omnium civium	6. toti saxo	10. celeris poena
3. aliud impedimentum	7. nullius timoris	
4. nova tela	8. ullam iniuriam	

171. Reading

Marcus Tullius Cicero

Cicero was born into an upper middle class family living near Arpinum, in Latium, the province in which Rome was located, in 106 B.C. He studied law, philosophy, and rhetoric in Rome, Athens, and Rhodes, and became consul in 63 B.C. It was in this office that he disclosed Catiline's conspiracy to overthrow the government and, in four orations delivered in the Senate, persuaded the Senators to decree the death penalty for the conspirators. After Caesar's assassination in 44 B.C. and the formation of the Second Triumvirate, Cicero was murdered in 43 B.C., while trying to escape from his political enemies.

O tempora! O mores! Senatus haec intellegit, consul vidit; hic tamen vivit. Vivit? Immo vero etiam in senatum venit, fit publici consili particeps, notat et designat oculis ad caedam unum quemque nostrum. Nos autem, fortes viri, satis facere rei publicae videmur, si istius furorem ac tela vitamus. Ad mortem te, Catilina, duci iussu consilis iam pridem oportebat; in te conferri pestem, quam tu in nos machinaris.

In Catilinam Oratio Prima, ii

Odo de Cerinton

The following two stories were written by Odo de Cerinton, who lived in the twelfth century and composed a work called **Narrationes**, which drew stories from various fables and other sources, giving a mystical interpretation to tales about animals.

DE HYDRO

Quoddam animal dicitur hydrus, cuius natura est se invovere luto, ut melius posset labi. Tandem in os crocodili, quando dormit, intrat et sic, ventrem eius ingrediens, cor eius mordet et sic crocodilum intermit.

Mistice: Hydrus significat filium Dei, qui assumpsit lutum nostrae carnis ut facilius laberetur in os diaboli, et sic, ventrem eius ingrediens et cor eius mordens, ipsum interficit.

DE ANTILOPE

Quoddam animal est quod vocatur antilops; quod cum virgultis ludit cum cornibus, tandem cornua eius implicantur cum virgultis quod non potest ea extrahere et tunc incipit clamare; quo audito veniunt venatores et interficiunt eum.

Mistice: Sic contigit quod plerique delectati sunt et ludunt cum negotiis huius mundi et sic in eisdem implicantur quod evelli non possunt et sic a venatoribus, id est a daemonibus, capiuntur et interficiuntur.

Familiar Phrases

status quo or **status in quo,** the state in which. That is, the existing condition.
mirabile dictu, wonderful to tell, wonderful to relate.
per se, by itself, of itself; by its own force.
cum grano salis, with a grain of salt.
modus vivendi, manner of living (often temporary).
post scriptum, written after. Abbreviated, **P.S.** or **p.s.**
inter nos, among us, among ourselves.
sine qua non, something indispensible or necessary. Literally, without which not.

---

172. New Reading Vocabulary

NOUNS
Orpheus, Orphei, m., Orpheus (a Greek name)
nihil or **nil, n.,** nothing **nihil** (or **nil**), has the same spelling in all cases (nihilist)
natura, naturae, f., nature (natural)
regnum, regni, n., kingdom (interregnum)
Eurydice, Eurydices, f., Eurydice (a Greek name)

ADJECTIVES
primus, prima, primum, first (prime, primary)
difficilis, difficile, difficult, hard (difficulty)

VERBS
audio, audire, audivi, auditus, hear (audio)
relinquo, relinquere, reliqui, relictus, leave, leave behind (relinquish)
discedo, discedere, discessi, discessus, withdraw, go away, leave
trado, tradere, tradidi, traditus, give up, surrender (tradition)
rego, regere, rexi, rectus, rule (regent)
educo, educere, eduxi, eductus, lead out (educate)
reduco, reducere, reduxi, reductus, lead back (reduce)

ADVERBS
parum, too little, not enough
magnopere, greatly

173. New Reading Grammar—Adverbs

A. IN LATIN, ADVERBS ARE GENERALLY FORMED FROM ADJECTIVES.

1. Adverbs formed from a- and o-declension adjectives end in -e.

Adjective	*Adverb*
altus, high	**alte**, high, on high
latus, wide	**late**, widely
longus, long	**longe**, far, distant
miser, wretched	**misere**, wretchedly
pulcher, beautiful	**pulchre**, beautifully

Note that when an adjective ending in **-er** in the masculine nominative singular keeps the **-e-** in all other forms, the adverb also keeps the **-e-**, as in the case of **misere**. When an adjective ending in **-er** in the masculine nominative singular drops the **-e-** in all other forms, the adverb also drops it, as in the case of **pulchre**.

2. Adverbs formed from i-declension adjectives end in -ter or -iter.

You will notice that the adverbial ending is added to the stem of the adjective, which is derived from the genitive singular.

Adjective		*Adverb*
Nom. Sing.	*Gen. Sing.*	
acer, keen	**acris**, of a keen man/woman/ object	**acriter**, keenly
audax, bold	**audacis**, of a bold man/woman/ object	**audacter**, boldly
celer, swift	**celeris**, of a swift man/woman/ object	**celeriter**, swiftly
fortis, brave	**fortis**, of a brave man/woman/ object	**fortiter**, bravely

3. Some adverbs are irregular.

Adjective	*Adverb*
bonus, good	**bene**, well
difficilis, difficult	**difficile**, with difficulty
facilis, easy	**facile**, easily
magnus, great	**magnopere**, greatly
malus, bad	**male**, badly
parvus, little	**parvum**, too little, not enough
primus, first	**primum**, at first, or **primo**, at first
solus, alone	**solum**, alone, only

4. Other adverbs are not based on any adjective; e.g.,

nunc, now **semper**, always **non**, not

174. New Reading Grammar—Fourth Conjugation Verbs

i-conjugation verbs, also known as fourth conjugation verbs, have **-i** as the predominant vowel between the stem and the endings. Consider the verb **audio**, *hear*.

1. PRINCIPAL PARTS: audio, audire, audivi, auditus.

<table>
<tr><td colspan="2">**2. PRESENT TENSE**</td><td colspan="2">**3. IMPERFECT TENSE**</td></tr>
<tr><td>*Active*</td><td>*Passive*</td><td>*Active*</td><td>*Passive*</td></tr>
<tr><td>**audio**, *I hear, do hear, am hearing*</td><td>**audior**, *I am being heard, I am heard*</td><td>**audiebam**, *I was hearing, heard*</td><td>**audiebar**, *I was being heard, was heard*</td></tr>
<tr><td>**audis**</td><td>**audiris**</td><td>**audiebas**</td><td>**audiebaris**</td></tr>
<tr><td>**audit**</td><td>**auditur**</td><td>**audiebat**</td><td>**audiebatur**</td></tr>
<tr><td>**audimus**</td><td>**audimur**</td><td>**audiebamus**</td><td>**audiebamur**</td></tr>
<tr><td>**auditis**</td><td>**audimini**</td><td>**audiebatis**</td><td>**audiebamini**</td></tr>
<tr><td>**audiunt**</td><td>**audiuntur**</td><td>**audiebant**</td><td>**audiebantur**</td></tr>
</table>

4. FUTURE TENSE

Active	*Passive*
audiam, *I shall hear*	**audiar**, *I shall be heard*
audies	**audieris**
audiet	**audietur**
audiemus	**audiemur**
audietis	**audiemini**
audient	**audientur**

You will note that fourth conjugation verbs are conjugated like **duco** or **capio** in the future tense. Latin thus forms the future tense in one of two ways: First and second conjugation verbs add **-bo/bi/bu** to the stem with the appropriate conjugation vowel, and add the endings to this, as in **amare: amabo, amabis, amabit,** etc. Third i-stem and fourth conjugation verbs use the stem plus **-am** for first person singular and **-e** plus the appropriate person ending for all of the other forms, as in **ducere: ducam, duces, ducet,** etc. Third i-stems and fourth conjugations show an **-i** throughout, as in **audire: audiam, audies, audiet,** etc.

<table>
<tr><td colspan="2">**5. PERFECT TENSE**</td><td colspan="2">**6. PLUPERFECT TENSE**</td></tr>
<tr><td>*Active*</td><td>*Passive*</td><td>*Active*</td><td>*Passive*</td></tr>
<tr><td>**audivi**, *I have heard, heard*</td><td>**auditus, -a, -um sum,** *I have been heard*</td><td>**audiveram**, *I had heard*</td><td>**auditus, -a, -um eram,** *I had been heard*</td></tr>
<tr><td>**audivisti**</td><td>**auditus, -a, -um es**</td><td>**audiveras**</td><td>**auditus, -a, -um eras**</td></tr>
<tr><td>etc.</td><td>etc.</td><td>etc.</td><td>etc.</td></tr>
</table>

7. FUTURE PERFECT TENSE

Active	*Passive*
audivero, *I shall have heard*	**auditus, -a, -um ero,** *I shall have been heard*
audiveris	**auditus, -a, -um eris**
etc.	etc.

175. Reading

Orpheus et Eurydice

1. Orpheus erat vir fortis, sed dolebat quod Eurydice morte capta erat et eum solum et miserum reliquerat.
2. Orpheus animalia omnia et naturam bene amabat et laetus esse simulabat, sed Eurydicen semper petebat.
3. Orpheus ipse sine ea esse non poterat. Itaque auxilium a deis petivit.
4. Nihil ab Iove facti poterat. Eurydice ab terra discesserat et apud Inferos nunc habitabat.
5. Iter ad regnum Plutonis erat difficile.
6. Pluto suos non saepe tradit, sed Orpheus erat audax et paene nullum timorem habebat.
7. Sub terram magna cum celeritate contendit. Ante regem, Plutonem, mox stat.
8. Orpheus ab Plutone petivit: "Cur Eurydicen hic tenes? Non solum ei amorem summum semper docebam sed etiam mors et non est idonea. Eurydice ipsa nihil fecerat."
9. Tum Pluto ipse pro illo acriter dolebat, sed Orpheum iussit: "Eam tradam, sed iter ex regno Inferorum difficile est. Ille ad terram tuam reduci poterit, sed eam spectare non debes. Cum primus eam ad terram educes, tum eam spectare poteris."
10. A Plutone grate discesserunt et iter ab illo loco malo celeriter faciebant.
11. Primo ille fortiter ambulabat, sed Orpheus amore regebatur. Non diu postea ad eam oculos suos vertit.
12. Ob eam causam Pluto magna cum celeritate illam cepit et eam ad Inferos reduxit.
13. Ab illo tempore in terra non visa est.

Orpheus and Eurydice

1. Orpheus was a brave man, but he grieved because Eurydice had been taken by death and had left him alone and wretched.
2. Orpheus loved all animals and nature very much and he pretended to be happy, but he always looked for Eurydice.
3. Orpheus himself could not be without her. And so, he sought help from the gods.
4. Nothing could be done by Jupiter. Eurydice had departed from the earth and was now living among Those Below.
5. The journey to the kingdom of Pluto was difficult.
6. Pluto does not often give up his own, but Orpheus was bold and had almost no fear.
7. He hurries below the earth with great speed. He soon stands before the king, Pluto.
8. Orpheus asked Pluto: "Why do you keep Eurydice here? Not only did I always show the greatest love for her, but also death is not suitable for her. Eurydice herself had done nothing."
9. Then Pluto himself felt keenly sorry for him, but he instructed Orpheus: "I shall give her up, but the way out of the kingdom of Those Below is difficult. She can be led back to your land, but you ought not to look at her. When you, going first, lead her back to earth, then you can look at her."
10. They departed from Pluto gratefully and quickly made the journey away from that evil place.
11. At first he walked bravely, but Orpheus was ruled by love. Not long afterwards, he turns his eyes toward her.
12. For this reason, Pluto seized her with great speed and led her back to Those Below.
13. From that time, she was not seen on earth.

176. Practice Exercises

No. 128. Form the adverbs and give the English meanings:

1. pulcher	5. acer	9. gratus	13. fortis
2. longus	6. gravis	10. audax	14. celer
3. magnus	7. brevis	11. miser	15. liber
4. novus	8. altus	12. proximus	

No. 129. Translate these verb forms:

1. portas	7. visi erant	13. audiet	19. capientur
2. habeo	8. auditi sunt	14. petiverunt	20. audieris
3. ducunt	9. acceptus es	15. audiunt	21. audiris
4. iacit	10. auditis eram	16. iuvabamini	22. fecit
5. audivistis	11. audiebant	17. audiebamur	23. rogabunt
6. liberatus est	12. paratus erit	18. vertebamus	24. audivimus

No. 130. Give the English for these phrases and clauses:

1. fortiter pugnant	3. difficile gessit	5. longe ambulat	7. facile cognovit
2. proxime vidimus	4. late accipientur	6. bene stant	8. magnopere amabat

No. 131. Translate these sentences:

1. Locus facile defendetur.
2. Primo nihil parari poterat.
3. Ob timorem non fortiter contendistis.
4. Utramque portam amas?
5. Terra natura difficile defensa est.
6. Non solum rex sed etiam regina id audivit.

177. New Reading Vocabulary

NOUNS

turris, turris, f., tower (turrium) (turret)
regio, regionis, f., region, boundary (regional)
Hellespontus, Hellesponti, m., Hellespont

Leander, Leandri, m., Leander
Hero, Herus, f., Hero (a Greek name)
inopia, inopiae, f., want, scarcity

PRONOUN AND ADJECTIVE

qui, quae, quod, who, which, that; which, what

VERBS

venio, venire, veni, ventus, come (venture)

pervenio, pervenire, perveni, perventus, arrive

accido, accidere, accidi, happen (accident)

reperio, reperire, repperi, repertus, find, discover (repertory)

conspicio, conspicere, conspexi, conspectus, observe (conspectus)

prohibeo, prohibere, prohibui, prohibitus, keep off, hinder, prohibit, prevent, forbid (prohibition)

cupio, cupere, cupivi, cupitus, desire, wish, want (cupidity)

vereor, vereri, veritus sum, fear

sequor, sequi, secutus sum, follow

morior, mori, mortuus sum, die (mortal)

impedio, impedire, impedivi, impeditus, hinder (impede)

hortor, hortari, hortatus sum, urge, encourage (exhort)

experior, experiri, expertus sum, try, test (experience)

ADVERBS

tamen, however, nevertheless   **iam,** already, now

CONJUNCTIONS

ut, as

PREFIXES

prae, before. **praepono,** put before.
re, again, back. **remitto, send back.**

con, together, with; very thoroughly. **convoco,** call together (convene). **conficio,** finish (thoroughly do). **pro,** out, forth. **provoco,** call forth.

178. New Reading Grammar—Relative Pronouns and Relative Clauses

A. ANTECEDENTS

An antecedent is a word or a group of words to which a pronoun refers. The word *antecedent* comes from the Latin word **antecedo,** which means *stand before* or *precede,* and an antecedent usually does precede the pronoun that refers to it. Consider the following sentence:

I saw the girl who was swimming.

The relative pronoun *who* refers to *the girl.* Thus, *the girl* is the antecedent of *who.* You will notice that the case of the pronoun is not necessarily the same as the case of its antecedent. While the relative pronoun must be the same gender and number as its antecdedent, its case is determined by its function in its own clause. In Latin, *the girl* will be in the accusative case, because it is the direct object of the verb *saw.* However, the pronoun *who* will be in the nominative case because it is the subject in its own clause of the verb *was swimming.*

B. A RELATIVE CLAUSE IS USED TO TELL SOMETHING ABOUT ITS ANTECEDENT; THE ENTIRE CLAUSE, THEREFORE, ACTS ADJECTIVALLY. A RELATIVE CLAUSE IS INTRODUCED BY A RELATIVE PRONOUN THAT HAS THE SAME NUMBER AND GENDER (BUT NOT NECESSARILY THE SAME CASE) AS ITS ANTECEDENT.

vir qui, the man who
Antecedent: **vir**
Relative pronoun: **qui**

puella quae, the girl who
Antecedent: **puella**
Relative pronoun: **quae**

bellum quod, the war that
Antecedent: **bellum**
Relative pronoun: **quod**

The case of a relative pronoun is determined by its use in its own clause.

vir quem video, the man whom I see
Antecedent: **vir**
Relative clause: **quem video**
Relative pronoun: **quem**
quem is accusative because it is used as the direct object of **video**. It is masculine and singular to agree with **vir.**

puella quam video, the girl whom I see
Antecedent: **puella**
Relative clause: **quam video**
Relative pronoun: **quam**
quam is accusative because it is used as the direct object of **video**. It is feminine and singular to agree with **puella.**

The relative pronoun is declined as follows:

Singular

Case	Masc.	Fem.	Neut.	
Nom.	**qui**	**quae**	**quod**	who, which, that
Gen.	**cuius**	**cuius**	**cuius**	whose, of which
Dat.	**cui**	**cui**	**cui**	to/for whom/which
Acc.	**quem**	**quam**	**quod**	whom, which, that
Abl.	**quo**	**qua**	**quo**	from/with/by/in which, whom

Plural

Case	Masc.	Fem.	Neut.	
Nom.	**qui**	**quae**	**quae**	who, which, that
Gen.	**quorum**	**quarum**	**quorum**	whose, of which
Dat.	**quibus**	**quibus**	**quibus**	to/for whom, which
Acc.	**quos**	**quas**	**quae**	whom, which, that
Abl.	**quibus**	**quibus**	**quibus**	from/with/by/in which, whom

To express *with,* **cum** is added to the end of the ablative case: **quocum, quacum, quibuscum.**

179. New Reading Grammar—Interrogative Adjective and Pronoun

The interrogative adjective **qui, quae, quod** modifies a noun and asks a question. It is, therefore, in the same case, number, and gender as the noun it modifies.

qui vir? which man?   **quae puella?** which girl?   **quod bellum?** which war?

Do not confuse the interrogative adjective **qui, quae, quod,** *who?* with the relative pronoun, **qui, quae, quod,** *who, which.* Although they have the same morphology, i.e., the same declensional pattern, they differ greatly in their usage. The interrogative adjective modifies a noun, and is in the same case, number, and gender. The relative pronoun introduces a relative clause, and is the same gender and number as its antecedent, but its case is determined by its use in its own clause. Both should be distinguished from the interrogative pronoun **quis**, **quid**, which introduces a question.

180. New Reading Grammar—Deponent and Semi-Deponent Verbs

1. **SEVERAL VERBS IN LATIN USE ONLY PASSIVE FORMS TO EXPRESS THE ACTIVE VOICE; THEY HAVE NO ACTIVE VOICE FORMS.**

   These verbs are called deponent verbs. They can easily be recognized from their prinicipal parts, which are passive in form, but active in meaning:

a-conjugation:	**hortor, hortari, hortatus sum**, urge, encourage (exhort)
e-conjugation:	**vereor, vereri, veritus sum**, fear
e/i-conjugation:	**sequor, sequi, secutus sum**, follow (sequential)
e/i-conjugation -io verbs:	**morior, mori, mortuus sum**, die (mortal)
i-conjugation:	**experior, experiri, expertus sum**, try, test (experience)

   You will notice that deponent verbs only have three principal parts. This is because deponent verbs lack active forms, and therefore do not need a perfect active stem (the normal third principal part).

2. **SINCE THE FORMS OF DEPONENT VERBS ARE THE SAME AS THE PASSIVE FORMS OF REGULAR VERBS, THE ONLY NEW FORM YOU NEED TO LEARN IS THE IMPERATIVE.**

   a. *The imperative singular is formed in the same way the present active infinitive is formed for a regular verb:*

   hortare, urge!
   morere, die!
   verere, fear!
   experire, try!
   sequere, follow!

   b. *The imperative plural is formed in the same way as the second person plural of the present tense. Remember that though the form is passive, the meaning is active.*

   hortamini, urge!
   morimini, die!
   veremini, fear!
   experimini, try!
   sequimini, follow!

3. **LATIN ALSO HAS FOUR VERBS THAT ARE KNOWN AS SEMI-DEPONENTS, NAMELY:**

   audeo, audere, ausus sum dare
   (con)fido, fidere, fisus sum trust, believe, confide

   gaudeo, gaudere, gavisus sum rejoice
   soleo, solere, solitus sum be accustomed to

   Semi-deponent verbs are active in meaning in all tenses. In the simple tenses (present, imperfect, and future), they are always active in form and meaning. In the perfect tenses (perfect, pluperfect, and future perfect), they are always passive in form but active in meaning. Like deponent verbs, these verbs have only three principal parts

181. Reading

Hero et Leander

1. Sunt multae fabulae de amore Leandri Herusque.
2. Haec fuit puella pulchra, quae in Graecia habitat et quae omnia in templo, quod erat in oppido suo, curabat.
3. Ille in altera regione, quae erat trans Hellespontum, pontem Graeciae, habitabat, sed, cum eam videre cupiebat, trans mare quod non erat latum natabat.
4. Ob leges templi cum ea videri non poterat, sed illa lex eum non impedivit. Itaque ad eam semper noctu veniebat.
5. Etiam longum et difficile iter trans aquam ab puella eum non prohibuit.
6. Hero ad mare de alto turri omnibus noctibus spectabat.
7. Leander sine periculo ullo saepe veniebat et tum Hero ipsa vero laeta erat, quod eum bene amabat.
8. Diu Leander bonam fortunam habebat et omnibus noctibus ad Graeciam facile natabat atque ad illam terram sine ullo periculo perveniebat.
9. Nullam inopiam celeritatis aut studi habebat. Ut accidit tamen uno tempore, cum natabat, tempestate magna victus est.
10. Primo trans aquam turris Herus ab illo videri poterat, sed iam iter erat difficile et mox tempestate sub mare mittebatur.
11. Hero totam noctem eum misere exspectabat.
12. Tum ad mare contendit et corpus illius petebat. Id primo non conspexit.
13. Tum in loco non longe ab mari corpus Leandri repperit.
14. Misera Hero in mare cucurrit et illa eum morte sua repperit.

Hero and Leander

1. There are many stories about the love of Hero and Leander.
2. She was a beautiful girl, who used to live in Greece and who took care of everything in the temple that was in her town.
3. He lived in another region, which was across the Hellespont, the sea of Greece, but, when he wished to see her, he used to swim across the sea, which was not wide.
4. Because of the laws of the temple, he could not be seen with her, but that law did not hinder him. And so, he used to come to her always at night.
5. Even the long and difficult journey across the water did not keep him from the girl.
6. Hero used to watch every night from a high tower toward the sea.
7. Leander often came without any danger and then Hero herself was truly happy, because she loved him well.
8. For a long time, Leander had good fortune and swam easily to Greece every night and came to that land without any danger.
9. He had no lack of speed or eagerness. As it happened, however, one time, when he was swimming, he was overcome by a great storm.
10. At first, Hero's tower could be seen by him across the water, but already the way was difficult and soon he was sent under the sea by the storm.
11. Hero waited for him unhappily all night.
12. Then she hurried to the sea and sought his body. She did not see it at first.
13. Then in a place not far from the sea, she found the body of Leander.
14. The unhappy Hero ran into the sea and she found him by her own death.

182. Practice Exercises

No. 132. In the following sentences, translate (a) the relative clause, and (b) the whole sentence:
1. Homines qui cum copiis suis iter faciunt sunt fortes.
2. Turris quam aedificavit ex oppido barbaros prohibebat.
3. Femina quacum ambulabam mater mea est.
4. Navis cuius nomen conspicere non possumus ad Italiam navigat.
5. Puer cui litteras dedi celeriter veniet.
6. Timor quem habebitis mox non memoria tenebitur.
7. Flumen ad quod fugiebant erat altum latumque.
8. Locus de quo scripsit longe est ab urbe.
9. Omnia quae habuit nunc mea sunt.
10. Viri quorum pueros vides sunt amici.

No. 133. Translate these phrases containing interrogative adjectives:

1. in quibus locis?	6. qua celeritate?	11. cum quibus militibus?
2. qui homo?	7. quo anno?	12. quorum civium?
3. quod oppidum?	8. cuius nominis?	13. quae impedimenta?
4. quae praeda?	9. qua hora?	14. cuius magnitudinis?
5. quos viros?	10. quo tempore?	15. quo consilio?

No. 134. Give the English for these verb forms:

1. faciunt	6. currebat	11. auditis	16. prohibuerunt
2. iubebit	7. fuerat	12. pervenisti	17. erunt
3. repperisti	8. cepit	13. contendebat	18. videbor
4. perveniet	9. conspexerunt	14. dederant	19. rogari
5. haberi	10. accidebat	15. videri	20. habebo

No. 135a. Translate these phrases and clauses:

1. non potuit	6. fortis populus	11. proximo anno
2. illius loci	7. ob tempestatem	12. mi amice
3. filios tuos	8. magno studio	13. omnes homines
4. alii veniunt	9. domi mansit	14. nihil timet
5. venire cupit	10. eius nationis	15. non solum mater tua

No. 135b. Translate these verb forms:

1. verebamini	6. hortor	11. hortabuntur	16. sequebamur
2. sequeris	7. veretur	12. experiris	17. mortuus est
3. experti erunt	8. morti eritis	13. verebuntur	18. moriemur
4. verita ero	9. hortata erat	14. expertus erat	19. secutus eram
5. sequuntur	10. moriebantur	15. hortabaris	20. experta est

Familiar Abbreviations

A.D., Anno Domini, in the year of (our) Lord.
a.m., ante meridiem, before noon.
p.m., post meridiem, after noon.
cf., confer, compare.

et al., et alii, or **et alia**, and other people or other things; **et alibi**, and elsewhere.
vs, v., versus, against.
c., circ., circa, circum, about. Used with dates.

---

183. New Reading Vocabulary

NOUNS

exercitus, exercitus, m., army (exercise)
impetus, impetus, m., attack (impetuous)
manus, manus, f., hand, group (manual)
res, rei, f., thing, matter, affair (re)
Persae, Persarum, m., the Persians
cornu, cornus, n., horn, wing (of an army) (cornucopia)
Athenae, Athenarum, f., Athens (declined in plural; meaning is singular)

domus, domus, f., house (domicile)
spes, spei, f., hope
acies, aciei, f., line of battle
passus, passus, m., pace (passage)
Sparta, Spartae, f., Sparta
dies, diei, m. or f., day (diet)
adventus, adventus, m., arrival, approach (adventure)

ADJECTIVES

Marathonius, Marathonia, Marathonium, of Marathon

VERBS

instruo, instruere, instruxi, instructus, draw up, form, train (instruct)

CONJUNCTIONS

neque, and . . . not
neque . . . neque, neither . . . nor

184. New Reading Grammar—Fourth Declension Nouns

A. NOUNS THAT END IN -us IN THE GENITIVE SINGULAR ARE OF THE u-DECLENSION, OR FOURTH DECLENSION.

With a few exceptions, fourth declension nouns ending in **-us** in the nominative singular are masculine; those ending in **-u** in the nominative singular are neuter. There are very few feminine gender fourth declension nouns.

The endings are:

Singular			*Plural*		
Case	*Masc. & Fem.*	*Neut.*	*Case*	*Masc. & Fem.*	*Neut.*
Nom.	-us	-u	Nom.	-us	-ua
Gen.	-us	-us	Gen.	-uum	-uum
Dat.	-ui	-u	Dat.	-ibus	-ibus
Acc.	-um	-u	Acc.	-us	-ua
Abl.	-u	-u	Abl.	-ibus	-ibus
Voc.	-us	-u	Voc.	-us	-ua

Thus, the declensions of **exercitus** and **cornu** are as follows:

Singular

Nom.	exercitus	the army	cornu	the horn, wing
Gen.	exercitus	of the army	cornus	of the horn, wing
Dat.	exercitui	to, for the army	cornu	to, for the horn, wing
Acc.	exercitum	the army		
			cornu	the horn, wing
Abl.	exercitu	from/with/by/in the army	cornu	from/with/by/in the horn, wing
Voc.	exercitus	O army	cornu	O horn, wing

Plural

Nom.	exercitus	the armies	cornua	the horns, wings
Gen.	exercituum	of the armies	cornuum	of the horns, wings
Dat.	exercitibus	to, for the armies	cornibus	to, for the horns, wings
Acc.	exercitus	the armies	cornua	the horns, wings
Abl.	exercitibus	from/with/by/in the armies	cornibus	from/with/by/in the horns, wings
Voc.	exercitus	O armies	cornua	O horns, wings

185. New Reading Grammar—The Noun *domus*

Domus, *house, home,* has endings in both the **second declension** and the **fourth declension**. Usage varies from author to author.

Case	Singular		Plural	
Nom.	**domus**	house	**domus**	houses
Gen.	**domus, domi**	of the house	**domuum, domorum**	of the houses
Dat.	**domui, domo**	to, for the house	**domibus**	to, for the houses
Acc.	**domum**	house	**domus, domos**	houses
Abl.	**domu, domo**	from/with/by/in the house	**domibus**	from/with/by/in the houses
Voc.	**domus**	O house	**domus**	O houses

Note that the nominative, dative, ablative, and vocative plurals use only the **u-declension** ending.

186. New Reading Grammar—Fifth Declension Nouns

Nouns that end in **-ei** in the genitive singular are of the **e-declension,** or fifth declension. These nouns are all feminine, except for **dies** (day), which is generally masculine.

The basic endings for this declension are:

Case	Singular	Plural
Nom.	-es	-es
Gen.	-ei	-erum
Dat.	-ei	-ebus
Acc.	-em	-es
Abl.	-e	-ebus
Voc.	-es	-es

Consider the declension of **spes, f.,** *hope:*

Case	Singular		Plural	
Nom.	**spes**	the hope	**spes**	the hopes
Gen.	**spei**	of the hope	**sperum**	of the hopes
Dat.	**spei**	to, for the hope	**spebus**	to, for the hopes
Acc.	**spem**	the hope	**spes**	the hopes
Abl.	**spe**	from, with, by, in the hope	**spebus**	from, with, by, in the hopes
Voc.	**spes**	O hope	**spes**	O hopes

187. Reading

Equus Troiae

1. **Graeci novem annos Troiam oppugnaverunt et iam domi esse cupiebant.**
2. **Bellum diu et fortiter gesserant, sed neque urbem ceperant neque illum locum relinquere potuerant.**
3. **Itaque consilium ceperunt. Magno studio laboreque equum magnum fecerunt. Multi milites Graeci, qui bene pugnare poterant, a sociis suis in equo ipso noctu locati sunt.**
4. **Exercitus urbis Troiae, qui post muros urbis erat, equum illa nocte non vidit.**
5. **Cives Troiae tamen, adventu solis in caelo, equum viderunt et eum in urbem duxerunt, sed mox Graeci, qui in equo positi erant, clamabant et in cives exercitumque Troiae impetum facibant.**

The Trojan Horse

1. The Greeks had attacked Troy for nine years and now they wanted to be at home.
2. They had carried on war for a long time and bravely, but they had neither captured the city nor had they been able to leave that place.
3. And so, they decided on a plan. With great zeal and work, they made a large horse. Many Greek soldiers, who were able to fight well, were placed in the horse itself by their comrades at night.
4. The army of the city of Troy, which was behind the walls of the city, did not see the horse that night.
5. The citizens of Troy, however, at the arrival of the sun in the sky, saw the horse and led it into the city, but soon the Greeks, who had been placed in the horse, shouted and made an attack on the citizens and army of Troy.

6. Populus terrebatur.
7. Graeci telis suis et igni urbem ceperunt. Tum Graeci ad mare, ubi alii Graeci naves suas instruxerant, cucurrerunt.
8. Post breve tempus, manus Graecorum cum captivis multis a Troia navigavit.

6. The people were terrified.
7. With their weapons and fire, the Greeks took the city. Then the Greeks ran to the sea, where the other Greeks had drawn up their ships.
8. After a short time, the band of Greeks sailed from Troy with many captives.

Proelium Marathonium

1. Anno XD Ante Christum, Graecis ab exercitu Persarum graviter oppugnabatur.
2. Persae trans mare ad Graeciam navigaverant et multa oppida occupaverant.
3. Hostes ad locum, qui non multa milia passuum Athenis erat, iam iter fecerant, et ob hanc rem cives Athenarum et in aliis urbibus propinquis illi loco adventum hostium timebant.
4. Populus Athenarum ad Spartam virum misit.
5. Ille totum iter cucurrit et ab populo Spartae auxilium petivit, sed Sparta legem habebat. Hac lege, illi sine luna in caelo bellum gerere non poterant, et illo tempore luna non erat.
6. Itaque milites soli Athenarum aciem suam instruxerunt et sagittis ac telis gravibus hostes vicerunt. Illo die populus Athenarum spem victoriae magnae videbat.
7. Postea ob virtutem viri, qui Athenis Spartam cucurrerat, ludos habebant. His ludis nomen proeli, quod in agro Marathonio fuerat, dederunt.
8. Etiam hodie ludo pedibus id nomen damus.

The Battle of Marathon

1. In the year 490 B.C., Greece was heavily attacked by the army of the Persians.
2. The Persians had sailed across the sea to Greece and had seized many towns.
3. The enemy had made the journey to a place which was not many miles from Athens, and for this reason, the citizens of Athens and in other cities near to that place feared the arrival of the enemy.
4. The people of Athens sent a man to Sparta.
5. He ran the whole way and sought help from the people of Sparta, but Sparta had a law. By this law, they were not able to carry on war without a moon in the sky, and at that time, there was no moon.
6. And so the soldiers of Athens drew up their battle line alone and conquered the enemy with arrows and heavy weapons. On that day, the people of Athens saw the hope of a great victory.
7. Afterwards, because of the courage of the man who had run from Athens to Sparta, they held games. To these games they gave the name of the battle that had been on the field of Marathon.
8. Even today, we give this name to a contest on foot.

187. Practice Exercises

No. 136. Give the English for these phrases:

1. multos passus
2. vestra manus
3. longum impetum
4. ob adventum eius
5. utrumque cornu
6. exercituum nostrorum
7. in cornu tuo
8. ex exercitu
9. in domum
10. sex milia passuum
11. contra exercitus
12. ob adventum tuum
13. impetus hostium
14. manus militum
15. ab exercitu

No. 137. Give the English for these phrases:

1. acies suas	6. totam rem	11. in qua acie?
2. multo die	7. unam diem	12. utriusque diei
3. proximo die	8. quarum rerum?	13. ob eam rem
4. ob has res	9. nostrae acies	14. in his aciebus
5. ullius spei	10. quas res?	15. multam spem

No. 138. Translate these verb forms:

1. ambulavit	6. reperit	11. relicti sunt
2. videmur	7. datum erat	12. pugnabunt
3. erant	8. potest	13. instruxit
4. fecerat	9. instructum est	14. iter facit
5. fugiebat	10. videri	15. audientur

No. 139. Translate these sentences:
1. Omnes res faciles esse videntur.
2. Post sex dies neuter miles ullam spem habebat.
3. Captivi quos reduxisti ex eorum exercitu venerunt.
4. Quis fortem impetum magnopere impedivit?
5. Una hora homines domum venient.
6. Quam ob rem aciem suam in colli instruebat?
7. Inter has res quas habemus est parva copia aquae.
8. Milites in illo cornu equos suos ad agrum vertunt.
9. Neque cornu neque acies spem videbat.
10. Quis inter hos populos regnum tenebat?

189. NEW READING VOCABULARY

NOUNS

Thermopylae, Thermopylarum, f. pl., Thermopylae
praesidium, praesidii or **praesidi, n.,** guard,
garrison (presidial, preside)
civitas, civitatis, f., state

VERBS

scio, scire, scivi, scitus, know (sciolist)
appello, appellare, appellavi, appellatus,
address, call, name (appellation)
conloco, conlocare, conlocavi, conlocatus,
place, station (collocate, collate)

PRONOUNS

ego, mei, I (e.g., egotist)
nos, nostrum, we (nostrum)
tu, tui, you (sing.)
vos, vestrum, you (pl.)

ADJECTIVES

decem, ten (decimal)

CONJUNCTIONS

enim, for. Never the first word in a
Latin sentence.

Legal Terms

a vinculo matrimonii, from the bond of marriage. Used in a decree of absolute divorce.

caveat emptor, let the buyer beware. The buyer buys at his or her own risk.

inter vivos, between the living. Used to indicate a gift from a living person to another living person.

compos mentis, sound or sane of mind; **non compos mentis** or **non compos,** not sound or sane of mind.

nolo contendere, I do not wish to contend. A plea by which a defendant is subject to conviction, but does not admit guilt.

nolle prosequi, to be unwilling to prosecute. Abbr. **nol pros.** A court record stating that the prosecutor will not carry the suit further.

non prosequitur, he or she does not prosecute. Abbr. **non pros.** Used to indicate a decision against a plaintiff who does not appear in court to prosecute.

obiter dictum, something said along the way. Used of remarks made by a judge that are not part of the legal decision, but are personal comments and observations on matters relating to the case and decision.

nisi, if not, unless. Used to indicate that an order or decree will go into effect at a specified time unless modified by further evidence or cause presented before that time.

sui iuris or **suo iure,** of one's own right or in one's own right. Used of a person who has full capacity and ability to act for him- or herself in legal proceedings.

190. New Reading Grammar—Personal Pronouns

Since the endings of verbs in Latin communicate the subject of the verb, personal pronouns are used primarily to show emphasis or to make a clear distinction.

Emphasis: **ego scio,** I (myself) know

Clarity: **ego et tu scimus,** I and you know

1. Personal Pronouns of the First Person

Case	Singular		Plural	
Nom.	**ego**	I	**nos**	we
Gen.	**mei**	of me	**nostrum** or **nostri**	of us
Dat.	**mihi**	to, for me	**nobis**	to, for us
Acc.	**me**	me	**nos**	us
Abl.	**me**	from, with, by, in me	**nobis**	from, with, by, in us

2. Personal Pronouns of the Second Person

Case	Singular		Plural	
Nom.	**tu**	you	**vos**	you
Gen.	**tui**	of you	**vestrum** or **vestri**	of you
Dat.	**tibi**	to, for you	**vobis**	to, for you
Acc.	**te**	you	**vos**	you
Abl.	**te**	from, with, by, in you	**vobis**	from, with, by, in you
Voc.	**tu**	O you	**vos**	O you

3. You have already learned the Personal Pronouns of the Third Person.

Singular		Plural	
is, ea, id	he, she, it	**ei, eae, ea,**	they
ille, illa, illud	he, she, it	**illi, illae, illa**	they
hic, haec, hoc	he, she, it	**hi, hae, haec**	they

191. New Reading Grammar—Possessive Adjectives

Adjectives are more commonly used to show possession than is the genitive case of the personal pronoun, except in the third person. In other words, *my horse* would be more likely to be expressed as **meus equus** than as **mei equus**.

1st person	**meus, mea, meum**	my, mine
	noster, nostra, nostrum	our, ours
2nd person	**tuus, tua, tuum**	your, yours
	vester, vestra, vestrum	your, yours

As always, these adjectives must agree with the nouns they modify in case, number, and gender.

But there are seeming exceptions to the rule when we use the genitive forms of the following pronouns:

3rd person	**eius, eius, eius**	his, her, its
	eorum, earum, eorum	their; *or*
	illius, illius, illius	his, her, its
	illorum, illarum, illorum	their; *or*
	huius, huius, huius	his, her, its
	horum, harum, horum	their

With these *pronouns*, the genitive of the third person is used, regardless of the case of the noun it modifies, e.g., **eius filiam**, *his (her) daughter.* Remember that these forms, while acting adjectivally to modify another noun, as all genitive forms do, are NOT themselves adjectives, and therefore need not agree with the nouns they modify. Note that this only applies when the third person possessor is not the same as the subject of the sentence, e.g., *The man loves his daughter*, where *his* does not refer to *The man.* If the third person possessor is the subject, then the reflexive adjective must be used:

suus, sua, suum   his, her, its, their (own)

Since **suus, sua, suum** is an adjective, it must agree with the noun it modifies in case, number, and gender, e.g., **suam filiam,** *his (her) own daughter.*

When **cum** is used, it is added to the end of the personal pronouns.

mecum, with me   **nobiscum,** with us

tecum, with you   **vobiscum,** with you

192. New Reading Grammar—Reflexive Pronouns

Reflexive pronouns reflect back to the subject and, therefore, have no nominative case.

Me video, I see myself   **Te vides,** you see yourself

1. REFLEXIVE PRONOUNS OF THE FIRST PERSON

Case	Singular		Plural	
Gen.	**mei**	of myself	**nostri**	of ourselves
Dat.	**mihi**	to/for myself	**nobis**	to/for ourselves
Acc.	**me**	myself	**nos**	ourselves
Abl.	**me**	from/with/by/in myself	**nobis**	from/with/by/in ourselves

2. REFLEXIVE PRONOUNS OF THE SECOND PERSON

Case	Singular		Plural	
Gen.	**tui**	of yourself	**vestri**	of yourselves
Dat.	**tibi**	to/for yourself	**vobis**	to/for yourselves
Acc.	**te**	yourself	**vos**	yourselves
Abl.	**te**	from/with/by/in yourself	**vobis**	from/with/by/in yourselves

3. THE REFLEXIVE PRONOUN FOR THE THIRD PERSON IS THE SAME IN LATIN FOR THE SINGULAR AND PLURAL. ONLY THE MEANING CHANGES.

Case	Singular and Plural	
Gen.	**sui**	of himself/herself/itself/themselves
Dat.	**sibi**	to/for himself/herself/itself/themselves
Acc.	**se**	himself, herself, itself, themselves
Abl.	**se**	from/with/by/in himself/herself/itself/themselves

193. Reading

Proelium Thermopylarum

1. Post decem annos Persae ad Graeciam navibus suos reduxerunt.
2. Proelium Marathonium anno XD Ante Christum fuerat.
3. Hic annus erat XXD Ante Christum et hoc proelium appellatur Proelium Thermopylarum.
4. Persae magnum copiam et cibi et frumenti, quam trans mare portare in animo habebant, decem annos paraverant atque exercitum fortem acremque habuerunt.
5. Illi in impetu hoc omnem spem suam posuerant, sed illo tempore erat apud Graecos nulla pax. Alia civitas contra aliam contendebat.
6. Itaque Athenae Spartaque Graeciam totam aegre defendere poterant.
7. Exercitus hostium ad partem montium quae Thermopylae appellata est pervenit.
8. Hic locus natura fortis est quod iter parvum inter montes ab non multis militibus teneri poterat.
9. In eo loco manus parva Graecorum conlocata erat et adventum hostium exspectabat.
10. Graeci in montibus facile pugnare poterant. Ei enim patriam suam bene sciebant.
11. Iter per montes erat difficile et angustum. Itaque Graeci praesidium ibi conlocaverant.
12. Hi contra milites fortes hostium, qui spem iam relinquebant, diu et fortiter contenderunt, sed erat unus homo, qui Persis auxilium dedit.
13. Hic vir hostibus iter, quod erat post locum ubi praesidium Graecum instructum erat, trans montes demonstravit.
14. Exercitus hostium ad locum post aciem Graecam noctu iter fecit.
15. Alii Graeci fugere potuerunt, sed alii milites Spartae et sociorum eius nullum timorem demonstraverunt.

The Battle of Thermopylae

1. After ten years, the Persians led their men back to Greece by ship.
2. The Battle of Marathon had been in the year 490 B.C.
3. This year was 480 B.C. and this battle is called the Battle of Thermopylae.
4. The Persians for ten years had prepared a great supply both of food and grain, which they intended to carry across the sea, and they also had a brave and keen army.
5. They had placed all their hope in this attack, but at that time there was no peace among the Greeks. One state was fighting against another.
6. And so, Athens and Sparta were able to defend all Greece with difficulty.
7. The army of the enemy came to the part of the mountains which is called Thermopylae.
8. This place is stong by nature because the small road between the mountains was able to be held by a few soldiers.
9. In this place, a small group of Greeks had been stationed and was waiting for the arrival of the enemy.
10. The Greeks were able to fight easily in the mountains. For they knew their native country well.
11. The way through the mountains was both difficult and narrow. And so the Greeks had stationed a garrison there.
12. They fought for a !ong time against the brave soldiers of the enemy, who were already giving up hope, but there was one man, who gave help to the Persians.
13. This man pointed out to the enemy a way across the mountains, which was in back of the place where the Greek guard had been drawn up.
14. The army of the enemy made its way at night to a place in back of the Greek battle line.
15. Some Greeks were able to escape, but other soldiers of Sparta and her allies showed no fear.

16. Hi gladiis et aliis telis pugnabant, sed post breve tempus Graeci omnes ab hostibus interfecti erant et Persae trans corpora eorum Athenas iter fecerunt.

16. These men fought for a time with swords and other weapons, but after a short time, all the Greeks had been killed by the enemy and the Persians made their way to Athens over their bodies.

194. Practice Exercises

No. 140. Give the English for these personal pronouns:

1. vos	7. te	13. vobis	19. illorum	25. illis
2. nos	8. ego	14. eos	20. ad vos	26. de his
3. a te	9. eum	15. illud	21. tibi	27. illa
4. eorum	10. mihi	16. huic	22. vestrum	28. cum ea
5. ea	11. nobiscum	17. eius	23. nostri	29. horum
6. ei	12. tu	18. tecum	24. de me	30. illos

No. 141. Give the English for these reflexive pronouns:

1. sibi	3. a me	5. se	7. mihi	9. me
2. te	4. vos	6. vobis	8. nobis	10. nos

No. 142. Translate these sentences:

1. Homo ipse nos non scit.
2. Ego tibi auxilium misi.
3. Nos in hoc loco te repperimus.
4. Venietisne vos mecum?
5. Tu nobis libros das.
6. Vos eum non auditis.
7. Illi ad nos fugiebant.
8. Is mihi haec misit.
9. Tecum domum ambulare non poterit.
10. Haec est patria nostra.
11. Tu id illis narrabis.
12. Nos hanc domum reducemus.
13. Illi ab his pacem petebant.
14. Ego a te et tuo gladio terrebar.
15. Nos illo tempore nos servaveramus.
16. Nonne tu nos iuvare potes?
17. Ille urbem eorum vidit.
18. Nos ipsi eos venire iubebimus.
19. Vos nobis ea demonstrabitis.
20. Animus eius me non diu terrebat.

Roman aqueducts still stand today in Spain and France.

REVIEW

195. Vocabulary Review

NOUNS

1. acies
2. adventus
3. Athenae
4. civitas
5. cornu
6. dies
7. domus
8. Eurydice
9. exercitus
10. Hellespontus
11. Hero
12. impetus
13. inopia
14. Leander
15. manus
16. natura
17. nihil, nil
18. Orpheus
19. passus
20. Persae
21. praesidium
22. regio
23. regnum
24. res
25. Sparta
26. spes
27. Thermopylae
28. turris

PRONOUNS

1. ego
2. nos
3. qui
4. tu
5. vos

ADJECTIVES

1. decem
2. difficilis
3. Marathonius
4. primus

VERBS

1. accido
2. appello
3. conloco
4. conspicio
5. cupio
6. discedo
7. educo
8. impedio
9. instruo
10. pervenio
11. prohibeo
12. reduco
13. rego
14. relinquo
15. reperio
16. scio

ADVERBS

1. iam
2. magnopere
3. parum
4. primum, primo
5. solum

CONJUNCTIONS

1. enim
2. neque
3. neque . . . neque
4. ut

196. Practice Exercises

No. 143. Give the adverbs of these adjectives, with their meanings:

1. latus
2. acer
3. difficilis
4. miser
5. longus
6. magnus
7. laetus
8. liber
9. parvus
10. angustus

No. 144. Translate these verbs:

1. veniam
2. sciebat
3. auditus est
4. perveniebamus
5. impedientur
6. reperiunt
7. audiebaris
8. scitum erat
9. cupiverunt
10. audieris

No. 145. Translate these pronouns:

1. cuius
2. quem
3. quae
4. qui
5. quibuscum
6. nos
7. mihi
8. me
9. vestrum
10. tibi
11. tecum
12. eius
13. eorum
14. illum
15. hanc

No. 146. Translate these nouns:

1. exercitui
2. res
3. cornus
4. aciem
5. spem
6. manuum
7. die
8. impetibus
9. adventum
10. domum
11. rebus
12. cornua
13. exercituum
14. manui
15. spei

197. Reading

PUBLIUS VERGILIUS MARO

Virgil was born in 70 B.C. near Mantua, in the north of Italy, and was educated in Milan, Rome, and Naples, where he studied philosophy and rhetoric. During the latter part of his life, he lived near Naples, where he composed his epic poem *The Aeneid*. Virgil died in 19 B.C. at Brundisium, while returning from Greece.

Ibant obscuri, sola sub nocte, per umbram
perque domos Ditis vacuas, et inania regna;
quale per incertam lunam sub luce maligna est
iter in silvis, ubi caelum condidit umbra Iuppiter,
et rebus nox abstulit atra colorem. Vestibulum
ante ipsum primisque in faucibus Orci
Luctus et ultrices posuere cubilia Curae,
pallentesque habitant Morbi, tristisque
Senectus,
et Metus, et malesuada Fames, ac turpis
Egestas, terribiles visu formae, Letumque
Labosque, tum consanguineus Leti Sopor, et
mala mentis Gaudia, mortiferumque adverso
in limine Bellum,
ferreique Eumenidum thalami, et Discordia
demens,
vipereum crinem vittis innexa cruentis.
Aeneidos VI, 268–281

JACQUES DE VITRY

These two stories are found in the sermons of Jacques de Vitry, who was the Cardinal Bishop of Tusculum and died in A.D. 1240. The stories were used to illustrate a point as well as to entertain the listeners.

De Arbore In Qua Se Suspendebant Mulieres

De quodam alio audivi, qui habebat arborem in horto suo, in qua duae eius uxores suspenderant semetipsas. Cui quidam eius vicinus ait: "Valde fortunata est arbor illa et bonum omen habet. Habeo autem uxorem pessimam; rogo te, da mihi surculum ex ea, ut plantem in horto meo."

De Bachone Qui Pendebat In Quadam Villa

Aliquando transivi per quandam villam in Francia, ubi suspenderant pernam seu bachonem in platea hac condicione ut, qui vellet iuramento firmare quod uno integro anno post contractum matrimonium permansisset cum uxore ita quod de matrimonio non paenituisset, bachonem haberet. Et cum per decem annos ibi pependisset non est unus solus inventus qui bachonem lucraretur, omnibus infra annum de matrimonio contracto paenitentibus.

NUMBERS AND COMPARISONS

More State Mottoes

E Pluribus Unum.
One From Many. (United States of America)

Nil Sine Numine.
Nothing Without Divine Power. (Colorado)

Qui Transtulit Sustinet.
He Who Has Transplanted Sustains. (Connecticut)

Scuto Bonae Voluntatis Tuae Coronasti Nos.
You Have Crowned Us With The Shield Of Thy Will. (Maryland)

Si Quaeris Paeninsulam Amoenam, Circumspice.
If You Seek A Pleasant Peninsula, Look Around. (Michigan)

Crescit Eundo.
It Increases As It Goes. (New Mexico)

Esse Quam Videri.
To Be Rather Than To Seem. (North Carolina)

Labor Omnia Vincit.
Labor Conquers All. (Oklahoma)

Alis Volat Propriis.
It Flies On Its Own Wings. (Oregon)

Animis Opibusque Parati.
Prepared In Mind And Resources. (South Carolina)

Sic Semper Tyrannis.
Thus Always To Tyrants. (Virginia)

---

198. New Reading Vocabulary

NOUNS

onus, oneris, n., burden, weight (onerous)
hiems, hiemis, f., winter
portus, portus, m., harbor (port)
multitudo, multitudinis, f., great number, multitude (multitudinous)

Creusa, Creusae, f., Creusa
ventus, venti, m., wind
aestas, aestatis, f., summer

VERBS

opprimo, opprimere, oppressi, oppressus, overcome, crush (oppressive)
convenio, convenire, conveni, conventus, come together, assemble (convene, convention)
incendo, incendere, incendi, incensus, set fire to, burn (incendiary)
cogo, cogere, coegi, coactus, collect, drive, compel (cogent)

recipio, recipere, recepi, receptus, take back, receive (reception)
dedo, dedere, dedidi, deditus, give up, surrender
suscipio, suscipere, suscepi, susceptus, take up, undertake (susceptible)

ADVERBS	CONJUNCTIONS
bis, twice (bicycle)	**nam**, for

199. New Reading Grammar—Cardinal and Ordinal Numbers

A. CARDINAL NUMBERS ARE ONE, TWO, THREE, FOUR, AND SO ON; THEY ANSWER THE QUESTION *how many?*

Ordinal numbers are first, second, third, fourth, and so on; they answer the question *which one?*

B. THE CARDINAL NUMBERS ONE TO TWENTY, ONE HUNDRED, AND ONE THOUSAND ARE AS FOLLOWS:

1—unus, una, unum	9—novem	17—septendecim
2—duo, duae, duo	10—decem	18—duodeviginti
3—tres, tria	11—undecim	19—undeviginti
4—quattuor	12—duodecim	20—viginti
5—quinque	13—tredecim	100—centum
6—sex	14—quattuordecim	1000—mille
7—septem	15—quindecim	
8—octo	16—sedecim	

The following cardinal numbers are declined:

Case	1			2			3		1000	
	Masc.	*Fem.*	*Neut.*	*Masc.*	*Fem.*	*Neut.*	*Masc.*	*Neut.*	*Singular*	*Plural*
Nom.	unus	una	unum	duo	duae	duo	tres	tria	mille	milia
Gen.	unius	unius	unius	duorum	duarum	duorum	trium	trium	mille	milium
Dat.	uni	uni	uni	duobus	duabas	duobus	tribus	tribus	mille	milibus
Acc.	unum	unam	unum	duos, duo	duas	duo	tres, tris	tria	mille	milia
Abl.	uno	una	uno	duobus	duabus	duobus	tribus	tribus	mille	milibus

1. **Unus** *is declined only in the singular.*

   Duo *and* **tres** *are declined only in the plural.* **Mille** *is declined in both the singular and the plural. The other cardinal numbers are not declined.*

2. *Mille is an adjective in the singular and a noun in the plural.*

   mille homines, a thousand men   **milia hominum**, thousands of men

3. *Note that most of the cardinal numbers are indeclinable.*

4. *The other cardinal numbers may be used as either adjectives or, like any adjective, can be used substantively as nouns.*

   tres homines, three men   **tres hominum**, three of the men
   tres de hominibus, three (from the) men   **tres ex hominibus**, three (from the) men

C. THE ORDINAL NUMBERS FIRST TO TENTH ARE AS FOLLOWS:

first	**primus, prima, primum**	sixth	**sextus, sexta, sextum**
second	**secundus, secunda, secundum**	seventh	**septimus, septima, septimum**
third	**tertius, tertia, tertium**	eighth	**octavus, octava, octavum**
fourth	**quartus, quarta, quartum**	ninth	**nonus, nona, nonum**
fifth	**quintus, quinta, quintum**	tenth	**decimus, decima, decimum**

All ordinal numbers are first and seond declension adjectives.

sexto die, on the sixth day

quartum annum, for the fourth year

200. Reading

Aeneas in Igni Troiae

1. **Aeneas in vias Troiae una nocte cucurrit et multitudinem militum Graecorum, qui vero laeti erant, quod urbem vicerant, ibi videbat.**
2. **Aeneas cum parva manu sociorum suorum contra hostes primo contendit, sed nihil faci poterat.**
3. **Tum patrem suum, qui domi erat, memoria tenuit et domum properavit.**
4. **Troia eo tempore acriter incendebatur. Populus Troiae dediderat. Bellum contra Graecos pugnatum erat.**
5. **Aeneas patrem suum secum venire coegit et in umeris suis totum onus corporis eius portabat. Hi tres, Aeneas atque pater suus atque suus filius parvus, ex igni contendebant.**
6. **Ob victoriam hostium magnopere opprimebantur.**
7. **Post breve tempus, Aeneas matrem fili sui, Creusam, memoria tenuit. Illa enim erat in urbe. Itaque in urbem celeriter cucurrit.**
8. **Bis centum tempora eam appellabat, sed illa ibi non erat. A Morte educta erat.**

Aeneas in the Fire of Troy

1. Aeneas ran into the streets of Troy one night and he saw there a great number of Greek soldiers, who were truly happy, because they had conquered the city.
2. Aeneas, with a small band of his comrades, at first struggled against the enemy, but nothing could be done.
3. Then he remembered his father, who was at home, and he hurried home.
4. Troy, at that time, was being fiercely burned. The people of Troy had surrendered. The war against the Greeks had been finished.
5. Aeneas had forced his father to come with him and he carried the whole burden of his body on his shoulders. These three, Aeneas and his father and his small son, hurried from the fire.
6. Because of the victory of the enemy, they were greatly oppressed.
7. After a short time, Aeneas remembered the mother of his son, Creusa. For she was in the city. And so, he ran quickly into the city.
8. He called her twice a hundred times, but she was not there. She had been carried off by Death.

Iter Ulixis

1. Decem annos Ulixes ab portu Troiae ad patriam suam navigabat. Ipse et socii sui ad multa loca illo tempore pervenerunt.
2. Primus locus erat eis acriter gratus idoneusque.
3. Secundus locus erat terra in qua Polyphemus habitabat.
4. Tertio in loco, venti eis ab rege ventorum dati sunt.
5. Quarto in loco, multi viri ab illo, quem ibi reppererunt, necati sunt.
6. Ob feminam pulchram ab quinto loco difficile se recipere potuerunt.
7. Sexto in loco, omnes qui apud Inferos convenerant viderunt.
8. Septimo in loco, multas res pulchras audiverunt et ibi manere cupiverunt.
9. Ab octavo loco celeriter fugerunt. Nam duo animalia ibi habitabant. Unum ex his erat serpens et alterum erat magnum equum.
10. Nono in loco animalia dei solis tenebantur.

11. Tum omnes socii eius in mari necati sunt. Itaque ille solus ad decimum locum pervenit.
12. Iter difficile susceperat, sed post decem aestates atque decem hiemes servatus erat et domum venit.

The Journey of Ulysses

1. Ulysses sailed for ten years from the harbor of Troy to his native country. He and his comrades arrived at many places during that time.
2. The first place was keenly pleasing and suitable to them.
3. The second place was the land in which Polyphemus lived.
4. In the third place, winds were given to them by the king of the winds.
5. In the fourth place, many of the men were killed by him, whom they found there.
6. They were able to depart from the fifth place with difficulty because of a beautiful woman.
7. In the sixth place, they say all those who had come together among Those Below.
8. In the seventh place, they heard many beautiful things and wished to stay there.
9. They fled from the eighth place quickly. For two animals lived there. One of these was a serpent and the other was a large horse.
10. In the ninth place, the animals of the god of the sun were held.

11. Then all his comrades were killed on the sea. And so, he arrived alone at the tenth place.
12. He had undertaken a difficult journey, but after ten summers and ten winters, he had been saved and he came home.

201. Practice Exercises

No. 147. Give the English forms for these cardinal numbers:

1. quindecim	6. decem	11. centum	16. tredecim
2. novem	7. tres	12. quattuordecim	17. septem
3. viginti	8. septendecim	13. octo	18. unus
4. quinque	9. quattuor	14. undeviginti	19. duodeviginti
5. sedecim	10. undecim	15. duo	20. mille

No. 148. Give the English forms for these ordinal numbers:

1. quartus	3. decimus	5. septimus	7. quintus	9. primus
2. octavus	4. tertius	6. secundus	8. nonus	10. sextus

No. 149. Translate these phrases, which contain cardinal numbers:

1. mille naves
2. tres homines
3. milium militum
4. quattuordecim dies
5. unius viri
6. viginti milia passuum
7. centum pueros
8. quinque annos
9. sex de militibus
10. septem horis
11. centum annis
12. octo ex pueris
13. duos dies
14. decem legum
15. tria loca
16. duae de provinciis
17. duodecim diebus
18. sex animalium
19. duodeviginti ex regibus
20. tribus annis

No. 150. Translate these phrases, which contain ordinal numbers:

1. decimae puellae
2. octavo die
3. sexta hora
4. septima navis
5. quinta aestate
6. tertium diem
7. decima hieme
8. septimus impetus
9. nonae horae
10. primo anno

202. New Reading Vocabulary

NOUNS
fons, fontis, m., spring, fountain (**fontium**) (font)
Psyche, Psyches, f., Psyche (a Greek name) (psychic)
oraculum, oraculi, n., oracle (oracular)
matrimonium, matrimonii or matrimoni, n., marriage (matrimony)
Cupido, Cupidinis, m., Cupid
difficultas, difficultatis, f., difficulty
soror, sororis, f., sister (sorority)
in matrimonium ducere, marry (literally, to lead into marriage)

VERBS
deligo, deligere, delegi, delectus, choose, select
dormio, dormire, dormivi, dormitus, sleep (dormant, dormitory)
tango, tangere, tetigi, tactus, touch (tangent)
constituo, constituere, constitui, constitutus, decide, establish (constitution)

ADJECTIVES
aequus, aequa, aequum, equal, level, fair (equality)
immortalis, immortale, immortal (immortality)
dulcis, dulce, sweet (dulcet)
similis, simile, like, similar (similarity)

ADVERBS
olim, formerly, once upon a time
quoque, also

CONJUNCTIONS
quamquam, although

Familiar Quotations

Laudator temporis acti. A praiser of past times. (Horace)

Abeunt studia in mores. Pursuits pass over into habits. (Ovid)

Factum fieri infectum non potest. What is done cannot be undone. (Terence)

O tempora! O mores! Oh the times! Oh the customs! (Cicero)

Tu ne cede malis. Do not yield to misfortunes. (Virgil)

Docendo discitur. We learn by teaching. (Seneca)

In hoc signo vinces. By this sign shalt thou conquer. (Constantine)

Non datur ad Musas currere lata via. It is not granted to run to the Muses on a wide road. (Propertius)

Est modus in rebus. There is a middle course in things. (Horace)

Forsan et haec olim meminisse iuvabit. Perhaps some time it will be pleasant to remember even these things. (Virgil)

---

203. New Reading Grammar—Comparative and Superlative Adjectives

A. ADJECTIVES HAVE THREE DEGREES OF COMPARISON—POSITIVE, COMPARATIVE, AND SUPERLATIVE.

	Positive	*Comparative*	*Superlative*
good:	*good* food	*better* food	the *best* food
pretty:	a *pretty* girl	a *prettier* girl	the *prettiest* girl
fast:	a *fast* train	a *faster* train	the *fastest* train
slow:	a *slow* boat	a *slower* boat	the *slowest* boat

In English, many adjectives end in *-er* in the comparative degree and in *-est* in the superlative degree. However, some adjectives modify their spelling in these two degrees. The comparative of *pretty* is *prettier*, and the superlative is *prettiest*. The *-y* becomes an *-i-*.

Some adjectives have irregular comparative and superlative degrees, for example, *good, better, best*, and *bad, worse, worst*.

B. IN LATIN, AS IN ENGLISH, MOST ADJECTIVES HAVE REGULAR ENDINGS IN THE COMPARATIVE AND SUPERLATIVE DEGREES. HOWEVER, SOME ADJECTIVES WILL HAVE MODIFIED SPELLINGS, WHILE OTHERS WILL BE IRREGULAR IN THESE DEGREES.

1. *The positive degree is always the simple form of the adjective.*

longus, longa, longum, long
miser, misera, miserum, wretched
acer, acris, acre, keen

fortis, forte, brave
pulcher, pulchra, pulchrum, pretty
facilis, facile, easy

The positive degree of an adjective is declined either in the first and second declensions (e.g., **longus, longa, longum**) or in the third (e.g., **acer, acris, acre**). All adjectives belong to either one or the other of these two types.

2. *The comparative degree of most adjectives has a stem that ends in -ior.*

This ending is typically added to the stem of the positive degree to form the comparative stem. Note that the neuter singular nominative and accusative forms end in **-ius**.

longior, longius, longer, rather long, too long, quite long
fortior, fortius, braver, rather brave, too brave, quite brave
miserior, miserius, more wretched, rather wretched, quite wretched
pulchrior, pulchrius, prettier, more pretty, rather pretty, quite pretty
acrior, acrius, keener, more keen, rather keen, quite keen
facilior, facilius, easier, more easy, rather easy, quite easy

The comparative degree is declined as follows:

Case	Singular		Plural	
	Masc./Fem.	*Neut.*	*Masc./Fem.*	*Neut.*
Nom.	**longior**	**longius**	**longiores**	**longiora**
Gen.	**longioris**	**longioris**	**longiorum**	**longiorum**
Dat.	**longiori**	**longiori**	**longioribus**	**longioribus**
Acc.	**longiorem**	**longius**	**longiores**	**longiora**
Abl.	**longiore**	**longiore**	**longioribus**	**longioribus**
Voc.	**longior**	**longius**	**longiores**	**longiora**

As you can see, the comparative degree uses regular (not i-stem) third declension endings. Since it is an adjective, it must agree in case, number, and gender with the word it modifies.

3. *The superlative degree of most adjectives has the endings -issimus, -a, -um.*

The superlative degree endings are as follows:

a. For most adjectives, the ending is **-issimus, -a, -um**.
    longissimus, -a, -um, very long, most long, longest
    fortissimus, -a, -um, very brave, bravest, most brave

b. For those adjectives that end in **-er, -rimus, -rima, -rimum**
    miserrimus, -a, -um, very wretched, most wretched
    pulcherrimus, -a, -um, very pretty, most pretty, prettiest
    acerrimus, -a, -um, very keen, most keen, keenest

c. For **facilis, difficilis,** and **similis**
    facillimus, -a, -um, very easy, most easy, easiest
    difficillimus, -a, -um, very difficult, most difficult
    simillimus, -a, -um, very similar, most similar

The superlative endings are added on to the stem of the positive degree. The superlative degree is declined regularly in the first and second declensions (**a-** and **o-declension**) and must agree with the word it modifies in case, number, and gender.

204. Reading

Cupido et Psyche

1. Erant olim tres sorores pulchrae, quae erant filiae regis reginaeque. Harum Psyche erat clarissima. Itaque fama eius in regionibus, quae finitimae erant domui suae, erat aequa illi Veneris.
2. Venus non solum immortalis sed etiam superbissima erat. Itaque contra puellam, quae neque dea neque immortalis erat, poenam reperire constituit.
3. Dea pulchra nullam inopiam consili habebat. Postquam ipsa iter ex hac difficultate delegerat, filium suum, Cupidem, deum amoris, ad se vocavit.
4. Ei difficultatem suam demonstrat et dicit: "Omnes Psychen petunt et illi nunc me adorare non etiam simulant. Ob iniurias, quas matri tuae fecit, poenas dare debet. Hoc opus tibi idoneum est."
5. Cupido matrem suam iuvare celeriter parabat.
6. Ad hortum Veneris, in quo erant duo fontes, quorum alter dulcis erat alterque non dulcis, properavit.
7. Postquam ex utroque fonte aquam obtinuerat, Psychen, quae domi dormiebat, petivit.
8. Ipse, ubi illam vidit, paene motus est quod pulcherrima erat, sed deus matrem memoria tenebat et puellam aqua, quae non dulcis erat, et sagitta sua tetigit.
9. Psyche incitata est, sed Cupidinem videre non poterat. Ipse territus est et in illa aquam dulcem posuit.
10. Postea Psyche, quamquam pulchra erat, miserrima quoque erat. Quod illa a Venere non amabatur nullus eam in matrimonium ducere cupiebat.
11. Itaque Psyche domi manebat et pater materque puellae simillimam inopiam spei demonstrabant.
12. Hoc ab oraculo dictum erat: "Non a viro, sed ab uno contra quem nullus stare potest tu in matrimonium duceris."

Cupid and Psyche

1. There were once three beautiful sisters, who were daughters of the king and queen. Of these, Psyche was the most famous. And so, her reputation in the regions that were neighboring to her home was equal to that of Venus.
2. Venus was not only immortal, but also very proud. And so, she decided to find a punishment against the girl, who was neither a goddess nor immortal.
3. The beautiful goddess had no lack of plan. After she had chosen a way out of this difficulty, she called her son, Cupid, the god of love, to her.
4. To him, she pointed out her difficulty and said: "All seek Psyche and they do not even pretend to worship me now. Because of the injuries which she has done to your mother, she ought to pay penalties. This work is suitable to you."
5. Cupid quickly prepared to help his mother.
6. He hurried to the garden of Venus, in which there were two fountains, one of which was sweet and the other not sweet.
7. After he had obtained water from each fountain, he sought Psyche, who was asleep at home.
8. He himself, when he saw her, was almost moved, because she was very pretty, but the god remembered his mother and touched the girl with the water that was not sweet and with his arrow.
9. Psyche was aroused, but she was not able to see Cupid. He was frightened and placed the sweet water on her.
10. Afterwards, Psyche, although she was pretty, was also very unhappy. Because she was not loved by Venus, no one wanted to marry her.
11. And so, Psyche remained at home and the father and mother of the girl showed a similar lack of hope.
12. This had been said by the oracle: "You will be married not by a man, but by one against whom no one can stand."

205. Practice Exercises

No. 151. Translate these phrases with positive degree adjectives:

1. iter difficile
2. domum miseram
3. virorum liberorum
4. timores acres
5. exercitus similes
6. diem longum
7. in monte alto
8. flumina celeria
9. vias latas
10. Puellarum puchrarum

No. 152. Translate these phrases with comparative degree adjectives:

1. viae angustiores
2. puer altior
3. puellarum laetiorum
4. populus amicior
5. iter longius
6. in locis gratioribus
7. sororum clariorum
8. hiemem longiorem
9. flumina latiora
10. virum audaciorem

No. 153. Translate these phrases with superlative degree adjectives:

1. fontis dulcissimi
2. ex hortis pulcherrimis
3. templum angustissimum
4. ob memoria miserrimas
5. oracula clarissima
6. civis laetissimus
7. ex agro latissimo
8. cum matribus pulcherrimis
9. in navi novissima
10. nomina brevissima

No. 154. Translate these sentences:

1. Is est locus miserrimus.
2. Fortissimi homines ad insulam pervenerunt.
3. Acerrimi equi erant inter primos.
4. Quid ad Graeciam est iter facilius?
5. Populus Italiae est liberrimus.
6. Haec est angustior pars aquae.
7. Hae res sunt quoque simillimae.
8. Flumen altissimum et latius vidimus.
9. Nostri ad urbem viam breviorem delegerunt.
10. Aedificium altum ab hoc loco videre potestis.

206. New Reading Vocabulary

NOUNS
maritus, mariti, m., husband (marital)
Zephyrus, Zephyri, m., Zephyr, west wind
vox, vocis, f., voice

ADJECTIVES
posterus, postera, posterum, next,
following (posterior)

ADVERBS
quam, than
multo, much
maxime, most, especially (maximum)
antea, before
magis, more

CONJUNCTIONS
aut . . . aut, either . . . or

Mathematical Terms Derived from Latin

plus, more, increased by.
minus, less, diminished by.
multiplication, from **multiplicare,** to make manifold or many fold.
division, from **dividere,** divide.
subtraction, from **subtrahere,** withdraw, draw from beneath.
addition, from **addere,** add to, or **additio,** adding.
ratio, from **ratio,** reason.
quotient, from **quotiens,** how often, how many times.
sum, from **summa,** sum or total, or **summus,** highest.
number and **numeral,** from **numerus,** number.
integer, from **integer,** whole, untouched.
fraction, from **frangere,** break.
percent and **per centum,** from **per centum,** by the hundred, in the hundred.

207. New Reading Grammar—Syntax of Comparisons

A.   LATIN HAS TWO WAYS TO SHOW COMPARISON BETWEEN TWO THINGS.

1. Use **quam,** *with the same case for the two things being compared.*
   Ego altior sum quam tu, I am taller than you.
   Ego and **tu** are both in the nominative case.
   amicior illi quam huic, more friendly to that one than to this one.
   illi and **huic** are both in the dative case.

2. Use the ablative case after the comparative degree, without **quam.**
   Ego altior sum te, I am taller than you.
   Ego is in the nominative case; **te** is in the ablative case.
   amicior illi hoc, more friendly to that one than to this one.
   illi is in the dative case; **hoc** is in the ablative case.

B.   SOME ADJECTIVES HAVE IRREGULAR COMPARATIVE AND SUPERLATIVE DEGREES; THIS IS KNOWN AS IRREGULAR COMPARISON.

Positive	*Comparative*	*Superlative*
bonus, -a, -um, good	**melior, melius,** better	**optimus, -a, -um,** best
magnus, -a, -um, large	**maior, maius,** larger	**maximus, -a, -um,** largest
malus, -a, -um, bad	**peior, peius,** worse	**pessimus, -a, -um,** worst
parvus, -a, -um, small	**minor, minus,** smaller	**minimus, -a, -um,** smallest
multus, -a, -um, much	—, **plus,** more	**plurimus, -a, -um,** most
multi, -ae, -a, many	**plures, plura,** more	**plurimi, -ae, -a,** most

The superlative degree of **posterus** is **postremus, -a, -um** or **postumus, -a, -um.**

Although the comparison of the above adjectives is irregular, the declension of the comparative and superlative degrees is regular, with the exception of **plus.**

C. PLUS IS A NEUTER NOUN IN THE SINGULAR AND AN ADJECTIVE IN THE PLURAL.

Case	Singular	Plural	
	Neut.	Masc./Fem.	Neut.
Nom.	plus	plures	plura
Gen.	pluris	plurium	plurium
Dat.	—	pluribus	pluribus
Acc.	plus	plures	plura
Abl.	plure	pluribus	pluribus
Voc.	plus	plures	plura

D. MOST ADJECTIVES ENDING IN A VOWEL AND -us ARE COMPARED IN THE FOLLOWING WAY:

Positive	Comparative	Superlative
idoneus, -a, -um	magis idoneus, -a, -um	maxime idoneus, -a, -um
suitable	more suitable	most suitable

idoneus, -a, -um is declined regularly in all three degrees (positive, comparative, and superlative). **Magis** and **maxime** are adverbs; therefore, they are not declined.

208. Reading

Cupido et Psyche (cont'd)

1. Locus, quem oraculum demonstraverat et in quo maritus illam exspectabat, summo in monte erat.
2. Illa ipsa etiam miserior aut patre aut matre erat. Itaque ad suam fortunam malam se dedere constituit.
3. Mox postea puella, cum matre patreque atque multis ex amicis suis, ad montem a populo oppidi, in quo habitabat, ducta est.
4. Hi eam solam ibi relinquerunt, quamquam pro ea magnopere dolebant, et se receperunt.
5. Psyche, quae summo in monte diu steterat et omnia in eo loco timebat, ab uno ex ventis, Zephyro, a monte ad terram pulcherrimam celeriter portata est.

Cupid and Psyche (cont'd)

1. The place which the oracle had pointed out and in which her husband was waiting for her, was on the top of a mountain.
2. She herself was more unhappy than either her father or mother. And so, she decided to surrender herself to her bad fortune.
3. Soon afterwards, the girl, with her mother and father and many of her friends, was led to the mountain by the people of the town in which she lived.
4. They left her there alone, although they felt very sorry for her, and departed.
5. Psyche, who had stayed on top of the mountain for a long time and was afraid of everything in that place, was carried quickly from the mountain to a very beautiful land by one of the winds, Zephyr.

6. Postquam breve tempus dormiverat, circum se spectabat et in silvam, quae propinqua erat agro, in quo a Zephyro relicta erat, audacter ambulavit.

7. In silva domum, quae pulchrior erat ulla quam antea viderat, repperit. Ad domum cucurrit.

8. Omnia in domo ei erant gratissima et ipsa tum vero laetissima erat.

9. Mox vocam audivit, sed neque virum neque mulierem vidit. Vox dixit: "Haec domus tua est et nos servi tui erimus. Omnia quae rogabis faciemus."

10. Postea in domo habitabat et laetior erat quam ulla puella in terra illa. Nil cupiebat.

11. Domum, servos, omnia bona, et maritum habebat, sed hunc non videbat. Noctu veniebat et ab ea ante diem properabat.

12. Quam ob rem maxime dolebat, sed maritum suum bene amabat. Ipse dixit: "Me nunc amas quod aequi sumus. Hoc iter optimum est."

13. Diu tamen laetissima erat, sed posteriore tempore matrem patremque sororesque quoque memoria tenebat et oppressa est quod ibi non erant.

14. Una nocte, ubi maritus eius venit, ab eo viam e difficultate sua petivit.

6. After she had slept for a short time, she looked around her and boldly walked into the forest, which was near the field in which she had been left by Zephyr.

7. In the forest, she found a house, which was prettier than any that she had seen before. She ran towards the house.

8. All the things in the house pleased her very much and she herself was then truly very happy.

9. Soon she heard a voice, but she saw neither man nor woman. The voice said: "This house is yours and we shall be your servants. We shall do everything that you ask."

10. Afterwards, she lived in the house and she was happier than any girl in that land. She wished for nothing.

11. She had a house, servants, all good things, and a husband, but she did not see him. He came at night and hurried away from her before day.

12. For this reason, she grieved greatly, but she loved her husband well. He said: "You love me now because we are equal. This way is best."

13. For a long time, however, she was very happy, but at a later time, she remembered her father and mother and also her sisters and was oppressed because they were not there.

14. One night, when her husband came, she sought from him a way out of her difficulty.

209. Practice Exercises

No. 155. Translate these sentences:

1. Hae turres altiores sunt quam illae.
2. Es altior patre tuo.
3. Illa itinera aliis faciliora non sunt.
4. Patri tuo quam matri similior es.
5. Homines multo fortiores mulieribus sunt.
6. Domus eius ruri novior est illa in urbe.
7. Puer laetior est quam soror.
8. Barbari multo audaciores sunt finitimis suis.
9. Ille vobis amicior quam mihi erit.
10. Estne manus celerior quam oculus?

No. 156. Give the English for these verb forms:

1. erunt
2. demonstratum est
3. constituit
4. parabitur
5. ducebant
6. relictus est
7. mittetur
8. portaris
9. videbamus
10. ambulavit

No. 157. Give the English for these adjectives:

1. plura	4. maioris	7. pluribus	10. maxime idoneum
2. melior	5. minorum	8. posteros	
3. pessimorum	6. plurimorum	9. magis idonei	

No. 158. Translate these adjective phrases:

1. in pluribus urbibus	6. plus aquae	11. die longiore
2. ex fontibus minoribus	7. tempus magis idoneum	12. plurimas civitates
3. virtutem maximam	8. rei pessimae	13. finem peiorem
4. vox optima	9. ad partem meliorem	14. annos optimos
5. de muris altioribus	10. cum maiore exercitu	15. soror minima

---

Geometric Terms Derived from Latin

perpendicular, from **per,** through, and **pendere,** hang.

circumference, from **circum,** around, and **ferre,** carry.

radius, from **radius,** staff, rod, ray.

arc, from **arcus,** bow, arc.

tangent, from **tangere,** touch.

angle, from **angulus,** angle, corner.

obtuse, from **obtundere,** strike.

acute, from **acuere,** sharpen.

triangle, from **tri,** three, and **angulus,** angle.

rectangle, from **rectus,** right, and **angulus,** angle.

Q. E. D., abbreviation of **quod erat demonstrandum,** which was to be demonstrated.

---

210. New Reading Vocabulary

NOUNS

imperium, imperii or **imperi, n.,** command (imperial)

verbum, verbi, n., word (verb)

uxor, uxoris, f., wife (uxorial)

lux, lucis, f., light (lucent)

ADJECTIVES

mortalis, mortale, mortal (mortality)

VERBS

conficio, conficere, confeci, confectus, finish, complete, carry out (confection)

plurimum posse, be most powerful

cado, cadere, cecidi, casurus, fall (cadence)

excito, excitare, excitavi, excitatus, arouse, stir up (excitement)

plus posse, be more powerful

ADVERBS

quam, as possible. With the superlative degree.

umquam, ever

supra, over, above. Also a preposition with the accusative case.

numquam, never

postridie, on the next day

CONJUNCTIONS

dum, while. With the present tense.

211. New Reading Grammar—Comparative and Superlative Adverbs

A. ADVERBS ARE COMPARED IN MUCH THE SAME WAY AS ADJECTIVES, BUT HAVE ONLY ONE FORM FOR EACH DEGREE. IN OTHER WORDS, ADVERBS ARE NOT DECLINED.

1. Regular adverbs are compared as follows:

Positive		*Comparative*		*Superlative*	
longe	far	**longius**	farther	**longissime**	farthest
misere	unhappily	**miserius**	more unhappily	**miserrime**	most unhappily
pulchre	beautifully	**pulchrius**	more beautifully	**pulcherrime**	most beautifully
acriter	keenly	**acrius**	more keenly	**acerrime**	most keenly
fortiter	bravely	**fortius**	more bravely	**fortissime**	most bravely
facile	easily	**facilius**	more easily	**facillime**	most easily

As you can see, in the positive degree, most adverbs end in **-e**, **-ter**, or **-iter**. In the comparative degree, most adverbs end in **-ius**, and in the superlative degree, most adverbs end in **-e**.

2. These adverbs are irregular:

Positive		*Comparative*		*Superlative*	
bene	well	**melius**	better	**optime**	best
magnopere	greatly	**magis**	more	**maxime**	most
male	badly	**peius**	worse	**pessime**	worst
multum	much	**plus**	more	**plurimum**	most
parum	little	**minus**	less	**minime**	least
diu	long	**diutius**	longer	**diutissime**	longest
saepe	often	**saepius**	more often	**saepissime**	most often

B. WHEN QUAM IS USED WITH THE SUPERLATIVE DEGREE OF AN ADJECTIVE OR ADVERB, IT MEANS *AS . . . AS POSSIBLE*.

quam pulcherrimus, as pretty (beautiful) as possible
quam pulcherrime, as prettily (beautifully) as possible

212. Reading

Cupido et Psyche (cont'd)

1. **Postridie ad Zephyrum quam celerrime contendit et illi id quod maritus suus dixerat narrabat.**
2. **Imperia Cupidinis facillime confecit et brevi tempore duae sorores eius ad domum eius a Zephyro celeriter portatae sunt.**

Cupid and Psyche (cont'd)

1. On the next day, she hurried as quickly as possible to Zephyr and told him what her husband had said.
2. He very easily carried out the commands of Cupid and in a short time, her two sisters were carried quickly to her house by Zephyr.

3. Psyche adventu earum laetissima erat et illis omnia sua demonstravit. Ipsae tamen postquam domum atque servos illius viderant inopiam eius bonae fortunae acerrime cognoverunt.

4. Multa rogabant: "Esne uxor laeta?" "Quis es maritus tuus?"

5. Magno cum studio verba eius audiebant. Vita eius melior quam vita earum esse videbatur.

6. Eam misserime conspiciebant. Eodem tempore spem maiorem videbant: "Num tu maritum tuum umquam vidisti? Maritus quem uxor numquam vidit optimus maritus esse non potest. Nonne verba oraculi memoria tenes? Ille aut serpens aut animal est."

7. Psyche consilio sororum suarum coacta est quod ab eis semper facillime ducebatur. Itaque lucem ac gladium cepit et haec in loco idoneo conlocavit.

8. Psyche consilium sororum suarum minime amabat, sed verba earum quam verba sua plus potereant. Illae plus facile quam ipsa dicere poterant.

9. Itaque ipsa lucem gladiumque paravit et maritus eius ad eam noctu venit. Ipsa maxime timebat, sed ei timorem suum non demonstrabat.

10. Dum ille dormit, lucem cepit et supra eum id tenebat. Quid vidit? Neque serpentem neque animal ante se conspexit. Erat unus ex deorum pulcherrimus atque gratissimus.

11. A timore liberata erat. Eum non diutius timebat, sed magis amabat.

12. Ut accidit tamen umerum eius luce tetegit et ille excitatus est. Ipse nullum verbum dixit, sed oculis suis eam monuit et alis celeribus eam reliquit.

13. Psyche ad terram cecidit. Cupido supra eam breve tempus volebat et dixit: "Contra imperia matris meae te amavi. Immortales mortales non saepe amant, sed te in matrimonium duxi et me interficere nunc cupis. Amor tuus minus fortis meo est."

14. His verbis puellam miserrimam reliquit et ad caelum volavit.

3. Psyche was very happy at their arrival and showed them all her possessions. They, however, after they had seen her house and servants, clearly recognized her lack of good fortune.

4. They asked many things: "Are you a happy wife?" "Who is your husband?"

5. They listened to her words with great eagerness. Her life seemed to be better than their life.

6. They looked at her most unhappily. At the same time, they saw a greater hope: "You haven't ever seen your husband, have you? A husband whom his wife has never seen can not be the best husband. You remember the words of the oracle, don't you? He is either a serpent or an animal."

7. Psyche was convinced by the plan of her sisters because she was always very easily influenced by them. And so, she took a light and a sword, and placed these things in a suitable place.

8. Psyche did not like her sisters' plan at all, but their words were more powerful than her own words. They were able to talk more easily than she.

9. And so she got the light and the sword ready, and her husband came to her at night. She was very much afraid, but she did not show her fear to him.

10. While he slept, she took the light and held it above him. What did she see? She saw in front of her neither a serpent nor an animal. He was one of the most handsome and pleasing of the gods.

11. She had been freed from fear. She no longer feared him, but loved him more.

12. As it happened, however, she touched his shoulder with the light and he was aroused. He said no word, but warned her with his eyes and left her on swift wings.

13. Psyche fell to the ground. Cupid flew above her for a short time and said: "I have loved you against the commands of my mother. Immortals do not often love mortals, but I married you and now, you want to kill me. Your love is less strong than mine."

14. With these words, he left the very unhappy girl and flew to the sky.

213. Practice Exercises

No. 159. Give the English for these adjectives and adverbs:

1. latus	8. libere	15. pulcherrimus	22. celerius
2. late	9. liberior	16. pulchre	23. celerrimus
3. latior	10. liberrimus	17. pulchrius	24. celerrime
4. latius	11. liberius	18. pulcherrime	25. acer
5. latissimus	12. liberrime	19. celer	26. acriter
6. latissime	13. pulcher	20. celeriter	27. acrior
7. liber	14. pulchrior	21. celerior	28. acrius

No. 160. Translate these sentences containing adverbs:

1. Gravissime oppugnabantur.
2. Fortius pugnat.
3. Celeriter incensi sunt.
4. Multo brevius dicent.
5. Audacissime monebitur.
6. Difficile aciem instruxerunt.
7. Acrius bellum gessit.
8. Superbe ambulant.
9. Gratius dabat.
10. Altissime laudatur.
11. Latius missis sunt.
12. Liberrime dedit.
13. Longissime navigat.
14. Miserius movet.
15. Nove videbantur.
16. Pulchrius movent.
17. Acerrime timebit.
18. Audacter capti sunt.
19. Brevissime dicebat.
20. Fortiter pugnant.

No. 161. Give the English for these adverbs:

1. bene	5. parum	9. plus	13. minus	17. diutissime
2. magnopere	6. diu	10. magis	14. saepius	18. saepissime
3. male	7. saepe	11. melius	15. maxime	19. optime
4. multum	8. diutius	12. peius	16. plurimum	20. pessime

No. 162. Translate these sentences containing adverbs:

1. Saepius perveniunt.
2. Quam diutissime pugnavit.
3. Magis excitatus est.
4. Plus impediebatur.
5. Optime amatus es.
6. Id saepissime auditum est.
7. Minus difficile ambulat.
8. Apud nos plurimum possunt.
9. Plus celeriter volat.
10. Multum diutius manebit.

REVIEW

214. Vocabulary Review

NOUNS

1. aestas
2. Creusa
3. Cupido
4. difficultas
5. fons
6. hiems
7. imperium
8. lux
9. maritus
10. matrimonium
11. multitudo
12. onus
13. oraculum
14. plus
15. portus
16. Psyche
17. soror
18. uxor
19. ventus
20. verbum

ADJECTIVES

1. aequus
2. dulcis
3. immortalis
4. maior
5. maximus
6. melior
7. minimus
8. minor
9. mortalis
10. optimus
11. peior
12. pessimus
13. plurimus
14. posterus
15. postumus

VERBS

1. cado
2. cogo
3. conficio
4. constituo
5. convenio
6. dedo
7. deligo
8. dormio
9. excito
10. incendo
11. opprimo
12. plurimum posse
13. plus posse
14. recipio
15. suscipio

ADVERBS

1. antea
2. bis
3. magis
4. maxime
5. multo
6. numquam
7. olim
8. postridie
9. quam
10. supra

CONJUNCTIONS

1. aut . . . aut
2. dum
3. nam
4. quamquam
5. quoque

215. Practice Exercises

No. 163. Translate these phrases:

1. una ex sororum
2. tria flumina
3. duos annos
4. mille anni
5. duas uxores
6. centum verba
7. unius vocis
8. viginti fontes
9. quarta hora
10. quinto die
11. secundo anno
12. septimum verbum
13. primum oraculum
14. in quarto portu
15. ex sexta porta

No. 164. Translate these adjective phrases:

1. longiorem hiemem
2. pulcherrima aestas
3. longissimorum annorum
4. dulcius verbum
5. onus simillimum
6. vocis immortalis
7. iter facilius
8. luces clariores
9. difficultatis acerrimae
10. maritorum fortiorum

No. 165. Give the English for these adjectives:

1. dulcis, dulcior, dulcissimus
2. acer, acrior, acerrimus
3. longus, longior, longissimus
4. similis, similior, simillimus
5. altus, altior, altissimus
6. liber, liberior, liberrimus
7. celer, celerior, celerrimus
8. latus, latior, latissimus
9. clarus, clarior, clarissimus
10. audax, audacior, audacissimus

No. 166. Give the English for these adjectives:

1. magnus, maior, maximus
2. parvus, minor, minimus
3. bonus, melior, optimus
4. malus, peior, pessimus
5. multus, plus, plurimus
6. multi, plures, plurimi

No. 167. Translate into English:

1. longius ambulabat
2. misere oppressus est
3. parum dormit
4. diutissime incendet
5. acrius excitati sunt
6. magis tangebant
7. facilius dediderunt
8. plurimum possunt
9. plus poterit
10. minus facile cogentur

216. Reading

PHAEDRUS

Phaedrus, a freedman of Augustus, lived in the first half of the first century A.D. Five books of his **Fables** are extant. These are based on early folk tales and on the Greek fables of Aesop. Phaedrus' work, in turn, furnished the material for the French fabulist, La Fontaine.

Qui se laudari gaudet verbis subdolis,
sera dat poenas turpes paenitentia.
Cum de fenestra corvus raptum caesum
comesse vellet, celsa residens arbore,
vulpes hunc vidit; deinde sic coepit loqui:
"O qui tuarum, corve, pinnarum est nitor.

Quantum decoris corpore et vultu geris.
Si vocem haberes, nulla prior ales foret."
At ille stultus, dum vult vocem ostendere,
emisit ore caesum, quem celeriter
dolosa vulpes avidis rapuit dentibus.
Tum demum ingemuit corvi deceptus stupor.

STABAT MATER

The thirteenth-century scholar and mystic St. Bonaventura is sometimes credited with writing the **Stabat Mater,** which has been set to music by many composers during the last three centuries.

Stabat mater dolorosa
iuxta crucem lacrimosa,
dum pendebat filius,
cuius animam gementem,
contristantem et dolentem
pertransivit gladius.
O quam tristis et afflicta
fuit illa benedicta
mater unigenti,
quae maerebat et dolebat
et tremebat, dum videbat
nati poenas incliti!
Quis est homo qui non fleret,
matrem Christi si videret
in tanto supplicio?
Quis non posset contristari
piam matrem contemplari
dolentem cum filio?
Pro peccatis suae gentis
vidit Iesum in tormentis

et flagellis subditum;
vidit suum dulcem natum
morientem, desolatum,
dum emisit spiritum
Eia mater, fons amoris!
Me sentire vim doloris
fac, ut tecum lugeam.
Fac ut ardeat cor meum
in amando Christum Deum,
ut sibi complaceam.
Sancta mater, istud agas,
crucifixi fige plagas
cordi meo valide;
tui nati vulnerati,
tam dignati pro me pati,
poenas mecum divide.
Fac me vere tecum flere,
crucifixo condolere,
donec ego vixero;
iuxta crucem tecum stare,

meque tibi sociare
in planctu desidero.
Virgo virginium praeclara,
mihi iam non sis amara,
fac me tecum plangere;
fac ut portem Christi mortem,
passionis fac consortem
et plagas recolere.
Fac me plagis vulnerari,
cruce had inebriari,
et cruore filii;
per te, Virgo, sim defensus
inflammatus et accensum
in die iudicii.
Fac me cruce custodiri
morte Christi praemuniri,
confoveri gratia.
Quando corpus morietur,
fac ut animae donetur
paradisi gloria.

INDIRECT STATEMENT

Medical Abbreviations Derived from Latin

R, recipe, take
d., da, give
gtt., guttae, drops
Lb., libra, pound
ol., oleum, oil
pulv., pulvis, powder
c, cum, with
os., os, ora, mouth
t.i.d., ter in die, three times a day
quotid., quotidie, every day
omn. hor., omni hora, every hour
noct., nocte, at night
t.i.n., ter in nocte, three times a night
h.s., hora somni, at the hour of sleep, at bedtime
non rep., non repetatur, do not repeat (literally, let it not be repeated)
Sig., S., signetur, let it be marked (direction to patient)
Q.v., quantum vis, as much as you wish
a.c, ante cibum, before food, before meals
Q.s., quantum sufficiat, a sufficient quantity

bib., bibe, drink
cap., capsula, capsule
gr., granum, grain
mist., mistura, mixture
ung., unguentum, ointment
aq., aqua, water
no., numero, number
p.o., per os, by mouth
q.i.d., quater in die, four times a day
stat., statim, immediately
H., hora, hour
omn. noct., omni nocte, every night
q.i.n., quater in nocte, four times a night
Q.h., quaque hora, every hour.
Q.2h., every two hours
p.r.n., pro re nata, as the occasion arises, as needed
alt. dieb., alternis diebus, every other day, on alternate days
rep., repetatur, let it be repeated
p.c., post cibum, after food, after meals

217. New Reading Vocabulary

NOUNS

numerus, numeri, m., number (numeral)
satis, n., enough. Same spelling in all cases, (satisfy)
modus, modi, m., manner, way (mode)
ordo, ordinis, m., rank, order (order, ordinal)

vulnus, vulneris, n., wound (vulnerable)
formica, formicae, f., ant
genus, generis, n., kind, class (genus)
dux, ducis, m., leader (duke)

VERBS

invenio, invenire, inveni, inventus, find, come upon (invent)

ADVERBS

tam, so
satis, enough (satisfaction)
tandem, finally

218. New Reading Grammar—Infinitives (Morphology)

REGULAR LATIN VERBS HAVE SIX DIFFERENT INFINITIVES, THREE IN THE ACTIVE VOICE, THREE IN THE PASSIVE.

All infinitives are formed on the same pattern. For example, the infinitives for **amo** are:

Active: **amare**, to love
          amavisse, to have loved
          amaturus esse, to be about to love
Passive: **amari**, to be loved
          amatus esse, to have been loved
          amatum iri, to be about to be loved

1. *The present active infinitive is the second principal part:*

   amare, to love   **posse**, to be able   **habere**, to have   **ire**, to go   **esse**, to be
   capere, to seize   **ferre**, to carry   **audire**, to hear   **ducere**, to lead **velle**, to wish

   The verb **fio** does not have a present active infinitive.

2. *The present passive infinitive ends in -i-. Note that the e/i-conjugation drops the -er-.*

   amari, to be loved   **fieri**, to be made   **audiri**, to be heard   **ferri**, to be carried
   capi, to be seized   **haberi**, to be had   **duci**, to be led

   The verbs **sum, possum, volo, nolo,** and **malo** do not have present passive infinitives, since only transitive verbs have passive forms. **Eo** does have a present passive infinitive, **iri**, but this is only used with the future passive infinitive.

3. *The perfect active infinitive is formed from the third principal part and the ending -isse.*

   amavisse, to have loved   **habuisse**, to have had   **duxisse**, to have led
   cepisse, to have seized   **audivisse**, to have heard   **fuisse**, to have been
   isse, to have gone   **voluisse**, to have wanted   **tulisse**, to have carried
   potuisse, to have been able

4. *The perfect passive infinitive is formed with the fourth principal part and esse, the present active infinitive of the verb sum.*

   amatus, -a, -um esse, to have been loved   **habitus, -a, -um esse**, to have been had
   ductus, -a, -um esse, to have been led   **capitus, -a, -um esse**, to have been seized
   auditus, -a, -um esse, to have been heard   **latus, -a, -um esse**, to have been carried
   factus, -a, -um esse, to have been made

   The verbs **sum, possum, eo, volo, nolo,** and **malo** do not have a perfect passive infinitive.

5. *The future active infinitive is formed by adding -ur- to the fourth principal part before the regular ending, together with esse.*

This modification of the fourth principal part creates the future active participle, which will be considered in the next chapter.

amaturus, -a, -um esse, to be about to love
habiturus, -a, -um esse, to be about to have
docturus, -a, -um esse, to be about to lead
capturus, -a, -um esse, to be about to seize

futurus, -a, -um esse, to be about to be
iturus, -a, -um esse, to be about to go
laturus, -a, -um esse, to be about to carry

The verbs **possum, volo, nolo,** and **malo** do not have a future active infinitive.

6. *There is a future passive infinitive in Latin, but this is rarely used.*

It is formed from the neuter nominative singular of the fourth principal part (technically, this is the accusative of the **supine**) and **iri,** the present passive infinitive of **eo.** The future passive participle does not decline.

amatum iri, to be about to be loved
ductum iri, to be about to be led
auditum iri, to be about to be heard
factum iri, to be about to be made

habitum iri, to be about to be had
captum iri, to be about to be seized
latum iri, to be about to be carried

219. New Reading Grammar—Infinitives (Syntax/Usage)

You have already met the complementary or completing infinitive.

Id capere cupit.   He wants *to take* it.
Amari cupit.   He wants *to be loved.*

The infinitive is also used to express:

1. A SUBJECT

Id invenire difficile est.   It is difficult *to find* it. *To find* it is difficult.

In this sentence, the infinitive, **invenire,** can be considered the subject of the verb, **est.** In such a case, the infinitive is considered a nominative singular neuter noun (strictly speaking, all infinitives are in fact verbal nouns).

2. A DIRECT OBJECT

Natare amat.   He likes *to swim.*

In this sentence, the infinitive, **natare,** is the direct object of the verb, **amat.** In such a case, the infinitive is considered an accusative singular neuter noun (again, strictly speaking, all infinitives are in fact verbal nouns).

3. *HISTORICAL INFINITIVES:* INFINITIVES CAN BE USED IN PLACE OF FINITE VERBS (IN ENGLISH THEY MUST STILL BE TRANSLATED AS THOUGH THEY ARE FINITE) TO EMPHASIZE THE PURE VERBAL ACTION OVER THE AGENT OF THE ACTION.

Such infinitives are called *historical infinitives* and are probably one of the earliest uses of the infinitive.

In viis urbis heri currere, clamare, fortiter pugnare.
In the streets of the city yesterday (there were) running, shouting and fighting bravely.
(Men were) running, shouting and fighting bravely in the streets of the city yesterday.
The subject of an historical infinitive is nominative.
Homo acriter pugnare, the man fought fiercely.

220. New Reading Grammar—Indirect Statement (Accusative /Infinitive)

If we say *the man is working,* we are giving a direct statement. If that direct statement is reported, for example, *he said that the man was working,* the sentence now includes two clauses, the second of which, *that the man was working,* is known as an indirect statement (**oratio oblique** in Latin).

An indirect statement can occur after a verb showing mental processes such as saying, thinking, knowing, or hearing. In English, an indirect statement is generally introduced by the word *that.* In Latin, the nominative subject of the original direct statement becomes an accusative subject, while the finite verb of the original direct statement becomes an infinitive. Indirect statement, therefore, is often referred to as the *accusative/infinitive* construction. You should be alert to the possibility that this construction is being used when you encounter an accusative after or together with a verb of mental process.

Virum laborare dico.   I say *that* the man *is working.*

virum laborare, *that the man is working,* is an indirect statement. A direct statement would be **vir laborat,** *The man is working.* Since the verb of mental process, **dico,** introduces an indirect statement, the nominative **vir** of the original direct statement must become the accusative **virum,** while the finite verb **laborat** of the original direct statement must become the infinitive **laborare.**

1. THE TENSE OF THE INFINITIVE IS RELATIVE TO THE TENSE OF THE MAIN VERB, AND IS DETEMINED BY WHEN THE ACTION OF THE INDIRECT STATEMENT TAKES PLACE.

    a. *If the action of the indirect statement takes place at the same time as the action of the main verb, the present infinitve is used, regardless of the tense of the main verb.*

Virum laborare dico.	I say that the man is working.
Virum laborare dixi.	I said that the man was working.
Virum laborare dicam.	I shall say that the man is working.
Virum amari dico.	I say that the man is loved.
Virum amari dixi.	I said that the man was loved.
Virum amari dicam.	I shall say that the man is loved.

b. *If the action of the indirect statement takes place earlier than the action of the main verb, the perfect infinitive is used, regardless of the tense of the main verb.*

Virum laboravisse dico.	I say that the man worked.
Virum laboravisse dixi.	I said that the man had worked.
Virum laboravisse dicam.	I shall say that the man worked.
Virum amatum esse dico.	I say that the man was loved.
Virum amatum esse dixi.	I said that the man had been loved.
Virum amatum esse dicam.	I shall say that the man was loved.

c. *If the action of the indirect statement takes place later than the action of the main verb, the future infinitive is used, regardless of the tense of the main verb. Note, however, that the future passive infinitive is rarely used.*

Virum laboraturum esse dico.	I say that the man will work.
Virum laboraturum esse dixi.	I said that the man would work.
Virum laboraturum esse dicam.	I shall say that the man will work.

2. SUBJECTS OF INFINITIVES, IN INDIRECT STATEMENT AND ELSEWHERE, ARE IN THE ACCUSATIVE CASE, WITH THE EXCEPTION OF THE *HISTORICAL INFINITIVE* AS NOTED ABOVE.

virum laborare   viros laborare   agrum arari   agros arari

3. WHEN THE PERFECT PASSIVE AND FUTURE ACTIVE INFINITIVES ARE USED IN INDIRECT STATEMENT, THE PARTICIPIAL PORTION (THE PART BASED ON THE FOURTH PRINCIPAL PART) MUST BE IN THE ACCUSATIVE TO AGREE WITH ITS ACCUSATIVE SUBJECTS.

Since participles are by definition adjectives, they must also agree in number and gender with their subjects. (Participles are covered in greater detail in Section 224 below.)

Agrum aratum esse dicit.	He says that the field has been plowed.
Agros aratos esse dicit.	He says that the fields have been plowed.
Virum laboraturum esse dicit.	He says that the man is going to work.
Viros laboraturos esse dicit.	He says that the men are going to work.

221. Reading

Cupido et Psyche (cont'd)

1. Postquam Cupido uxorem suam tam celeriter reliquerat, illa circum se spectavit. Omnis spes ab ea interea cecidit atque sua vita laeta discessit, nam horti pulchri ac domus magna nunc ibi non erant.

2. Non longe ab urbe, ubi antea habitaverat, erat sola. Maxime dolebat.

3. Sorores fabulam eius magno cum studio audiverunt. Sibi dixerunt: "Cupido unam ex nobis nunc certe deliget."

Cupid and Psyche (cont'd)

1. After Cupid had left his wife so quickly, she looked around her. All hope fell from her meanwhile and her happy life departed, for the beautiful gardens and large house were not there now.

2. She was alone, not far from the city where she had lived before. She grieved very much.

3. Her sisters heard her story with great eagerness. They said to themselves: "Cupid will now certainly choose one of us."

4. Prima luce postridie illae duae ad montem properaverunt et Zephyrum audacissime appellabant. Utraque tamen ad terram sub monte cecidit et interfecta est, quod deus venti eam non iuvit.

5. Psyche interea maritum suum noctu dieque petebat. Montem altissimum, in quo templum magnum erat, conspexit. Eratne templum Cupidinis?

6. In templo aliud genus rei invenit. Omnibus in partibus aedifici frumentum videbat.

7. Quo modo multa genera frumenti in ordine ponere poterit?

8. Nunc etiam magis dolebat, sed erat puella fortissima.

9. Dum illa laborat, Ceres, dea frumenti, in templum venit, nam id erat templum Cereris. Ceres puellam miserrimam iuvare cupiebat quod Psyche bene laboraverat et frumentum in templo in ordine bene posuerat.

10. Dea ei auxilium dare cupiebat quod illa pro ea satis iam fecerat. Dixit: "Venus tibi auxilium non dat. Dea bona est, sed filium suum, maritum tuum, maxime amat et eum dedere non cupit."

11. Psyche nullam spem habebat, sed tamed ad domum deae pulcherrimae properavit.

12. Ibi Venerem superbam invenit, quae dixit: "Nonne tu me tandem memoria tenes? Maritus tuus vulnus quod tu luce ei dedisti nunc curat. Postquam hunc laborem confecisti tibi eum dare cupio."

13. Hoc opus erat: Magnum numerum et multa genera frumenti sine ordine ante se videbat.

14. Mors melior quam hoc opus esse videbatur. Ipsa nil fecit. Labor maximus erat, sed Cupido uxorem suam mox vidit et ei auxilium misit.

15. Parva formica, quae erat dux sociorum amicorumque suorum, ad eam venit.

16. Omnes hae formicae brevissimo tempore frumentum in ordine conlocaverunt. Fugerunt postquam hoc fecerant.

4. At dawn the next day, those two hurried to the mountain and very boldly called Zephyr by name. Each, however, fell to the ground at the foot of the mountain and was killed, because the god of the wind did not help her.

5. Psyche, meanwhile, sought her husband night and day. She saw a very high mountain, on which there was a large temple. Was it the temple of Cupid?

6. In the temple, she found another kind of thing. In all parts of the building, she saw grain.

7. How will she be able to put many kinds of grain in order?

8. Now she grieved even more, but she was a very brave girl.

9. While she was working, Ceres, the goddess of grain, came into the temple, for this was the temple of Ceres. Ceres wished to help the very unhappy girl, because Psyche had worked well and had put the grain in the temple in order well.

10. The goddess wished to give help to her because she had already done enough for her. She said: "Venus does not give help to you. The goddess is good, but she loves her son, your husband, very much and does not want to give him up."

11. Psyche had no hope, but nevertheless, she hurried to the house of the very beautiful goddess.

12. There she found the proud Venus, who said: "You finally remember me, don't you? Your husband is now caring for the wound that you gave him with the light. After you have finished this work, I want to give him to you."

13. This was the task: She saw in front of her a great amount and many kinds of grain without order.

14. Death seemed to be better than this task. She did nothing. The work was very great, but Cupid soon saw his wife and sent help to her.

15. A small ant, that was the leader of his comrades and friends, came to her.

16. All these ants placed the grain in order in a very short time. They fled after they had done this.

222. Practice Exercises

No. 168. Give the English for these infinitives:

1. monere
2. auxisse
3. iaci
4. positurum esse
5. fugisse
6. impedire
7. natavisse
8. territurum esse
9. manisse
10. auditurum esse
11. scripsisse
12. pugnaturum esse
13. laudaturum esse
14. excitari
15. petitum esse
16. mittere
17. tangi
18. oppugnatum esse
19. sciri
20. gesturum esse
21. accipi
22. victum esse
23. dici
24. ambulaturum esse

No. 169. Change these infinitives to the active and give the English meanings:

1. peti
2. captum esse
3. haberi
4. rectum esse
5. portari
6. vocatum esse
7. ferri
8. datum esse
9. instrui
10. verti

No. 170. Change these infinitives to the passive and give the English meanings:

1. narrare
2. defendisse
3. videre
4. iuvare
5. pugnavisse
6. movisse
7. vocare
8. invenire
9. necavisse
10. relinquere

No. 171. Give the future active infinitive of these verbs and the English meanings:

1. esse
2. iubere
3. facere
4. defendere
5. oppugnare
6. properare
7. capere
8. invenire
9. dare
10. ponere

No. 172. Translate these sentences:

1. Illi milites viros auxilium portaturos esse dixerunt.
2. Putatisne opus vestrum factum esse?
3. Nos hostes quam celerrime venturos esse sperabamus.
4. Puellae latae esse videntur.
5. Hic rex bene regere cupiebat.
6. Ille appellari non cupiet.
7. Oppidum nostrum defendere optimum est.
8. Spem habuisse melius erat quam se recepisse.
9. Celeritatem augeri posse nuntiavit.
10. Nos locum meliorem invenire iussit.

Familiar Abbreviations

i.e., id est, that is.
pro and **con, pro et contra,** for and against.
etc., et cetera, and the rest; and so forth.
e.g., exempli gratia, for (the sake of) example.
no., numero, by number.

viz., videlicet, namely, that is to say; introduces further explanation.
d.v. or **D.V., Deo volente,** God willing; if God is willing.
vox pop., vox populi, the voice of the people.

223. New Reading Vocabulary

NOUNS
lana, lanae, f., wool
ovis, ovis, f., sheep
pulchritudo, pulchritudinis, f., beauty (pulchritude)

ADJECTIVES
utilis, utile, useful (utility)

VERBS
spero, sperare, speravi, speratus, hope (aspire)
puto, putare, putavi, putatus, think, believe (putative)
reporto, reportare, reportavi, reportatus, carry back, bring back (reporter)

224. New Reading Grammar—Participles

A. REGULAR LATIN VERBS HAVE FOUR PARTICIPLES OR VERBAL ADJECTIVES: THE PRESENT ACTIVE, THE PERFECT PASSIVE, THE FUTURE ACTIVE, AND THE FUTURE PASSIVE.

They have some of the qualities of verbs (tense, voice, and mood) and some of the qualities of adjectives (case, number, and gender). They are not used as the main verb of a sentence, but in addition to the main verb. In English, participles generally end in -*ing*: singing, dancing, having, going, doing. The participles of **amo** are:

Active:	**amans**	loving	**amaturus** about to love
Passive:	**amatus**	having been loved	**amandus** deserving to be loved, being loved

1. *The present active participle is formed from the present stem and -ns/nt.*

   The -**ns** only shows in the nominative singular of all three genders, and the accusative singular of neuters. All other forms have -**nt**, as indicated later.

amans	loving	**habens**	having	**nolens**	not wishing
ducens	leading	**capiens**	seizing	**ferens**	carrying
audiens	hearing	**potens**	having		
iens	going	**volens**	wishing		

   Sum, malo, and **fio** do not have present active participles.

   The action of the present active participle occurs at the same time as the action of the main verb, as in the sentence *I am carrying the book.*

2. *The perfect passive participle is the fourth principal part.*

amatus, -a, -um	having been loved	**habitus, -a, -um**	having been had
ductus, -a, -um	having been led	**captus, -a, -um**	having been seized
auditus, -a, -um	having been heard	**factus, -a, -um**	having been made
latus, -a, -um	having been carried		

   Sum, possum, volo, nolo, and **malo** do not have perfect passive participles. The perfect passive participle of **eo** is **itus, -a, -um.**

   The action of the perfect passive participle occurs before the action of the main verb, as in *The woman, having been loved, was happy.*

3. *The future active participle is formed from the fourth principal part, ending in -urus, -a, -um.*

amaturus, -a, -um	about to love	**habiturus, -a, -um**	about to have
ducturus, -a, -um	about to lead	**capturus, -a, -um**	about to seize
auditurus, -a, -um	about to hear	**futurus, -a, -um**	about to be
iturus, -a, -um	about to go	**laturus, -a, -um**	about to carry

Futurus, the future active participle, is used as the fourth principal part of **sum.** Many dictionaries frequently list future active participles as the fourth principal part of verbs that are not transitive (i.e., they cannot have passive forms). These future active participles are readily identifiable by the **-urus** ending. The verbs **possum, volo, nolo, malo,** and **fio** do not have future active participles.

The action of the future active participle occurs after the action of the main verb, as in *The army was about to seize the town.*

4. *The future passive participle is formed from the present stem and -ndus.*

amandus, -a, -um	deserving to be loved, being loved
habendus, -a, -um	deserving to be had, being had
ducendus, -a, -um	deserving to be led, being led
capiendus, -a, -um	deserving to be taken, being taken
audiendus, -a, -um	deserving to be heard, being heard
eundus, -a, -um	deserving to be gone, being gone
faciendus, -a, -um	deserving to be made, being made
ferendus, -a, -um	deserving to be carried, being carried

Sum, possum, volo, molo, and **malo** do not have future passive participles.

The action of the future passive participle occurs after the action of the main verb, as in *the song, deserving to be heard/being heard/worthy to be heard.*

The future passive participle, also known as the gerundive, normally carries with it a sense of obligation or necessity. You will learn more about this participle in Section 230 later in this chapter.

B. IT IS IMPORTANT TO REMEMBER THAT PARTICIPLES ARE VERBAL ADJECTIVES.

Thus, like verbs, they have voice, tense, and mood, (participle *is* the mood), and like adjectives, they must agree with their nouns in case, number, and gender.

1. *Present participles have a stem ending generally in -nt and take third declensional ending (i-stem), as follows:*

Case	Singular		Plural		
	Masc./Fem.	Neut.	Masc./Fem.	Neut.	
Nom.	**amans**	**amans**	**amantes**	**amantia**	the loving
Gen.	**amantis**	**amantis**	**amantium**	**amantium**	of the loving
Dat.	**amanti**	**amanti**	**amantibus**	**amantibus**	to, for the loving
Acc.	**amantem**	**amans**	**amantes**	**amantia**	the loving
Abl.	**amanti**	**amanti**	**amantibus**	**amantibus**	from/with/by/in the loving

Note with **eo** that the genitive of **iens** is **euntis** (and the stem used for the remainder of the declensional pattern is therefore **eunt-**).

2. The perfect passive and future active and passive participles decline as first and second declension adjectives.

C. PARTICIPLES OFTEN ARE BEST TRANSLATED BY A SUBORDINATE CLAUSE IN ENGLISH BEGINNING WITH *when, who, because, if,* OR *although.*

Miles captus non timebat.	The soldier, although he was captured, was not afraid.
Miles captus timebat.	The soldier, because he was captured, was afraid.
Miles pugnans necatus est.	The soldier, when he was fighting, was killed, *or* The soldier, who was fighting, was killed.

225. Reading

Cupido et Psyche (cont'd)

1. **Venus ad templum suum multo die venit et ad illam partem templi ubi puellam reliquerat sine mora properavit. Ipsa puellam miseram ante se etiam tum laborem difficile habere sperabat.**

2. **Ubi laborem confectum esse vidit, filium suum id fecisse putabat et puellae cibum minimum dedit.**

3. **Postridie puellam ad se venire iussit. Dea ad silvam in qua erant multae oves, quarum lana erat aurea, currere et lanam reportare illam iussit.**

4. **Cum illa ad flumen pervenit non solum oves sed etiam deum fluminis invenit.**

5. **Ille dixit flumen celerrimum esse atque oves die maxime inimicas esse, sed demonstravit oves noctu futuras esse dulciores. Quam ob rem illa ad noctem exspectavit et oves dormire invenit.**

6. **Labor eius facillimus erat quod lana ovium in arboribus erat. Oves non etiam tetigerat, sed auxilio dei multam lanam auream ab arboribus obtinuit et eodem die ad. Venerem, dominam suam, properavit, quod pro illa omnia bene facere cupiebat.**

7. **Postquam ad Venerem venerat et sub pedibus illius lanam posuerat, Psyche deam eam liberaturam esse atque se maritum suum recepturam esse sperabat.**

8. **Qua de causa spes eius celeriter fugit nam domina eius illam sine auxilio alterius lanam non obtinuisse dixit.**

Cupid and Psyche (cont'd)

1. Venus came to her temple late in the day and hurried without delay to that part of the temple where she had left the girl. She hoped that the unhappy girl had difficult work ahead of her even then.

2. When she saw that the work had been finished, she thought that her son had done it and she gave the girl very little food.

3. On the next day, she ordered the girl to come to her. The goddess ordered her to run to the forest in which there were many sheep, whose wool was golden, and to bring back the wool.

4. When she came to the river, she found not only the sheep, but also the god of the river.

5. He said that the river was very swift and the sheep were especially unfriendly in the daytime, but he pointed out that the sheep would be more gentle at night. For this reason, she waited until night and found that the sheep were sleeping.

6. Her work was very easy because the wool of the sheep was on the trees. She had not even touched the sheep, but with the help of the god, she obtained much golden wool from the trees and the same day she hurried to Venus, her mistress, because she wished to do everything well for her.

7. After she came to Venus and placed the wool at her feet, Psyche hoped that the goddess would free her and that she would get back her husband.

8. For this reason, her hope quickly fled, for her mistress said that she had not obtained the wool without the help of another.

9. Puellam esse utilem cupiebat. Itaque eam apud Inferos iter facere iussit. Ei arcam parvam dedit.

10. Psyche miser templum Veneris reliquit et se mortem certe inventuram esse putabat quod dea partem pulchritudinis Proserpinae ex terra mortis ad se reportari cupiebat.

11. Psyche tamen fortissima erat et ad turrem altissimam venit. Celerrimum iter ad Inferos petebat, sed vox ex turre eam appellavit et ipsam illo modo se necare non debere dixit.

12. Vox quoque id ei futurum esse postremum laborem nuntiavit. Puellae iter facile celereque ad regnum Plutonis demonstravit et illa ex timore ab eodem amico qui eam antea servaverat nunc liberata est.

9. She wanted the girl to be useful. And so, she ordered her to make a journey among Those Below. She gave her a small box.

10. The unhappy Psyche left the temple of Venus and thought that she would certainly find death, because the goddess wished a part of Proserpina's beauty to be brought back to her from the land of death.

11. Psyche, however, was very brave and came to a very high tower. She was seeking the fastest way to Those Below, but a voice out of the tower called to her and said that she ought not to kill herself in that manner.

12. The voice also announced that this would be the last task for her. It pointed out to the girl an easy and quick way to the kingdom of Pluto and she was now freed from fear by the same friend who had saved her before.

Familiar Quotations

Veni, vidi, vici, I came, I saw, I conquered. (Caesar)
Vae victis, Woe to the vanquished. (Livy)
In medias res, Into the middle of things. (Horace)
Finis coronat opus, The end crowns the work. (Ovid)
Non omnia possumus omnes, We can't all do everything. (Virgil)
Diem perdidi, I have lost a day. (Titus)
Pares cum paribus facillime congregantur, Equals very easily congregate with equals. (Cicero)

226. Practice Exercises

No. 173. Translate these participles:

1. vocans
2. motus
3. missurus
4. accipiens
5. venturus
6. spectatus
7. perveniens
8. capturus
9. ponens
10. nuntiatus

No. 174. Translate these participial phrases:

1. naves navigantes
2. ducem iussurum
3. illi oppugnati
4. viros perventuros
5. petentes pacem
6. canem currentem
7. urbes captae
8. templa aedificata
9. portus inventos
10. flumina currentia

No. 175. Translate these sentences:

1. Populus urbium captarum quam fortissimus erat.
2. Viri perventuri iter quam celerrime faciebant.
3. Rex patriam vestram nunc regens timidus esse videtur.
4. Mulier difficultatem tuam videns auxilium dabit.
5. Tempestas non auctura non acerrima erit.
6. Pater filios suos visurus magnum gaudium habebat.
7. Ei nostros timentes quam celerrime currebant.
8. Homines victi maxime territi sunt.
9. In oppido perveniens illa fabulam suam narravit.
10. Illi portam defendentes amici non erant.

No. 176. Translate these adverbs:

1. fortiter	3. minime	5. acrius
2. quam celerrime	4. diutissime	6. difficile

7. facillime	9. male
8. melius	10. magnopere

227. New Reading Vocabulary

NOUNS

carcer, carceris, n., prison (incarcerate)
gaudium, gaudii or **gaudi, n.**, joy (gaudy)
Cerberus, Cerberi, m., Cerberus
somnus, somni, m., sleep (insomnia)
canis, canis, m. and f., dog (canine)
Charon, Charontis, m., Charon

ADJECTIVES

timidus, timida, timidum, timid (timidity)
reliquus, reliqua, reliquum, remaining, rest of
apertus, aperta, apertum, open (aperture)

228. New Reading Grammar—Clauses and Sentence Types

The fundamental components of a grammatical sentence are not really the individual words. Words must be grouped in either phrases or clauses. A phrase can have a subject or a verb, but not both; e.g., *on the table* is a prepositional phrase, *singing a song* is a participial phrase. A clause, on the other hand, is a group of words that contains both a subject and a verb (remember, however, that the subject of a Latin verb can be expressed by its personal ending).

A. CLAUSES CAN BE INDEPENDENT OR DEPENDENT.

1. *If the clause can stand alone, as a complete sentence, it is called a primary clause, or an independent clause:*

   I went to the city.

2. *If the clause cannot stand alone, it is called a subordinate clause, or a dependent clause:*

   While I was going to the city,

This clause has a subject, *I*, and a verb, *was going*. However, it is not a complete sentence. It needs a main clause, for example, *I lost my watch*. Therefore, the second clause is a subordinate clause.

In the sentence *I saw the woman who was speaking*, the main clause is *I saw the woman*, because this clause can stand alone as a complete sentence. The clause *who was speaking* is a subordinate clause because it cannot do this. Subordinate clauses stand in any number of relationships to the main verb, but can be generally thought to substitute for either a noun, an adverb, or an adjective. An indirect statement, for example, acts like the direct object (i.e., a noun) of the verb of mental process of the main clause. Relative clauses always act like adjectives modifying their antecedents. Most subordinate clauses act adverbially, e.g, *when my mother called me,* or *because I was tired,* to modify the action of the main verb.

B. SENTENCES CAN BE CLASSIFIED ACCORDING TO THE NATURE AND NUMBER OF THEIR CLAUSES, AS FOLLOWS.

Simple: One and only one independent clause. *I saw the man.*

Complex: One and only one independent clause, together with one or more dependent clauses. *I saw the man who likes my sister.*

Compound: More than one independent clause, but no dependent clauses. *I went to the store and I carried the groceries home.*

Compound-Complex: More than one independent clause and one or more dependent clauses. *Because my mom asked me to, I went to the store and I carried the groceries home.*

229. New Reading Grammar—Ablative Absolutes

A participle modifying a noun or a pronoun, both in the ablative case, may be translated as though they were equivalent to a subordinate clause, although this construction, known as the *ablative absolute,* technically has no grammatical relationship with the rest of the sentence (absolute is from **absolutus,** the fourth principal part of **absolvo,** *to free, release*).

A. THE ABLATIVE ABSOLUTE CONSTRUCTION MUST HAVE A NOUN OR PRONOUN SUBJECT THAT IS DIFFERENT FROM THE SUBJECT OF THE MAIN PART OF THE SENTENCE; IT MUST BE GRAMMATICALLY "FREE" FROM THE REST OF THE SENTENCE.

B. THE ABLATIVE ABSOLUTE CONSTRUCTION MAY BE TRANSLATED WITH ANY NUMBER OF ADVERBIAL RELATIONSHIPS, DEPENDING ON THE CONTEXT, E.G., *because, when, although,* **OR** *if.*

C. SINCE THE VERB sum, esse DOES NOT HAVE A PRESENT PARTICIPLE, IT IS POSSIBLE TO HAVE AN ABLATIVE ABSOLUTE THAT CONSISTS OF TWO NOUNS OR A NOUN AND AN ADJECTIVE, WITH THE PARTICIPLE "being" UNDERSTOOD.

Oppidis captis, pacem petebant.	When the towns had been captured, they sought peace.
Hoc viro duce, vincemur.	If this man is leader, we shall be conquered.
Navibus gravibus, celerius navigabant.	Although the ships were heavy, they were sailing quite quickly.

230. New Reading Grammar—The Gerundive and the Gerund

1. YOU HAVE ALREADY LEARNED ABOUT THE gerundive, OR THE FUTURE PASSIVE PARTICIPLE, EARLIER IN THIS CHAPTER (Section 224).

The gerundive is a verbal adjective, used to express an action that ought to be done, or that will be done. When used to express an action that should or must be taken, the gerundive is usually in the nominative case, although it may occasionally be in the accusative case instead.

Puella tibi amanda est.	The girl must be loved by you, *or* You must love the girl.
Dico puellam tibi amandam est.	I say that the girl must be loved by you, *or* I say that you must love the girl.

You will notice that the person or object who must perform the action is put in the dative case. This is referred to as a *dative of agent*.

2. THE gerund IS A VERBAL NOUN, AND HAS CHARACTERISTICS OF BOTH VERBS AND NOUNS.

It is formed in the same way as the gerundive. However, since it is a verbal noun, it has gender, just like a noun does. The gerund is neuter. It is conjugated only in the singular, and it does not have a nominative or a vocative form (the infinitive acts as its nominative form). It is declined by adding the following endings to the present tense stem, with the appropriate vowel depending on the conjugational pattern of the verb involved:

Case	*Ending*		Thus, the gerund of **amo** is:
Gen.	**-ndi**	Gen. **amandi**	of loving
Dat.	**-ndo**	Dat. **amando**	to, for loving
Acc.	**-ndum**	Ace. **amandum**	loving
Abl.	**-ndo**	Abl. **amando**	from, with, by, in loving

As you can see, the gerund is essentially a participle used substantively as a noun.

a. *The gerund is used in the accusative with the preposition* **ad** *to express purpose.*

Aures ad audiendum facti sunt.	Ears were made for hearing.

b. *The gerund is used in the genitive with the preposition* **causa,** *or to modify another noun. Note that the preposition* **causa** *usually comes after the noun it governs.*

Ars amandi.	The art of loving.
Pugnandi causa venerunt.	They came in to fight.

c. *The gerund is used in the ablative with a preposition, or without a preposition as an ablative of means or instument.*

In dormiendo tempus terebant.	They wasted time in sleeping.
Audiendo disces.	You learn by listening.

d. *The gerund can take a direct object because it is a verbal noun. However, in practice, when a gerund would take a direct object, Latin uses the gerundive instead, in the appropriate case as determined by the context.*

Spes est casam inveniendi.	There is hope of finding the house.
Spes est casae inveniendae.	There is hope of finding the house.

The first sentence uses the gerund; the second uses the gerundive. Both mean the same thing, although the second sentence would be found most often. Note that when the gerund takes a direct object, the object is put into the accusative case, as **casam** is. However, when the gerundive is used, the noun is put into the case that the gerund would have taken (the genitive in this example). Remember that because it is a verbal adjective, the gerundive must agree with the noun.

231. New Reading Grammar—The Supine

In addition to the gerund, Latin has one other verbal noun, the **supine.** The supine is formed from the fourth principal part (which some texts call the supine stem). The supine only exists in two cases, the accusative singular and the ablative singular, both of which have very specific and limited uses. The supine's most common use, in fact, is in combination with the verb **iri** to form the future passive infinitive (e.g., **amatum iri**).

The supine declines like a fourth declension noun but, again, only in the accusative and ablative singular. The accusative of the supine (**-um**) is used without a preposition after verbs of motion to express purpose:

Eunt urbem captum. *They came to capture the city.*

The ablative of the supine (**-u**) is used with certain adjectives (e.g., **difficulis, facilis, mirabilis**) as an *ablative of respect*:

Hic liber facilis est lectu. *This book is easy with respect to reading. This book is easy to read.*

232. Reading

Cupido et Psyche (concl'd)

1. **Psyche, timida videri non cupiens, verba vocis magno cum gaudio audivit et hunc laborem difficillimum futurum esse sperabat.**
2. **Itaque haec omnia, quae demonstraverant, facere contendit. Sine plurimo periculo enim ad regnum Inferorum iter facere magnopere cupiebat.**
3. **Cerberus, ante portam quae ad terram mortis ducit positus, canis erat audacissimus qui tria capita habebat, sed Psyche voce monita eum non timebat.**
4. **Charon tum nave minima trans flumen illam, in regnum Plutonis venturam, duxit.**
5. **Ante Proserpinam, reginam pulcherrimam Inferorum, stans illa Venerem donum cupire nuntiavit.**
6. **Regina arcam a puella cepit et in eandem arcam partem parvam suae pulchritudinis posuit. Dea, puella arcam dans, illam monuit.**

Cupid and Psyche (concl'd)

1. Psyche, who did not wish to seem timid, heard the words of the voice with great joy and hoped that this task would be very difficult.
2. And so, she hurried to do all these things that they had pointed out to her. For she greatly wished to make the journey to the kingdom of Those Below without very great danger.
3. Cerberus, who was placed in front of the door that leads to the land of death, was a very bold dog who had three heads, but Psyche, because she had been warned by the voice, was not afraid of him.
4. Charon then led her, as she was about to come into the kingdom of Pluto, across the river in a very small boat.
5. Standing in front of Proserpina, the very beautiful queen of Those Below, she reported that Venus wanted a gift.
6. The queen took the box from the girl and put a small part of her own beauty into the same box. The goddess, as she gave the box to the girl, warned her.

7. Illam in arcam spectantem, in periculum magnum casuram esse dixit, sed Psyche, ex terra Inferorum iter facere cupiens, verbis reginae ad timorem non excitata est.

8. Ad terram mortalium eadem viam cepit, sed postquam ad lucem pervenerat in arcam spectare et pulchritudinem videre atque habere cupiebat, sed nil pulchritudinis ib invenit, arca aperta.

9. Psyche dolens pulchritudinem ibi non invenit quod id quod Proserpina in arca posuerat somnus altus Inferorum erat.

10. Somno ex carcere suo liberato, puella somno celeriter capta est et ipsa sine ulla mora, modo simili corpori quod a Morte delectum, erat, media in via cecedit. Nil sciebat atque nil faciebat. Solum dormiebat.

11. Cupido tamen, vulnerre eius curato, magno cum gaudio uxorem suam vidit. Ad locum ubi illa dormiebat quam celerrime volavit.

12. Ipse, supra illam stans, somnum qui illam opprimebat cepit et, hoc in arca posito, una ex sagittis suis uxorem tetegit.

13. Ipse dixit: "Tu, multis temporibus e morte servata, omnes labores tuos conficere debes. His factis, omnia reliqua faciam."

14. Illa satis poena habuerat. Hic ad Iovem properavit et ab eo auxilium petivit. Iuppiter ad Venerem eodem die iter fecit et illa tandem puellam dedidit.

15. Psyche, ad regnum deorum a Mercurio ducta, immortalis facta est.

16. Matrimonium ab illo tempore ad finem temporis omnis, illa immortali facta, laetissimum erat.

17. Mortales hac fabula animum esse immortalem atque se gaudium per omnes difficultates semper inventuros esse docentur.

7. She said that she would fall into great danger, if she looked into the box, but Psyche, who wished to make the journey out of the land of Those Below, was not aroused to fear by the words of the queen.

8. She took the same road to the land of mortals, but after she had arrived at the light, she wished to look into the box and to see and have the beauty, but she found no beauty there, when the box was opened.

9. The grieving Psyche did not find beauty there, because what Proserpina had placed in the box was the deep sleep of Those Below.

10. When sleep had been freed from its prison, the girl was quickly overcome by sleep and without any delay, in a manner similar to a body that had been chosen by Death, she fell in the middle of the road. She knew nothing and she did nothing. She only slept.

11. Cupid, however, when his wound had been healed, saw his wife with great joy. He flew as quickly as possible to the place where she was sleeping.

12. He, standing above her, took the sleep that was oppressing her and, when this had been placed in the box, he touched his wife with one of his arrows.

13. He said: "You, because you have been saved from death many times, ought to finish all your tasks. When these have been done, I shall do all the other things."

14. She had had enough punishments. He hurried to Jupiter and begged aid from him. Jupiter made the journey to Venus the same day and, at last, she surrendered the girl.

15. Psyche, after she had been led to the kingdom of the gods by Mercury, was made immortal.

16. The marriage from that time to the end of all time was very happy, because she had been made immortal.

17. Mortals are taught by this story that the spirit is immortal and that they will always find joy through all difficulties.

233. Practice Exercises

No. 177. Translate these sentences:

1. Multi, oraculo audito, ad terram nostram venire constituerunt.
2. Signo dato, in agrum impetum fecerunt.
3. Homines, armis non multis, tamen fortiter pugnaverunt.
4. Militibus multis interfectis, duces pacem petiverunt.
5. Viri, praeda magna, magno cum gaudio domi accipientur.
6. Hac re gesta, pueri domum venient.
7. Illo duce, id sine difficultate faciemus.
8. His mihi nuntiatis, ex urbe iter facere cupiebam.
9. His necatis, populus melius regetur.
10. Die dicto, omnia quam celerrime paraverunt.
11. Porta aperta, in casam venire potuit.
12. Nullam spem habebat, oppido capto.
13. His rebus factis, rex plus poterat.
14. Reliquis visis, ad silvam curremus.
15. Patre eius duce, omnia audacter faciunt.
16. Pace facta, ab insula navigabit.
17. Multis timidis, flumina invenire non poterunt.
18. Tempore nunc brevi, nullum auxilium perveniet.
19. Loco idoneo, hic diutius manere cupitis.
20. Auxilio dato, gaudium magnum erat.
21. Arma utila est pugnando.
22. Habes spem natandi.
23. Ierant urbis oppugnandae causa.
24. Veni ad audiendum.

The ruins of the Coliseum have become a symbol of ancient Rome.

REVIEW

234. Vocabulary Review

NOUNS

1. canis	4. Charon	7. gaudium	10. modus	13. ovis
2. carcer	5. dux	8. genus	11. numerus	14. pulchritude
3. Cerberus	6. formica	9. lana	12. ordo	15. satis

ADJECTIVES	VERBS	ADVERBS
1. apertus	1. invenio	1. satis
2. reliquus	2. puto	2. tam
3. timidus	3. reporto	3. tandem
4. utilis	4. spero	

235. Practice Exercises

No. 178. Translate these infinitives:

1. esse	6. putavisse	11. duci	16. cupi
2. fuisse	7. reportare	12. duxisse	17. potuisse
3. inventurum esse	8. reportaturum esse	13. habitum esse	18. posse
4. inveniri	9. speravisse	14. habere	19. pugnavisse
5. putatum esse	10. speraturum esse	15. cupere	20. pugnatum esse

No. 179. Translate these participles:

1. ducens	8. inventa	15. venientium	22. missus
2. ducturus	9. reportantium	16. ventura	23. visuris
3. habentes	10. reportaturus	17. timenti	24. videntium
4. habitos	11. sperantia	18. territus	25. dicturos
5. putata	12. speratam	19. posituros	26. dicens
6. putaturis	13. moturos	20. ponentibus	27. monentes
7. invenientem	14. moventes	21. mittens	28. moniti

No. 180. Translate these ablative clauses:

1. eis visis	5. viris timentibus	9. somno venienti	13. verbo audito
2. illo capto	6. puella ambulanti	10. carcere magno	14. spe inventa
3. his dictis	7. ducibus timidis	11. urbe capta	15. generibus multis
4. bello facto	8. numero parvo	12. reliquis dicentibus	

236. Reading

QUINTUS HORATIUS FLACCUS

Horace, the son of a freedman, was born in 65 B.C. at Venusia, in southern Italy, and studied in Rome and Athens. He was a friend of Virgil and of Augustus, through his literary patron, Maecenas. Before his death in 8 B.C., he had gained enduring popularity from the quality and universality of his poetry and philosophy.

Integer vitae scelerisque purus
non eget Mauris iaculis neque arcu
nec venenatis gravida sagittis, Fuscae, pharetra,
sive per Syrtis iter aestuosas
sive facturus per inhospitalem
Caucasum vel quae loca fabulosus lambit Hydaspes.

Carminum Liber Primus, xxii

CARMINA BURANA

In the early nineteenth century, a thirteenth-century manuscript was found in the monastery of Benedictburen in Bavaria. These **carmina,** or songs, called **Carmina Burana** after the monastery (Buren), were mostly poems, chiefly in Latin or German, or a combination of both, composed by the goliards, or wandering students and monks, on a wide variety of topics. By the Middle Ages, the classical pronunciation and meter had changed and the use of rhyme had been introduced in poetry. These poems provided both inspiration and text for the German composer Carl Orff's famous "Carmina Burana."

Omnia sol temperat
purus et subtilis,
nova mundo reserat
facies Aprilis,
ad amorem properat
animus erilis,
et iucundis imperat
deus puerilis.
Rerum tanta novitas
in sollemni vere
et veris auctoritas
iubet nos gaudere,
vias praebet solitas,
et in tuo vere
fides est et probitas
tuum retinere.
Ama me fideliter,
fidem meam nota,

de corde totaliter
et ex mente tota,
sum praesentialiter
absens in remota;
quisquis amat taliter,
volvitur in rota.
Ecce gratum
et optatum
ver reducit gaudia,
purpuratum
floret pratum,
sol serenat omnia,
iam iam cedunt tristia.
aestas redit,
nunc recedit
hiemis saevitia.
Iam liquescit
et decrescit

grando, nix, et cetera,
bruma fugit,
et iam sugit
ver aestatis ubera;
illi mens est misera,
qui nec vivit,
nec lascivit
sub aestatis dextera.
Gloriantur
et laetantur
in melle dulcedinis
qui conantur
ut utantur
praemio Cupidinis;
simus iussu Cypridis
gloriantes
et laetantes
pares esse Paridis.

SUBJUNCTIVE

237. New Reading Grammar—Introducing the Subjunctive Mood

A listing of all the moods in Latin includes indicative, infinitive, imperative, participle, gerund, supine, and subjunctive. So far, we've covered each of these in turn, in both the active and passive voices, with the single exception of the subjunctive. As its name implies (from **subiunctus,** the fourth principal part of **subiungo,** *to yoke beneath, to attach under*), the subjunctive's main use is in subordinate clauses, although there are several uses of the subjunctive as the main verb in independent clauses as well.

The subjunctive has four tenses: present, perfect, imperfect, and pluperfect in both the active and the passive voice. There are no future or future perfect tenses in the subjunctive. In general, the subjunctive (depending on the tense and voice) is used to express doubt, hope, probability, improbability, and unreal situations or events. First we will learn the forms of the subjunctive and the sequences of tenses, and then we will consider specific uses of this mood.

238. NEW READING GRAMMAR—PRESENT SUBJUNCTIVE:

1. ACTIVE VOICE

amem	habeam	ducam	capiam	audiam
ames	habeas	ducas	capias	audias
amet	habeat	ducat	capiat	audiat
amemus	habeamus	ducamus	capiamus	audiamus
ametis	habetis	ducatis	capiatis	audiatis
ament	habeant	ducant	capiant	audiant

2. PASSIVE VOICE

amer	habear	ducar	capiar	audiar
ameris	habearis	ducaris	capiaris	audiaris
ametur	habeatur	ducatur	capiatur	audiatur
amemur	habeamur	ducamur	capiamur	audiamur
amemini	habeamini	ducamini	capiamini	audiamini
amentur	habeantur	ducantur	capiantur	audiantur

As you can see, for **First Conjugation** verbs the basic endings are added to the present stem after the vowel -a- of the present stem is changed to -e-. For the other conjugations, the basic endings are added to the present stem plus the vowel -a-. The active and passive personal endings are the same as in the indicative.

3. PRESENT SUBJUNCTIVE OF sum.

The verb **sum** has no passive voice. The active voice of the present subjunctive is as follows:

Singular:	*Plural:*
sim	simus
sis	sitis
sit	sint

239. New Reading Grammar—Perfect Subjunctive

1. ACTIVE VOICE

amaverim	habuerim	duxerim	ceperim	audiverim
amaveris	habueris	duxeris	ceperis	audiveris
amaverit	habuerit	duxerit	ceperit	audiverit
amaverimus	habuerimus	duxerimus	ceperimus	audiverimus
amaveritis	habueritis	duxeritis	ceperitis	audiveritis
amaverint	habuerint	duxerint	ceperint	audiverint

You will notice that the perfect active subjunctive is formed in the same way as the future active indicative, with the exception of the first person singular. However, there is no danger of confusing the two tenses. The context will always provide you with enough information to figure out which tense is being used.

2. PASSIVE VOICE

The perfect passive subjunctive is formed by using the fourth principal part and the present subjunctive of **sum**.

amatus, -a, -um sim	habitus, -a, -um sim	ductus, -a, -um sim	captus, -a, -um sim	auditus, -a, -um sim
amatus, -a, -um sis	habitus, -a, -um sis	ductus, -a, -um sis	captus, -a, -um sis	auditus, -a, -um sis
amatus, -a, -um sit	habitus, -a, -um sit	ductus, -a, -um sit	captus, -a, -um sit	auditus, -a, -um sit
amati, -ae, -a simus	habiti, -ae, -a simus	ducti, -ae, -a simus	capti, -ae, -a simus	auditi, -ae, -a simus
amati, -ae, -a sitis	habiti, -ae, -a sitis	ducti, -ae, -a sitis	capti, -ae, -a sitis	auditi, -ae, -a sitis
amati, -ae, -a sint	habiti, -ae, -a sint	ducti, -ae, -a sint	capti, -ae, -a sint	auditi, -ae, -a sint

3. THE PERFECT SUBJUNCTIVE OF sum IS FORMED REGULARLY ON THE PERFECT ACTIVE STEM.

Singular:	*Plural:*
fuerim	fuerimus
fueris	fueritis
fuerit	fuerint

240. New Reading Grammar—Imperfect Subjunctive

1. ACTIVE VOICE

The imperfect active subjunctive is formed by adding the basic active endings onto the second principal part, the present active infinitive.

amarem	haberem	ducerem	caperem	audirem
amares	haberes	duceres	caperes	audires
amaret	haberet	duceret	caperet	audiret
amaremus	haberemus	duceremus	caperemus	audiremus
amaretis	haberetis	duceretis	caperetis	audiretis
amarent	haberent	ducerent	caperent	audirent

2. PASSIVE VOICE

The imperfect passive subjunctive is formed by adding the passive endings onto the second principal part, the present active infinitive.

amarer	haberer	ducerer	caperer	audirer
amareris	habereris	ducereris	capereris	audireris
amaretur	haberetur	duceretur	caperetur	audiretur
amaremur	haberemur	duceremur	caperemur	audiremur
amaremini	haberemini	duceremini	caperemini	audiremini
amarentur	haberentur	ducerentur	caperentur	audirentur

3. THE IMPERFECT SUBJUNCTIVE OF sum IS FORMED REGULARLY BY ADDING ACTIVE ENDINGS ONTO THE SECOND PRINCIPAL PART.

Singular:	*Plural:*
essem	essemus
esses	essetis
esset	essent

241. New Reading Grammar—Pluperfect Subjunctive

1. ACTIVE VOICE

The pluperfect active subjunctive is formed by using the perfect active infinitive (the third principal part plus -isse-) and the basic active endings.

amavissem	habuissem	duxissem	cepissem	audivissem
amavisses	habuisses	duxisses	cepisses	audivisses
amavisset	habuisset	duxisset	cepisset	audivisset
amavissemus	habuissemus	duxissemus	cepissemus	audivissemus
amavissetis	habuissetis	duxissetis	cepissetis	audivissetis
amavissent	habuissent	duxissent	cepissent	audivissent

2. PASSIVE VOICE

The pluperfect passive subjunctive is formed by using the fourth principal part and the imperfect subjunctive of **sum**.

amatus, -a, -um essem	ductus, -a, -um essem	auditus, -a, -um essem
amatus, -a, -um esses	ductus, -a, -um esses	auditus, -a, -um esses
amatus, -a, -um esset	ductus, -a, -um esset	auditus, -a, -um esset
amati, -ae, -a essemus	ducti, -ae, -a essemus	auditi, -ae, -a essemus
amati, -ae, -a essetis	ducti, -ae, -a essetis	auditi, -ae, -a essetis
amati, -ae, -a essent	ducti, -ae, -a essent	auditi, -ae, -a essent

habitus, -a, -um essem	captus, -a, -um essem
habitus, -a, -um esses	captus, -a, -um esses
habitus, -a, -um esset	captus, -a, -um esset
habiti, -ae, -a essemus	capti, -ae, -a essemus
habiti, -ae, -a essetis	capti, -ae, -a essetis
habiti, -ae, -a essent	capti, -ae, -a essent

3. THE PLUPERFECT SUBJUNCTIVE OF sum IS FORMED NORMALLY.

Singular:	*Plural*:
fuissem	fuissemus
fuisses	fuissetis
fuisset	fuissent

242. New Reading Grammar—Sequences of Tenses

The subjunctive, as its name implies, is primarily used in subordinate clauses. Normally, the main verb of a sentence will be in the indicative (although it can also be imperative or an independent use of the subjunctive). The tense of the verb in the subjunctive will be relative to that of the main verb. The name given to this relationship of tenses is **Sequence of Tenses.**

Latin has two sequences of verbs. The primary sequence consists of verbs whose action takes place either in the **present** or in the **future.** The secondary sequence consists of verbs whose action takes place in the **past.** When the subjunctive is used in the same sentence as the indicative, the subjunctive must be of the same sequence as the indicative, primary in primary sequence, and secondary in secondary sequence. Examples of this will follow.

Primary Sequence. In the indicative, the primary tenses are the present, future, and future perfect. The imperative is also considered a primary tense. In the subjunctive, the primary tenses are the present and the perfect. When both the indicative and subjunctive verbs of a sentence are in *primary* sequence, (1) the **present subjunctive** is used if the action of the subjunctive verb takes place at the same time as the action of the indicative verb and, (2) the **perfect subjunctive** is used if the action of the subjunctive verb takes place or is completed prior to the action of the indicative verb.

Secondary Sequence. In the indicative, the secondary tenses are the imperfect, perfect, and pluperfect. (Note that the perfect tense can be either primary or secondary depending on context; it is normally secondary.) In the subjunctive, the secondary tenses are the imperfect and the pluperfect. When both the indicative and subjunctive verbs of a sentence are in *secondary* sequence, (1) the **imperfect subjunctive** is used if the action of the subjunctive verb takes place at the same time as the action of the indicative verb and, (2) the **pluperfect subjunctive** is used if the action of the subjunctive verb takes place or is completed prior to the action of the indicative verb.

To look at it another way, **present** (in primary sequence) and **imperfect** (in secondary sequence) subjunctives are used to indicate actions that take place at the same time as the main verb, while **perfect** (primary sequence) and **pluperfect** (secondary sequence) subjunctives are used to indicate actions that took place prior to the action of the main verb.

The above information can be summarized as follows:

PRIMARY SEQUENCE

Indicative	*Subjunctive*
Present	Present—if action takes place at the same time
Future	Perfect—if action takes place earlier
Future Perfect	

Thus, if the action of the subjunctive verb takes place at the same time as the action of the indicative verb, you will see a sentence like this using the present subjunctive:

Rogo/Rogabo/Rogavero quid mulier audiat.

I ask/will ask/shall have asked what the woman hears.

However, if the action of the subjunctive verb takes place earlier than the action of the indicative verb, you will see a sentence like this using the perfect subjunctive:

Rogo/Rogabo/Rogavero quid mulier audiverit.

I ask/will ask/shall have asked what the woman heard.

SECONDARY SEQUENCE

Indicative	*Subjunctive*
Imperfect	Imperfect—if action takes place at the same time
Perfect	
Pluperfect	Pluperfect—if action takes place earlier

Thus, if the action of the subjunctive verb takes place at the same time as the action of the indicative verb, you will see a sentence like this using the imperfect subjunctive:

Rogabam/Rogavi/Rogaveram quid mulier audiret.

I was asking/have asked/had asked what the woman heard.

However, if the action of the subjunctive verb takes place earlier than the action of the indicative verb, you will see a sentence like this using the pluperfect subjunctive:

Rogabam/Rogavi/Rogaveram quid mulier audivissit.

I was asking/have asked/had asked what the woman had heard.

Note that the tense of the subjunctive verbs is not determined only by the tense of the indicative verb, but also by when the action of the subjunctive takes place relative to the action of the main verb. Thus, if the main verb is from the primary sequence and the action of the subjunctive occurs at the same time, the present tense of the subjunctive is used, regardless of whether the main primary sequence verb is in the present, future, or future perfect.

243. Practice Exercises

No. 181. Change these verbs to the subjunctive:

1. debuerunt	6. facis	11. ventae estis	16. debes
2. relinquebat	7. iacta erant	12. fuit	17. fuerat
3. oppugnatis	8. debitus sum	13. rogamini	18. oppungnabant
4. es	9. veniebat	14. conspicimur	19. relicta est
5. eram	10. relinquebamur	15. veni	20. debebatur

No. 182. Change these verbs to the indicative:

1. sint	6. debeam	11. debita esses	16. conspecti essetis
2. veniamus	7. fuerimus	12. reliquerit	17. fuissem
3. rogata sint	8. conspexissent	13. rogaverit	18. oppugnaveris
4. oppugnaret	9. veniretur	14. venisses	19. relinquas
5. conspicerem	10. debuerim	15. esses	20. deberetur

No. 183. Tell which tense of the subjunctive would be used to indicate the following:

1. ACTION HAPPENING AT THE SAME TIME AS ONE REQUIRING A PRESENT TENSE VERB.
2. ACTION HAPPENING BEFORE ONE REQUIRING A PLUPERFECT TENSE VERB.
3. ACTION HAPPENING BEFORE ONE REQUIRING A FUTURE TENSE VERB.
4. ACTION HAPPENING AT THE SAME TIME AS ONE REQUIRING A PERFECT TENSE VERB.

No. 184.
1. Give the present subjunctive, active and passive, of **laudo.**
2. Give the perfect subjunctive, active and passive, of **video.**
3. Give the imperfect subjunctive, active and passive, of **peto.**
4. Give the pluperfect subjunctive, active and passive, of **dormio.**

244. New Reading Vocabulary

NOUNS

severitas, severitatis, f., severity, strictness (severe)

coniuratio, coniurationis, f., conspiracy, plot

res publica, rei publicae, f., republic, common good

desiderium, desiderii, or **desideri, n.,** longing loss, need (desire)

vespera, vesperae, f., evening

senatus, senatus, m., senate (senator)

lenitas, lenitatis, f., mercy, mildness, gentleness gentleness (lenient)

ADJECTIVES

Aurelius, Aurelia, Aurelium, Aurelian

tantus, tanta, tantum, so great

pristinus, pristina, pristinum, former, earlier (pristine)

superior, superius, higher, past, preceding (superior). Comparative of **superus,** high, upper

hesternus, hesterna, hesternum, yesterday

tot, so many (indeclinable)

perpetuus, perpetua, perpetuum, continuous, perpetual, uninterrupted (perpetuity)

VERBS

accelero, accelerare, acceleravi, acceleratus, hurry (accelerate)

concedo, concedere, concessi, concessum, grant, allow, withdraw (concede)

erro, errare, erravi, erratus, be mistaken, lose one's way (error)

patefacio, patefacere, patefeci, patefactus, throw open, bring to light. Conjugated like facio; the passive verb is **patefio, patefieri, patefactus sum,** which is conjugated like **fio.**

patior, pati, passus sum, allow, grant, suffer (patience)

proficiscor, proficisci, profectus sum, go forth, depart

tabesco, tabescere, tabescui, decay, melt away

adsequor, adsequi, adsecutus sum, gain, obtain, reach

consequor, consequi, consecutus sum, follow, catch up with (consequence)

exeo, exire, exii, exitus, avoid, go away, depart (exit). Conjugated like **eo.**

profugio, profugere, profugi, run away, flee, escape

perfero, perferre, pertuli, perlatus, report. Conjugated like **ferro.**

pertimesco, pertimescere, pertimui, fear, be alarmed at

sentio, sentire, sensi, sensus, feel, perceive, realize (sense)

flagito, flagitare, flagitavi, flagitatus, demand

ADVERBS

ita, so

vehementer, violently, eagerly (vehemently)

sic, so, thus

ADVERB AND CONJUNCTION

ut, or **uti,** as; that, so that

CONJUNCTIONS

ne, that not, lest

245. New Reading Grammar—Overview of Uses of the Subjunctive

You have learned that the indicative mood is used to state a fact or to ask a direct question, and the imperative mood is used to give commands. The subjunctive mood has many different uses. This is why only the briefest explanation about the uses of the subjunctive was given ealier in this chapter. When you meet or use the subjunctive in Latin, you must determine how it is being used before you can decide how to translate it. The uses can be categorized under two main headings:

Independent Subjunctives can be used as the main verb in an independent clause. These include what are known as the jussive, hortatorical, optative, deliberative, and potential uses. Each of these uses will be discussed in turn.

Dependent Subjunctives perform any of numerous possible functions within dependent or subordinate clauses, including purpose, result, indirect commands, indirect questions, fear, doubt, hindrance, and prevention, as well as causal, concessive, and circumstantial relationships. Our text will touch upon each of these uses as well.

246. New Reading Grammar—Jussive and Hortatory Subjunctive

The jussive subjunctive is one of the uses of the **Independent Subjunctive.** The word *jussive* is derived from the Latin verb **iubeo,** meaning *command.* However, in Latin, as you have already learned, you use the imperative mood to issue commands. In fact, the jussive subjunctive is used to recommend an action strongly; not quite a command, but stronger than a suggestion. For this reason, the jussive subjunctive is often called the *hortatory* subjunctive. The word comes from the verb **hortor,** meaning *urge.* When the subjunctive is translated into English, the word *let* is supplied. This construction uses only the present subjunctive, usually in the first person plural or in the third person. Some texts restrict the term hortatory to first person usage and reserve jussive for third person, but the two uses are essential identical.

Vocemus eum.	Let us call him.
Dicat.	Let him (her) speak.
Mulieres id audiant.	Let the women hear it.

The hortatory subjunctive can also be used to strongly recommend that an action not be taken. In this case, the word **ne** is used to express the negative.

Ne vocemus virum.	Let us not call the man.
Ne dicat.	Let him (her) not speak.
Mulieres id ne videant.	Let the women not see it.

247. New Reading Grammar—Purpose Clauses

In English, the infinitive is used to express purpose:

I am going to the store to buy food.

The infinitive, *to buy,* expresses the purpose of going to the store. You could also say, *I am going to the store for the purpose of buying food,* or, *I am going to the store so that I can buy food.*

In Latin, the infinitive is not used to express purpose. Instead, you use the present and the imperfect tenses of the subjunctive in a subordinate clause (one of the uses of the Dependent Subjunctive). As the previous chapter stated, the **present tense** is used if the main verb is from the primary sequence, and the **imperfect tense** is used if the main verb is from the secondary sequence. The word **ut** is usually used to introduce purpose clauses.

Urbam eunt ut matrem suam videant.	They go to the city to see (in order to see, for the purpose of seeing, so that they might see) their mother.
Urbem ibis ut patrem tuum videas.	You will go to the city to see your father.
Urbem iero ut sorores meas videam.	I shall have gone to the city to see my sisters.
Urbem ductus est ut a sorore sua videretur.	He was led to the city to be seen by his sister.
Urbem ibam ut viros audirem.	I was going to the city to hear the men.
Currerant ut ludos viderent.	They had run to see the games.
Milites pugnabant ut liberaremur.	The soldiers were fighting so that we might be made free.

If the purpose clause is negative, the word **ne** is used instead of **ut.**

Pugnant ne necentur.	They fight so that they will not be killed (in order not to be killed, for the purpose of not being killed).
Domi manebam ne viros audirem.	I remained at home so that I would not hear the men.

248. New Reading Grammar—Result Clauses

Another use of the Dependent Subjunctive is in result clauses. Result clauses show the result of an action.

I ran so fast that I caught the train.

The result clause is *that I caught the train.* You could also say: *I ran so fast with the result that I caught the train,* or *I ran so fast that the result was that I caught the train.*

Result clauses are formed in the same way as purpose clauses. Often, you will have to decide from the context whether a clause expresses result or purpose. However, there are two instances when this will be easier.

The first instance is if the clause is negative. A negative purpose clause uses the word **ne.** A negative result clause uses the words **ut** and **non** in the same sentence.

Purpose Clause:	**Pugnant ne necentur.**
	They fight so that they will not be killed.
Result Clause:	**Pugnant ut non necentur.**
	They fight with the result that they are not killed.

The other instance is when certain words appear in the main clause that precedes the result clause. These words are **ita**, *so;* **tam**, *so;* **tantus**, *so great;* **tot**, *so many;* **talis**, *such;* and **sic**, *so.*

Purpose Clause:	**Pugnabant bene ne necarentur.**
	They fought well so that they would not be killed.
Result Clause:	**Pugnabant tam bene ut non necarentur.**
	They fought so well that they were not killed.
Purpose Clause:	**Cucurreram celeriter ut eam viderem.**
	I had run swiftly so that I might see her.
Result Clause:	**Cucurreram ita celeriter ut eam viderem.**
	I had run so swiftly that I saw her.

249. New Reading Grammar—Subjunctive of Irregular Verbs

1. **YOU HAVE ALREADY LEARNED THE SUBJUNCTIVE OF** sum.

Like **sum**, the verbs **possum, eo, volo, nolo,** and **malo** only have the active voice.

a. *Present Subjunctive*

possim	eam	velim	nolim	malim
possis	eas	velis	nolis	malis
possit	eat	velit	nolit	malit
possimus	eamus	velimus	nolimus	malimus
possitis	eatis	velitis	nolitis	malitis
possint	eant	velint	nolint	malint

The present tense is the most irregular; the other three subjunctive tenses are more straightforward.

b. *Perfect Subjunctive*

potuerim	ierim	voluerim	noluerim	maluerim
potueris	ieris	volueris	nolueris	malueris
potuerit	ierit	voluerit	noluerit	maluerit
potuerimus	ierimus	voluerimus	noluerimus	maluerimus
potueritis	ieritis	volueritis	nolueritis	malueritis
potuerint	ierint	voluerint	noluerint	maluerint

c. *Imperfect Subjunctive*

possem	irem	vellem	nollem	mallem
posses	ires	velles	nolles	malles
posset	iret	vellet	nollet	mallet
possemus	iremus	vellemus	nollemus	mallemus
possetis	iretis	velletis	nolletis	malletis
possent	irent	vellent	nollent	mallent

d. Pluperfect Subjunctive

potuissem	issem	voluissem	noluissem	maluissem
potuisses	isses	voluisses	noluisses	maluisses
potuisset	isset	voluisset	noluisset	maluisset
potuissemus	issemus	voluissemus	noluissemus	maluissemus
potuissetis	issetis	voluissetis	noluissetis	maluissetis
potuissent	issent	voluissent	noluissent	maluissent

2. THE VERB fio ONLY HAS THE PASSIVE VOICE IN THE SUBJUNCTIVE.

Present	*Perfect*	*Imperfect*	*Pluperfect*
fiam	factus, -a, -um sim	fierem	factus, -a, -um essem
fias	factus, -a, -um sis	fieres	factus, -a, -um esses
fiat	factus, -a, -um sit	fieret	factus, -a, -um esset
fiamus	facti, -ae, -a simus	fieremus	facti, -ae, a essemus
fiatis	facti, -ae, -a sitis	fieretis	facti, -ae, a essetis
fiant	facti, -ae, -a sint	fierent	facti, -ae, a essent

Note that, although the imperfect of **fio** is translated as passive, it is formed by adding the active endings to **fier-**. Only the stem of the second principal part is used, not the whole infinitive.

3. THE VERB fero HAS BOTH THE ACTIVE AND THE PASSIVE VOICE IN THE SUBJUNCTIVE.

Present		*Perfect*	
Active	*Passive*	*Active*	Passive
feram	ferar	tulerim	latus, -a, -um sim
feras	feraris	tuleris	latus, -a, -um sis
ferat	feratur	tulerit	latus, -a, -um sit
feramus	feramur	tulerimus	lati, -ae, -a simus
feratis	feramini	tuleritis	lati, -ae, -a sitis
ferant	ferantur	tulerint	lati, -ae, -a sint

Imperfect		*Pluperfect*	
Active	*Passive*	*Active*	*Passive*
ferrem	ferrer	tulissem	latus, -a, -um essem
ferres	ferreris	tulisses	latus, -a, -um esses
ferret	ferretur	tulisset	latus, -a, -um esset
ferremus	ferremur	tulissemus	lati, -ae, -a essemus
ferretis	ferremini	tulissetis	lati, -ae, -a essetis
ferrent	ferrentur	tulissent	lati, -ae, -a essent

4. REGULAR DEPONENT VERBS FORM THE SUBJUNCTIVE WITH THE USUAL PASSIVE ENDINGS. THEY ARE, OF COURSE, TRANSLATED IN THE ACTIVE VOICE.

250. Reading

From this point on, the readings will all be drawn directly from actual writings in Classical Latin. Some of the more complicated constructions will occasionally be simplified, but for the most part, you will be reading the same words that literate citizens of the Roman Empire read centuries ago.

Often, words that would be used in English are left out in Latin. Such words are supplied in the translation where necessary. If they are not obvious, they are placed in square brackets [ ].

In the Sixth Review Section, you read an excerpt from Cicero's First Oration Against Cataline, who had formed a conspiracy to overthrow the government. This excerpt is taken from Cicero's second oration against Cataline, which was delivered before the people of Rome. In this section, Cicero is trying to convince Cataline's fellow conspirators to leave Rome. Refer to the Sixth Review Section to refresh your memory on Cicero and Cataline.

In Catilinam II, 6–7.

Omnia superioris noctis consilia ad me perlata esse sentiunt, patefeci in senatu hesterno die, Catalina ipse pertimuit, profugit: hi quid exspectant?
Ne illi vehementer errant, si illam meam pristinam lenitatem perpetuam sperant futuram. Quod exspectavi iam sum adsecutus, ut vos omnes factam esse aperte coniurationem contra rem publicam videretis. Non est iam lenitati locus; severitatem res ipsa flagitat.

Unum etiam nunc concedam: exeant, proficiscantur, ne patiantur desidero sui Catalinam miserum tabescere. Demonstrabo iter: Aurelia via profectus est; si accelerare volent, ad vesperam consequentur.

Against Cataline 2, 6–7,
adapted from the Second Oration Against Cataline, delivered before the people.
They realize that all their plans of the past night have been reported to me; I brought them to light yesterday in the senate; Cataline himself was alarmed; he fled: for what do these men wait? Indeed, they are violently mistaken if they hope that earlier mildness of mine will exist forever. What I have waited for I have now obtained: that you all may see that a conspiracy has been made openly against the republic. There is not now a place for mildness; the matter itself demands severity.
I will grant one thing even now: let them go away; let them depart; let them not allow wretched Cataline to waste away from their lack. I will point out the road: He has set out by the Aurelian Road; if they wish to hurry, they will catch up at evening.

Church Hours

When monasteries were established during the Middle Ages, the religious rules required the monks to say prayers at specific times of the day. The names of the prayers, derived from Latin, reflected the names of the times at which they were recited. These times were the seven canonical hours. Time keeping was not fixed and standard in the Middle Ages, and often depended on the time of year and on the location of the monastery. However, the following is an approximate guide to the canonical hours.

Matins, from the adjective **matutinus,** *of the morning.* Despite the meaning, Matins is supposed to be recited at midnight, although it is often recited at dawn instead. As a canonical hour, Matins falls between midnight and 3 a.m.

Lauds, from **laus,** *praise.* This refers to the prayers said at dawn, and to an hour within the 3 A.M. to 6 A.M. period.

Prime, from **primus,** *first.* This refers to the first daylight hour, falling between 6 A.M. and 9 A.M. It begins at sunrise.

Terce, from **tertius,** *third.* This refers to the third hour after sunrise, and to the prayers recited then. This hour falls between 9 A.M. and noon.

Sext, from **sextus,** *sixth.* This refers to the sixth hour after sunrise, or noon, and to the prayers recited then. It falls between noon and 3 p.m.

Nones, from **nonus,** *ninth.* This refers to the ninth hour of daylight and to the prayers recited then. It falls between 3 P.M. and 6 p.m.

Vespers, from **vesper,** *the evening.* This refers to the evening hour, which falls between 6 P.M. and 9 P.M., and to the prayers recited then. It starts at sunset.

Compline, from **completus,** the fourth principal part of the verb **compleo,** *complete.* This refers to the final canonical hour and to the prayers recited then. It falls between 9 P.M. and midnight.

The canonical hours do not last for sixty minutes. Their duration, as well as their starting and finishing times, is determined by the times of sunrise, midday, sunset, and midnight.

251. Practice Exercises

No. 185. Change these indicative tenses to the subjunctive:

1. possum
2. eunt
3. tulit
4. fiebatis
5. volueramus
6. non vult
7. isti
8. malebant
9. potuit
10. noluistis
11. factus est
12. ferebantur
13. malo
14. ierant
15. potueras
16. volebat
17. maluit
18. fio
19. fertis
20. nolueritis

No. 186. Translate these jussive clauses:

1. concedamus
2. ne veniat
3. pugnebant
4. profugiant
5. maneamus
6. ne scribat
7. ne arment
8. ne flagitemus
9. conficiat
10. dormiamus

No. 187. Translate these sentences containing purpose clauses:

1. Pugnant ut urbem capiant.
2. Accelerabam ut consequerer.
3. Daedalus alas paraverat ut ipse et filius suus volarent.
4. Urbem existi ne pugnares.
5. Haec patefacit ut sciamus.
6. Instruimus ut cognoscatis.
7. Audiunt ut cognoscant.
8. Mulier profugerat ne necerat.

No. 188. Translate theses sentences containing result clauses:

1. Cicero tam bene narravit ut Catilina Roma profisceretur.
2. Catalina pertimescebam ut non urbem oppugnaret.
3. Psyche Cupidinem tam magnopere amavit ut ad Inferos iret.
4. Cupid Psychem tam magnopere amavit ut non verba matris suae audiret.
5. Vidistis tam longe ut coniurationem inveniretis.
6. Viri tam celere cucurrerant ut consequerent.
7. Severitas rei tanta erat ut non lenitas daretur.
8. Soror tua ita bene instruit ut multo cognoscamus.

252. Reading Vocabulary

NOUNS

Allobroges, Allobrogum, m. pl., Allobroges
fames, famis, f., famine, hunger
Helvetii, Helvetiorum, m. pl., Helvetii
Latobrigi, Latobrigorum, m. pl., Latobrigi
bonitas, bonitatis, f., goodness, kindness, benevolence

deditio, deditionis, f., surrender
fructus, fructus, m., produce, fruit
vicus, vici, m., village, street
obses, obsidis, m., or **f.,** hostage
Tulingi, Tulingorum, m. pl., Tulingi
Rhenus, Rheni, m., the Rhine

ADJECTIVES

quantus, quanta, quantum, how much

VERBS

accipio, accipere, accepi, acceptus, take, receive (accept)
amitto, amittere, amisi, amissum, lose
dubito, dubitare, dubitavi, dubitatus doubt, hesitate, be uncertain (dubious)
permitto, permittere, permisi, permissus, allow, permit (permission)
purgo, purgare, purgavi, purgatus, clean, remove, excuse (purge)
rescisco, resciscere, rescii, rescitus, learn, find out
revertor, reverti, reversus sum, turn back, return (revert)
vaco, vacare, vacavi, vacatus, be empty (vacant)
transeo, transire, transivi, transitus, pass over, cross, desert. Conjugated like **eo.**

conquiro, conquirere, conquisivi, conquisitus, look for, collect
incolo, incolere, incolui, live in, reside
impero, imperare, imperavi, imperatus, command, order (imperial)
persuadeo, persuadere, persuasi, persuasus, persuade (persuasion)
restituo, restituere, restitui, restitutus, restore rebuild (restitution)
oro, orare, oravi, oratus, beg, pray
tolero, tolerare, toleravi, toleratus, bear, endure (tolerate)
veto, vetare, vetavi, vetatus, forbid (veto)

ADVERBS

unde, from where, whence

CONJUNCTIONS

an, or
si, if
num, whether

253. New Reading Grammar—Noun Clauses: Indirect Commands

Many uses of the Dependent Subjunctive occur in a group of clauses known as noun clauses. These clauses function in the sentence as though they were a noun, usually as the subject or the direct object.

A. INDIRECT COMMANDS ARE ONE OF THESE NOUN CLAUSES.

A direct command, which would use the imperative in Latin, would be something like *Go to Rome!* In an indirect command, the original command is expressed by a subjunctive verb, and the entire clause acts as the object of the main verb, e.g., *He told her to go to Rome.* The main verb usually expresses an action of commanding or asking. The main verb is in the indicative, and the subordinate verb is in the subjunctive. If the noun clause is positive, **ut** is used; if negative, **ne** is used.

Imperaverunt nobis ut hoc faceremus.	They commanded us to do this.
Eam rogis ut Romam eat.	You ask her to go to Rome.
Ab eis petivi ne pugnarent.	I begged of them not to fight.
Moneat ne illud facias.	He (she) warns you not to do that.

As you see, indirect commands are formed the same way as purpose clauses. However, you will not confuse the two because the indicative verb will show what kind of clause you are dealing with.

The following are some of the verbs that can be used with indirect commands:

constituo	decide
moneo	warn
permitto	allow
peto	ask, seek
impero	command
oro	beg
persuadeo	persuade
rogo	ask

The following verbs are *not* used in indirect commands:

volo	wish
malo	prefer
iubeo	command
veto	forbid
nolo	wish not
cupio	desire
patior	allow

Instead, these verbs are used with the accusative and the complementary infinitive:

Vos manere iubeo.	I order you to remain.
Te amari volo.	I want you to be loved.

B. NEW READING GRAMMAR—NOUN CLAUSES: CLAUSES OF PREVENTING, FORBIDDING, AND HINDERING

Verbs that express actions of preventing, forbidding, and hindering also use the dependent subjunctive in noun clauses. These clauses are introduced by **ne**, **quin**, or **quominus**. They are otherwise identical with indirect commands.

Timent ne milites veniant.	They fear that the soldiers will come, *or* They fear lest the soldiers come.
Timent ut milites veniant.	They fear that the soldiers will not come.

C. NEW READING GRAMMAR—NOUN CLAUSES: CLAUSES OF FEARING

Verbs that express fear form noun clauses with the dependent subjunctive and the word **ne** if the clause is positive. If the clause is negative, the word **ut** is used. Note that this is the opposite of the way most noun clauses are formed.

Timent ne milites veniant.	They fear that the soldiers will come, *or*
	They fear lest the soldiers come.
Timent ut milites veniant.	They fear that the soldiers will not come.

D. NEW READING GRAMMAR—NOUN CLAUSES: CLAUSES OF DOUBT

Verbs expressing doubt form noun clauses with the dependent subjunctive and **quin** if the clause is negative. If the clause is positive, **an**, *whether;* **num**, *whether;* or **si**, *if* is used.

Non dubitat quin puella pulchra sit.	He (she) does not doubt that the girl is pretty.
Dubito si veniam.	I doubt if I shall come.

E. NEW READING GRAMMAR—NOUN CLAUSES: INDIRECT QUESTIONS

Where are you going? is a direct question.

I ask where you are going is an indirect question.

You already know that a direct question is formed by using the indicative mood and adding **-ne** to the end of the first word, as in **Amatne vir mulierem?** *Does the man love the woman?* Direct questions can also start with an interrogatory word, with **num** (expecting a *no* answer) and **nonne** (expecting a *yes* answer).

An indirect question is formed by using the indicative for the main verb, which expresses the action of asking, knowing, showing, or perceiving. The dependent subjunctive is used for the other verb. The entire clause acts as the direct object of the verb of asking. This is different from an indirect statement, where the infinitive is used instead of the subjunctive.

Remember to use the proper sequence of tenses in indirect questions.

Scio quid velis.	I know what you want, *or* I know what you will want.
Scio quid volueris.	I know what you wanted.
Rogavi ubi irent.	I have asked where they were, *or*
	I have asked where they would be.
Rogavi ubi issent.	I have asked where they had been.
Rogabunt quid faciamus.	They will ask what we are doing, *or*
	They will ask what we will do.
Rogabunt quid fecerimus.	They will ask what we did.
Cognoscebatis cur oppugnarentur.	You learned why they attacked, *or*
	You learned why they were attacked.
Cognoscebatis cur oppugnati essent.	You learned why they had been attacked.

It is easy to recognize an indirect question. One of the following words will generally be present in the sentence:

quis, who (relative pronoun)
ubi, where, when (adverb)
cur, why (adverb)

quid, what (relative pronoun)
unde, whence, from where (adverb)
quantus, -a, -um, how much (adjective)

qui, quae, quod, which (interrogative adjective)

quo modo, how, in what way (interrogative adjective plus noun)

254. Reading

In the third review section, you read an excerpt from Book I of Caesar's *Commentaries on the Gallic War.* Gaul was the name of what is now France. The Helvetii had surrendered to Caesar. However, one group attempted to sneak away and escape across the upper Rhine.

Comentarii de Bello Gallico I

Quod ubi Caesar resciit, quorum per fines ierant, his uti conquirerent et reducerent, si sibi purgati esse vellent, imperavit. Reductos in hostium numero habuit; reliquos omnes obsidibus, armis, perfugis traditis in deditionem accepit.
Helvetios, Tulingos, Latobrigos in fines suos, unde erant profecti, reverti iussit, et quod omnibus fructibus amissis domique nihil erat, quo famem tolerarent, Allobrogios imperavit ut his frumenti copiam facerent.
Ipsos oppida vicosque, quos incenderant, restituere iussit quod noluit eum locum, unde Helvetii discesserant vacare, ne propter bonitatem agrorum Germani, qui trans Rhenum incolunt, e suis finibus in Helvetiorum fines transirent et finitimi Galliae provinciae Allobrogibusque essent.

Commentaries on the Gallic War 1, adapted from chapter 28.
When Caesar learned this, he ordered those [tribes] through whose borders they [the Helvetii] had gone to look for them and lead them back, if they wanted to be excused. He held the men led back into the number of the enemy; he received all those remaining in surrender, when the hostages, weapons, and deserters were handed over.
He ordered the Helvetii, the Tulingi, and the Latobrigi to return to their own borders from where they had set forth, and, because they had lost all their produce and nothing was at home by which they might endure famine, he ordered the Allobroges to make an abundance of grain for them.
He ordered them [the tribes] to rebuild themselves the towns and villages which they had burned, because he did not wish that place from where the Helvetii had departed to be empty, lest, on account of the goodness of the fields, the Germans, who live across the Rhine, cross over from their own borders into the borders of the Helvetii and be neighbors to the province of Gaul and to the Allobroges.

258. Practice Exercises

No. 189. Translate these sentences:

1. Monuerat ne Romam veniretis.
2. Tulingos persuadetis ut arma sua tradant.
3. Oro ne patrem meum necatur.
4. Mater tua imperavit ne equos amitteres.
5. Caesar milites suos reverti vetat.
6. Caesar Allobroges prohibuit ne urbem captam rescicerent.
7. Timemus ne vici vacent.
8. Cicero pertimescet ut Catilina Roma proficiscatur.
9. Helvetii dubitant si Caesar deditiones suas accipiat.
10. Non dubitant quin Germani fines suos transeant.

No. 190. Translate the following sentences, which contain indirect questions:

1. Non scio quis sis.
2. Cicero vos narrabit cur Catilina Roma discesseris.
3. Mulier rogavit quo modo hoc rescisses.
4. Rescierant quid cuperemus.
5. Sciamus unde milites oppugnent.
6. Cognosco cur mulierem ames.
7. Me dixisti quo modo vici restituissentur.
8. Rogabas querm amavero.
9. Vir scit quid soror tua viderit.
10. Helvetii casa incenderant in quos incoluerint.

No. 191.

1. Give the present subjunctive, active and passive, of **accipio**.
2. Give the perfect subjunctive of **revertor**.
3. Give the imperfect subjunctive of **eo**.
4. Give the pluperfect subjunctive, active and passive, of **veto**.

The Months of the Year

The names of all of our months come from Latin.

January, from **Januarius**. Named after Janus, the two-headed god of beginnings.

February, from **Februarius**. Named from the Latin februa, offerings of expiation or atonement.

March, from **Martius**. Named after Mars, the god of war, it was originally the first month of the Roman year.

April, from **Aprilis**. Probably named after **Apru**, the Etruscan equivalent to Venus, the goddess of love.

May, from **Maius**. Named after Maia, the mother of Mercury, the messenger of the gods.

June, from **Junius**. Named after Juno, the queen of the gods.

July, from **Julius**. Named after Julius Caesar, the month was originally called **Quintilis**, a word related to the adjective **quintus**, meaning *fifth*. **Quintilis** was the fifth month of the year when the calender started with **Martius**.

August, from **Augustus**. Named after Augustus Caesar, this month was originally called **Sextilis**, related to **sextus**, *sixth*, because it was originially the sixth month of the year.

September, **October**, **November**, and **December** are taken directly from Latin. The words for these months are related to **septimus**, **octavus**, **nonus**, and **decimus**, because they were originally the seventh, eighth, ninth, and tenth months of the year.

255. New Reading Vocabulary

NOUNS

ius, iuris, n., right, authority

Nicaea, Nicaeae, f., Nicaea

annua, annuorum, n. pl., pension, yearly pay (annuity)

magnitudo, magnitudinis, f., greatness, vastness (magnitude)

nemo, neminis, m. or **f.,** no one, nobody

Nicomedia, Nicomediae, f., Nicomedia

officium, officii or **offici, n.,** official job, official position

ministerium, ministerii or **ministeri, n.,** service, work, employment (ministry)

PRONOUNS

quidam, quaedam, quiddam, a certain one; pl., some. Declined like the relative pronoun plus **dam**, except that the neuter nominative, accusative, and vocative singular are **quid.**

aliquis, aliquid, someone, something; anyone, anything. Declined like the interrogative pronoun **quis, quid.**

ADJECTIVES

publicus, publica, publicum, public, common

salvus, salva, salvum, safe, well (salvation)

otiosus, otiosa, otiosum, free, at leisure, not working

plerusque, plerasque, plerumque, most. Declined like **plerus** plus **que.**

inutilis, inutile, useless, harmful

senex, senis, old, aged (senile)

periculosus, periculosa, periculosum, dangerous, perilous

honestus, honesta, honestum, honored, respected (honest)

VERBS

adfirmo, adfirmare, adfirmavi, adfirmatus, strengthen, affirm, assert

arbitror, arbitrari, arbitratus sum, think, judge (arbitrate)

comperio, comperire, comperi, compertus, learn, ascertain (compare)

credo, credere, credidi, creditus, believe, trust (credit, credence)

damno, damnare, damnavi, damnatus, condemn, find guilty (damnation)

descendo, descendere, descendi, descensus, descend, come down (descent)

evenio, evenire, eveni, evenitus, happen, come out

existimo, existimare, existimavi, existimatus, think, judge

exsolvo, exsolvere, exsolvi, exsolutus, release, free

fungor, fungi, functus sum, perform, do

haesito, haesitare, haesitavi, haesitatus, hesitate, be at a loss (hesitant)

lego, legere, legi, lectus, read (legible)

nescio, nescire, nescivi, nescitus, not know, be ignorant of

pascor, pasci, pastus sum, feed on, eat

quaero, quaerere, quaesivi, quaesitus, ask, look for (quest, question)

reddeo, reddere, reddidi, reditus, return, restore

refero, referre, retuli, relatus, report, bring back (refer). Conjugated like **fero.**

retineo, retinere, retinui, retentus, keep back, retain

vivo, vivere, vixi, victus, live (vivacious)

oportet, oportere, oportuit, it is right, it is proper. This is an impersonal verb. The subject is always *it;* thus, it is used only in the third person.

ADVERBS

fortasse, perhaps
modeste, moderately, modestly
quantum, as much as
frugaliter, temperately, frugally (frugal)
nimis, very much, too much
rursus, backward, on the other hand

CONJUNCTIONS

utinam, if only, would that
vel, or **vel . . . vel,** either . . . or

256. New Reading Grammar—Relative Clauses of Characteristic

In a sentence containing a relative clause of characteristic, the clause tells you something about its antecedent. It is like an adjective in this way, like any relative clause. In sentences using relative clauses of characteristic, however, the antecedent is usually indefinite, negative, general, or interrogative rather than specific, and the verb of the clause is put into the subjunctive.

Nemo est qui te credat.   There is no one who believes you.

In this sentence, the relative characteristic clause is: *who believes you.* It describes a characteristic of *no one,* the antecedent. Thus, the sentence might be translated as follows: There is no one with the characteristic of believing you. Other examples follow:

Aliquis est qui puerum nesciat?   Is there anyone who does not know the boy?
Multi sunt qui illa credant.   There are many who believe those things.
Sunt qui libros legant.   There are those who have read the books.
Hic est vir quem omnes ament.   He is the kind of man whom all like.

Note that, in the last example, **omnes,** *all,* is the subject of the relative clause and of the verb **ament; quem,** which is masculine and singular in agreement with its antecedent **vir,** is in the accusative case because it is the direct object of the verb **ament.**

257. New Reading Grammar—Optative Subjunctive

With the optative subjunctive we find another use of the subjunctive in an Independent Clause. The optative subjunctive expresses a wish (from the Latin **opto, optare,** *to wish* or *desire*). The word **ne** is used when the wish is negative. The adverbs **utinam** (if only, would that), **ut,** or **uti** may be used whether the optative is positive or negative. Wishes either can/cannot or did/did not come true; Latin represents this range of possibilities through the tense of the subjunctive that is used in the optative clause.

1. **IF IT IS** *possible* **FOR THE WISH TO COME TRUE, THE PRESENT SUBJUNCTIVE IS USED.**

   Utinam may or may not be used. It is easy to recognize the optative, whether or not **utinam** is used.

   Utinam veniant!   If only they would come!
   Ne miles necetur!   May the soldier not die!

2. **IF THE WISH REFERS TO THE PRESENT TIME, AND IT *cannot* COME TRUE, THE IMPERFECT SUBJUNCTIVE IS USED.**

Note that this is different from the usual sequence of tenses.

Utinam regina diceret!	If only the queen were speaking!
Utinam ne ibi essem!	If only I were not here!

3. **IF THE WISH REFERS TO THE PAST, AND IF IT *did not* COME TRUE, THE PLUPERFECT SUBJUNCTIVE IS USED.**

If the wish refers to the past and it did come true, it no longer qualifies as a wish, and would not use a subjunctive construction.

Utinam casam vidissetis!	If only you had seen the house!
Utinam ne Romam venissent!	If only they had not come to Rome!

258. New Reading Grammar—*cum* Clauses and the Subjunctive

A. **YOU HAVE ALREADY LEARNED THAT, WHEN IT IS A SUBORDINATING CONJUNCTION, cum CAN BE USED WITH THE INDICATIVE MOOD.**

In this case, **cum** means *when* or *while,* and the verb is in the present or future tense. This is known as the *temporal* use of the conjunction **cum** (from **tempus, temporis,** *time*).

Cum Romam eo, patrem meum video.	When I go to Rome, I see my father.

If the verb is in the past, the indicative is used if the clause with **cum** refers to the point in time at which something occurred.

Cum Romam veni, patrem meum vidi.	When I went to Rome, I saw my father, *or* At the time when I went to Rome, I saw my father.

B. **THE SUBJUNCTIVE IS USED IN A cum CLAUSE IF THE ACTION TOOK PLACE IN THE PAST AND THE CLAUSE REFERS TO THE SITUATION OR THE *CIRCUMSTANCES* UNDER WHICH THE MAIN ACTION TOOK PLACE.**

The verb describing the main action stays in the indicative. In this context, the word **cum** can be translated as *when, since,* or *although.* The subjunctive **cum** clause is used in almost the same way as the ablative absolute and can often be replaced by it.

As always, the proper sequence of tenses must be followed. Since the main verb will be in one of the past tenses (otherwise, there would be no need for the subjunctive), the imperfect is used if the action of **cum** clause occurs at the same time as the main action. The pluperfect is used if the action of the clause occurs before the action of the main verb. This use of **cum** with the subjunctive is known as a *cum circumstantial clause.*

Cum pugnarent, timebamus.	When they were fighting, we were afraid.
Cum bene pugnarent, timebamus.	Although they were fighting well, we were afraid.
Cum bene pugnarent, non timebamus.	Since they fought well, we were not afraid.
Cum dixissem, mansisti.	When I had spoken, you remained.
Cum bene pugnavissent, urbs capta est.	Since they had fought well, the city was captured, *or* Although they had fought well, the city was captured.

You will notice that it is not always immediately obvious how **cum** is to be translated. You will have to rely on the context of the sentence for help.

259. Reading

Gaius Plinius Caecilius Secundus, known as Pliny the Younger, was born in North Italy in A.D. 61 or 62. In A.D. 109, he was appointed by the Emperor Trajan to represent him in the province of Bithynia, in northern Turkey. Pliny wrote several letters to Trajan, discussing the various problems of Bithynia.

Gaius Plinius Traiano Imperatori

Salva magnitudine tua, domine, descendas oportet ad meas curas, cum ius mihi dederis referendi ad te, de quibus dubito. In plerisque civitatibus, maxime Nicomediae et Nicaeae, quidam vel in opus damnati vel in ludum similiaque his genera poenarum publicorum servorum officio ministerioque funguntur, atque etiam ut publici servi annua accipiunt. Quod ego cum audissem, diu multumque haesitavi, quid facere deberem. Nam et reddere poenae post longum tempus plerosque iam senes et, quantum adfirmatur, frugaliter modesteque viventes nimis severum arbitrabar, et in publicis officiis retinere damnatos non satis honestum putabam; eosdem rursus a re publica pasci otiosos inutile, non pasci etiam periculosum existimabam.

Quares fortasse quem ad modum evenerit, ut poenis in quas damnati erant exsoluerentur: et ego quaesivi, sed nihil comperi quod adfirmare tibi possim.

Gaius Pliny to Emperor Trajan, adapted from Pliny's Letters, 10, 31.

Saving your greatness, lord, it is right that you should descend to my cares, since you have given to me the right of reporting to you about what I am in doubt. In most cities, especially those of Nicomedia and Nicaea, some of those condemned either to work or to the [gladiatorial] games and types of punishments similar to these, perform the job and ministry of public servants, and even receive a pension as public servants.

When I had heard this, I was for long at a great loss as to what I ought to do. Now, I thought that to return them to punishment after a long time, most of them already old and, as far as can be affirmed, living frugally and moderately, [would be] too severe, and I thought that to retain the condemned men in public jobs was not sufficiently honest; on the other hand, I thought for these same men to eat at [the expense of] the republic wasteful; [for them] not to eat, [I thought] even perilous.

You will ask, perhaps, in what way it happened that those condemned to these penalties were freed, and I have asked, but I learned nothing which I am able to affirm to you.

Note: Trajan's response to Pliny was that the elderly men, and those who had been sentenced more than ten years ago, could be employed in jobs traditionally reserved for criminals, but that the rest of those sentenced must return until they had completed the term of their sentences.

260. Practice Exercises

No. 192. Translate these sentences:

1. Nemo erat qui haec existimaret.
2. Illa est quam omnes credunt.
3. Aliquis est qui non exsolutus sit?
4. Sunt quo illud adfirment.
5. Utinam pater meus viveret!
6. Utinam reddeant!
7. Utinam libros meos legisses!
8. Ne haec quaerant!
9. Ne in ludum damnatus esset!
10. Ne pugnandi nescirem!

No. 193. Translate the following sentences, which contain cum clauses:

1. Cum armes obsidesque tradidissent, Caesar vicos restituit.
2. Cum damnatus esset, miserus erat.
3. Cum exsolutae essent, non laetae erant.
4. Cum mulierem amarem, urbem exii.
5. Cum periculosum esset, non pertimescimus.
6. Cum acceleravissent, non consecuti sunt.
7. Cum acceleravisset, consecutus est.
8. Cum Cicero erraret, bene dixit.
9. Cum agri incensi essent, Helvetii non ibi incolebant.
10. Cum id concessum esset, Catilina Roma discessit.

No. 194.

1. Give the present indicative of **consequor.**
2. Give the imperfect subjunctive, active and passive, of **erro.**
3. Give the perfect subjunctive, active and passive, of **perfero.**
4. Give the pluperfect indicative, active and passive, of **flagito.**

Special Days in the Roman Months

Each month in the Roman calendar had three special days that were used to keep track of when an event had happened or was to happen.

Kalendae, the *Kalends,* fell on the first day of every month. It is abbreviated **Kal.**

Idus, the *Ides,* fell on the fifteenth in March, May, July, and October, and on the thirteenth in all other months. It is abbreviated to **Id.** One of the most famous dates in Roman history is the Ides of March, the date of the assassination of Julius Caesar.

Nonae, the *Nones,* comes from the adjective **nonus,** *ninth.* It fell on the ninth day before the Ides. However, when the Romans counted days, they added in the day they started with and the day they ended with (inclusively). Thus, the Nones fell on the seventh in March, May, July, and October, and on the fifth of all other months.

The names of these days are given in the plural. **Kalendae** and **Nonae** are first declension nouns. **Idus** is a fourth declension noun.

Days were counted backwards from whichever of these three days was closest. The starting and ending days were counted as well. Thus, **ante diem septimum Kalendas Augustas,** *the seventh day before the Kalends of August,* would be July 26. The Latin would be abbreviated to A.D. VII. Kal. Aug. You will notice that the date is put into the accusative.

The day immediately before one of the three special days is indicated by using the word **pridie,** followed by the accusative. Thus, **pridie Idus Martias** is March 14.

261. New Reading Vocabulary

NOUNS

aspectus, aspectus, m., look, sight (aspect)
misericordia, misericordiae, f., sympathy, pity
odium, odii, or odi, n., hatred (odius)
praesentia, praesentiae, f., presence, effect
sensus, sensus, m., sense, sensation, feeling
iudicium, iudicii, or iudici, n., judgment, sentence
contumelia, contumeliae, f., mistreatment, outrage, injury
necessarius, necessarii, or necessari, m., or **necessaria, necessariae, f.**, relative, friend
frequentia, frequentiae, f., crowd
mens, mentis, f., mind (mental)
pactum, pacti, n., way, manner
parens, parentis, m. or f., parent
ratio, rationis, f., manner, fashion, reason
taciturnitas, taciturnitatis, f., silence (taciturn)
parricidium, parricidii or parricidi, n., parricide, murder, treason

PRONOUN AND ADJECTIVE

iste, ista, istud, that, that one of yours.

Conjugated like **ille, illa, illud,** this generally has negative or derogatory connotations.

ADJECTIVES

infestus, infesta, infestum, threatening, dangerous, hostile (infested)
communis, commune, common, public

VERBS

absum, abesse, abfui, be absent, be away from
careo, carere, carui, be without, be absent from
loquor, loqui, locutus sum, say, speak (loquacious)
opinor, opinari, opinatus sum, think, suppose (opinion)
placo, placare, placavi, placatus, calm, reconcile (placate)
saluto, salutare, salutavi, salutatus, greet, welcome (salute, salutations)
suspicio, suspicere, suspexi, suspectus, mistrust, suspect (suspicion)

metuo, metuere, metui, fear, be afraid
permoveo, permovere, permovi, stir, move
vito, vitare, vitavi, vitatus, avoid
adsum, adesse, adfui, be present, be here. Conjugated like **sum.**
cogito, cogitare, cogitavi, cogitatus, consider, think (cogitate)
iudico, iudicare, iudicavi, iudicatus, judge, sentence, examine
vulnero, vulnerare, vulneravi, vulneratus, wound, hurt (vulnerable)

ADVERBS

paulo, a little

CONJUNCTIONS

etiamsi, even if
quamvis, although
etsi, even if, although
tametsi, even if
nisi, if not, unless

INTERJECTIONS

mehercule, by Hercules!

262. New Reading Grammar—Conditional Sentences

A sentence is conditional if it speaks of an action that will occur if another action occurs.

If he eats, he will not be hungry.

If he eats is the conditional clause of the sentence; the technical term is the **protasis**. The conclusion or consequence, *he will not be hungry,* is known as the **apodosis**. The apodosis (the *then* part) is an independent clause, while the protasis (the *if* part) is always a subordinate clause describing the circumstances according to which the conclusion is foreseeable. The protasis modifies the rest of the sentence adverbially.

In Latin the protasis (the *if* part) of a conditional sentence is introduced by the following words:

si, if   **tametsi**, even if
nisi, if not, unless   **etiamsi**, even if
etsi, even if

There are three basic types of conditional sentences in Latin, each with its own rules for what tenses and moods are appropriate.

1. SIMPLE CONDITIONAL SENTENCES

The indicative is used in both the protasis and the apodosis if the conditional sentence refers to a definite fact. The same tense is used in both halves of the sentence. Because simple conditional sentences refer to facts, the future and future perfect tenses are not used.

Si audit, multa cognoscit.	If he is listening, he is learning many things.
Etsi audivit, nulla congnovit.	Even if he has listened, he has learned nothing.
Si audiet, multa cognoscet.	If he will listen, he will learn many things.

2. FUTURE CONDITIONAL SENTENCES

Within future conditionals there are three subdivions. If a conditional sentence deals with a future event that probably **will not** happen, the present subjunctive is used in both the protasis and the apodosis. This kind of conditional sentence is called the **future less vivid,** and is usually translated as *"if this should happen, then that would happen."* They are sometimes referred to as *should/would* clauses.

If, on the other hand, there is a high probability of the condition being fulfilled, the future indicative is used in both the protasis and apodosis. This type is known as **future more vivid,** and is translated as *"if this happens, then that will happen."*

Once in a while one runs across a **future most vivid** conditional, which has a future perfect indicative in the apodosis, and a future indicative in the apodosis. To the Roman mind, the future perfect emphasized the necessity of the first act being completed before the second could occur. These, like the future more vivid, are best translated as *"If this happens, then that will happen."*

Si audiat, cognoscat.	If he should listen (he will not), he would learn.
Si ad urbem eas, laetus sim.	If you should come to the city, I would be happy.
Tametsi non ad urbem eas, laetus sim.	Even if you should not come to the city, I would be happy.

3. CONTRARY TO FACT CONDITIONALS

The third kind of conditional sentence deals with conditions contrary to fact. The condition expressed in the apodosis of the sentence has not been or cannot be met. Some texts refer to these as Contrafactual Conditions.

If the action takes place in the present, the *imperfect subjunctive* is used in both parts of the sentence. Note that this does not break the rules for sequences of tenses since the rules for sequence of tenses only apply when the main verb of the independent clause is in the indicative. Present contrary to fact conditionals are usually best translated *"If this were to happen, then that would happen."*

Si veniret, adesset.	If he were coming, he would be here.
Nisi oppugnarent, non timeremus.	If they were not attacking, we should not be afraid.

If the action takes place in the past, the *pluperfect subjunctive* is used in both parts of the sentence. Past contrary to fact conditionals are usually best translated as *"If this had happened, then that would have happened."*

Si adfuisset, eam vidisses.	If she had been here, you would have seen her.
Nisi hoc dixisset, non oppugnavissent.	If he had not said this, they would not have attacked.

Sometimes you will run across a mixed conditional sentence, one that does not seem to follow the above rules. For example:

Si laboravisset, felix esset.	If he had worked, he would be happy.

Generally, such mixed conditionals have been constructed by their authors as the sense seemed to demand. In the above example, the author is suggesting that if he had worked in the past (which he did not, hence the need for the pluperfect of the past contrary to fact), then he would be happy now in the present (which he apparently is not, hence the imperfect of the present contrary to fact).

263. New Reading Grammar—Concessive Clauses

Concessive clauses are adverbial subordinate clauses that are introduced by words such as *although, nevertheless, even though, despite the fact that,* and so forth. You have already learned how **cum** is used in a concessive clause in the subjunctive and how the ablative absolute is used like a concessive clause with a participle. The words **quamquam, etsi, tametsi, etiamsi,** or **quamvis** may also be used in this construction. The word **tamen,** *nevertheless,* is often used in the second half of the sentence, the portion that contains the independent clause.

1. **IF quamquam IS USED, OR IF etsi, MEANING *ALTHOUGH,* IS USED, THEN THE SENTENCE DEALS WITH A DEFINITE FACT AND THE INDICATIVE MOOD IS USED IN BOTH THE INDEPENDENT AND THE DEPENDENT CLAUSES.**

   Quamquam diu acriterque vidimus, mulierem non invenimus.
   Although we have looked for a long time and keenly, we have not found the woman.
   Etsi bene pugnabunt, tamen urbs capietur.
   Although they will fight well, nevertheless, the city will be captured.

2. IF **quamvis** IS USED, THEN THE SENTENCE DEALS WITH A POSSIBILITY INSTEAD OF WITH A FACT.

In that event, the subjunctive is used in the dependent concessive clause and the indicative is used for the main verb of the independent clause.

Quamvis mulierem non veniamus, diu acriterque videbimus.
Although we may not find the woman, we shall look long and keenly.

3. IF **etiamsi, tametsi,** OR **etsi** MEANING *EVEN IF* ARE USED, THEN THE SENTENCE IS A CONDITIONAL SENTENCE, AND FOLLOWS THE RULES FOR CONDITIONALS GIVEN ABOVE.

264. Reading

The following section is taken from Cicero's First Oration Against Cataline. In this passage, he attempts to convince Cataline, as he will later attempt to convince Cataline's cohorts, to leave Rome.

In Catalinam II

Against Cataline 2,16–18, adapted from the Second Oration Against Cataline, delivered in the senate.

Nunc vero quae tua est ista vita? Sic enim iam tecum loquar, non ut odio permotus esse videar, quo debeo, sed ut misericordia quae tibi nulla debetur.

Now, truly, what is this life of yours? For I shall speak with you thus, not as if I seemed to be moved by hatred, which I ought, but as if by pity, of which none is owed to you.

Venisti paulo ante in senatum. Quis te ex hac tanta frequentia, tot ex tuis amicis ac necessariis salutavit? Vocis exspectas contumeliam, cum sis gravissimo iudicio taciturnitatis oppressus?

You came, a little before, into the Senate. Who welcomed you out of such a crowd as this, out of so many of your friends and relatives? Do you wait for an insult of the voice when you have been crushed by the most grave judgment of silence?

Servi mehercule mei si me isto pacto metuerent ut te metuunt omnes cives tui, domum meam relinquerem: tu tibi urbem non arbitraris? Et si me meis civibus suspectum tarn graviter viderem, carere civium quam infestis omnium oculis conspici mallem: dubitas quorum mentus sensusque vulneras, eorum aspectum praesentiamque vitare?

By Hercules, if my slaves feared me in that manner as all your fellow citizens fear you, I should leave my house: Do you not think that [you should leave] the city? And if I saw that I was suspected so gravely by my fellow citizens, I should prefer to avoid my fellow citizens than to see the unfriendly eyes of all: Do you hesitate to avoid the looks and the presence of those whose minds and senses you are wounding?

Si te parentes timerent tui neque eos ratione ulla placere posses, ut opinor, ab eorum oculis concederes. Nunc te patria quae communis est parens omnium nostrum metuit et iam diu nihil te iudicat nisi de parricidio suo cogitare.

If your parents feared you, nor were you able to calm them by any manner, you would withdraw from their eyes, as I think. Now your native land, which is the common parent of all of us, fears you and judges that for a long time now, you consider nothing except her murder.

265. Practice Exercises

No. 195. Translate these conditional sentences:

1. Si me vulneraveris, te vitavero.
2. Tametsi non salutatus esset, venisset.
3. Nisi metuerim, pugnaverim.
4. Tametsi milites Caesaris metuissent, urbes vicosque Helvetiorum oppugnavissent.
5. Tametsi Catilina non Roma discedat, Cicero populum de coniuratio eius moneat.
6. Si te amavissem, te narravissem.
7. Si illa adfuerit, nos crediderit.
8. Tametsi ibi adfuisses, nihil fecisses.
9. Tametsi litteras scribamus, non eas legant.
10. Nisi Allobroges arma tradidissent, Caesar casas suas incendisset.

No. 196. Translate the following sentences, which contain concessive clauses:

1. Quamquam me suspicis, tamen te credo.
2. Etsi mulieram nescivisti, eam audivisti.
3. Quamvis non audiant, Cicero loquetur.
4. Quamvis Catilina non salutetur, tamen in senatum veniet.
5. Etsi miles vitatus est, vivit.
6. Quamvis urbs capiatur, tamen non metuemus.
7. Quamquam corpus tuum adest, mens tua abest.

No. 197.

1. Give the present subjunctive of **adsum**.
2. Give the future perfect indicative, active and passive, of **exsolvo**.
3. Give the pluperfect subjunctive, active and passive, of **suscipio**.
4. Give the imperfect subjunctive, active and passive, of **vulnero**.
5. Give the perfect indicative, active and passive, of **vivo**.

An Overview of Latin Literature

Latin literature is usually divided into six periods. The first of these is the *Early Period,* and it covers Latin literature before 80 B.C. The second period, the *Golden Age,* lasted from 80 B.C. until A.D. 14. During this period, Classical Latin reached its height as a written language. The Golden Age is further subdivided into the *Ciceronian* period and the *Augustan* period. The Ciceronian period, named after the orator Cicero, whose command of Latin few could equal, ran from 80 B.C. through 43 B.C. The Augustan period, named after Augustus Caesar, lasted from 43 B.C. until A.D. 14.

The *Silver Age* of Latin literature ran from A.D. 14 through A.D. 138. It shows a decline in standards. The fourth period, called the *Patristic Period,* ran from the late second century through the fifth century. The major writers included the Church Fathers (**patres**). During this period the Romance languages were developing from local dialects of Latin. The fifth period ran from the sixth through the fourteenth centuries. It is called the *Medieval Period,* and the literature of this period was written in looser, more flexible Medieval Latin rather than in Classical Latin. However, your knowledge of Classical Latin will enable you to read the literature of this period with little difficulty.

The sixth and final period runs from the fifteenth century until the present day. It is called the *Modern Period.* Much of the literature from this period is written in Classical Latin, as people rediscovered the literature of the earlier periods.

266. New Reading Vocabulary

NOUNS

Carnutes, Carnutum, m. pl., Carnutes

initium, initii or **initi, n.,** beginning, start (initiation)

maiores, maiorum, m. pl., ancestors, forefathers

salus, salutis, f., health, safety (salutary)

casus, casus, m., downfall, overthrow, fate

Acco, Acconis, m., Acco

pollicitatio, pollicitationis, f., promise

legio, legionis, f., legion

NOUN AND ADJECTIVE

princeps, principis, m., (as noun) chief; first, foremost (principal)

ADJECTIVES

postremus, postrema, postremum, last, finally

clandestinus, clandestina, clandestinum, secret, hidden (clandestine)

vetus, veteris, old, aged (veteran)

VERBS

recido, recidere, reccidi recoil, fall

sancio, sancire, sanxi, sanctus, consecrate

absum, abesse, abfui, be absent, be away from

recupero, recuperare, recuperavi, recuperatus, recover, get back (recuperate)

vindico, vindicare, vindicavi, vindicatus, defend, protect; **in libertatem vindicare,** set free

deleo, delere, delevi, deletus, destroy, obliterate (delete)

effero, efferre, extuli, elatus, carry forth, bring out. Conjugated like **fero.**

intercludo, intercludere, interclusi, interclusus, shut off, stop

misereor, misereri, miseritus sum, pity, feel sorry for

profiteor, profiteri, professus sum, declare, acknowledge, say

recuso, recusare, recusavi, recusatus, refuse, reject (recusant)

posco, poscere, poposci, ask, beg, demand

audeo, audere, ausus sum, dare (audacity)

polliceor, polliceri, pollicatus sum, promise

agito, agitare, agitavi, agitatus, consider, discuss

caveo, cavere, cavi, cautus, beware of, guard against (caution)

desero, deserere, deserui, deseritus, desert, abandon

egredior, egredi, egressus sum, quit, surpass, go beyond (e.g., ress)

iureiuro, iureiurare, iureiuravi, iureiuratus, swear by an oath

praesto, praestare, praestavi, praestatus, be better than, be superior to

queror, queri, questus sum, complain about (querulous)

CONJUNCTIONS

priusquam, before

quoniam, because, now that

267. New Reading Grammar—Subjunctive in Indirect Statement

The subjunctive mood is also used in subordinate clauses within indirect statements (*accusative/infinitive* constructions). This is perhaps easiest to see if we walk through the steps.

A direct statement uses the indicative:

Urbs deleta est.   The city was destroyed.

An indirect statement uses the indicative for the main verb and the infinitive in the subordinate clause. The subject of the infinitive is put into the accusative case:

Putavi urbem deli.   I thought that the city was destroyed.

However, if the indirect statement has its own subordinate clause, the subjunctive is used in that clause, even if the indicative would be used in direct speech.

Putavi urbem qui capta esset deli.   I thought that the city which had been captured was destroyed.

The subordinate clause is **qui capta esset**, *which had been captured.* **qui** is in the nominative because it is the subject of this clause. The verb, **capta esset,** is in the pluperfect subjunctive because the action in the subordinate clause takes place before the action of the main verb, which is from the secondary sequence.

More examples follow.

1. **DIRECT SPEECH**

Scribit libros.	He writes the books.
Scripsit libros.	He wrote the books.

2. **DIRECT SPEECH WITH A SUBORDINATE CLAUSE**

Scribit libros quos legis.	He writes the books *which you read.*
Scribit libros quos legisti.	He writes the books *which you have read.*
Scipsit libros quos legis.	He wrote the books *which you read.*
Scripsit libros quos legisti.	He wrote the books *which you have read.*

   You will note that the subordinate clauses in the sentences above are in the indicative, because this is direct speech.

3. **INDIRECT SPEECH**

Dico eum libros scribere.	I say that he writes the books.
Dico eum libros scripsisse.	I say that he wrote the books.
Dixi eum libros scribere.	I said that he wrote the books.
Dixi eum libros scripsisse.	I said that he had written the books.

   Both **eum** and **libros** are in the accusative. **libros** is accusative because it is the direct object of the infinitve, and **eum** is accusative because it is the subject of the infinitive. The present infinitive is used when the action takes place at the same time as that of the main verb, **dico.** The perfect infinitive is used when the action takes place before that of the main verb.

4. **INDIRECT SPEECH WITH A SUBORDINATE CLAUSE**

Dico eum libros quos legas scribere.	I say that he writes the books which you read.
Dixi eum libros quos lectus sis scribere.	I said that he wrote the books which you read.
Dixi eum libros quos lectus esses scripsisse.	I said that he had written the books which you had read.

268. New Reading Grammar—Subjunctive by Attraction

Subordinate clauses within subjunctive clauses often change to the subjunctive mood, through a process known as attraction (think of the attraction between a magnet and a piece of iron), especially when the subordinate clause is an integral part of the idea of the main clause. For example:

Direct Question: **Cur puella quem amat abest?**
Why is the girl whom he loves not here?

Indirect Question: **Rogabat cur puella quem amaret abesset.**
He asked why the girl whom he loved was not here.

In the second sentence, the orginal indicative **abest** has become the subjunctive **abesset** according to the rules for indirect questions. The original indicative **amat** of the relative clause has become the subjunctive **amaret** by attraction. The tenses follow the rules for Sequence of Tenses.

269. READING

The following is another excerpt from Caesar's *Commentaries on the Gallic War*. This reading is drawn from the seventh book, where the leaders of the Gauls are attempting to conspire against Caesar.

Commentarii de Bello Gallico

Inter se principes Galliae de Acconis morte queruntur; posse hunc casum ad ipsos recidere demonstrant, miserantur communem Galliae fortunam, omnibus pollicitationibus ac praemiis deposcunt qui belli initium faciant et sui capitis periculo Galliam in libertatem vindicent.

In primis rationem esse habendam dicunt, priusquam eorum clandestina consilia efferantur, ut Caesar ab exercitu intercludatur. Id esse facile quod neque legiones audeant absente imperatore egredi, neque imperator sine praesidio ad legiones pervenire possit. Postremo in acie praestare interfici quam non veterem belli gloriam libertatemque quam a maioribus acceperint recuperare.

His rebus agitatis profitentur Carnutes se nullum periculum communis salutis causa recusare principesque ex omnibus bellum facturos pollicentur et, quoniam in praesentia obsidibus cavere inter se non possint ne res efferatur, ut iureiurando sanciatur, petunt, ne facto initio belli ab reliquis deserantur.

Commentaries on the Gallic War,
adapted from 7, 1–2.

The chiefs of Gaul complained among themselves about the death of Acco; they pointed out that this fate could fall on themselves; they pitied the common fortune of Gaul; they asked with all [kinds of] promises and rewards for those who would make a beginning of the war and free Gaul at the risk of their own heads. First, they said that there would have to be a way, before their secret plans were carried abroad, for Caesar to be shut off from the army. [They said that] this would be easy because neither would the legions dare to go out when the general was absent nor could the general arrive at the legions without a guard. At last, [they said that] to die in battle is better than not to recover the old glory of war and freedom which they had received from their ancestors.

When these matters had been considered, the Carnutes said that they themselves refused no danger for the cause of the common safety and they promised that they, first of all, would make war, and, because in the present situation, they could not guard against [betrayal] among themselves with hostages, lest the matter be carried abroad, they sought that it be consecrated by swearing an oath, lest, when a beginning of war had been made, they be deserted by those remaining.

270. Practice Exercises

No. 198. Translate these sentences:
1. Dixit Helvetios qui in agris incolerent urbem delevisse.
2. Dicunt mulierem quam sciam non adesse.
3. Professus est milites quos Caesar imperavisset arma obsidesque tradidisse.
4. Dico puellas quae haec pollicatae sint in libertatem vindicatas esse.
5. Dices sagittam quae puerum necaverit in silva amissam esse.
6. Putaverunt legionem quae Caesarem deservisset redituram esse.
7. Putamus coniurationem quam Cicero patefecerit Romam volneraturam esse.
8. Sentio verbi qui a te narreris ab omnibus credi.
9. Putavisti pollicitationes quae ab frequentia Carnutum factae essent parricidium cauturas esse.
10. Imperavit virum qui filios filiasque eius pastus sit laudari.

No. 199.
1. Give all six infinitives of **recido.**
2. Give the four participles of **recuso.**
3. Give the imperfect active indicative of **queror.**
4. Give the perfect subjunctive, active and passive, of **praesto.**

275. Vocabulary Review

NOUNS

1. Acco	11. desiderium	21. lenitas	31. obses	41. res publica
2. Allobroges	12. fames	22. magnitudo	32. odium	42. Rhenus
3. annua	13. frequentia	23. maiores	33. officium	43. salus
4. aspectus	14. fructus	24. mens	34. pactum	44. senatus
5. bonitas	15. Helvetii	25. ministerium	35. parens	45. sensus
6. Carnutes	16. initium	26. misercordia	36. parricidium	46. severitas
7. casus	17. iudicium	27. necessarius	37. pollicitatio	47. taciturnitas
8. coniuratio	18. ius	28. nemo	38. praesentia	48. Tulingi
9. contumelia	19. Latobrigi	29. Nicaea	39. princeps	49. vespera
10. deditio	20. legio	30. Nicomedia	40. ratio	50. vicus

PRONOUNS

1. aliquis, aliquid
2. iste, ista, istud
3. quidam, quaedam, quiddam

ADJECTIVES

1. Aurelius	6. infestus	11. perpetuus	16. publicus
2. clandestinus	7. inutilis	12. plerusque	17. quantus
3. communis	8. iste	13. postremus	18. salvus
4. hesternus	9. otiosus	14. princeps	19. senex
5. honestus	10. periculosus	15. pristinus	20. superior

VERBS

1. **absum**	17. **consequor**	33. **haesito**	49. **patior**	65. **recido**
2. **accelero**	18. **credo**	34. **impero**	50. **perfero**	66. **recupero**
3. **accipio**	19. **damno**	35. **incolo**	51. **permitto**	67. **recuso**
4. **adfirmo**	20. **deleo**	36. **intercludo**	52. **permoveo**	68. **reddeo**
5. **adsequor**	21. **descendo**	37. **iudico**	53. **persuadeo**	69. **refero**
6. **adsum**	22. **deseo**	38. **iureiuro**	54. **pertimesco**	70. **rescisco**
7. **agito**	23. **dubito**	39. **lego**	55. **placo**	71. **restituo**
8. **amitto**	24. **effero**	40. **loquor**	56. **polliceor**	72. **retineo**
9. **arbitror**	25. **egredior**	41. **metuo**	57. **posco**	73. **revertor**
10. **audeo**	26. **erro**	42. **misereor**	58. **praesto**	74. **saluto**
11. **careo**	27. **evenio**	43. **nescio**	59. **proficiscor**	75. **sentio**
12. **caveo**	28. **exeo**	44. **opinor**	60. **profiteor**	76. **suspicio**
13. **cogito**	29. **existimo**	45. **oportet**	61. **profugio**	77. **tabesco**
14. **comperio**	30. **exsolvo**	46. **oro**	62. **purgo**	78. **tolero**
15. **concedo**	31. **flagito**	47. **pascor**	63. **quaero**	79. **transeo**
16. **conquiro**	32. **fungor**	48. **patefacio**	64. **queror**	80. **vulnero**

ADVERBS

1. **fortasse**	4. **modeste**	7. **quantum**	10. **unde**
2. **frugaliter**	5. **nimis**	8. **rursus**	11. **ut, uti**
3. **ita**	6. **paulo**	9. **sic**	12. **vehementer**

CONJUNCTIONS

1. **an**	5. **nisi**	9. **quoniam**	13. **utinam**
2. **etiamsi**	6. **num**	10. **si**	14. **vel . . . vel**
3. **etsi**	7. **priusquam**	11. **tametsi,**	
4. **ne**	8. **quamvis**	12. **ut, uti**	

INTERJECTIONS

1. **mehercule**

276. Practice Exercises

No. 200.

1. Give all the subjunctive forms of **loquor**.
2. Give all the infinitives of **oro**.
3. Give all the participles of **concedo**
4. Give all the subjunctive forms of **possum**.
5. Give all the indicative forms of **sentio**.

277. Reading

PUBLIUS VERGILIUS MARO

You have already read one passage from *The Aeneid* in the Seventh Review Section. In the following passage, Jupiter prophesies the founding of Rome to Venus, the mother of Aeneas.

Parce metu, Cytherea, manent immota tuorum
fata tibi; cernes urbem et promissa Lavini
moenia sublimemque feres ad sidera caeli
magnanimum Aenean; neque me sententia
vertit. Hic tibi (fabor enim, quando haec te
cura remordet, longius et volvens fatorum
arcana movebo) bellum ingens geret Italia
populosque ferocis contundet moresque viris
et moenia ponet, tertia dum Latio regnantem
viderit aestas, ternaque transierint Rutulis
hiberna subactis. At puer Ascanius, cui nunc
cognomen Iulo additur (Ilus erat, dum res
stetit Ilia regno), triginta magnos volvendis
mensibus orbis imperio explebit, regnumque
ab sede Lavini transferet, et Longam multa vi
muniet Albam. Hic iam ter centum totos
regnabitur annos gente sub Hectorea, donec
regina sacerdos Marte gravis geminam partu
dabit Ilia prolem. Inde lupae fulvo nutricis
tegmine laetus Romulus excipiet gentem et
Mavortia condet moenia Romanosque suo de
nomine dicet.

His ego nec metas rerum nec tempora pono;
imperium sine fine dedi. Quin aspera Juno,
quae mare nunc terrasque metu caelumque
fatigat, consilia in melius referet, mecumque
fovebit Romanos, rerum dominos gentemque
togatam. Sic placitum. Veniet lustris
labentibus aetas cum domus Assaraci
Phthiam clarasque Mycenas servitio premet ac
victis dominabitur Argis. Nascetur pulchra
Troianus origine Caesar, imperium Oceano,
famam qui terminet astris, Iulius, a magno
demissum nomen Iulo. Hunc tu olim caelo
spoliis Orientis onustum accipies secura;
vocabitur hic quoque votis. Aspera tum
positis mitescent saecula bellis; cana Fides et
Vesta, Remo cum fratre Quirinus iura dabunt;
dirae ferro et compagibus artis claudentur
Belli portae; Furor impius intus saeva sedens
super arma et centum vinctus aenis post
tergum nodis fremet horridus ore cruento.

Aeneidos, I, 257–296

278. Congratulations

If you've made use of **Latin Made Simple** correctly, making sure that you were fairly confident in your understanding of one section before moving on to the next, doing regular drills on the various inflectional endings, and honestly working through the readings to help build your vocabulary, then you have successfully completed the equivalent of two years of high school Latin, perhaps even a year of college-level. Good for you.

You certainly have been exposed to nearly all of the morphology of the language and to all of the important syntactical rules. There aren't really any additional inflectional forms to learn, and you can always learn more of the fine points of any language, even English. Through the readings and exercises in **Latin Made Simple,** you should have developed a working Latin vocabulary of about 850 words or so, and certainly, you have learned the most common vocabulary items that you will encounter as you, now, begin to engage with genuine Latin texts. Reading the Latin texts that are out there—Caesar, Cicero, Ovid, Horace, Vergil, Catullus, the Bible, *et cetera*—is the best way to build on the skills you've already developed. Find a good dictionary, keep your **Latin Made Simple** text (with its helpful charts) within easy reach as a reference tool, and you should be fine as you continue the adventure you've begun so well. Congratulations once again. *Vive valeque!*

—DOUG JULIUS

ANSWERS

Chapter One

Grammar Practice No. 1

puella	the girl
puellae	of the girl
puellae	to/for the girl
puellam	the girl
puella	from/with/by/in the girl
puella	O girl
puellae	the girls
puellarum	of the girls
puellis	to/for the girls
puellas	the girls
puellis	from/with/by/in the girls
puellae	O girls
terra	the land
terrae	of the land
terrae	to/for the land
terram	the land
terra	from/with/by/in the land
terra	O land
terrae	the lands
terrarum	of the lands
terris	to/for the lands
terras	the lands
terris	from/with/by/in the lands
terrae	O lands

aqua	the water
aquae	of the water
aquae	to/for the water
aquam	the water
aqua	from/with/by/in the water
aqua	O water
aquae	the waters
aquarum	of the waters
aquis	to/for the waters
aquas	the waters
aquis	from/with/by/in the waters
aquae	O waters

casa	the cottage
casae	of the cottage
casae	to/for the cottage
casam	the cottage
casa	from/with/by/in the cottage
casa	O cottage
casae	the cottages
casarum	of the cottages
casis	to/for the cottages
casas	the cottages
casis	from/with/by/in the cottages
casae	O cottages

femina	the woman
feminae	of the woman
feminae	to/for the woman
feminam	the woman
femina	from/with/by/in the woman
femina	O woman
feminae	the women
feminarum	of the women
feminis	to/for the women
feminas	the women
feminis	from/with/by/in the women
feminae	O women

agricola	the farmer
agricolae	of the farmer
agricolae	to/for the farmer
agricolam	the farmer
agricola	from/with/by/in the farmer
agricola	O farmer
agricolae	the farmers
agricolarum	of the farmers
agricolis	to/for the farmers
agricolas	the farmers
agricolis	from/with/by/in the farmers
agricolae	O farmers

Grammar Practice No. 2

porto	I carry, do carry, am carrying
portas	you carry
portat	he/she/it carries
portamus	we carry
portatis	you carry
portant	they carry
laboro	I work, do work, am working
laboras	you work
laborat	he/she/it works
laboramus	we work
laboratis	you work
laborant	they work
laudo	I praise, do praise, am praising
laudas	you praise
laudat	he/she/it praises
laudamus	we praise
laudatis	you praise
laudant	they praise
voco	I call, do call, am calling
vocas	you call
vocat	he/she/it calls
vocamus	we call
vocatis	you call
vocant	they call

Practice Exercise No. 1

1. **aquas,** the waters
2. **puellarum,** of the girls
3. **terrae,** the lands
4. **agricolis,** for the farmers
5. **stellis,** by the stars
6. **vocant,** they call
7. **laboratis,** you work
8. **portamus,** we carry

Practice Exercise No. 2

1. of the farmers
2. the, a girl
3. the cottages
4. for the woman
5. by the lands
6. he/she/it is praising
7. you call
8. they are working
9. we like

Practice Exercise No. 3

1. we
2. he/she/it
3. I
4. you
5. they

Practice Exercise No. 4

1. direct object, acc.
2. prepositional phrase, abl.
3. subject, nom.
4. indirect object, dat.
5. possession, gen.

Practice Exercise No. 5

1. **portamus**
2. **amat**
3. **porto**
4. **laudamus**
5. **vocant**
6. **laboratis**
7. **portat**
8. **vocas**
9. **amamus**
10. **laudatis**

Practice Exercise No. 6

1. **casam parvam**
2. **mearum filiarum**
3. **pulchras stellas**
4. **tua terra**
5. **filiae malae**
6. **casis Romanis**
7. **puellas parvas**
8. **aquam bonam**
9. **feminae parvae**
10. **casarum pulchrarum**

Practice Exercise No. 7

1. you are
2. he/she/it is; there is
3. they are; there are
4. I am
5. you are
6. we are

Practice Exercise No. 8

1. **natantne?** Do they swim?
2. **portasne?** Are you carrying?
3. **amamusne?** Do we like?
4. **laboratne?** Does he (she, it) work?
5. **vocatisne?** Are you calling?
6. **suntne?** Are they? Are there?
7. **natamusne?** Do we swim?
8. **portatne?** Is he (she, it) carrying?
9. **estisne?** Are you?
10. **laudasne?** Do you praise?
11. **laudatne?** Does he (she, it) praise?
12. **vocantne?** Are they calling?
13. **estne?** Is he (she, it) there? Is there?
14. **natasne?** Do you swim?
15. **amantne?** Do they love?

Practice Exercise No. 9

1. you love/are loving/do love
2. we praise
3. you call
4. I work
5. they love
6. you call
7. he (she, it) swims
8. we carry
9. you work
10. he (she, it) praises

Roman Numeral Practice No. 1

13	1100	43	502	120
300	25	610	420	10300
9	900	36	95	74

Roman Numeral Practice No. 2

LIX	XLII	LXV	MMCCXXII	DCCCXVIII or
CCCIV	VXL	MLXVI	XXVI	CCMXVIII
LXXXV, XXCV	MCDXCII	DCCLIII	CMLX	CCLXXI
				CI

Practice Exercise No. 10

1. the girl's cottage
2. a supply of water
3. the farmers' land
4. the women's cottages
5. the sailor's native country
6. the sailor's island
7. the farmer's daughter
8. the sailors' cottages
9. an abundance of stars

Practice Exercise No. 11

1. **Feminae,** the women
2. **Puella,** the girl
3. **Agricolae,** the farmers
4. **Nauta,** the sailor
5. **Agricola,** the farmer
6. **Filiae,** the daughters
7. **Patria,** the native country
8. **Insulae,** the islands
9. **Filia,** the daughter

Practice Exercise No. 12

1. **magna,** big
2. **pulchrae,** pretty
3. **bonae,** good
4. **Romanae,** Roman
5. **mala,** bad
6. **tua,** yours
7. **parvae,** small
8. **pulchra,** beautiful
9. **bona,** good

Practice Exercise No. 13

1. **agricola**, a farmer
2. **nautae**, sailors
3. **patria**, native country
4. **casae**, cottages
5. **nauta**, a sailor
6. **feminae**, women
7. **puella**, a girl
8. **agricolae**, farmers
9. **silva**, a forest

Practice Exercise No. 14

1. toward the road
2. in the cottage
3. with the woman
4. into the wood
5. out of the cottages
6. away from the land
7. away from the cottages
8. out of the forests
9. into the islands
10. toward the streets
11. into the forests
12. with the girl
13. in or on the water
14. toward the water
15. away from the girls
16. toward the island
17. out of the land
18. with the farmer
19. in the native country
20. with the girls

Practice Exercise No. 15

1. **aquam**, water
2. **fabulam**, a story
3. **aquam**, water
4. **Nautam**, the sailor
5. **Agricolas**, the farmers
6. **fabulam**, a story
7. **viam**, the road
8. **Terram**, the land
9. **terram**, the land

Practice Exercise No. 16

1. **Feminae**, to the women
2. **Nautae**, to the sailor
3. **Nautis**, to the sailors
4. **Puellae**, to the girl
5. **Puellis**, to the girls
6. **Feminis**, to the women
7. **Agricolis**, to the farmers
8. **Feminae**, to the woman
9. **Puellis**, to the girls

Practice Exercises No. 17

1. you walk; you are walking, you do walk
2. he/she/it tells/is telling/does tell
3. they walk; they do walk; they are walking
4. I dwell; I am dwelling; I do dwell
5. we sail; we are sailing; we do sail
6. you give; you are giving; you do give
7. he/she/it gives/is giving/does give
8. they call; they are calling; they do call
9. you work; you are working; you do work
10. we carry; we are carrying; we do carry
11. you praise; you are praising; you do praise
12. they love; they are loving; they do love
13. you are
14. we are
15. they swim; they are swimming; they do swim
16. you swim; you are swimming; you do swim
17. he/she/it fights/is fighting/does fight
18. we fight; we are fighting; we do fight
19. I attack; I am attacking; I do attack
20. they attack; they are attacking; they do attack

Chapter One Review

VOCABULARY REVIEW

NOUNS

1. farmer
2. water
3. Britain
4. cottage
5. supply, abundance
6. troops
7. Europe
8. story
9. rumor, renown, report
10. woman
11. daughter
12. Germany
13. inhabitant
14. island
15. Italy
16. Julia
17. sailor
18. peninsula
19. native country
20. girl
21. forest, woods
22. star
23. land, earth
24. road, way, street

ADJECTIVES

1. ancient, old
2. good
3. clear, bright, famous
4. wide
5. long
6. large, great
7. bad, evil
8. my, mine
9. much
10. many
11. small
12. pretty, beautiful
13. Roman
14. your, yours

VERBS

1. walk
2. love, like
3. give
4. dwell, live
5. help, aid
6. work
7. praise
8. point out, show
9. tell, relate
10. swim
11. sail, cruise
12. attack
13. carry
14. fight
15. be
16. call

ADVERBS
1. well
2. why
3. badly
4. not

PREPOSITIONS
1. from, away from
2. to, toward
3. with
4. from, out from
5. in, on; into

CONJUNCTIONS
1. and
2. because

Practice Exercise No. 18

1. **Europam antiquam**
2. **aquae pulchrae**
3. **silvis parvis**
4. **stellas claras**
5. **insularum multarum**
6. **terra Romana**
7. **filias bonas**
8. **famam malam**
9. **puellarum pulchrarum**
10. **incolis multis**

Practice Exercise No. 19

1. casae, f.	6. insulae, f.	11. terrae, f.	16. patriae, f.
2. feminae, f.	7. puellae, f.	12. Britanniae, f.	17. incolae, m. or f.
3. stellae, f.	8. copiae, f.	13. famae, f.	18. Europae, f.
4. aquae, f.	9. filiae, f.	14. Italiae, f.	19. agricolae, m.
5. fabulae, f.	10. nautae, m.	15. silvae, f.	20. viae, f.

Practice Exercise No. 20

1. amare	6. oppugnare	11. narrare
2. laudare	7. monstrare	12. laborare
3. navigare	8. dare	13. natare
4. esse	9. habitare	14. pugnare
5. vocare	10. portare	15. ambulare

Practice Exercise No. 21

1. Nominative Case: Subject; Predicate Noun or Adjective
   Genitive Case: Possession
   Dative Case: Indirect Object

   Accusative Case: Direct Object; Prepositional Phrases
   Ablative Case: Prepositional Phrases
   Vocative Case: Direct Address

2. **insula lata**, wide island
   insulae latae, of the wide island
   insulae latae, to/for the wide island
   insulam latam, wide island
   insula lata, from/with/by/in the wide island
   insula lata, O wide island

   insulae latae, wide islands
   insularum latarum, of the wide islands
   insulis latis, to/for the wide islands
   insulas latas, wide islands
   insulis latis, from/with/by/in the wide islands
   insulae latae, O wide islands

   via longa, long road
   viae longae, of the long road
   viae longae, to/for the long road
   viam longam, long road
   via longa, from/with/by/in the long road
   via longa, O long road

   viae longae, long roads
   viarum longarum, of the long roads
   viis longis, to/for the long roads
   vias longas, long roads
   viis longis, from/with/by/in the long roads
   viae longae, O long roads

3. **laboro,** I work; I am working; I do work
    laboras, you work; you are working; you do work
    laborat, he/she/it works; he/she/it is working;
        he/she/it does work
    laboramus, we work; we are working; we do work
    laboratis, you work; you are working; you do work
    laborant, they work; they are working; they do work
    laudo, I praise; I am praising; I do praise
    laudas, you praise; you are praising; you do praise
    laudat, he/she/it praises; he/she/it is praising;
        he/she/it does praise
    laudamus, we praise; we are praising; we do praise
    laudatis, you praise; you are praising; you do praise
    laudant, they praise; they are praising; they do praise
    sum, I am
    es, you are
    est, he/she/it is; there is
    sumus, we are
    estis, you are
    sunt, they are; there are

Chapter Two

Practice Exercise No. 22

1. we are
2. they conquer
3. he/she/it stands
4. he/she/it is; there is
5. you wait for
6. he/she/it builds
7. they are; there are
8. we swim
9. he/she/it overcomes
10. they sail
11. you give
12. you call
13. we build
14. they walk
15. you stand

Practice Exercise No. 23

1. in Italy
2. toward Britain
3. with the women
4. toward Italy
5. in the province
6. with the troops
7. on the peninsula
8. in front of the cottages
9. behind the cottages
10. with the girl
11. in the woods
12. toward the road

Practice Exercise No. 24

1. of the inhabitant; to/for the inhabitant; the inhabitants; O inhabitants
2. Why do they work?
3. You help your native country.
4. He is carrying the booty.
5. He fights well.
6. They are pretty.
7. of many victories
8. a famous native country
9. a long story
10. out of the cottage
11. away from the road
12. Where is he (she, it)?
13. Here I am.
14. in front of the island
15. after the victory
16. with the troops
17. out of the provinces
18. There are troops here.
19. toward the streets
20. There is the province.
21. There are the women.
22. There is glory.
23. There are many girls.
24. Where are they?
25. Here they are.

Practice Exercise No. 25

1. to/for, from/with/by/in the field
2. to/for, from/with/by/in the wars
3. of the battles
4. of the boy; the boys
5. the ally
6. the friends
7. the camp
8. the swords
9. the help, aid
10. to/for/from/with/by/in the message/messenger
11. the dangers
12. of the weapons, arms
13. of the town
14. the man
15. the enemies

Practice Exercise No. 26

1. **amici,** the friends
2. **puerorum,** of the boys
3. **agris,** to/for, from/with/ by/in the fields
4. **bellorum,** of the wars
5. **oppida,** the towns
6. **viri,** the men
7. **pericula,** dangers
8. **gladiorum,** of the swords
9. **nuntios,** messengers
10. **auxiliis,** to/for, from/with/ by/in the aids
11. **nuntiis,** to/for, from/with/ by/in the messages
12. **viris,** to/for, from, with, by, in the men
13. **periculis,** to/for, from/ with/by/in the danger
14. **agri,** the fields
15. **bella,** the wars

Practice Exercise No. 27

1. of the
2. the, an
3. the, a
4. about
5. through
6. of the
7. of
8. the
9. the
10. of

Practice Exercise No. 28

1. out of the field
2. Are they arming?
3. a narrow street
4. friends
5. with the boy
6. He plows there.
7. behind the camp
8. of the friends
9. with the man
10. They fight a war.
11. They point out the towns.
12. They give arms to the man.
13. We tell stories about the war.
14. He likes dangers.
15. The camp is in the field.

Practice Exercise No. 29

1. My friend is there.
2. toward your cottages
3. out of the deep ditches
4. with famous men
5. in front of the Roman camp
6. in back of my fields
7. about good water
8. through the large forest
9. of the bad friend; the bad friends

Practice Exercise No. 30

1. **virorum multorum**
2. **filiae meae**
3. **frumento bono**
4. **meis filiis**
5. **pueros agros**
6. **puellae miserae**
7. **soci liberi**
8. **feminam miseram**
9. **agris pulchris**

Practice Exercise No. 31

Column I

1. many **viros**
2. sick **pueri**
3. pretty **oppidum**
4. many **servorum**
5. happy **puellam**
6. good **fili**
7. bad **famam**
8. wretched **equis**
9. Roman **terrae**
10. happy **agricola**

Column II

3. **multos**
5. **aegri**
1. **pulchrum**
2. **multorum**
4. **laetam**
6. **boni**
8. **malam**
9. **miseris**
10. **Romanae**
7. **laetus**

Practice Exercise No. 32

1. **curamus**
2. **liberas**
3. **laboratis**

4. **portat**
5. **aro**
6. **necant**

7. **nuntiat**
8. **occupamus**
9. **statis**

Practice Exercise No. 33

1. They are free.
2. of the happy mistress
3. into deep water
4. concerning great cares
5. in wide fields

6. about good masters
7. Why are you happy?
8. There are many people.
9. We are ill.
10. with good friends

11. in free lands
12. She is pretty.
13. Are they pretty?
14. He is unhappy.
15. many things

Practice Exercise No. 34

1. **nostram**
2. **tuas**
3. **sua**

4. **sua**
5. **vestrae**
6. **nostram**

7. **sui**
8. **suarum**
9. **meam**

Practice Exercise No. 35

1. I fear
2. he/she/it sees
3. you fear (plural)
4. he/she/it adores
5. they rule

6. you see (singular)
7. they fear
8. we have
9. we rule
10. they have

11. he/she/it fears
12. you see (plural)
13. I have
14. you rule (singular)
15. you adore (plural)

Practice Exercise No. 36

1. ancient gods
2. of/to/for the Roman goddess; Roman goddesses
3. of my friends
4. your booty
5. our daughters
6. his, her, its, their master
7. his, her, their son
8. his/her/its/their wisdom; from/with/by/in his/her/its/their wisdom
9. our glory

Practice Exercise No. 37

1. Your glory is not great.
2. Why do you kill your enemy?
3. Is the messenger telling many things?
4. The men are walking across their own fields.
5. The women are in their cottages.
6. Your daughters are sick today.
7. Many people sail across the ocean.
8. They are our goddesses.
9. They are our gods.
10. The woman cares for her daughters.
11. I am standing in front of the cottages.
12. He does not have many things.
13. We are telling about the moon.
14. Your fortune is good.
15. The slaves fear their masters.
16. Why are you not afraid?
17. We see a beautiful temple.
18. He has a camp there.
19. We see the boys in the back of the ditch.
20. You have great wisdom.

Chapter Two Review

VOCABULARY REVIEW

NOUNS

1. field
2. friend
3. arms, weapons
4. aid, help
5. war
6. sky, heaven
7. camp
8. care
9. goddess
10. god
11. mistress
12. master
13. horse
14. son
15. fortune, fate, luck
16. ditch
17. grain
18. sword
19. glory
20. Greece
21. Spain
22. (personal) enemy
23. moon
24. messenger, message
25. ocean
26. town
27. danger
28. booty, plunder
29. battle
30. province
31. boy
32. queen
33. wisdom
34. slave, servant
35. comrade, ally

ADJECTIVES

1. sick, ill
2. high, deep
3. narrow
4. happy
5. free
6. wretched, unhappy
7. our, ours
8. his, hers, its, their
9. your, yours

VERBS

1. worship, adore
2. build
3. arm
4. plow
5. care for, cure
6. await, expect, wait for
7. have, hold
8. free, set free
9. kill
10. announce, report
11. seize, take possession of
12. rule
13. stand
14. surpass, overcome
15. fear, be afraid of

ADVERBS

1. even, also
2. here, in this place
3. today
4. there, in that place
5. often
6. where, when

PREPOSITIONS

1. before, in front of
2. about, concerning, down from
3. through
4. behind, in back of
5. across

CONJUNCTIONS

1. but

Practice Exercise No. 38

1. aedificare
2. nuntiare
3. exspectare
4. superare
5. videre
6. liberare
7. regnare
8. arare
9. stare
10. curare
11. necare
12. adorare
13. timere
14. habere
15. occupare

Practice Exercise No. 39

1. deae, f.
2. proelii or proeli, n.
3. provinciae, f.
4. belli, n.
5. oceani, m.
6. socii or soci, m.
7. fortunae, f.
8. amici, m.
9. inimici, m.
10. reginae, f.
11. pueri, m.
12. agri, m.
13. castrorum, n.
14. periculi, n.
15. victoriae, f.
16. viri, m.
17. gladii or gladi, m.
18. curae, f.
19. praedae, f.
20. equi, m.

Practice Exercise No. 40

1. a. **Cur viris frumentum non datis?**

    b. **Datne incolis insularum curam bonam?**

2. **sto**	I stand; I am standing; I do stand
stas	you stand; you are standing; you do stand
stat	he/she/it stands; he/she/it is standing; he/she/it does stand
stamus	we stand; we are standing; we do stand
statis	you stand; you are standing; you do stand
stant	they stand; they are standing; they do stand
timeo	I fear; I am fearing; I do fear
times	you fear; you are standing; you do stand
timet	he/she/it fears; he/she/it is fearing; he/she/it does fear
timemus	we fear; we are fearing; we do fear
timetis	you fear; you are fearing; you do fear
timent	they fear; they are fearing; they do fear

Practice Exercise No. 41

1. our farmers
2. of the happy daughters
3. high sky
4. of, to/for a free country; free countries
5. your slave
6. his, her, their sons
7. wretched people
8. narrow roads
9. your messenger; your message
10. my fortune; from/with/ by/in my fortune
11. many people
12. small boy
13. of the wide fields
14. good care; from/with/ by/in good care
15. of the long sword

Practice Exercise No. 42

1. O friends
2. O wars
3. O goddesses
4. O god
5. O master
6. O mistress
7. O son
8. O glory
9. O messengers
10. O my slave
11. O good man
12. O good girl
13. O many friends
14. O good farmer
15. O our friend

READING

Give me a thousand kisses, then a hundred,
then another thousand, then a second hundred,
then up to a thousand more, then a hundred.
At the last, when we have given many
thousands, we shall mix their count, lest we
know, or lest any wicked person might envy
us,when he learns our kisses are so many.

CATULLUS 5

I hate and I love. Why I do this, perhaps you ask.

I do not know, but I feel it happen and I am
tortured.

Catullus 8

THE VULGATE BIBLE

In the beginning was the Word, and the Word was with God, and the Word was God. The same was in the beginning with God. All things were made by him; and without him was not any thing made that was made; in him was life, and the life was the light of men. And the light shineth in darkness; and the darkness comprehended it not. There was a man sent from God, whose name was John. The same came for a witness, to bear witness of the Light, that all men through him might believe. He was not that Light, but was sent to bear witness of that Light. That was the true Light, which lighteth every man that cometh into the world. He was in the world, and the world was made by him, and the world knew him not. Gospel According to St. John, 1, 1–10

Chapter Three

Practice Exercise No. 43
1. You have friends, haven't you? Certainly.
2. Are they building cottages? Yes. They are building cottages.
3. You are indeed afraid, aren't you? I am indeed afraid.
4. The people are not fighting, are they? The people are not fighting.
5. The roads are not long, are they? The roads are not at all long.
6. Why are they walking toward the town?
7. Is the man staying in the building? The man is staying in the building.
8. Is the province free? The province is truly free.
9. He isn't sailing on the ocean, is he? He is not sailing on the ocean.

Practice Exercise No. 44

1. videtis	7. iuvat	13. possunt
2. potest	8. manent	14. aedificas
3. habeo	9. habes	15. oppugnant
4. adoras	10. statis	16. ambulatis
5. video	11. parant	17. timet
6. eunt	12. debemus	18. properat

Practice Exercise No. 45

1. ambulare	5. vocare	9. oppugnare
2. pugnare	6. natare	10. manere
3. necare	7. iuvare	11. navigare
4. superare	8. laborare	12. ire

Practice Exercise No. 46

1. Why is he preparing grain there?
2. You like the Latin language, don't you?
3. Where do your buildings stand?
4. You ought not to give swords to the boys.
5. The gods also have their own weapons.
6. They tell the story about the long war of Troy.
7. Aeneas is sailing with his men to Italy.
8. The god helps the people of Greece.
9. Why do the Romans fear their allies?
10. He sees the clear moon in the sky.

Practice Exercise No. 47

1. deb**ebamus**
2. par**abam**
3. proper**abant**
4. man**ebant**
5. tim**ebat**
6. vid**ebas**
7. cur**abam**
8. ador**abamus**
9. loc**abas**
10. d**abatis**
11. hab**ebatis**
12. st**abat**
13. laud**abam**
14. man**ebas**
15. vid**ebamus**
16. hab**ebas**
17. port**abatis**
18. iuv**abat**
19. voc**abat**
20. tim**ebamus**

Practice Exercise No. 48

1. he/she/it was pointing out
2. I call
3. we prepare
4. you were ruling
5. you ought
6. you fear
7. he/she/it was; there was
8. you fight
9. I was hurrying
10. they used to see
11. you were praising
12. you carry
13. we were going
14. I was able
15. we remain
16. he/she/it was saving
17. I was placing
18. you were attacking
19. you were having
20. you were; you used to be
21. he/she/it was able
22. they were going
23. you were conquering
24. they tell

Practice Exercise No. 49

1. when he was standing
2. with the daughter
3. when we work
4. when I wait for; when I await
5. with friends
6. when he/she/it conquers
7. with a wolf
8. when you see
9. when he/she/it was; when there was
10. when you were fighting
11. with the girl
12. when they were; when there were
13. with my uncle
14. with the Romans
15. with many women

Practice Exercise No. 50

1. He does not have many men in camp, does he?
2. We were preparing today to be there.
3. Your friend has a good reputation in our town.
4. I was preparing to stay with the girls.
5. He often kills many wolves in the forests, doesn't he?
6. The Romans ought not to fear the swords of the Sabines.
7. When they build a town, they place temples and buildings there.
8. Why do they give rewards to their slaves?
9. The farmer was in the field with his friend.
10. You are without water, aren't you?

Practice Exercise No. 51

1. he/she/it attacks
2. they were setting free
3. I shall see
4. he/she/it will remain
5. they were; they used to be
6. they are; there are
7. they ought; they owe
8. to love; to like
9. you will have
10. you were fighting
11. they were giving
12. he/she/it will be; there will be
13. they will stir up
14. he/she/it will warn
15. to carry
16. he/she/it will fear
17. you will fight
18. we shall conquer
19. we were preparing
20. they will be; there will be
21. they will tell
22. he/she/it was inciting
23. you were warning
24. we are
25. we were attacking
26. he/she/it will arouse
27. they were swimming
28. you were placing
29. you will save
30. you will help
31. you will go
32. I will be able

Practice Exercise No. 52

1. down from a clear sky
2. neighboring to my country
3. near to the island
4. with our friend
5. toward the high buildings
6. in the wide ditches
7. pleasing to his comrade
8. in front of the fields
9. friendly to the slaves
10. after the war
11. unfriendly to the queen
12. concerning your victory
13. through many battles
14. suitable to the man
15. without booty

Practice Exercise No. 53

1. present
2. future
3. imperfect
4. present
5. imperfect
6. imperfect
7. future
8. present
9. future
10. future
11. future
12. imperfect
13. future
14. imperfect
15. future
16. imperfect
17. future
18. imperfect
19. imperfect
20. future

Practice Exercise No. 54

1. He (she) will walk toward the narrow streets.
2. They were standing in front of the temples.
3. You were swimming out of the ocean.
4. They will fight on the water.
5. She was pleasing to the women.
6. They ought to have a free country.
7. The girls will swim.
8. He liked his neighbors.
9. You will save your uncles.
10. They will praise the queen.
11. Where ought you to be?
12. You were calling the boy.
13. He will be unfriendly to the messenger.
14. It is not near to the province.
15. We shall not fear your swords.
16. Your slaves are helping.
17. The man will remain there.
18. We were preparing a deep ditch.
19. The master will tell a story.
20. We shall plow the field.

Practice Exercise No. 55

1. walk! sing.	6. sail! pl.	11. stand! pl.	16. conquer! pl.
2. love! pl.	7. give! pl.	12. have! pl.	17. stand! sing.
3. swim! pl.	8. dwell! sing.	13. hold! sing.	18. help! pl.
4. fight! sing.	9. fear! pl.	14. rule! sing.	19. warn! pl.
5. praise! pl.	10. see! sing.	15. hold! pl.	20. stay! sing.

Practice Exercise No. 56

1. a farmer	4. a girl	7. enemies
2. sailors	5. our allies	8. a friend
3. Britain	6. a boy	9. boys

Practice Exercise No. 57

1. The sick boy, your son, will stay in the town.
2. You ought to have allies in the battle, O friend.
3. Arouse your men, O Roman people, against war.
4. Warn the inhabitants of Gaul, O messengers.
5. I shall call the Sabines, our neighbors, to the games.
6. See the temple, O girls, beautiful buildings.
7. Rome, a town in Italy, will be famous.
8. Remember Gaul, O my son.
9. Shall we have a big forum, O friends?
10. I shall wait for my uncles, the messengers.

Chapter Three Review

VOCABULARY REVIEW

NOUNS

1. building	7. Gaul	13. language	19. river bank
2. chest, box	8. a Gaul	14. game	20. Rome
3. uncle	9. a German	15. wolf	21. a Roman
4. barbarian	10. Latinus	16. memory	22. the Sabines
5. neighbor	11. Latium	17. people	23. Troy
6. forum, market place	12. lieutenant, legate	18. reward	24. life

ADJECTIVES

1. friendly	4. pleasing	7. Latin
2. savage, uncivilized, barbarian	5. fit, suitable	8. near
3. neighboring	6. unfriendly	

VERBS

1. owe, ought
2. arouse, stir up, incite
3. place, put
4. remain, stay
5. warn, advise
6. prepare, get ready
7. hurry, hasten
8. save, preserve
9. hold, keep, have
10. remember
11. go
12. be able, can

ADVERBS

1. certainly, indeed, surely
2. tomorrow
3. thus, so; yes
4. not at all, by no means
5. expects the answer "yes"
6. expects the answer "no"
7. now
8. then
9. truly, in truth

PREPOSITIONS

1. against
2. on account of, because of
3. for, in behalf of
4. without

CONJUNCTIONS

1. and also, and

Practice Exercise No. 58

1. simple question
2. simple question
3. simple question
4. answer "no"
5. answer "yes"
6. answer "no"
7. simple question
8. simple question
9. simple question

Practice Exercise No. 59

1. debebam
2. locabas
3. incitabat
4. parabatis
5. tenebamus
6. servabas
7. tenebam
8. manebamus
9. monebat

Practice Exercise No. 60

1. videbo
2. stabunt
3. timebis
4. necabitis
5. habebimus
6. aedificabo
7. superabis
8. curabimus
9. nuntiabunt

Practice Exercise No. 61

1. serva, servate
2. mone, monete
3. incita, incitate
4. naviga, navigate
5. para, parate
6. tene, tenete
7. propera, properate
8. neca, necate
9. pugna, pugnate

Practice Exercise No. 62

1. popule, populi
2. memoria, memoriae
3. legate, legati
4. amice, amici
5. femina, feminae
6. bellum, bella
7. avuncule, avunculi
8. vir, viri
9. fili, filii
10. agricola, agricolae

READING

GAIUS IULIUS CAESAR

The entire nation of the Gauls is quite devoted to religious rites . . . They worship the god Mercury especially. There are very many statues of him; they say he is the inventor of all the arts; they believe he is the guide on roads and journeys, and that he has the greatest power over money transactions and merchants. After him come Apollo and Mars and Jupiter and Minerva. About these, they have almost the same idea as other races: Apollo dispels diseases; Minerva hands down the skills of handcrafts and arts; Jupiter holds the power over the gods, and Mars rules over wars.

Commentaries on the Gallic War, 6, 16, 17

THE BIBLE

In the beginning, God created the heaven and the earth. And the earth was without form, and void; and darkness was upon the face of the deep. And the Spirit of God moved upon the face of the waters.
And God said: Let there be light. And there was light. And God saw the light, that it was good; and God divided the light from the darkness. And God called the light Day, and the darkness he called Night. And the evening and the morning were the first day.
And God said: Let there be a firmament in the midst of the waters, and let it divide the waters from the waters. And God made the firmament, and divided the waters which were under the firmament from the waters which were above the firmament. And it was so. And God called the firmament Heaven. And the evening and morning were the second day.

And God said: Let the waters under the heaven be gathered together unto one place, and let the dry land appear. And it was so. And God called the dry land Earth; and the gathering together of the waters he called Seas. And God saw that it was good. And God said: Let the earth bring forth grass, the herb yielding seed, and the fruit tree yielding fruit after his kind, whose seed is in itself, upon the earth. And it was so. And the earth brought forth grass, and herb yielding seed after his kind, and the tree yielding fruit, whose seed was in itself, after his kind. And God saw that it was good. And the evening and morning were the third day.

Genesis I, 1–13

Chapter Four

Practice Exercise No. 63

1. you will be feared
2. I was praising
3. I am being cared for
4. they are praised
5. they will be related; they will be told
6. I shall stand
7. he/she/it was being armed
8. you are plowing
9. he/she/it will be seized
10. you will stand
11. he was killing
12. they will be built
13. I shall overcome; I shall conquer; I shall surpass
14. he will sail
15. I was living in
16. I was being pointed out
17. they were walking
18. he/she/it will be given
19. you are being helped; you are being aided
20. I shall be called

Practice Exercise No. 64

1. exspectabar
2. tenentur
3. monebitur
4. videbatur
5. amabitur
6. habetur
7. videbamini
8. portabitur
9. movebimini
10. parantur
11. laudabuntur
12. locamini
13. properabuntur
14. timemur
15. incitor
16. monebaris
17. servaris
18. debebatur
19. videntur
20. monebantur

Practice Exercise No. 65

1. with the lieutenant
2. with a sword
3. by the boys
4. with ditches
5. by friends
6. by a messenger
7. with uncles
8. by wars
9. by the masters
10. with a comrade
11. with horses
12. by arrows
13. by an archer
14. by a goddess
15. with a slave
16. with wisdom
17. by the people
18. with enemies
19. with water
20. by a man

Practice Exercise No. 66

1. Money will be given to the man and the girl because the boy is ill.
2. I was remembered when I was moving to the neighboring town.
3. They seem to grieve, but a gift will be brought.
4. On account of the dangers, the men were afraid of the letters.
5. Fight well for Britain, your native country.
6. Many people were walking toward the temples of the gods.
7. Where (when) will the game be given by your friend?
8. We were living in the cottage where you see the girls.
9. The man will not be attacked by a sword, will he?
10. The people were preparing to move camp, weren't they?

Practice Exercise No. 67

1. of the long peace
2. for the soldier
3. famous soldiers
4. Roman peace
5. your heads
6. to/for their dictators
7. your head
8. by happy men
9. suitable part
10. in an ancient city
11. of our sea
12. strong soldiers
13. good men
14. long peace
15. on their heads
16. against dictators
17. with the men
18. without your soldiers
19. about pleasing peace
20. friendly man

Practice Exercise No. 68

1. of the soldiers
2. of peace
3. the, a head
4. the, a part
5. in, on the cities
6. the seas
7. with the soldier
8. of the bridges
9. the enemy
10. about slaughter

Practice Exercise No. 69

1. **paces**, the peaces
2. **militibus**, from/with/by/in the soldiers
3. **capitibus**, to/for the heads
4. **partes**, parts
5. **hostibus**, to/for the enemy
6. **urbium**, of the cities
7. **caedes**, slaughters
8. **pontes**, bridges
9. **homines**, men
10. **capita**, heads
11. **militum**, of the soldiers
12. **partium**, of the parts
13. **homines**, the men
14. **pacum**, of peace
15. **dictatores**, the dictators
16. **pontibus**, to/for the bridges
17. **marium**, of the seas
18. **pontium**, of the bridges
19. **hostes**, the enemy
20. **urbibus**, from/with/by/in the cities

Practice Exercise No. 70

1. Cincinnatus was being called from his field and was giving aid.
2. Men rule on earth, but the gods rule heaven and earth.
3. Rewards will be given to a great man by the Roman people.
4. The Latin language will always be preserved.
5. He will not plow tomorrow, but he will soon save our country.
6. He was swimming toward the river bank because the bridge was not standing.
7. Fight well, O Horatius, for your country with your sword.
8. The soldiers, O my sons, will be armed with swords.
9. Because of the dangers, you ought to save your water.
10. The sailor loves the sea but the farmer loves his fields.

Practice Exercise No. 71

1. gods and goddesses
2. the god and the goddess
3. we have and we give
4. he (she, it) had and he (she, it) gave
5. a man and women
6. of the men and of the women
7. toward the sun and moon
8. toward the sun and moon
9. from the sea and land
10. from the land and sea
11. with force and weapons
12. with force and weapons

Practice Exercise No. 72

1. in the middle of the roads
2. in many towns
3. in a great war
4. on the tops of the buildings
5. in a good part
6. on (in) wide oceans
7. in many lands
8. in the middle of the sky
9. on top of the sea

Practice Exercise No. 73

1. toward the sea
2. from the cities
3. with their fathers
4. in front of the forum
5. behind the temple
6. concerning the box
7. without a plan, without advice
8. across the ocean
9. through the seas
10. because of wings
11. for your queen
12. against the people
13. among the enemy
14. by (away from) the men
15. away from the towns
16. in front of the camp
17. through the dangers
18. toward the master
19. across the field
20. concerning peace

Practice Exercise No. 74

1. he/she/it will be; there will be
2. he/she/it will be frightened
3. he/she/it was flying
4. he/she/it will swim
5. they grieve
6. we are being carried
7. he/she/it was being held
8. we shall be loved
9. I shall move
10. they were being praised
11. he/she/it was fighting
12. you will place
13. I shall be called
14. we were being warned
15. they will work
16. they are being stirred up
17. he/she/it will owe; he, she it ought
18. they are preparing
19. they were being cared for
20. you will be freed

Practice Exercise No. 75

1. The man, my uncle
2. O good friends
3. O good son
4. Of the nations, Italy and Germany
5. Because of the money, the reward
6. Of the women, of the queens
7. O famous man
8. The boy, a slave
9. to/for the girls, my daughters
10. O our father

Practice Exercise No. 76

1. **vocare**, to call
2. **debere**, to owe
3. **ambulare**, to walk
4. **ire**, to go
5. **esse**, to be
6. **monere**, to warn
7. **timere**, to fear
8. **narrare**, to tell
9. **curare**, to take care of
10. **dolere**, to grieve
11. **nuntiare**, to announce
12. **volare**, to fly
13. **terrere**, to frighten
14. **adorare**, to worship
15. **movere**, to move
16. **parare**, to prepare
17. **servare**, to preserve, to save
18. **laudare**, to praise
19. **dare**, to give
20. **videre**, to see

Practice Exercise No. 77

1. **paravi**, I have prepared
2. **incitavi**, I have aroused
3. **aravi**, I have plowed
4. **debui**, I have owed
5. **liberavi**, I have freed
6. **ii, ivi** I have gone
7. **terrui**, I have frightened
8. **aedificavi**, I have built
9. **habitavi**, I have lived in
10. **monui**, I have warned
11. **properavi**, I have hurried
12. **habui**, I have held
13. **dedi**, I have given
14. **tenui**, I have held; I have kept
15. **servavi**, I have preserved; I have saved
16. **monstravi**, I have shown; I have pointed out
17. **timui**, I have feared
18. **natavi**, I have swum
19. **movi**, I have moved
20. **mansi**, I have remained; I have stayed

Practice Exercise No. 78

1. **amatus**, having been loved
2. **habitus**, having been had
3. **liberatus**, having been freed
4. **necatus**, having been killed
5. **monitus**, having been warned
6. **exspectatus**, having been waited for
7. **narratus**, having been told
8. **territus**, having been frightened
9. **occupatus**, having been seized
10. **portatus**, having been carried
11. **datus**, having been given
12. **monitus**, having been warned
13. **servatus**, having been saved
14. **iutus**, having been helped
15. **visus**, having been seen; having seemed
16. **adoratus**, having been worshipped
17. **motus**, having been moved
18. **spectatus**, having been seen
19. **obtentus**, having been obtained
20. **locatus**, having been placed; having been put

Practice Exercise No. 79

1. Both your mother and your father were giving advice about courage.
2. In the middle of the town, there were many buildings.
3. The report about my nation will be carried by the messengers.
4. The girl and the boy are swimming under the water.
5. We ought to walk around the city and see many things.
6. You remember many bad things, don't you?
7. The sun seemed to be on the top of the water.
8. The nations of Europe will not always fight.
9. Sailors sail on seas and oceans.
10. Roman soldiers have great courage.

Chapter Four Review

VOCABULARY REVIEW

NOUNS

1. wing
2. amphitheater
3. animal
4. year
5. slaughter
6. captive
7. head
8. speed, swiftness
9. wax
10. Ceres
11. Cincinnatus
12. the Colosseum
13. plan, advice
14. Crete
15. Daedalus
16. dictator
17. gift
18. gladiator
19. man
20. Horatius
21. enemy
22. Icarus
23. Those Below
24. Jupiter
25. work, toil, labor
26. letter
27. size, great size
28. sea
29. mother
30. Mercury
31. soldier
32. nation
33. part
34. father
35. peace
36. money
37. Pluto
38. bridge
39. Proserpina
40. arrow
41. archer
42. sun
43. star
44. city
45. courage, valor

ADJECTIVES
1. middle, middle of
2. strong, robust
3. greatest, highest, top of

VERBS
1. grieve
2. move
3. secure, obtain
4. look at, watch
5. frighten, terrify, scare

ADVERBS
1. long, for a long time
2. soon, presently
3. always

PREPOSITIONS
1. by; away from, from
2. around, about
3. among, between
4. under

CONJUNCTIONS
1. or
2. both . . . and
3. and

Practice Exercise No. 80

1. dolere	6. dare	11. debere	16. parare
2. terrere	7. spectare	12. timere	17. occupare
3. movere	8. volare	13. habere	18. stare
4. vocare	9. laudare	14. videre	19. iuvare
5. obtinere	10. manere	15. necare	20. monere

Practice Exercise No. 81

1. spectavi	3. moneo	5. motus	7. servatus	9. habito
2. curare	4. dedi	6. paravi	8. territus	10. laudare

Practice Exercise No. 82

1. of the animals and men
2. by the father
3. by the mothers
4. the sea and star
5. fathers and mothers
6. of speed and size
7. by Mercury
8. by the soldiers
9. by Pluto
10. war and peace

Practice Exercise No. 83

1. he/she/it was being praised
2. they will grieve
3. we were being warned
4. they are being killed
5. you are being called
6. they will be; there will be
7. we shall obtain; we shall secure
8. you are being seen; you seem
9. you were helping
10. I shall have; I shall hold
11. you will be moved
12. you can; you are able
13. they are being occupied; they are being seized
14. they were being feared
15. he/she/it will be prepared
16. you will give
17. you are being saved
18. they used to go
19. we were being prepared
20. it will be owed
21. you were being cared for
22. we were being watched; we were being looked at
23. they will frighten; they will terrify
24. I used to be; I was

READING

EUTROPIUS

He [Anthony] also stirred up a great Civil War, with his wife Cleopatra, queen of Egypt, urging it, since she hoped, with a womanly desire, to rule also in the City [Rome]. He was defeated by Augustus in a famous and glorius naval battle near Actium, which is a place in Epirus, from which he escaped to Egypt and, because his future was without hope, since everyone was going over to the side of Augustus, he killed himself. Cleopatra let a snake bite her and died from its poison. Egypt was added to the Roman Empire by Octavius Augustus and Gaius Cornelius Gallus was put in command of it. Egypt had him as its first Roman judge.

Brevarium, Book 7, 7

THE BIBLE

A Psalm of David, When He Fled from Absalom His Son

Lord, how are they increased that trouble me!
Many are they that rise up against me;
many there be which say of my soul:
There is no help for him in God.
But thou, O Lord, art a shield for me;
my glory, and the lifter up of mine head.
I cried unto the Lord with my voice,
and he heard me out of his holy hill.

I laid me down and slept;
I awaked; for the Lord sustained me.
I will not be afraid of ten thousands of people
that have set themselves against me round about.
Arise, O Lord; save me, O my God;
for thou hast smitten all mine enemies upon
the cheek bone;
thou hast broken the teeth of the ungodly.
Salvation belongeth unto the Lord; thy blessing
is upon thy people.

Psalm 3

Chapter Five

Practice Exercise No. 84

1. **ambulavi**
2. **laudavi**
3. **monui**
4. **debui**
5. **portavi**
6. **servavi**
7. **vocavi**
8. **movi**
9. **dedi**
10. **rogavi**

Practice Exercise No. 85

1. he/she/it has asked
2. they have watched
3. we have warned, advised
4. I have helped, aided
5. you have been
6. you have killed
7. you have told, related
8. I have lived in, dwelt
9. I have seen
10. they have feared
11. you have grieved
12. you have had, held
13. we have owed, ought
14. they have worked
15. you have overcome, conquered
16. he/she/it has pointed out, shown
17. they have told, related
18. you have occupied, seized
19. we have prepared
20. he/she/it has flown

Practice Exercise No. 86

1. I had walked
2. they had adored
3. he/she/it had plowed
4. they had moved
5. we had remained, stayed
6. you had seen
7. you had prepared
8. you had given
9. you had held, kept
10. I had stood
11. he/she/it had prepared
12. they had placed
13. you had stirred up, aroused
14. you had cared for
15. I had swum
16. we had grieved
17. he/she/it had asked
18. they had watched, looked at
19. he/she/it had seen
20. you had called

Practice Exercise No. 87

1. you will have loved
2. he/she/it will have cared for
3. I shall have praised
4. we shall have placed
5. they will have had
6. he/she/it will have frightened
7. he/she/it will have moved
8. they will have given
9. you will have stood
10. he/she/it will have held
11. we shall have called
12. I shall have saved
13. he/she/it will have carried
14. they will have prepared
15. you will have announced
16. we shall have told, related
17. you will have had
18. he/she/it will have owed
19. they will have worshipped
20. you will have walked

Practice Exercise No. 88

1. they have been
2. he, she has walked
3. he has been carried
4. they have been loved
5. you have been cared for
6. they have been praised
7. I have been warned
8. we have owed, ought to have
9. you have stood
10. it has been related, told
11. we have been called
12. I have swum
13. you have been saved
14. it has been announced
15. they have been moved
16. you have feared
17. he has been prepared
18. they have been placed
19. they have praised
20. you have moved

Practice Exercise No. 89

1. they had given
2. he/she/it had moved
3. he had been frightened
4. you had remained, stayed
5. you had held
6. he/she/it had fought
7. I had been praised
8. they had been cared for
9. you had been loved
10. you had been aroused, incited
11. they had been prepared
12. you had been occupied, seized
13. you had been freed
14. he had been killed
15. we had been saved
16. he had warned, advised
17. you had had
18. you had held, kept
19. we had been helped
20. they had worshipped

Practice Exercise No. 90

1. I shall have warned, advised
2. he/she/it will have been
3. it will have been carried
4. they will have been warned
5. they will have had
6. you will have frightened
7. we shall have moved
8. you will have been seen
9. he/she/it will have feared
10. she, will have been moved
11. we shall have given
12. they will have stood
13. we shall have been
14. you will have been killed
15. we shall have been praised
16. you will have been armed
17. they will have been cared for
18. it will have been placed
19. they will have been; there will have been
20. she will have been saved

Practice Exercise No. 91

1. it had been had
2. I shall have seen
3. they will have been attacked
4. you will have been praised
5. you had been carried
6. it will have been owed
7. they had owed
8. you have waited for
9. you have seen
10. it has been pointed out, shown
11. they have been warned, advised
12. we have been asked
13. they have looked at, watched
14. we have been moved
15. we had prepared
16. he has been warned, advised
17. he/she/it had stood
18. they had been given
19. they have told, related
20. I shall have held, kept

Practice Exercise No. 92

1. for many years
2. in the next year
3. for many hours
4. in the next hour
5. for seven hours
6. in the middle of the year
7. in six hours
8. for long years
9. in an hour
10. for twelve hours

Practice Exercise No. 93

1. to the cities
2. from the towns
3. from Rome
4. to Rome
5. into the camp
6. in front of the forum
7. in back of the garden
8. in the field
9. into the fields
10. down from the hills
11. out of the cottage
12. in the country
13. at home
14. away from the river
15. under the sea
16. under the walls
17. into the ditch
18. away from the temple
19. out of the roads
20. about, down from the sun

Practice Exercise No. 94

1. I shall see
2. he/she/it had fought
3. you were standing
4. we shall work
5. he/she/it had been; there had been
6. they will obtain
7. we were swimming
8. he/she/it will be; there will be
9. we see
10. it has been looked at; it has seemed
11. he/she/it will be moved
12. they had been built
13. you have been
14. we were being attacked
15. they have remained, stayed
16. he/she/it wants; he/she/it is willing
17. you do not want; you are not willing
18. I prefer to have; I prefer to hold
19. I was preferring
20. you will not want; you will be unwilling

Practice Exercise No. 95

1. Next year, we shall move to Rome.
2. For six hours, they remained in the city.
3. They had been attacked half way up the hill.
4. I stayed in Italy for many hours.
5. He (she) will be there for an hour.
6. They will work for many years, won't they?
7. He walked toward the town for many long hours.
8. He has not been freed by the king.
9. Are they in the garden with the boys?
10. I moved seven miles from the city.
11. Do not go to the city!
12. I prefer to remain in town.

Practice Exercise No. 96

1. they are sending
2. I have been shown, taught
3. we are being sought
4. he/she/it ought; owes
5. you had been warned
6. they will have been prepared
7. he/she/it has led
8. you have freed
9. I was worshipping
10. he/she/it will have sent
11. he/she/it will order
12. we were being watched, looked at
13. you are showing
14. they will ask
15. you were leading
16. he/she/it will send
17. I have been saved, preserved
18. you had feared
19. you had sought
20. they had remained, stayed

Practice Exercise No. 97

1. on account of the injury
2. from the battles
3. for six hours
4. on the road, march, journey
5. out of the territory
6. toward Gaul
7. away from the hill
8. in the letter
9. by the men; away from the men
10. into the river bank

Practice Exercise No. 98

1. I seek them.
2. of these (those) books
3. his, her garden
4. I gave these (those) things to them.
5. He was fighting.
6. You have seen him.
7. in these (those) places
8. to/for his (her) father
9. They are being sent by him.
10. You sent them.
11. this, that hour; in this, that hour
12. her, his, their own signals
13. out of these (those) cities
14. this (that) woman
15. We are being led by them.
16. their apples
17. his, her, their own kings
18. with them
19. this, that road, journey
20. this (that) cause

Practice Exercise No. 99

1. **ducitur**
2. **ductus sum**
3. **ducebam**
4. **duxerunt**
5. **ducar**
6. **missus es**
7. **mittebant**
8. **mittetis**
9. **misisti**
10. **missus erat**
11. **petiti sunt**
12. **petiverimus**
13. **petetur**
14. **petit**
15. **petebas**
16. **currentur**
17. **cursus est**
18. **currit**
19. **currebantur**
20. **cucurrerat**

Chapter Five Review

VOCABULARY REVIEW

NOUNS

1. love
2. Apollo
3. Atalanta
4. Atlas
5. boldness, bravery, daring
6. cause, reason
7. hill
8. body
9. Eurystheus
10. territory
11. end, border
12. river
13. Hercules
14. the Hesperides
15. Hippomenes
16. hour
17. garden
18. fire
19. journey, march, way, route
20. Juno
21. law
22. book
23. place
24. miles
25. a mile
26. mountain, mount
27. delay
28. woman
29. wall
30. name
31. night
32. foot
33. apple
34. price
35. fight
36. Pythia
37. king
38. snake, serpent
39. signal, standard
40. Tarquinius

PRONOUNS

1. he
2. she
3. it

ADJECTIVES

1. golden
2. twelve
3. nine
4. next, nearest
5. seven
6. six
7. Sibylline
8. proud, haughty
9. last, farthest
10. this, that

VERBS

1. increase, enlarge
2. run
3. point out, show
4. speak, say
5. teach, show
6. lead
7. order, command
8. prefer
9. send
10. be unwilling, wish not to
11. seek
12. ask, ask for

ADVERBS

1. at home
2. almost, nearly
3. afterwards
4. how long
5. in the country

PREPOSITIONS

1. into, onto; in, on

CONJUNCTIONS

1. after, when

Practice Exercise No. 100

1. in, on the feet
2. away from the hill
3. toward the rivers
4. out of the fields
5. into the fire
6. in, on the walls
7. about the body
8. in the country
9. from Rome
10. to Rome
11. at home
12. out of the night

Practice Exercise No. 101

1. he/she/it had been; there had been
2. we have ruled
3. he has been asked
4. you will have carried
5. they have given
6. they have placed
7. they have been given
8. you have sent
9. it will have been sought
10. it had been increased
11. we have moved
12. we have been
13. they had been aroused
14. you had hurried
15. they will have been; there will have been
16. I have been asked
17. he/she/it stood
18. you have called
19. we shall have been praised
20. he had had
21. he/she/it has preferred
22. they have wanted; they have been willing
23. I had preferred
24. you will not have wanted; you will not have been willing

Practice Exercise No. 102

1. in the next year
2. for seven hours
3. in the next hours
4. late in the year
5. for six years
6. on this (that) night
7. for these (those) nights
8. for these (those) years
9. in this (that) year
10. in this (that) hour

Practice Exercise No. 103

1. his, her, its
2. them
3. they
4. to/for him, her, it; they
5. it
6. them
7. she; they; them; from/with/by/in her
8. their
9. to/for, from/with/by/in them
10. him
11. they
12. from/with/by/in him, it

Practice Exercise No. 104

1. this (that) love
2. of this (that) boldness
3. these (those) names
4. these (those) causes
5. to/for, from/with/by/in these (those) territories
6. of these (those) journeys
7. these (those) apples
8. to/for this (that) woman
9. this (that) body
10. of this (that) place
11. to/for this (that) king
12. this (that) night

READING

MARCUS VALERIUS MARTIALIS

I do not love thee, Sabidius, nor can I tell you why;
this only I can say: I do not love thee.
Epigrams, 1, 32

Tomorrow you will live, tomorrow, you always say, Postumus.
Tell me when, Postumus, is that tomorrow coming?
How far away is your tomorrow, where is it? Or where must it be sought?
It doesn't lie hidden among the Parthians and Armenians, does it?

Already that tomorrow of yours has the years of Priam or Nestor.
Tell me, for how much could that tomorrow of yours be bought?
You will live tomorrow? Today it is already too late to live, Postumus;
he is wise, whoever has lived yesterday, Postumus.

Epigrams, 5, 58

THE BIBLE

To everything there is a season, and a time to every purpose under the heaven:
A time to be born, and a time to die;
a time to plant, and a time to pluck that which is planted;
a time to kill, and a time to heal;
a time to break down, and a time to build up;
a time to weep, and a time to laugh;
a time to mourn, and a time to dance;
a time to cast away stones, and a time to gather stones together;

a time to embrace, and a time to refrain from embracing;
a time to get, and a time to lose;
a time to keep, and a time to cast away;
a time to rend, and a time to sew;
a time to keep silence, and a time to speak;
a time to love, and a time to hate;
a time of war and a time of peace.
What profit hath he that worketh in that wherein he laboureth?

Ecclesiastes, 3, 1–9

Chapter Six

Practice Exercise No. 105

1. because of the delay
2. because of my care
3. because of the dangers
4. because of fear
5. because of death
6. because of diligence
7. because of speed
8. because of boldness
9. because of the delays
10. because of the time

Practice Exercise No. 106

1. with zeal, eagerness
2. with great care
3. with great diligence, care
4. with great fear
5. with speed
6. with much zeal, eagerness
7. with great zeal, eagerness
8. with delay
9. with great speed
10. with great delay

Practice Exercise No. 107

1. **posui**
2. **superare**
3. **dedi**
4. **capere**
5. **servatus**
6. **facio**
7. **verti**
8. **terrui**
9. **duco**
10. **tuli**

Practice Exercise No. 108

1. he/she/it has ordered
2. you have led
3. they have shown
4. I was asking
5. we have made, done
6. he/she/it is being shown
7. you are being sent; will be sent
8. you are being taken, seized
9. he/she/it will look at, watch
10. we shall increase
11. they will seek
12. they were carrying
13. you were obtaining, getting
14. he/she/it was being turned
15. he/she/it had terrified
16. you had sought
17. they had taken, seized
18. they will have been moved
19. we had been led
20. he/she/it was taking, seizing

Practice Exercise No. 109

1. because of the hour
2. because of the weapon
3. in front of the camp
4. from fear
5. down from the tree; about the tree
6. by the king; away from the king
7. out of the trees
8. into this (that) place
9. with the father
10. with care
11. in, on the water
12. under the ocean
13. around the walls
14. against him
15. between, among the towns
16. through the field
17. in back of the camp
18. without them
19. across the sea
20. about, concerning the men

Practice Exercise No. 110

1. this wall
2. that city
3. in that place
4. these leaders
5. to/for those soldiers
6. to/for that lieu-tenant
7. these commanders
8. those plans
9. of that ocean
10. of these men
11. in that garden
12. that goddess
13. of that foot soldier
14. about this master
15. out of that tree
16. this hindrance
17. to/for these fathers
18. these ships
19. that book
20. to that girl
21. these weapons
22. of these parts
23. about that peace
24. of those sands
25. in these years
26. for that hour
27. that sign, standard
28. of this horse

Practice Exercise No. 111

1. his, her, its
2. he
3. to/for him, her, it; they
4. them
5. to/for, from/with/by/in them
6. of them, their
7. it; from/with/by/in him, it
8. to/for him, her, it
9. she; from/with/by/in her; them; they
10. they
11. she; them; they
12. her
13. them
14. him
15. them

Practice Exercise No. 112

1. the goddess herself, the very goddess
2. out of the temples themselves, out of the very temples
3. the same city
4. the men themselves, the very men
5. by the same youth
6. the same name, the very name
7. of the same nation
8. on the very night, in the night itself
9. the same roads, ways
10. to/for, from/with/by/in the same men
11. out of the field itself, out of the very field
12. in the years themselves, in the very years
13. the boys themselves, the very boys
14. of the lieutenant himself, of the very lieutenant
15. the same hour, in the same hour
16. the law itself, the very law
17. the mountain itself, the very mountain
18. the girls themselves, the very girls
19. the same journey, road, way
20. by the women themselves, by the very women
21. at the same time
22. peace itself, the very peace
23. the same towns
24. in the cities themselves, in the very cities
25. of the same people
26. the same men
27. out of the same place
28. in the same years

Practice Exercise No. 113

1. to/for him (himself), her (herself), it (itself); they (themselves)
2. of (the same) him, her, it
3. (the same) it
4. she (herself); they (themselves); them (themselves)
5. them (themselves)
6. (the same) she; they; them; from, with, by, in her
7. (the same) him
8. of (the same) them
9. out of (the same) them
10. of him (himself), her (herself), it (itself)

Practice Exercise No. 114

1. they were able to lead
2. you can stay
3. he, she was not able to worship
4. he/she/it will be able to free
5. they can care for
6. we were not able to kill
7. I had been able to order
8. you can show, point out
9. we were able to ask
10. I was not able to increase
11. we shall be able to help
12. you will be able to fight
13. they have not been able to call
14. I can not work
15. you have been able to stay
16. they become; they are made
17. he has been made; he has become
18. you will become; you will be made
19. they had become; they had been made
20. I was becoming; I was made
21. we make; we do
22. you will make; you will do
23. they make; they do
24. they were making; they were doing

Practice Exercise No. 115

1. in one year
2. no care
3. of which gift
4. to/for any ship
5. for all the years
6. with the father alone
7. of no deaths
8. to neither nation
9. in the other road
10. with, by another name
11. to which river
12. of any hill
13. to/for one book
14. for no reasons
15. by neither man

Practice Exercise No. 116

1. they had feared
2. you have been
3. they will send
4. he/she/it took
5. he/she/it will fear
6. they were looking at
7. they will be held
8. I shall be sent
9. they have been praised
10. it had become, been done, been made
11. you were sailing
12. they were being given
13. he/she/it carries on, bears
14. they had been; there had been
15. they have had

Practice Exercise No. 117

1. one is a boy, the other is not
2. at no time
3. of any war
4. toward which camp
5. the women themselves alone
6. of neither youth
7. other cities
8. one part
9. about neither girl
10. another road, journey, way

Practice Exercise No. 118

1. in a short hour
2. of a bold slave
3. swift horse
4. in, on a swift river
5. by bold men
6. for all times; all times
7. by a keen lieutenant
8. short life
9. at all hours
10. in a swift ship
11. bold work
12. in a short time
13. active troops
14. of a swift horse
15. active women
16. swift death, quick death
17. short journeys, roads
18. to a bold man
19. for a short year
20. in every, each place

Practice Exercise No. 119

1. of the golden sun
2. out of neither place
3. on the top of the mountain
4. of an easy journey
5. any hours
6. grave punishments
7. of the nearest nations
8. bold citizen
9. strong body
10. of swift rivers
11. Latin books
12. other men
13. your ship
14. of many fathers
15. of each king

Practice Exercise No. 120

1. Who are you?
2. To whom did he give those things?
3. Whom shall I see?
4. Whose eyes?
5. What things does he know?
6. With whom does he (she) walk?
7. By whom has he been captured?
8. Who is shouting?
9. Who is fighting?
10. Whose weapons?
11. What do you have?
12. Whom has he killed?
13. To whom shall I give it?
14. What has been asked?
15. To whom have you sent the gift?
16. Whom do you like?
17. Who is fleeing?
18. What is easy?
19. Whose is it?
20. With whom?
21. Whom will he send?
22. What is he doing?
23. Who are struggling?
24. By whom has it been carried out?

Practice Exercise No. 121

1. **pugnare**
2. **mittere**
3. **regere**
4. **dare**
5. **laudare**
6. **rogare**
7. **scribere**
8. **videre**
9. **cognoscere**
10. **necare**
11. **capere**
12. **timere**
13. **habere**
14. **movere**
15. **parare**
16. **ducere**
17. **augere**
18. **servare**
19. **vincere**
20. **terrere**

Practice Exercise No. 122

1. **demonstrari**	6. **armari**	11. **mitti**	16. **interfici**
2. **duci**	7. **amari**	12. **geri**	17. **iuvari**
3. **moveri**	8. **ferri**	13. **accipi**	18. **teneri**
4. **iuberi**	9. **doceri**	14. **timeri**	19. **cognosci**
5. **verti**	10. **occupari**	15. **vocari**	20. **simulari**

Chapter Six Review

VOCABULARY REVIEW

NOUNS

1. youth
2. Africa
3. mind, spirit
4. tree
5. sand
6. Ariadne
7. gold
8. Bacchus
9. food
10. citizen
11. fleet
12. Cyclops
13. diligence, care
14. horseman, knight
15. flight, escape
16. Hannibal
17. Homer
18. hindrance
19. commander, general, emperor
20. injury, harm
21. labyrinth
22. Midas
23. Minos
24. the Minotaur
25. death
26. ship
27. eye
28. work
29. foot soldier
30. punishment, fine
31. poet
32. Polyphemus
33. gate, door, entrance
34. stone, rock
35. Silenus
36. zeal, eagerness
37. weapons
38. storm, bad weather
39. time
40. Theseus

PRONOUNS

1. he/she/it (this one)
2. he/she/it (the same one)
3. he/she/it (that one)
4. he himself, she herself, it itself

ADJECTIVES

1. sharp, active, keen
2. other, another
3. the one, the other
4. bold
5. short, brief
6. quick, swift
7. easy
8. brave, strong
9. heavy, severe, serious
10. this
11. the same
12. that
13. very, himself, herself, itself
14. neither
15. new
16. no, none
17. all, every
18. alone, only
19. all, whole
20. any

VERBS

1. take, seize, capture
2. shout, cry
3. learn, recognize, know
4. hasten, strive, contend
5. make, do
6. carry, bear
7. be made, be done, become
8. flee, run away, escape
9. carry on, wage
10. throw
11. kill
12. put, place
13. write
14. pretend
15. turn

ADVERBS
1. meanwhile
2. at night

PREPOSITIONS
1. among, in the presence of
2. in front of; for, instead of
3. because of, on account of

CONJUNCTIONS
1. and so, therefore

Practice Exercise No. 123

1. they take, seize
2. it had been learned
3. they have been conquered
4. they will turn
5. we were killing
6. they have done, made
7. you had taken, seized
8. he/she/it was fleeing
9. he/she/it will be put
10. they will have carried on, waged
11. he/she/it writes
12. you throw
13. they will hurry
14. they have been put
15. it has been carried on, waged
16. you become, are made

Practice Exercise No. 124

1. because of death
2. because of injury
3. with great diligence
4. because of the general
5. because of food
6. because of the fleets
7. with a small punishment, fine
8. with great zeal, eagerness
9. because of the hindrance
10. because of the sand

Practice Exercise No. 125

1. him
2. his, her, its
3. them
4. that
5. he
6. their
7. the same things; she
8. his, hers, its
9. he
10. their
11. whom
12. what
13. whose
14. to/for whom
15. with whom

Practice Exercise No. 126

1. he/she/it was able to shout
2. they were able to take
3. you can do, make
4. we can put, place
5. you have been able to conquer
6. he/she/it will be able to hurry
7. they have been able to write
8. we were able to recognize, learn
9. you are able to turn
10. they are able to carry on, wage

Practice Exercise No. 127

1. of one work
2. of all the citizens
3. another hindrance
4. new weapons
5. in a short time
6. to/for the whole stone
7. of no fear
8. any injury
9. bold horsemen, knights
10. swift punishment

READING

MARCUS TULLIUS CICERO

Oh what times these are! Oh what habits we have! The Senate knows these things, the consul sees them; this man, however lives. Does he live? Indeed, he even comes into the Senate, he becomes a participant in the public plans, he notes and designates with his eyes each single one of us for murder. We, however, brave men, seem to do enough for the Republic if we avoid the fury and weapons of this man. You, Catiline, should have been lead to your death by the order of the consul long ago; the destruction that you are plotting against us should have been brought against you.

First Oration Against Catiline, 2

ORO DE CERINTON

About the Hydra

There is a certain animal, called the hydra, whose nature it is to bury itself in the mud so that it might be better able to glide. Finally, it enters the mouth of a crocodile, when it is sleeping, and thus, entering its stomach, it eats its heart and thus kills the crocodile.
Mystical interpretation: The hydra signifies the son of God, who has assumed the mud of our flesh so that he might slip more easily into the mouth of the devil, and thus, entering his stomach and eating his heart, he kills him.

About the Antelope

There is a certain animal that is called the antelope; when this animal plays in a thicket with its horns, finally its horns are entangled with the thicket so that it is not able to extricate them and then, it begins to cry aloud; when this is heard, hunters come and kill him.
Mystical interpretation: Thus it happens that many people are delighted and play with the occupations of this world and thus are entangled in these things so that they can not be torn away and thus by hunters, that is, by demons, they are taken and killed.

Chapter Seven

Practice Exercise No. 128

1. **pulchre,** beautifully
2. **longe,** far, distant
3. **magnopere,** greatly
4. **nove,** recently, newly
5. **acriter,** keenly
6. **graviter,** seriously
7. **breviter,** briefly
8. **alte,** on high
9. **grate,** with pleasure
10. **audacter,** boldly
11. **misere,** wretchedly
12. **proxime,** next, most recently
13. **fortiter,** bravely
14. **celeriter,** swiftly
15. **libere,** freely

Practice Exercise No. 129

1. you carry, do carry
2. I have, hold
3. they lead, are leading
4. he throws, is throwing
5. you have heard
6. he has been freed
7. they had been seen; had seemed
8. they had been heard
9. you have been received
10. I had been heard
11. they were hearing
12. he will have been prepared
13. he/she/it will hear
14. they have sought
15. they hear, do hear
16. you were being helped
17. we were being heard
18. we were turning
19. they will be taken, seized
20. you will be heard
21. you are being heard
22. he/she/it has done, made
23. they will ask
24. we have heard

Practice Exercise No. 130

1. they are fighting bravely
2. we saw very recently
3. he/she/it carried on with difficulty
4. they will be widely received
5. he, she walks far
6. they stand well
7. he easily recognized
8. he, she liked greatly

Practice Exercise No. 131

1. The place will be defended easily.
2. At first, nothing could be prepared.
3. Because of fear, you did not fight bravely.
4. Which door do you like?
5. The land by nature has been defended with difficulty.
6. Not only the king, but also the queen heard it.

Practice Exercise No. 132

1. a. who are making the journey with their forces
   b. The men, who are making the journey with their forces, are brave.

2. a. which he built
   b. The tower, which he built, was keeping the barbarians from the town.

3. a. with whom I was walking
   b. The woman, with whom I was walking, is my mother.

4. a. whose name we can not see
   b. The ship, whose name we can not see, is sailing toward Italy.

5. a. to whom I gave the letter
   b. The boy, to whom I gave the letter, will come quickly.

6. a. which you will have
   b. The fear, which you will have, will soon not be remembered.

7. a. to which they were fleeing
    b. The river, to which they were fleeing, was deep and wide.

8. a. about which he wrote
    b. The place, about which he wrote, is far from the city.

9. a. which he had
    b. Everything, which he had, now is mine.

10. a. whose boys you see
     b. The men, whose boys you see, are friends.

Practice Exercise No. 133

1. in what place?
2. which man?
3. what town?
4. what booty?
5. which men?
6. with what speed?
7. in what year?
8. of what name?
9. at what hour?
10. at what time?
11. with what soldiers?
12. of what citizens?
13. what baggage? what hindrances?
14. of what size?
15. with what plan?

Practice Exercise No. 134

1. they make, do
2. he/she/it will order
3. you have found, learned
4. he/she/it will arrive
5. to be had
6. he/she/it was running
7. he/she/it had been
8. he/she/it took, seized
9. they have looked at
10. it was happening
11. you hear
12. you have arrived
13. he/she/it was fighting, hurrying
14. they had given
15. to be seen; to seem
16. they have prohibited
17. they will be; there will be
18. I shall be seen; I shall seem
19. to be asked
20. I shall have

Practice Exercise No. 135a

1. he/she/it has not been able
2. of that place
3. your sons
4. others come; some come
5. he, she wishes to come
6. brave people
7. because of the storm
8. with great zeal
9. he, she remained at home
10. of this, that nation
11. in the next year
12. O my friend
13. all men
14. he, she fears nothing
15. not only your mother

Practice Exercise No. 135b

1. you were fearing; fear!
2. you will follow
3. they will have tried
4. I shall have feared
5. they follow
6. I urge
7. he/she/it fears
8. you will have died
9. she had urged
10. they were dying
11. he/she/it will urge
12. you try
13. they will fear
14. he had tried
15. you were urging
16. we were following
17. he has died
18. we shall die
19. I had followed
20. she has tried

Practice Exercise No. 136

1. for many paces
2. your group; your hand
3. long attack
4. because of his arrival
5. each wing
6. of our armies
7. on your wing
8. out of the army
9. into the house
10. for six miles
11. against the armies
12. because of your arrival
13. the attack (attacks) of the enemy
14. group (groups) of soldiers
15. by the army

Practice Exercise No. 137

1. their battle lines
2. late in the day
3. on the next day
4. because of these things
5. of any hope
6. the whole thing
7. for one day
8. of what things?
9. our battle lines
10. what things?
11. in what battle line?
12. of each day
13. because of this (that) thing
14. in these battle lines
15. much hope

Practice Exercise No. 138

1. he, she has walked
2. we are seen; we seem
3. they were; there were
4. he/she/it had done, made
5. he, she was fleeing
6. he/she/it finds
7. it had been given
8. he/she/it can, is able
9. it has been drawn up
10. to be seen; to seem
11. they will have been left behind
12. they will fight
13. he/she/it has drawn up
14. he, she makes a journey
15. they will be heard

Practice Exercise No. 139

1. All things seem to be easy.
2. After six days, neither soldier had any hope.
3. The captives whom you led back came out of their army.
4. Who greatly hindered the strong attack?
5. In one hour, the men will come home.
6. For what reason was he drawing up his battle line on the hill?
7. Among these things which we have is a small supply of water.
8. The soldiers in that wing are turning their horses toward the field.
9. Neither the wing nor the battle line saw hope.
10. Who among these peoples was holding the royal power?

Practice Exercise No. 140

1. you
2. we; us
3. by you
4. their; of them
5. she; they; them; from, with her
6. to/for her, him, it; they
7. you; from/with/by/in you
8. I
9. him
10. to/for me

11. with us
12. you
13. to/for you; from, with you
14. them
15. that; it
16. to him, her, it
17. his, hers, its
18. with you
19. their; of them
20. toward you
21. to you

22. your; of you
23. our; of us
24. about me
25. to/for them; from, with, by, in them
26. about them
27. she; from them; from, with, by, in her; they; them
28. with her
29. their; of them
30. them

Practice Exercise No. 141

1. to/for himself, herself, itself; to/for themselves
2. yourself; from/with/by/in yourself
3. by myself
4. yourselves

5. himself, herself, itself; themselves; from/with/by/in himself, herself, itself, themselves
6. to/for yourselves; from/with/by/in yourselves
7. to/for myself
8. to/for ourselves; from/with/by/in ourselves

Practice Exercise No. 142

1. The man himself does not know us.
2. I sent help to you.
3. We found you in this place.
4. Will you come with me?
5. You give books to us.
6. You do not hear him.
7. They were fleeing toward us.
8. He sent these things to me.
9. He (She) will not be able to walk home with you.
10. This is our native country.

11. You will tell this (that) to them.
12. We shall lead her home.
13. They were seeking peace from them.
14. I was being terrified by you and your sword.
15. We had saved ourselves at that time.
16. You can help us, can't you?
17. He saw their city.
18. We ourselves shall order them to come.
19. You will point out these things to us.
20. His spirit did not frighten me long.

Chapter Seven Review

VOCABULARY REVIEW

NOUNS

1. line of battle
2. arrival, approach
3. Athens
4. state
5. horn, wing
6. day
7. house, home
8. Eurydice
9. army
10. Hellespont
11. Hero
12. attack
13. want, scarcity
14. Leander
15. hand, group
16. nature
17. nothing
18. Orpheus
19. pace
20. the Persians
21. guard, garrison
22. region, boundary
23. kingdom
24. thing, matter, affair
25. Sparta
26. hope
27. Thermopylae
28. tower

PRONOUNS
1. I
2. we
3. who, which, that; which, what
4. you (sing.)
5. you (pl.)

VERBS
1. happen
2. address, call, name
3. place, station
4. observe
5. desire, wish, want
6. withdraw, go away, leave
7. lead out
8. hinder

ADVERBS
1. now, already
2. greatly
3. too little, not enough
4. first, at first
5. alone, only

ADJECTIVES
1. ten
2. difficult, hard
3. of Marathon
4. first

9. draw up, form, train
10. arrive
11. keep off, hinder, prohibit, prevent, forbid
12. lead back
13. rule
14. leave, leave behind
15. find, discover
16. know

CONJUNCTIONS
1. for
2. and not
3. neither . . . nor
4. as

Practice Exercise No. 143
1. **late,** widely
2. **acriter,** keenly
3. **difficile,** with difficulty
4. **misere,** wretchedly
5. **longe,** far
6. **magnopere,** greatly
7. **laete,** happily
8. **libere,** freely
9. **parum,** too little, not enough
10. **anguste,** narrowly

Practice Exercise No. 144
1. I shall come
2. he, she knew
3. he has been heard
4. we were arriving
5. they will be hindered
6. they find, discover
7. you were being heard
8. it had been known
9. they have wished
10. you will be heard

Practice Exercise No. 145
1. whose
2. whom
3. who, which, that
4. who
5. with whom
6. we; us; ourselves
7. to/for me, myself
8. me; myself; from/with/by/in me, myself
9. of you
10. to/for you, yourself
11. with you, yourself
12. his, her, its
13. their, of them
14. him
15. her

Practice Exercise No. 146

1. to/for the army
2. the thing; things
3. of the horn, wing
4. the battle line
5. hope
6. of the hands, bands
7. on, from, with, by the day
8. to/for, from/with/by/in the attacks
9. the arrival
10. home; the house
11. to/for, from/with/by/in the things
12. horns, wings
13. of the armies
14. to/for the hand, group
15. to/for hope

READING

PUBLIUS VERGILIUS MARO

They walked obscured by darkness, in the lonely night, through the shadows and through the vacant kingdoms of Pluto, and the empty homes; just as under the dim light of a wavering moon is a journey in the woods, when Jupiter has hidden the sky in shadows and black night has taken away the color from things. Before the very entrance and in the very jaws of Orcus Grief and avenging Cares have placed their couches, and pale Diseases dwell, and sad Old Age, and Fear, and Hunger persuading-evil, also base Want, forms terrible to see, both Death and Toil, then Sleep, the kinsman of Death, and evil Pleasures of the mind, and death-bearing War on the threshold opposite, and the iron chambers of the Furies, and mad Discord, entwining her snaky hair with bloody fillets.

Aeneid 6, 268–281

JACQUES DE VITRY

ABOUT A TREE ON WHICH WOMEN WERE HANGING

I have heard about a certain other man, who had a tree in his garden, on which two of his wives had hanged themselves. A certain one of his neighbors said to him: "Certainly that tree is lucky and holds a good omen. I, however, have a very bad wife; I ask you, give me a young shoot from it, so that I may plant it in my garden."

ABOUT A SIDE OF BACON WHICH WAS HANGING IN A CERTAIN TOWN

Once I passed through a certain town in France, where they had hung a ham or side of bacon in the street with this condition that, whoever might wish to swear on oath that he had lived one whole year with his wife after the marriage had been contracted in such a way that he had not regretted the marriage, might have the side of bacon. And although it had hung there for ten years, not one single man was found who might win the side of bacon, because all, inside of a year from the contract of marriage, regretted it.

Chapter Eight

Practice Exercise No. 147

1. fifteen	6. ten	11. one hundred	16. thirteen
2. nine	7. three	12. fourteen	17. seven
3. twenty	8. seventeen	13. eight	18. one
4. five	9. four	14. nineteen	19. eighteen
5. sixteen	10. eleven	15. two	20. one thousand

Practice Exercise No. 148

1. fourth	3. tenth	5. seventh	7. fifth	9. first
2. eigth	4. third	6. second	8. ninth	10. sixth

Practice Exercise No. 149

1. a thousand ships
2. three men
3. of thousands of soldiers
4. for fourteen days
5. of one man
6. twenty miles
7. a hundred boys
8. for five years
9. six of the soldiers
10. in seven hours
11. in a hundred years
12. eight of the boys
13. for two days
14. of ten laws; ten of the laws
15. three places
16. two of the provinces
17. in twelve days
18. of six animals
19. eighteen of the kings
20. in three years

Practice Exercise No. 150

1. to/for, of the tenth girl
2. on the eighth day
3. in the sixth hour; the sixth hour
4. the seventh ship
5. in the fifth summer
6. for the third day
7. in the tenth winter
8. the seventh attack
9. to/for, of the ninth hour; ninth hour
10. in the first year

Practice Exercise No. 151

1. a difficult way, road
2. a wretched home
3. of the free men
4. keen fears
5. similar armies
6. on a long day, for a long day
7. on a high mountain
8. swift rivers
9. wide streets
10. of pretty girls

Practice Exercise No. 152

1. narrower streets
2. a taller boy
3. of happier girls
4. a friendlier people
5. a longer road, way
6. in more pleasing places
7. of more famous sisters
8. a longer winter, for a longer winter
9. wider rivers
10. bolder man

Practice Exercise No. 153

1. of a very sweet spring
2. out of very pretty gardens
3. a very narrow temple
4. because of very wretched memories
5. very famous oracles
6. a very happy citizen
7. out of a very wide field
8. with very pretty mothers
9. on a very new ship
10. very short names

Practice Exercise No. 154

1. This is a very wretched place.
2. The bravest men arrived at the island.
3. The very keen horses were among the first.
4. What is an easier way to Greece?
5. The people of Italy are very free.
6. This is the narrower part of the water.
7. These things are also very similar.
8. We saw a very deep and rather wide river.
9. Our men chose a shorter way to the city.
10. You can see a high building from this place.

Practice Exercise No. 155

1. These towers are higher than those.
2. You are taller than your father.
3. Those roads are not easier than others.
4. You are more like your father than your mother.
5. Men are much stronger than women.
6. His house in the country is newer than that in the city.
7. The boy is happier than his sister.
8. The barbarians are much bolder than their neighbors.
9. He will be friendlier to you than to me.
10. Is the hand quicker than the eye?

Practice Exercise No. 156

1. they will be; there will be
2. it has been shown
3. he/she/it decided
4. he/she/it will be prepared
5. they were leading
6. he has been left behind
7. he/she/it will be sent
8. you are being carried
9. we were seeing
10. he, she has walked

Practice Exercise No. 157

1. more things
2. better
3. of the worst
4. of a bigger
5. of smaller
6. of very many
7. to/for, from/with/by/in more
8. the next
9. more suitable, of more suitable
10. most suitable

Practice Exercise No. 158

1. in very many cities
2. out of smaller springs
3. the greatest courage
4. best voice
5. down from higher walls
6. more water
7. more suitable time
8. of the worst thing; to/for the worst thing
9. toward a better part
10. with a bigger army
11. on a longer day
12. very many states
13. worse end
14. best years
15. smallest sister

Practice Exercise No. 159

1. wide
2. widely
3. wider
4. more widely
5. very wide
6. very widely
7. free
8. freely
9. freer
10. very free
11. more freely
12. very freely
13. pretty
14. more pretty
15. very pretty
16. prettily
17. more prettily
18. very prettily
19. swift
20. swiftly
21. swifter
22. more swiftly
23. very swift
24. very swiftly
25. keen
26. keenly
27. keener
28. more keenly

Practice Exercise No. 160

1. They were being attacked most severely.
2. He fights more bravely.
3. They have been burned quickly.
4. They will speak much more briefly.
5. He will be warned very boldly.
6. They drew up the battle line with difficulty.
7. He waged war more keenly.
8. They walk proudly.
9. He gave more pleasingly.
10. He is praised very highly.
11. They have been sent more widely.
12. He gave very freely.
13. He sails very far.
14. He moves more wretchedly.
15. They were seen recently.
16. They move more beautifully.
17. He will fear very keenly.
18. They have been taken boldly.
19. He was speaking very briefly.
20. They fight bravely.

Practice Exercise No. 161

1. well
2. greatly
3. badly
4. much
5. little
6. long
7. often
8. longer
9. more
10. more
11. better
12. worse
13. less
14. more often
15. most
16. most
17. longest
18. most often
19. best
20. worst

Practice Exercise No. 162

1. They arrive more often.
2. He fought as long as possible.
3. He has been aroused more.
4. He was being hindered more.
5. You have been loved best.
6. It has been heard most often.
7. He walks with less difficulty.
8. They are very powerful among us.
9. He flies more swiftly.
10. He will stay much longer.

Chapter Eight Review

VOCABULARY REVIEW

NOUNS

1. summer
2. Creusa
3. Cupid
4. difficulty
5. spring, fountain
6. winter
7. command
8. light
9. husband
10. marriage
11. great number, multitude
12. burden, weight
13. oracle
14. more
15. harbor, port
16. Psyche
17. sister
18. wife
19. wind
20. word

ADJECTIVES

1. equal, level, fair
2. sweet
3. immortal
4. larger
5. largest
6. better
7. smallest
8. smaller
9. mortal
10. best
11. worse
12. worst
13. most
14. next, following
15. next, following

VERBS

1. fall
2. collect, drive, compel
3. finish, complete, carry out
4. decide, establish
5. come together, assemble
6. give up, surrender
7. choose, select
8. sleep
9. arouse, stir up
10. set fire to, burn
11. overcome, crush
12. be most powerful
13. be more powerful
14. take back, receive
15. take up, undertake

ADVERBS

1. before
2. twice
3. more
4. most, especially
5. much, by much
6. never
7. formerly, once upon a time
8. on the next day
9. as possible; than
10. over, above

CONJUNCTIONS

1. either . . . or
2. while
3. for
4. although
5. also

Practice Exercise No. 163

1. one of the sisters
2. three rivers
3. two years; for two years
4. a thousand years
5. two wives
6. a hundred words
7. of one voice
8. twenty springs, fountains
9. the fourth hour;
   in the fourth hour
10. on the fifth day
11. in the second year
12. the seventh word
13. the first oracle
14. in the fourth harbor, port
15. out of the sixth gate, door

Practice Exercise No. 164

1. the longer winter; for the longer winter
2. the very pretty summer
3. of the longest years
4. the sweeter word
5. a very similar burden
6. of an immortal voice
7. easier way, journey
8. clearer lights
9. of a very keen difficulty
10. of stronger husbands

Practice Exercise No. 165

1. sweet, sweeter, sweetest
2. keen, keener, keenest
3. long, longer, longest
4. similar, more similar, most similar
5. high, higher, highest
6. free, freer, freest
7. swift, swifter, swiftest
8. wide, wider, widest
9. clear, clearer, clearest
10. bold, bolder, boldest

Practice Exercise No. 166

1. big, bigger, biggest
2. small, smaller, smallest
3. good, better, best
4. bad, worse, worst
5. much, more, most
6. many, more, very many

Practice Exercise No. 167

1. he was walking farther
2. he has been oppressed miserably
3. he sleeps little
4. it will burn for a very long time
5. they have been more keenly aroused
6. they were touching more
7. they have surrendered more easily
8. they are very powerful
9. it, he, she will be more powerful
10. they will be forced less easily

READING

PHAEDRUS

He who rejoices that he is praised by words of flattery,
too late pays his penalty with lowly repentance.
When a crow started to eat the cheese
he snatched from a window, perching in a lofty tree, a wolf saw him; thus, with flattery, he began to speak:
"Oh what a brightness, crow, that your feathers have.
What grace of body, what charms of looks you possess.

If you should have a voice, no bird would be above you."
Then he, foolish one, while he tried to show off his voice,
dropped the cheese from his mouth. This quickly the tricky fox snatched in his greedy teeth.
Then the crow, deceived by his stupidity, groaned, but too late.

Phaedrus I, 13

STABAT MATER

At the Cross her station keeping,
Stood the mournful Mother weeping,
Close to Jesus at the last.
Though her soul, of joy bereaved,
Bowed with anguish, deeply grieved,
Now at length the sword hath passed.
Oh how sad and sore distressed
Was that Mother, highly blest,
Of the sole begotten One!
Oh that silent, ceaseless mourning,
Oh those dim eyes, never turning
From that wondrous, suffering Son!
Who on Christ's dear Mother gazing,
In her trouble so amazing,
Born of woman, would not weep?
Who on Christ's dear Mother thinking,
Such a cup of sorrow drinking,
Would not share her sorrow deep?
For the sins of his own nation,
Saw him hang in desolation
Till his Spirit forth he sent;
Bruised, derided, cursed, defiled,
She beheld her tender Child,
All with bloody scourges rent.
O, thou Mother, fount of love!
Touch my spirit from above,
Make my heart with thine accord.
Make me feel as thou hast felt;
Make my soul to glow and melt
With the love of Christ my Lord.

Holy Mother, pierce me through.
In my heart each wound renew
Of my Savior crucified;
Let me share with thee his pain,
Who for all my sins was slain,
Who for me in torment died.
Let me mingle tears with thee,
Mourning him who mourned for me,
All the days that I may live.
By the cross with thee to stay,
There with thee to weep and pray,
Is all I ask of thee to give.
Virgin of all virgins blest,
Listen to my fond request;
Let me share thy grief divine.
Let me to my latest breath,
In my body bear the death
Of that dying Son of thine.
Wounded with his every wound,
Steep my soul till it hath swooned
In his very blood away.
Be to me, O Virgin, nigh,
Lest in flames I burn and die
In his awful judgment day.
Christ, when thou shalt call me hence,
Be thy Mother my defense,
Be thy cross my victory.
While my body here decays
May my soul thy goodness praise
Safe in Paradise with thee.

Chapter Nine

Practice Exercise No. 168

1. to warn
2. to have increased
3. to be thrown
4. to be about to place
5. to have fled
6. to hinder
7. to have swum
8. to be about to frighten
9. to have remained
10. to be about to hear
11. to have written
12. to be about to fight
13. to be about to praise
14. to be aroused
15. to have been sought
16. to send
17. to be touched
18. to have been attacked
19. to be known
20. to be about to carry on
21. to be received
22. to have been conquered
23. to be said
24. to be about to walk

Practice Exercise No. 169

1. **petere,** to seek
2. **cepisse,** to have taken
3. **habere,** to have
4. **rexisse,** to have ruled
5. **portare,** to carry
6. **vocavisse,** to have called
7. **ferre,** to carry
8. **dedisse,** to have given
9. **instruere,** to draw up
10. **vertere,** to turn

Practice Exercise No. 170

1. **narrari,** to be told
2. **defensus, -a, -um esse,** to have been defended
3. **videri,** to be seen; to seem
4. **iuvari,** to be helped
5. **pugnatus, -a, -um esse,** to have been fought
6. **motus, -a, -um esse,** to have been moved
7. **vocari,** to be called
8. **inveniri,** to be found
9. **necatus, -a, -um esse,** to have been killed

Practice Exercise No. 171

1. **futurus, -a, -umm esse,** to be about to be
2. **iussurus, -a, -um esse,** to be about to order
3. **facturus, -a, -um esse,** to be about to make
4. **defensurus, -a, -um esse,** to be about to defend
5. **oppugnaturus, -a, -um esse,** to be about to attack
6. **properaturus, -a, -um esse,** to be about to hurry
7. **capturus, -a, -um esse,** to be about to take
8. **inventurus, -a, -um esse,** to be about to find
9. **daturus, -a, -um esse,** to be about to give
10. **positurus, -a, -um esse,** to be about to place

Practice Exercise No. 172

1. Those soldiers said that the men would carry aid.
2. Do you think that your work has been done?
3. We were hoping that the enemy would come as quickly as possible.
4. The girls seem to be happy.
5. This king wished to rule well.
6. He will not want to be called.
7. To defend our town is best.
8. To have had hope was better than to have retreated.
9. He announced that the speed could be increased.
10. He ordered us to find a better place.

Practice Exercise No. 173

1. calling
2. having been moved
3. about to send
4. receiving
5. about to come
6. having been watched
7. arriving
8. about to take
9. placing, putting
10. having been announced

Practice Exercise No. 174

1. the ships, sailing
2. the leader, about to order
3. they, having been attacked
4. the men, about to arrive
5. seeking peace
6. the dog, running
7. the cities, having been captured
8. the temple, having been built
9. the harbors, having been found
10. the rivers, running

Practice Exercise No. 175
1. The people of the cities, which had been captured, were as brave as possible.
2. The men, who were about to arrive, were making the trip as quickly as possible.
3. The king, who is now ruling your country, seems to be timid.
4. The woman will give aid, when (if) she sees your difficulty.
5. The storm will not be very fierce, if it does not increase.
6. The father had great joy, because he was about to see his sons.
7. They were running as fast as possible, because they fear our men.
8. The men, who (because they) had been defeated, were especially frightened.
9. When she arrived in the town, she told her story.
10. They, who are defending the gate, were not friends.

Practice Exercise No. 176

1. bravely
2. as quickly as possible
3. least, not at all
4. for a very long time
5. more keenly
6. with difficulty
7. very easily
8. better
9. badly
10. greatly

Practice Exercise No. 177
1. When the oracle had been heard, many people decided to come to our land.
2. When the signal had been given, they made an attack onto the field.
3. The men, although their weapons were not many, nevertheless fought bravely.
4. Because many soldiers had been killed, the leaders sought peace.
5. The men, because the booty is large, will be received at home with great joy.
6. When this thing has been done, the boys will come home.
7. If he is the leader, we shall do it without difficulty.
8. When these things had been reported to me, I wanted to make the trip from the city.
9. If these have been killed, the people will be better ruled.
10. When the day had been set, they prepared everything as quickly as possible.
11. Because the door was open, he was able to come into the cottage.
12. He had no hope, because the city had been captured.
13. When these things had been done, the king was more powerful.
14. If the rest have been seen, we shall run toward the forest.
15. When his father is the leader, they do everything boldly.
16. When peace has been made, he will sail away from the island.
17. If many are timid, they will not be able to find the rivers.
18. Because the time is now short, no help will arrive.
19. Because the place is suitable, you wish to stay here longer.
20. Because help was given, there was great joy.
21. Weapons are useful for fighting.
22. You have hope of swimming.
23. They went for the purpose of attacking the city.
24. I came to listen.

Chapter Nine Review

VOCABULARY REVIEW

NOUNS

1. dog
2. prison
3. Cerberus
4. Charon
5. leader
6. ant
7. joy
8. kind, class
9. wool
10. manner, way
11. number
12. rank, order
13. sheep
14. beauty
15. enough

ADJECTIVES

1. open
2. remaining, rest of
3. timid
4. useful

VERBS

1. find, come upon
2. think, believe
3. carry back, bring back
4. hope

ADVERBS

1. enough
2. so
3. finally

Practice Exercise No. 178

1. to be
2. to have been
3. to be about to find out
4. to be found out
5. to have been thought
6. to have thought
7. to carry back, report
8. to be about to carry back, report
9. to have hoped
10. to be going to hope
11. to be led
12. to have led
13. to have been had
14. to have
15. to wish, want
16. to be wished, wanted
17. to have been able
18. to be able
19. to have fought
20. to have been fought

Practice Exercise No. 179

1. leading
2. about to lead
3. having, holding
4. having been had
5. having been thought
6. about to think
7. finding out
8. having been found out
9. carrying back, reporting
10. about to carry back, report
11. hoping
12. having been hoped
13. about to move
14. moving
15. coming
16. about to come
17. fearing
18. having been frightened
19. about to place, put
20. putting, placing
21. sending
22. having been sent
23. about to see
24. seeing
25. about to say
26. saying
27. warning
28. having been warned

Practice Exercise No. 180

1. they having been seen
2. he, it having been captured
3. these having been said
4. the war having been made
5. the men fearing
6. the girl walking
7. the leaders being afraid
8. the number being small
9. sleep coming
10. the prison being big
11. the city having been captured
12. the remaining speaking
13. the word having been heard
14. hope having been found
15. the kinds being many

READING

QUINTUS HORATIUS FLACCUS

He who is upright of life and free from crime
needs neither Moorish javelins nor a bow
nor a quiver heavy with poisoned arrows,
Fuscus,
whether he is going to journey through the hot
Quicksands
or through the inhospitable
Caucasus or the places which the storied
Hydaspes laps.

First Book of Odes, 22

CARMINA BURANA

The sun, pure and clear,
Tempers everything,
A new world resows
The appearance of April;
The sweetheart's spirit
Hurries to love,
And over pleasant things rules
The boyish god, Cupid.
So much newness of nature
In the festive springtime
And the power of the spring
Orders us to rejoice,
Shows us the accustomed ways,
And in your own springtime
There is trust and the right
To cling to your loved one.
Love me faithfully,
Mark my trust,
In my heart completely,
And with my whole mind
I am in your presence,
Even when absent at a distance;
Whoever loves in such a way,
Is turned on a wheel of torture.
Behold, pleasing
And longed for,
The spring brings back our joys;
Clad in purple

The meadow is in flower,
The sun makes all serene,
Now, now, sorrows depart,
Summer returns,
Now retreats
The severity of winter.
Now there melts
And disappears
All hail, snow, and such,
Winter flees,
And now the spring
Sucks in the richness of summer;
His heart is wretched,
Who neither lives,
Nor plays
Under the joys of summer.
They glory
and delight
In the honey of sweetness
Who try
To use
The favor of Cupid;
Let us be, at the command of Venus,
Boasting
And rejoicing
To be the equals of Paris.

Chapter Ten

Practice Exercise No. 181

1. debuerint
2. relinqueret
3. oppugnetis
4. sis
5. essem
6. facias
7. iacta essent
8. debitus sim
9. veniret
10. relinqueremur
11. ventae sitis
12. fuerit
13. rogemini
14. conspiciamur
15. venerim
16. debeas
17. fuisset
18. oppugnarent
19. relicta sit
20. deberetur

Practice Exercise No. 182

1. sunt
2. venimus
3. rogata sunt
4. oppugnabat
5. conspiciebam
6. debeo
7. fuimus
8. conspexerant
9. veniebatur
10. debui
11. debita eras
12. reliquit
13. rogavit
14. venieras
15. eras
16. conspecti eratis
17. fueram
18. oppugnavisti
19. relinquis
20. debebatur

Practice Exercise No. 183

1. Present subjunctive
2. Pluperfect subjunctive
3. Perfect subjunctive
4. Imperfect subjunctive

Practice Exercise No. 184

1.

Active	Passive
laudem	lauder
laudes	lauderis
laudet	laudetur
laudemus	laudemur
laudetis	laudemini
laudent	laudentur

2.

Active	Passive
viderim	visus, -a, -um sim
videris	visus, -a, -um sis
viderit	visus, -a, -um sit
viderimus	visi, -ae, -a simus
videritis	visi, -ae, -a sitis
viderint	visi, -ae, -a sint

3.

Active	Passive
peterem	peterer
peteres	petereris
peteret	peteretur
peteremus	peteremur
peteretis	peteremini
peterent	peterentur

4.

Active	Passive
dormivissem	dormitus, -a, -um essem
dormivisses	dormitus, -a, -um esses
dormivisset	dormitus, -a, -um esset
dormivissemus	dormi, -ae, -a essemus
dormivissetis	dormi, -ae, -a essetis
dormivissent	dormi, -ae, -a essent

Practice Exercise No. 185

1. possim
2. eant
3. tulerit
4. fieretis
5. voluissemus
6. nolit
7. ieris
8. mallent
9. potuerit
10. nolueritis
11. factus sit
12. ferrentur
13. malim
14. issent
15. potuisses
16. vellet
17. maluerit
18. fiam
19. feratis
20. noluissetis

Practice Exercise No. 186

1. let us allow; let us withdraw
2. let him (her) not go
3. let them fight
4. let them flee
5. let us remain
6. let him (her) not write
7. let them not arm
8. let us not demand
9. let him (her) finish
10. let us sleep

Practice Exercise No. 187

1. They fight in order to seize the city.
2. I was hurrying in order to catch up.
3. Daedalus had prepared wings in order that he himself and his son might fly.
4. You have left the city in order not to fight.
5. He brings these things in order for us to know them.
6. We teach so that you might learn.
7. They listen so that they might learn.
8. The woman ran away so she would not be killed.

Practice Exercise No. 188

1. Cicero spoke so well that Catiline left the city.
2. Catiline was so alarmed that he did not attack the city.
3. Psyche loved Cupid so greatly that she went to Those Below.

4. Cupid loved Psyche so greatly that he did not listen to the words of his mother.
5. You have looked so long that you have found the conspiracy.
6. The men ran so fast that they caught up.
7. The severity of the matter was so great that mercy was not given.
8. Your sister teaches so well that we learn much.

Practice Exercise No. 189
 1. He warned you not to come to Rome.
 2. You will persuade the Tulingi to surrender.
 3. I pray that my father not be killed.
 4. Your mother has commanded that you not lose the horses.
 5. Caesar forbids his soldiers to turn back.
 6. Caesar has forbidden the Allobroges to rebuild the captured city.
 7. We fear lest the villages be empty.
 8. Cicero fears that Catiline will not depart from Rome.
 9. The Helvetii doubt if Caesar will receive their surrender.
10. You do not doubt whether the Germans will pass over their own borders.

Practice Exercise No. 190
 1. I do not know who you are.
 2. Cicero will tell you why Catiline left Rome.
 3. The woman has asked how you learned this.
 4. They learned what we wanted.
 5. We know whence the soldiers will attack.
 6. I understand why you like the woman.
 7. You told me how the villages had been restored.
 8. You were asking me whom I loved.
 9. The man knows what your sister saw.
10. The Helvetii burned the houses in which they lived.

Practice Exercise No. 191
1.

Active	Passive
accipiam	accipiar
accipias	acciparis
accipiat	accipatur
accipiamus	accipamur
accipiatis	accipamini
accipiant	accipantur

2.

Active

reversus, -a, -um sim
reversus, -a, -um sis
reversus, -a, -um sit
reversi, -ae, -a simus
reversi, -ae, -a sitis
reversi, -ae, -a sint
There is no passive; **revertor** is a deponent verb.

3.

Active

irem
ires
iret
iremus
iretis
irent
The verb **eo** has no passive forms.

4.

Active	*Passive*
vetavissem	**vetatus, -a, -um essem**
vetavisses	**vetatus, -a, -um esses**
vetavisset	**vetatus, -a, -um esset**
vetavissemus	**vetati, -ae, -a essemus**
vetavissetis	**vetati, -ae, -a essetis**
vetavissent	**vetati, -ae, -a essent**

Practice Exercise No. 192
1. There was no one who thought this.
2. She is a woman whom all believe.
3. Is there anyone who has not been freed?
4. There are those who assert that.
5. If only my father were alive!
6. If only they would return!
7. If only you had read my books!
8. May they not ask this!
9. If only he had not been condemned to the games!
10. If only I were not ignorant of fighting!

Practice Exercise No. 193
1. When (Since) they had surrendered weapons and hostages, Caesar rebuilt the towns.
2. Since he had been condemned, he was wretched.

3. Although the women had been freed, they were not happy.
4. Since (Although) I loved the woman, I left the city.
5. Although it was dangerous, we were not alarmed.
6. Although they had hurried, they did not catch up.
7. Since he had hurried, he caught up.
8. Although Cicero was mistaken, he spoke well.
9. Since the fields had been burned, the Helvetii were not living there.
10. When (Since) it had been granted, Catiline left the city.

Practice Exercise No. 194

1.
Active
consequor
consequeris
consequitur
consequimur
consequimini
consequuntur

There are no passive forms.

2.

Active	*Passive*
errarem	**errarer**
errares	**errareris**
erraret	**erraretur**
erraremus	**erraremur**
erraretis	**erraremini**
errarent	**errarentur**

3.

Active	*Passive*
pertulerim	**perlatus, -a, -um sim**
pertuleris	**perlatus, -a, -um sis**
pertulerit	**perlatus, -a, -um sit**
pertulerimus	**perlati, -ae, -a simus**
pertuleritis	**perlati, -ae, -a sitis**
pertulerint	**perlati, -ae, -a sint**

4.

Active	Passive
flagitaveram	**flagitus, -a, -um eram**
flagitaveras	**flagitus, -a, -um eras**
flagitaverat	**flagitus, -a, -um erat**
flagitaveramus	**flagiti, -ae, -a eramus**
flagitaveratis	**flagiti, -ae, -a eratis**
flagitaverant	**flagiti, -ae, -a erant**

Practice Exercise No. 195

1. If you were to hurt me, I would avoid you.
2. Even if he had not been welcomed, he would have come.
3. If I were not afraid, I would fight.
4. Even if Caesar's soldiers had been afraid, they would have attacked the cities and villages of the Helvetii.
5. Even if Catiline will not leave Rome, Cicero will warn the people of his conspiracy.
6. If I loved you, I would tell you.
7. If she were here, she would believe us.
8. Even if you had been there, you would have done nothing.
9. Even if we were to write letters, they would not read them.
10. If the Allobroges had not surrendered their weapons, Caesar would have burned their houses.

Practice Exercise No. 196

1. Although you mistrust me, nevertheless, I believe you.
2. Although you did not know the woman, you listened to her.
3. Although they may not listen, Cicero will speak.
4. Although Catiline may not be welcomed, nevertheless, he will come into the senate.
5. Although the soldier has been wounded, he is alive.
6. Although the city may be captured, nevertheless, we shall not be afraid.
7. Although your body is present, your mind is absent.

Practice Exercise No. 197

1.

Active
adsum
adsis
adsit
adsimus
adsitis
adsint

2.

Active	Passive
exsolvero	exsolutus, -a, -um ero
exsolveris	exsolutus, -a, -um eris
exsolverit	exsolutus, -a, -um erit
exsolverimus	exsoluti, -ae, -a erimus
exsolveritis	exsouti, -ae, -a eritis
exsolverint	exsoluti, -ae, -a erunt

3.

Active	Passive
suspexissem	suspectus, -a, -um essem
suspexisses	suspectus, -a, -um esses
suspexisset	suspectus, -a, -um esset
suspexissemus	suspecti, -ae, -a essemus
suspexissetis	suspecti, -ae, -a essetis
suspexissent	suspecti, -ae, -a essent

4.

Active	Passive
vulnerarem	vulnerarer
vulnerares	vulnerareris
vulneraret	vulneraretur
vulneraremus	vulneraremur
vulneraretis	vulneraremini
vulnerarent	vulnerarentur

5.

Active	Passive
vixi	victus, -a, -um sum
vixisti	victus, -a, -um es
vixit	victus, -a, -um est
viximus	victi, -ae, -a sumus
vixitis	victi, -ae, -a estis
vixerunt	victi, -ae, -a sunt

Practice Exercise No. 198
1. He said that the Helvetii, who lived in the fields, had destroyed the city.
2. They say that the woman, whom I know, is not here.
3. He said that the soldiers whom Caesar had commanded had surrendered weapons and hostages.
4. I say that the girls who promised these things were set free.
5. You will say that the arrow which had killed the boy was lost in the forest.
6. They thought that the legion which had deserted Caesar would return.

7. We think that the conspiracy which Cicero brought to light will hurt Rome.
8. I feel that the words which are spoken by you are believed by all.
9. You thought that the promises which had been made by the crowd of Carnutes would guard against murder.
10. He ordered that the man who fed his sons and daughters be praised.

Practice Exercise No. 199

1.
Present active infinitive: **recidere**
Present passive infinitive: **recidi**
Perfect active infinitive: **recepisse**
Perfect passive infinitive: **receptus, -a, -um esse**
Future active infinitive: **recepturus, -a, -um esse**
Future passive participle: **receptum iri**

2.
Present active participle: **recusans, recusantis**
Perfect passive participle: **recusatus, -a, -um**
Future active participle: **recusaturus, -a, -um**
Future passive participle: **recusandus, -a, -um**

3.
Active
querebar
querebaris
querebatur
querebamur
querebamini
querebantur

4.

Active	*Passive*
praestaverim	**praestatus, -a, -um sim**
praestaveris	**praestatus, -a, -um sis**
praestaverit	**praestatus, -a, -um sit**
praestaverimus	**praestati, -ae, -a simus**
praestaveritis	**praestati, -ae, -a sitis**
praestaverint	**praestati, -ae, -a sint**

Chapter Ten Review

VOCABULARY REVIEW

NOUNS

1. Acco
2. Allobroges
3. pension, yearly pay
4. look, sight
5. goodness, kindness, benevolence
6. Carnutes
7. downfall, fate
8. conspiracy, plot
9. mistreatment, outrage, injury
10. surrender
11. longing, loss, need
12. famine, hunger
13. crowd
14. produce, fruit
15. Helvetii
16. beginning, start
17. judgment, sentence
18. right, authority
19. Latobrigi
20. legion
21. mercy, mildness, gentleness
22. greatness, vastness
23. ancestors, forefathers
24. mind
25. service, work
26. sympathy, pity
27. relative, friend
28. no one
29. Nicaea
30. Nicomedia
31. official job, official position
32. hostage
33. hatred
34. way, manner
35. parent
36. parricide, murder, treason
37. promise
38. chief
39. presence, effect
40. manner, fashion, reason
41. republic, common good
42. the Rhine
43. health, safety
44. senate
45. sense, sensation, feeling
46. severity, strictness
47. silence
48. Tulingi
49. evening
50. village, street

PRONOUNS

1. someone, something; anyone, anything
2. that, that one of yours
3. a certain one; pl., some

ADJECTIVES

1. Aurelian
2. secret, hidden
3. common, public
4. yesterday
5. honored, respected
6. threatening, dangerous, hostile
7. useless, harmful
8. that, that one of yours
9. free, at leisure, not working
10. dangerous, perilous
11. continuous, perpetual, uninterrupted
12. most, the largest part
13. last, finally
14. first, foremost
15. former, earlier
16. public, common
17. how much
18. safe, well
19. old, aged
20. higher, past, preceding

VERBS

1. be absent, be away from
2. take, receive
3. hurry
4. strengthen, affirm, assert
5. gain, obtain, reach
6. be present, be here
7. consider, discuss
8. lose
9. think, judge
10. dare
11. be without, be absent from
12. beware of, guard against
13. consider, think
14. learn, ascertain
15. grant, allow, withdraw
16. look for, collect
17. follow, catch up with
18. believe, trust
19. condemn, find guilty
20. destroy, obliterate
21. descend, come down
22. desert, abandon
23. wound, hurt
24. doubt, hesitate, be uncertain
25. carry forth, bring out
26. quit, surpass, go beyond
27. be mistaken, lose one's way
28. happen, come out
29. avoid, go away, depart
30. think, judge
31. release, free
32. demand
33. perform, do
34. hesitate, be at a loss
35. command, order
36. live in, reside
37. shut off, stop
38. judge, sentence, examine
39. swear
40. read
41. say, speak
42. fear, be afraid
43. pity, feel sorry for
44. not know, be ignorant of
45. think, suppose
46. it is right, it is proper
47. beg, pray
48. feed on, eat
49. throw open, bring to light
50. allow, grant, suffer
51. report
52. allow, permit
53. stir, move
54. persuade
55. fear, be alarmed at
56. calm, reconcile
57. promise
58. ask, beg, demand
59. be better than, be superior to
60. go forth, depart
61. declare, acknowledge, say
62. run away, flee, escape
63. clean, remove, excuse
64. ask, look for
65. complain about
66. recoil, fall
67. recover, get back
68. refuse, reject
69. return, restore
70. report, bring back
71. learn, find out
72. restore, rebuild
73. keep back, retain
74. turn back, return
75. greet, welcome
76. feel, perceive, realize
77. mistrust, suspect
78. decay, melt away
79. bear, endure
80. pass over, cross, desert

ADVERBS

1. perhaps
2. temperately, frugally
3. so
4. moderately, modestly
5. very much, too much
6. a little
7. as much as
8. backward, on the other hand
9. so, thus
10. from where, whence
11. as
12. violently, eagerly

CONJUNCTIONS

1. or
2. even if
3. even if, although
4. that not, lest
5. if not, unless
6. whether
7. before
8. although
9. because, now that
10. if
11. even if
12. that, so that
13. if only, would that
14. either . . . or

INTERJECTIONS

1. by Hercules!

Practice Exercise No. 200

1.

Present	Perfect	Imperfect	Pluperfect
loquar	locutus, -a, -um sim	loquerer	locutus, -a, -um essem
loquaris	locutus, -a, -um sis	loquereris	
loquatur	locutus, -a, -um sit	loqueretur	locutus, -a, -um esses
loquamur	locuti, -ae, -a simus	loqueremur	locutus, -a, -um esset
loquamini	locuti, -ae, -a sitis	loqueremini	locuti, -ae, -a essemus
loquantur	locuti, -ae, -a sint	loquerentur	locuti, -ae, -a essetis
			locuti, -ae, -a essent

2.
Present active infinitive: **orare**
Present passive infinitive: **orari**
Perfect active infinitive: **oravisse**
Perfect passive infinitive: **oratus, -a, -um esse**
Future active infinitive: **oraturus, -a, -um esse**
Future passive infinitive: **oratum iri**

3.
Present active participle: **concedens, concedentis**
Perfect passive participle: **concessus, -a, -um**
Future active participle: **concessurus, -a, -um**
Future passive participle: **concendus, -a, -um**

4.

Note that **possum** has no passive forms.

Present	*Perfect*	*Imperfect*	*Pluperfect*
possim	potuerim	possem	potuissem
possis	potueris	posses	potuisses
possit	potuerit	posset	potuisset
possimus	potuerimus	possemus	potuissemus
possitis	potueritis	possetis	potuissetis
possint	potuerint	possent	potuissent

5.

Present

Active	*Passive*
sentio	sentior
sentis	sentiris
sentit	sentitur
sentimus	sentimur
sentitis	sentimini
sentiunt	sentiuntur

Imperfect

Active	*Passive*
sentiebam	sentiebar
sentiebas	sentiebaris
sentiebat	sentiebatur
sentiebamus	sentiebamur
sentiebatis	sentiebamini
sentiebant	sentiebantur

Future

Active	*Passive*
sentiam	sentiar
senties	sentieris
sentiet	sentietur
sentiemus	sentiemur
sentietis	sentiemini
sentient	sentientur

Perfect

Active	*Passive*
sensi	sensus, -a, -um sum
sensisti	sensus, -a, -um es
sensit	sensus, -a, -um est
sensimus	sensi, -ae, -a sumus
sensistis	sensi, -ae, -a estis
senserunt	sensi, -ae, -a sunt

Pluperfect

Active	*Passive*
senseram	sensus, -a, -um eram
senseras	sensus, -a, -um eras
senserat	sensus, -a, -um erat
senseramus	sensi, -ae, -a eramus
senseratis	sensi, -ae, -a eratis
senserant	sensi, -ae, -a erant

Future Perfect

Active	*Passive*
sensero	sensus, -a, -um ero
senseris	sensus, -a, -um eris
senserit	sensus, -a, -um erit
senserimus	sensi, -ae, -a erimus
senseritis	sensi, -ae, -a eritis
senserint	sensi, -ae, -a erunt

READING

PUBLIUS VERGILIUS MARO

Spare your fear, Cythera; the Fates remain unmoved
for your children; you will see the city and the promised
walls of Lavinium and you will carry aloft to the starry sky
great Aeneas; nor has intent changed me.
Your son (for indeed, I will speak, since this care troubles you,
and rolling them farther, I will consider the secrets of the Fates)
will wage a great war on Italy and will crush fierce peoples
and will establish customs for the people, and walls,
until the third summer will have seen him ruling at Latium
and three winters will have passed since the Rutulians were subdued.
But the boy Ascanius, to whom now the cognomen Iulus
is added (He was Iulus, while the matter stood with Ilian ruling),
For thirty great circles with rolling months
will fulfill his rule from the seat of Lavinium,
and, with great force, he will fortify Alba Longa.
Here now for three hundred entire years, it will be ruled
by the race of Hector, until a royal priestess
will give to Mars, heavy in birth, twins, the offspring of Ilian.
Then with the yellow skin of the nurturing she-wolf, happy
Romulus will take up the race, and will establish
the walls of Mars, and he will call the Romans by his own name.

For these, I place neither limits of space nor time;
I have given them rule without end. Even harsh Juno,
who now wearies the sea and the shores and the sky with her dread,
will turn to better plans, and with me, she will cherish
the Romans, lords of the world and the toga-clad race.
So it has pleased me. There will come a time, as the seasons glide by,
when the house of Assaracus will repress Phthia
and the famous Mycenas and will rule over the conquered Argos.
A Trojan Caesar will be born, of beautiful origin,
Who will limit his rule with the ocean, his fame with the stars,
Julius, a name descended from great Iulus.
Him, at some time, laden with the spoils of the East,
You untroubled, will receive in heaven; he also will be called in prayers.
Then the harsh ages will become mild when wars have ceased;
Hoary Faith and Vesta, Romulus with his brother Remus
will give justice; the awful doors of war will be closed
with iron and close-fitting seams; impious Fury within
sitting over fierce weapons and with a hundred bonds of bronze
knotted behind his back shall roar horrible with his bloody mouth.
Aeneid, 1, 257–296

Nouns

First Declension

Feminine (most)
aqua, water

	Singular	*Plural*
Nom.	**aqua**	**aquae**
Gen.	**aquae**	**aquarum**
Dat.	**aquae**	**aquis**
Acc.	**aquam**	**aquas**
Abl.	**aqua**	**aquis**
Voc.	**aqua**	**aquae**

Second Declension

Masculine

servus, slave

Nom.	**servus**	**servi**
Gen.	**servi**	**servorum**
Dat.	**servo**	**servis**
Acc.	**servum**	**servos**
Abl.	**servo**	**servis**
Voc.	**serve**	**servi**

puer, boy

Nom.	**puer**	**pueri**
Gen.	**pueri**	**puerorum**
Dat.	**puero**	**pueris**
Acc.	**puerum**	**pueros**
Abl.	**puero**	**pueris**
Voc.	**puer**	**pueri**

Neuter
periculum, danger

Nom.	periculum	pericula
Gen.	periculi	periculorum
Dat.	periculo	periculis
Acc.	periculum	pericula
Abl.	periculo	periculis
Voc.	periculum	pericula

Third Declension (regular)

Masculine or Feminine

miles, m., soldier

Nom.	miles	milites
Gen.	militis	militum
Dat.	militi	militibus
Acc.	militem	milites
Abl.	milite	militibus
Voc.	miles	milites

Neuter
caput, head

Nom.	caput	capita
Gen.	capitis	capitum
Dat.	capiti	capitibus
Acc.	caput	capita
Abl.	capite	capitibus
Voc.	caput	capita

Third Declension (i-stem)

Masculine or Feminine

urbs, f., city

Nom.	urbs	urbes
Gen.	urbis	urbium
Dat.	urbi	urbibus
Acc.	urbem	urbes
Abl.	urbe	urbibus
Voc.	urbs	urbes

Neuter
animal, n., animal

Nom.	animal	animalia
Gen.	animalis	animalium
Dat.	animali	animalibus
Acc.	animal	animalia
Abl.	animali	animalibus
Voc.	animal	animalia

Irregular Noun
vis, force

Nom.	vis	vires
Gen.	vis	virium
Dat.	vi	viribus
Acc.	vim	vires
Abl.	vi	viribus

Fourth Declension

Masculine

passus, pace

Nom.	passus	passus
Gen.	passus	passuum
Dat.	passui	passibus
Acc.	passum	passus
Abl.	passu	passibus
Voc.	passus	passus

Neuter
cornu, horn

Nom.	cornu	cornua
Gen.	cornus	cornuum
Dat.	cornu	cornibus
Acc.	cornu	cornua
Abl.	cornu	cornibus
Voc.	cornu	cornua

Fifth Declension
spes, hope

Nom.	spes	spes
Gen.	spei	sperum
Dat.	spei	spebus
Acc.	spem	spes
Abl.	spe	spebus
Voc.	spes	spes

Adjectives

First and Second Declension
bonus, good

Singular

	Masc.	Fem.	Neut.
Nom	bonus	bona	bonum
Gen.	boni	bonae	boni
Dat.	bono	bonae	bono
Acc.	bonum	bonam	bonum
Abl.	bono	bona	bono
Voc.	bone	bona	bonum

Plural

	Masc.	Fem.	Neut.
Nom	boni	bonae	bona
Gen.	bonorum	bonarum	bonorum
Dat.	bonis	bonis	bonis
Acc.	bonos	bonas	bona
Abl.	bonis	bonis	bonis
Voc.	boni	bonae	bona

liber, free

Singular

	Masc.	Fem.	Neut.
Nom	liber	libera	liberum
Gen.	liberi	liberae	liberi
Dat.	libero	liberae	libero
Acc.	liberum	liberam	liberum
Abl.	libero	libera	libero
Voc.	liber	libera	liberum

Plural

	Masc.	*Fem.*	*Neut.*
Nom	liberi	liberae	libera
Gen.	liberorum	liberarum	liberorum
Dat.	liberis	liberis	liberis
Acc.	liberos	liberas	libera
Abl.	liberis	liberis	liberis
Voc.	liberi	liberae	libera

pulcher, pretty

Singular

	Masc.	*Fem.*	*Neut.*
Nom	pulcher	pulchra	pulchrum
Gen.	pulchri	pulchrae	pulchri
Dat.	pulchro	pulchrae	pulchro
Acc.	pulchrum	pulchram	pulchrum
Abl.	pulchro	pulchra	pulchro
Voc.	pulcher	pulchra	pulchrum

Plural

	Masc.	*Fem.*	*Neut.*
Nom	pulchri	pulchrae	pulchra
Gen.	pulchrorum	pulchrarum	pulchrorum
Dat.	pulchris	pulchris	pulchris
Acc.	pulchros	pulchras	pulchra
Abl.	pulchris	pulchris	pulchris
Voc.	pulchri	pulchrae	pulchra

Third Declension (one ending):

audax, bold

Singular

	Masc. & Fem.	*Neut.*
Nom.	audax	audax
Gen.	audacis	audacis
Dat.	audaci	audaci
Acc.	audacem	audax
Abl.	audaci	audaci
Voc.	audax	audax

Plural

	Masc. & Fem.	*Neut.*
Nom.	audaces	audacia
Gen.	audacium	audacium
Dat.	audacibus	audacibus
Acc.	audaces	audacia
Abl.	audacibus	audacibus
Voc.	audaces	audacia

Third Declension (*two endings*):
brevis, breve, short

Singular

	Masc. & Fem.	*Neut.*
Nom.	brevis	breve
Gen.	brevis	brevis
Dat.	brevi	brevi
Acc.	brevem	breve
Abl.	brevi	brevi
Voc.	brevis	breve

Plural

	Masc. & Fem.	*Neut.*
Nom.	breves	brevia
Gen.	brevium	brevium
Dat.	brevibus	brevibus
Acc.	breves	brevia
Abl.	brevibus	brevibus
Voc.	breves	brevia

Third Declension (*three endings*):

celer, celeris, celere, quick

Singular

	Masc.	*Fem.*	*Neut.*
Nom.	celer	celeris	celere
Gen.	celeris	celeris	celeris
Dat.	celeri	celeri	celeri
Acc.	celerem	celerem	celere
Abl.	celeri	celeri	celeri
Voc.	celer	celeris	celere

Plural

	Masc. & Fem.	Neut.
Nom.	celeres	celeria
Gen.	celerium	celerium
Dat.	celeribus	celeribus
Acc.	celeres	celeria
Abl.	celeribus	celeribus
Voc.	celeres	celeria

Comparative Adjectives

facilior, facilius, easier

Singular

	Masc. & Fem.	Neut.
Nom.	facilior	facilius
Gen.	facilioris	facilioris
Dat.	faciliori	faciliori
Acc.	faciliorem	facilius
Abl.	faciliore	faciliore
Voc.	facilior	facilius

Plural

	Masc. & Fem.	Neut.
Nom.	faciliores	faciliora
Gen.	faciliorum	faciliorum
Dat.	facilioribus	facilioribus
Acc.	faciliores	faciliora
Abl.	facilioribus	facilioribus
Voc.	faciliores	faciliora

Pronouns

Personal Pronouns

First Person

	Singular	Plural
Nom.	ego	nos
Gen.	mei	nostrum, nostri
Dat.	mihi	nobis
Acc.	me	nos
Abl.	me	nobis

Second Person

	Singular:	Plural:
Nom.	tu	vos
Gen.	tui	vestrum, vestri
Dat.	tibi	vobis
Acc.	te	vos
Abl.	te	vobis

Third person (reflexive):

	Singular:	Plural:
Nom.	—	—
Gen.	sui	sui
Dat.	sibi	sibi
Acc.	se	se
Abl.	se	se

Demonstrative Pronouns
1. hic

Singular

	Masc.	Fem.	Neut.
Nom.	hic	haec	hoc
Gen.	huius	huius	huius
Dat.	huic	huic	huic
Acc.	hunc	hanc	hoc
Abl.	hoc	hac	hoc

Plural

	Masc.	Fem.	Neut.
Nom.	hi	hae	haec
Gen.	horum	harum	horum
Dat.	his	his	his
Acc.	hos	has	haec
Abl.	his	his	his

2. ille

Singular

	Masc.	Fem.	Neut.
Nom.	ille	illa	illud
Gen.	illius	illius	illius
Dat.	illi	illi	illi
Acc.	ilium	illam	illud
Abl.	illo	illa	illo

Plural

	Masc.	Fem.	Neut.
Nom.	illi	illae	illa
Gen.	illorum	illarum	illorum
Dat.	illis	illis	illis
Acc.	illos	illas	illa
Abl.	illis	illis	illis

Remember that **hic** and **ille** can also be used as adjectives.

Intensive Pronoun: *ipse*

Singular

	Masc.	Fem.	Neut.
Nom.	ipse	ipsa	ipsum
Gen.	ipsius	ipsius	ipsius
Dat.	ipsi	ipsi	ipsi
Acc.	ipsum	ipsam	ipsum
Abl.	ipso	ipsa	ipso

Plural

	Masc.	Fem.	Neut.
Nom.	ipsi	ipsae	ipsa
Gen.	ipsorum	ipsarum	ipsorum
Dat.	ipsis	ipsis	ipsis
Acc.	ipsos	ipsas	ipsa
Abl.	ipsis	ipsis	ipsis

Remember that **ipse** is also an adjective.

Relative Pronoun: *qui*

Singular

	Masc.	Fem.	Neut.
Nom.	qui	quae	quod
Gen.	cuius	cuius	cuius
Dat.	cui	cui	cui
Acc.	quem	quam	quod
Abl.	quo	qua	quo

Plural

	Masc.	Fem.	Neut.
Nom.	qui	quae	quae
Gen.	quorum	quarum	quorum
Dat.	quibus	quibus	quibus
Acc.	quos	quas	quae
Abl.	quibus	quibus	quibus

Remember that **qui** is also the interrogative adjective.

Interrogative Pronoun: *quis*

Singular

	Masc. & Fem.	Neut.
Nom.	quis	quid
Gen.	cuius	cuius
Dat.	cui	cui
Acc.	quem	quid
Abl.	quo	quo

Plural

The plural of the interrogative pronoun is the same as the plural of the relative pronoun.

Verbs

Regular Verbs:
First Conjugation: **amo**
Second Conjugation: **habeo**
Third Conjugation: **pono**
Third Conjuation "**io**" verb: **capio**
Fourth Conjugation: **audio**

Principal Parts:
amo, amare, amavi, amatus
habeo, habere, habui, habitus
pono, ponere, posui, positus
capio, capere, cepi, captus
audio, audire, audivi, auditus

Indicative Mood

Active Voice

Present

amo	habeo	pono	capio	audio
amas	habes	ponis	capis	audis
amat	habet	ponit	capit	audit
amamus	habemus	ponimus	capimus	audimus
amatis	habetis	ponitis	capitis	auditis
amant	habent	ponunt	capiunt	audiunt

Imperfect

amabam	habebam	ponebam	capiebam	audiebam
amabas	habebas	ponebas	capiebas	audiebas
amabat	habebat	ponebat	capiebat	audiebat
amabamus	habebamus	ponebamus	capiebamus	audiebamus
amabatis	habebatis	ponebatis	capiebatis	audiebatis
amabant	habebant	ponebant	capiebant	audiebant

Future

amabo	habebo	ponam	capiam	audiam
amabis	habebis	pones	capies	audies
amabit	habebit	ponet	capiet	audiet
amabimus	habebimus	ponemus	capiemus	audiemus
amabitis	habebitis	ponetis	capietis	audietis
amabunt	habebunt	ponent	capient	audient

Perfect

amavi	habui	posui	cepi	audivi
amavisti	habuisti	posuisti	cepisti	audivisti
amavit	habuit	posuit	cepit	audivit
amavimus	habuimus	posuimus	cepimus	audivimus
amavistis	habuistis	posuistis	cepistis	audivistis
amaverunt	habuerunt	posuerunt	ceperunt	audiverunt

Pluperfect

amaveram	habueram	posueram	ceperam	audiveram
amaveras	habueras	posueras	ceperas	audiveras
amaverat	habuerat	posuerat	ceperat	audiverat
amaveramus	habueramus	posueramus	ceperamus	audiveramus
amaveratis	habueratis	posueratis	ceperatis	audiveratis
amaverant	habuerant	posuerant	ceperant	audiverant

Future Perfect

amavero	habuero	posuero	cepero	audivero
amaveris	habueris	posueris	ceperis	audiveris
amaverit	habuerit	posuerit	ceperit	audiverit
amaverimus	habuerimus	posuerimus	ceperimus	audiverimus
amaveritis	habueritis	posueritis	ceperitis	audiveritis
amaverint	habuerint	posuerint	ceperint	audiverint

Passive Voice

Present

amor	habeor	ponor	capior	audior
amaris	haberis	poneris	caperis	audiris
amatur	habetur	ponitur	capitur	auditur
amamur	habemur	ponimur	capimur	audimur
amamini	habemini	ponimini	capimini	audimini
amantur	habentur	ponuntur	capiuntur	audiuntur

Imperfect

amabar	habebar	ponebar	capiebar	audiebar
amabaris	habebaris	ponebaris	capiebaris	audiebaris
amabatur	habebatur	ponebatur	capiebatur	audiebatur
amabamur	habebamur	ponebamur	capiebamur	audiebamur
amabamini	habebamini	ponebamini	capiebamini	audiebamini
amabantur	habebantur	ponebantur	capiebantur	audiebantur

Future

amabor	habebor	ponar	capiar	audiar
amaberis	habeberis	poneris	capieris	audieris
amabitur	habebitur	ponetur	capietur	audietur
amabimur	habebimur	ponemur	capiemur	audiemur
amabimini	habebimini	ponemini	capiemini	audiemini
amabuntur	habebuntur	ponentur	capientur	audientur

Perfect

amatus, -a, -um sum	habitus, -a, -um sum	positus, -a, -um sum
amatus es	habitus es	positus es
amatus est	habitus est	positus est
amati, -ae, -a sumus	habiti, -ae, -a sumus	positi, ae, -a sumus
amati estis	habiti estis	positi estis
amati sunt	habiti sunt	positi sunt

captus, -a, -um sum	auditus, -a, -um sum
captus es	auditus es
captus est	auditus est
capti, -ae, -a sumus	auditi, -ae, -um sumus
capti estis	auditi estis
capti sunt	auditi sunt

Pluperfect

amatus, -a, -um eram	habitus eram	positus eram	captus eram	auditus eram
amatus eras	habitus eras	positus eras	captus eras	auditus eras
amatus erat	habitus erat	positus erat	captus erat	auditus erat
amati, -ae, -a eramus	habiti eramus	positi eramus	capti eramus	auditi eramus
amati eratis	habiti eratis	positi eratis	capti eratis	auditi eratis
amati erant	habiti erant	positi erant	capti erant	auditi erant

Future Perfect

amatus, -a, -um ero	habitus ero	positus ero	captus ero	auditus ero
amatus eris	habitus eris	positus eris	captus eris	auditus eris
amatus erit	habitus erit	positus erit	captus erit	auditus erit
amati, -ae, -a erimus	habiti erimus	positi erimus	capti erimus	auditi erimus
amati eritis	habiti eritis	positi eritis	capti eritis	auditi eritis
amati erunt	habiti erunt	positi erunt	capti erunt	auditi erunt

Subjunctive Mood

Active Voice

Present

amem	habeam	ponam	capiam	audiam
ames	habeas	ponas	capias	audias
amet	habeat	ponat	capiat	audiat
amemus	habeamus	ponamus	capiamus	audiamus
ametis	habeatis	ponatis	capiatis	audiatis
ament	habeant	ponant	capiant	audiant

Perfect

amaverim	habuerim	posuerim	ceperim	audiverim
amaveris	habueris	posueris	ceperis	audiveris
amaverit	habuerit	posuerit	ceperit	audiverit
amaverimus	habuerimus	posuerimus	ceperimus	audiverimus
amaveritis	habueritis	posueritis	ceperitis	audiveritis
amaverint	habuerint	posuerint	ceperint	audiverint

Imperfect

amarem	haberem	ponerem	caperem	audirem
amares	haberes	poneres	caperes	audires
amaret	haberet	poneret	caperet	audiret
amaremus	haberemus	poneremus	caperemus	audiremus
amaretis	haberetis	poneretis	caperetis	audiretis
amarent	haberent	ponerent	caperent	audirent

Pluperfect

amavissem	habuissem	posuissem	cepissem	audivissem
amavisses	habuisses	posuisses	cepisses	audivisses
amavisset	habuisset	posuisset	cepisset	audivisset
amavissemus	habuissemus	posuissemus	cepissemus	audivissemus
amavissetis	habuissetis	posuissetis	cepissetis	audivissetis
amavissent	habuissent	posuissent	cepissent	audivissent

Passive Voice

Present

amer	habear	ponar	capiar	audiar
ameris	habearis	ponaris	capiaris	audiaris
ametur	habeatur	ponatur	capiatur	audiatur
amemur	habeamur	ponamur	capiamur	audiamur
amemini	habeamini	ponamini	capiamini	audiamini
amentur	habeantur	ponantur	capiantur	audiantur

Perfect

amatus, -a, -um sim	habitus, -a, um sim	positus, -a, -um sim
amatus sis	habitus sis	positus sis
amatus sit	habitus sit	positus sit
amati, -ae, -a simus	habiti, -ae, -a simus	positi, -ae, -a simus
amati sitis	habiti sitis	positi sitis
amati sint	habiti sint	positi sint

captus, -a, -um sim	auditus, -a, -um sim
captus sis	auditus sis
captus sit	auditus sit
capti, -ae, -a simus	auditi, -ae, -a simus
capti sitis	auditi sitis
capti sint	auditi sint

Imperfect

amarer	haberer	ponerer	caperer	audirer
amareris	habereris	ponereris	capereris	audireris
amaretur	haberetur	poneretur	caperetur	audiretur
amaremur	haberemur	poneremur	caperemur	audiremur
amaremini	haberemini	poneremini	caperemini	audiremini
amarentur	haberentur	ponerentur	caperentur	audirentur

Pluperfect

amatus, -a, -um essem	habitus essem	positus essem	captus essem	auditus essem
amatus esses	habitus esses	positus esses	captus esses	auditus esses
amatus esset	habitus esset	positus esset	captus esset	auditus esset
amati, -ae, -a essemus	habiti essemus	positi essemus	capti essemus	auditi essemus
amati essetis	habiti essetis	positi essetis	capti essetis	auditi essetis
amati essent	habiti essent	positi essent	capti essent	auditi essent

Imperative Mood

Singular	*Plural*
ama	amate
habe	habete
pone	ponite
cape	capite
audi	audite

Infinitives

Active Voice

Present	amare	habere	ponere	capere	audire
Perfect	amavisse	habuisse	posuisse	cepisse	audivisse
Future	amaturus esse	habiturus esse	positurus esse	capturus esse	auditurus esse

Passive Voice

Present	amari	haberi	poni	capi	audiri
Perfect	amatus esse	habitus esse	positus esse	captus esse	auditus esse
Future	amatum iri	habitum iri	positum iri	captum iri	auditum iri

Participles

Active Voice

Present	amans	habens	ponens	capiens	audiens
Future	amaturus	habiturus	positurus	capturus	auditurus

Passive Voice

Perfect	amatus	habitus	positus	captus	auditus
Future	amandus	habendus	ponendus	capiendus	audiendus

Irregular Verbs: *sum, possum,* and *eo*

None of these verbs has a passive voice.

Principal parts: **sum, esse, fui, futurus; possum, posse, potui; eo, ire, ii** or **ivi, itus**

Indicative Mood

Present

sum	possum	eo
es	potes	is
est	potest	it
sumus	possumus	imus
estis	potestis	itis
sunt	possunt	eunt

Imperfect

eram	poteram	ibam
eras	poteras	ibas
erat	poterat	ibat
eramus	poteramus	ibamus
eratis	poteratis	ibatis
erant	poterant	ibant

Future

ero	potero	ibo
eris	poteris	ibis
erit	poterit	ibit
erimus	poterimus	ibimus
eritis	poteritis	ibitis
erunt	poterunt	ibunt

Perfect

fui	potui	ii or ivi
fuisti	potuisti	isti
fuit	potuit	iit
fuimus	potuimus	iimus
fuistis	potuistis	istis
fuerunt	potuerunt	ierunt

Pluperfect

fueram	potueram	ieram
fueras	potueras	ieras
fuerat	potuerat	ierat
fueramus	potueramus	ieramus
fueratis	potueratis	ieratis
fuerant	potuerant	ierant

Future Perfect

fuero	potuero	iero
fueris	potueris	ieris
fuerit	potuerit	ierit
fuerimus	potuerimus	ierimus
fueritis	potueritis	ieritis
fuerint	potuerint	ierint

Subjunctive Mood

Present

sim	possim	eam
sis	possis	eas
sit	possit	eat
simus	possimus	eamus
sitis	possitis	eatis
sint	possint	eant

Perfect

fuerim	potuerim	ierim
fueris	potueris	ieris
fuerit	potuerit	ierit
fuerimus	potuerimus	ierimus
fueritis	potueritis	ieritis
fuerint	potuerint	ierint

Imperfect

essem	possem	irem
esses	posses	ires
esset	posset	iret
essemus	possemus	iremus
essetis	possetis	iretis
essent	possent	irent

Pluperfect

fuissem	potuissem	issem
fuisses	potuisses	isses
fuisset	potuisset	isset
fuissemus	potuissemus	issemus
fuissetis	potuissetis	issetis
fuissent	potuissent	issent

Imperative Mood

Only **sum** has the imperative mood.

Singular	es
Plural	este

Infinitives

Present	esse	posse	ire
Perfect	fuisse	potuisse	isse
Future	futurus esse	—	iturus esse

Participles

Present	—	potens	iens
Future	futurus	—	iturus

Note that the genitive of **iens** is **euntis**.

Irregular Verbs: *nolo, volo, malo*

Note that none of these verbs has a passive voice.

Principal parts: **volo, velle, volui**   **nolo, nolle, nolui**   **malo, malle, malui**

Indicative Mood

Present

volo	nolo	malo
vis	non vis	mavis
vult	non vult	mavult
volumus	nolumus	malumus
vultis	non vultis	mavultis
volunt	nolunt	malunt

Imperfect

volebam	nolebam	malebam
volebas	nolebas	malebas
volebat	nolebat	malebat
volebamus	nolebamus	malebamus
volebatis	nolebatis	malebatis
volebant	nolebant	malebant

Future

volam	nolam	malam
voles	noles	males
volet	nolet	malet
volemus	nolemus	malemus
voletis	noletis	maletis
volent	nolent	malent

Perfect

volui	nolui	malui
voluisti	noluisti	maluisti
voluit	noluit	maluit
voluimus	noluimus	maluimus
voluistis	noluistis	maluistis
voluerunt	noluerunt	maluerunt

Pluperfect

volueram	nolueram	malueram
volueras	nolueras	malueras
voluerat	noluerat	maluerat
volueramus	nolueramus	malueramus
volueratis	nolueratis	malueratis
voluerant	noluerant	maluerant

Future Perfect

voluero	noluero	maluero
volueris	nolueris	malueris
voluerit	noluerit	maluerit
voluerimus	noluerimus	maluerimus
volueritis	nolueritis	malueritis
voluerint	noluerint	maluerint

Subjunctive Mood

Present

velim	nolim	malim
velis	nolis	malis
velit	nolit	malit
velimus	nolimus	malimus
velitis	nolitis	malitis
velint	nolint	malint

Perfect

voluerim	noluerim	maluerim
volueris	nolueris	malueris
voluerit	noluerit	maluerit
voluerimus	noluerimus	maluerimus
volueritis	nolueritis	malueritis
voluerint	noluerint	maluerint

Imperfect

vellem	nollem	mallem
velles	nolles	malles
vellet	nollet	mallet
vellemus	nollemus	mallemus
velletis	nolletis	malletis
vellent	nollent	mallent

Pluperfect

voluissem	noluissem	maluissem
voluisses	noluisses	maluisses
voluisset	noluisset	maluisset
voluissemus	noluissemus	maluissemus
voluissetis	noluissetis	maluissetis
voluissent	noluissent	maluissent

Imperative Mood

Only **nolo** has the imperative mood.

Singular	noli
Plural	nolite

Infinitives

Present	**velle**	nolle	malle

Perfect	voluisse	noluisse	maluisse

Participles

Present	volens	nolens	—

Irregular Verb: *fio*

Note that the verb **fio** has no active voice. Principal parts: **fio, fieri, factus sum**

Indicative Mood

Present	*Imperfect*	*Future*
fio	fiebam	fiam
fis	fiebas	fies
fit	fiebat	fiet
—	fiebamus	fiemus
—	fiebatis	fietis
fiunt	fiebant	fient

Perfect	*Pluperfect*	*Future Perfect*
factus sum	factus eram	factus ero
factus es	factus eras	factus eris
factus est	factus erat	factus erit
facti sumus	facti eramus	facti erimus
facti estis	facti eratis	facti eritis
facti sunt	facti erant	facti erunt

Subjunctive Mood

Present	*Perfect*
fiam	factus sim
fias	factus sis
fiat	factus sit
fiamus	facti simus
fiatis	facti sitis
fiant	facti sint

Imperfect	*Pluperfect*
fierem	factus essem
fieres	factus esses
fieret	factus esset
fieremus	facti essemus
fieretis	facti essetis
fierent	facti essent

Imperative Mood

Singular   fi

Plural   fite

	Infinitives	*Participles*
Present	fieri	factus
Perfect	factus esse	faciendus
Future	factum iri	

Irregular Verb: *fero*

Principal Parts:

fero, ferre, tuli, latus

Indicative Mood

Present

Active	*Passive*
fero	feror
fers	ferris
fert	fertur
ferimus	ferimur
fertis	ferimini
ferunt	feruntur

Imperfect

Active	*Passive*
ferebam	ferebar
ferebas	ferebaris
ferebat	ferebatur
ferebamus	ferebamur
ferebatis	ferebamini
ferebant	ferebantur

Future

Active	*Passive*
feram	ferar
feres	fereris
feret	feretur
feremus	feremur
feretis	feremini
ferent	ferentur

Perfect

Active	*Passive*
tuli	latus sum
tulisti	latus es
tulit	latus est
tulimus	lati sumus
tulistis	lati estis
tulerunt	lati sunt

Pluperfect

Active	*Passive*
tuleram	latus eram
tuleras	latus eras
tulierat	latus erat
tuleramus	lati eramus
tuleratis	lati eratis
tulerant	lati erant

Future Perfect

Active	*Passive*
tulero	latus ero
tuleris	latus eris
tulerit	latus erit
tulerimus	lati erimus
tuleritis	lati eritis
tulerint	lati erunt

Subjunctive Mood

Present

Active	*Passive*
feram	ferar
feras	feraris
ferat	feratur
feramus	feramur
feratis	feramini
ferant	ferantur

Perfect

Active	*Passive*
tulerim	latus sim
tuleris	latus sis
tulerit	latus sit
tulerimus	lati simus
tuleritis	lati sitis
tulerint	lati sint

Imperfect

Active	*Passive*
ferrem	ferrer
ferres	ferreris
ferret	ferretur
ferremus	ferremur
ferretis	ferremini
ferrent	ferrentur

Pluperfect

Active	*Passive*
tulissem	latus essem
tulisses	latus esses
tulisset	latus esset
tulissemus	lati essemus
tulissetis	lati essetis
tulissent	lati essent

Imperative Mood

Singular **fer**   *Plural* **ferte**

Infinitives

	Active	*Passive*
Present	ferre	ferri
Perfect	tulisse	latus esse
Future	laturus esse	latum iri

Participles

	Active	Passive
Present	ferens	
Perfect		latus
Future	laturus	ferendus

Numbers

Cardinal	Ordinal	Arabic	Roman
unus, una, unum	primus, -a, -um	1	I
duo, duae, duo	secundus, -a, um	2	II
tres, tria, tria	tertius, -a, um	3	III
quattuor	quartus	4	IIII, IV
quinque	quintus	5	V
sex	sextus	6	VI
septem	septimus	7	VII
octo	octavus	8	VIII
novem	nonus	9	VIIII, IX
decem	decimus	10	X
undecim	undecimus	11	XI
duodecim	duodecimus	12	XII
tredecim	tertius decimus	13	XIII
quattuordecim	quartus decimus	14	XIIII, XIV
quindecim	quintus decimus	15	XV
sedecim	sextus decimus	16	XVI
septendecim	septimus decimus	17	XVII
duodeviginti	duodevicesimus	18	XVIII
undeviginti	undevicesimus	19	XVIII, XIX
viginti	vicesimus	20	XX
viginti unus, unus et	unus et vicesimus	21	XXI
triginta	tricesimus	30	XXX
quadraginta	quadragesimus	40	XXXX, XL
quinquaginta	quinquagesimus	50	L
sexaginta	sexagesimus	60	LX
septuaginta	septuagesimus	70	LXX
octoginta	octogesimus	80	LXXX
nonaginta	nonagesimus	90	LXXXX, XC
centum	centesimus	100	C

BIBLIOGRAPHY

The following list is by no means exhaustive. Many other Latin books have been translated into English, most of them by several different translators.

Metamorphoses, by Apuleius. Based on the story *Lucius, or the Ass,* by Lucian, this book is also known as *The Golden Ass.* One of the only two surviving Roman novels, it tells the story of a man transformed into an ass.

Satyricon, by Petronius Arbiter. This is the other surviving Roman novel, though only fragments of the full work remain. The longest of these is called *Cena Trimalchionis,* or *The Feast of Trimalchio.*

Commentarii de Bello Gallico, by Gaius Julius Caesar.

Poems, by Gaius Valerius Catullus.

Narrationes, by Odo de Cerinton.

In Catilinam I—IV, by Marcus Tullius Cicero.

Brevarium, by Eutropius. This is a history of Rome from 753 B.C. to A.D. 364.

Odes, by Quintus Horatius Flaccus.

Lucius, or the Ass, by Lucian. This was Apuleius' source for *The Golden Ass.*

De Rerum Natura, by Titus Lucretius Carus (Lucretius). As the title suggests, this is a poem discussing *The Nature of Things.*

Epigrams, by Marcus Valerius Martialis.

Metamorphoses, by Publius Ovidius Naso (Ovid). Don't confuse this with Apuleius' work of the same name. This is not a novel, but a long poem that tells the stories of people tranformed into something else.

Fables, by Phaedrus.

Menaechmi, by Titus Maccius Plautus (Plautus). This play is a comedy about twin brothers.

The Letters of Pliny the Younger, by Gaius Plinius Caecilius Secundus.

The Aeneid, by Publius Vergilius Maro.

Sermons, by Jacques de Vitry.

The Vulgate Bible, translated into Latin by St. Jerome.

PRINCIPAL PARTS FOR ALL VERBS
INCLUDED IN *LATIN MADE SIMPLE*

Learning the principal parts of verbs is critical in trying to understand the Latin language, since all of the possible forms which a verb can take can be generated from its principal parts. The reverse, unfortunately, is not true. If you encounter, for example, the form **tulerant** in a passage, you will look for it in vain in the dictionary, since **tulerant** is formed from the third principal part of **fero, ferre.** It is essential, therefore, to learn the principal parts of a verb when learning vocabulary. Fortunately, principal parts do tend to fall into one of several fairly predictable patterns based on the third principal part (the first person singular, perfect active indicative), as indicated in the following list. Within each category, verbs are listed alphabetically. Deponents and semi-deponents, which have no perfect active forms, are listed separately.

Type I—Perfect Stem Ending in *–vi* or *–ui*

accelero, accelerare, acceleravi, acceleratus hurry

adfirmo, adfirmare, adfirmavi, adfirmatus strengthen, affirm, assert

administro, administrare, administravi, administratus manage, control, rule

adoro, adorare, adoravi, adoratus worship, adore

aedifico, aedificare, aedificavi, aedificatus build

agito, agitare, agitavi, agitatus consider, discuss

ambulo, ambulare, ambulavi, ambulatus walk

amo, amare, amavi, amatus like, love

appello, appellare, apellavi, appellatus address, call, name

armo, armare, armavi, armatus arm

aro, arare, aravi, aratus plow

careo, carere, carui, caritus be without, be absent from

clamito, clamitare, clamitavi, clamitatus proclaim, cry aloud

clamo, clamare, clamavi, clamatus shout, cry

cogito, cogitare, cogitavi, cogatatus consider, think

cognosco, cognoscere, cognovi, cognitus learn, recognize, know

comparo, comparare, comparavi, comparatus bring together, compare

concilio, conciliare, conciliavi, conciliatus reconcile, win, win over

confirmo, confirmare, confirmavi, confirmatus establish, strengthen, confirm

congrego, congregare, congregavi, congregatus assemble, gather together

conloco, conlocare, conlocavi, conlocatus place, station

conquiro, conquirere, conquisivi, conquisitus look for, collect

conservo, conservare, conservavi, conservatus keep safe, preserve

cupio, cupere, cupivi, cupitus desire, wish, want

curo, curare, curavi, curatus care for, cure

damno, damnare, damnavi, damnatus condemn, find guilty

debeo, debere, debui, debitus owe, ought

deleo, delere, delevi, deletus destroy, obliterate

demonstro, demonstrare, demonstravi, demonstratus point out, show

desero, deserere, deserui, deseritus desert, abandon

deterreo, deterrere, deterrui, deterritus frighten off, deter, prevent, hinder

doceo, docere, docui, doctus teach, show

doleo, dolere, dolui, dolitus grieve, be sorry

dormio, dormire, dormivi, dormitus sleep

dubito, dubitare, dubitavi, dubitatus doubt, hesitate, be uncertain

enuntio, enuntiare, enuntiavi, enuntiatus speak out, reveal, make known

erro, errare, erravi, erratus be mistaken, lose one's way

excito, excitare, excitavi, excitatus arouse, stir up

existimo, existimare, existimavi, existimatus think, judge

expono, exponere, exposui, expositus set forth, exhibit, explain

exspecto, exspectare, exspectavi, exspectatus await, expect, wait for

firmo, firmare, firmavi, firmatus strengthen, make firm

flagito, flagitare, flagitavi, flagitatus demand

habeo, habere, habui, habitus have, hold

habito, habitare, habitavi, habitatus dwell, live

haesito, haesitare, haesitavi, haesitatus hesitate, be at a loss

ignoro, ignorare, ignoravi, ignoratus not know, be ignorant

illustro, illustrare, illustravi, illustratus make clear, reveal

impedio, impedire, impedivi, impeditus hinder

impero, imperare, imperavi, imperatus command, order

incito, incitare, incitavi, incitatus arouse, stir up, incite

incolo, incolere, incolui live in, reside

iudico, iudicare, iudicavi, iudicatus judge, sentence, examine

iureiuro, iureiurare, iureiuravi, iureiuratus swear

laboro, laborare, laboravi, laboratus work

laudo, laudare, laudavi, laudatus praise

libero, liberare, liberavi, liberatus free, set free

loco, locare, locavi, locatus place, put

metuo, metuere, metui fear, be afraid

moneo, monere, monui, monitus warn, advise

monstro, monstrare, monstravi, monstratus point out, show

narro, narrare, narravi, narratus tell, relate

nato, natare, natavi, natatus swim

navigo, navigare, navigavi, navigatus sail, cruise

neco, necare, necavi, necatus kill
nescio, nescire, nescivi, nescitus not know, be ignorant of
nuntio, nuntiare, nuntiavi, nuntiatus announce, report
obtineo, obtinere, obtinui, obtentus secure, obtain
occupo, occupare, occupavi, occupatus seize, take possession of
oportet, oportere, oportuit (Impersonal verb) it is right, it is proper
oppugno, oppugnare, oppugnavi, oppugnatus attack
oro, orare, oravi, oratus beg, pray
paro, parare, paravi, paratus prepare, get ready
pertimesco, pertimescere, pertimui fear, be alarmed at
peto, petere, petivi or petii, petitus seek
placo, placare, placavi, placatus calm, reconcile
pono, ponere, posui, positus put, place
porto, portare, portavi, portatus carry
praesto, praestare, praestavi, praestatus be better than, be superior to
prohibeo, prohibere, prohibui, prohibitus keep off, hinder, prohibit, prevent
propero, properare, properavi, properatus hurry, hasten
purgo, purgare, purgavi, purgatus clean, remove, excuse
puto, putare, putavi, putatus think, believe
quaero, quaerere, quaesivi, quaesitus ask, look for
recupero, recuperare, recuperavi, recuperatus recover, get back
recuso, recusare, recusavi, recusatus refuse, reject
regno, regnare, regnavi, regnatus rule
reporto, reportare, reportavi, reportatus carry back, bring back
retineo, retinere, retinui, retentus keep back, retain
saluto, salutare, salutavi, salutatus greet, welcome
scio, scire, scivi, scitus know
servo, servare, servavi, servatus save, preserve
simulo, simulare, simulavi, simulatus pretend
specto, spectare, spectavi, spectatus hope
supero, superare, superavi, superatus surpass, overcome, conquer
tabesco, tabescere, tabescui (or tabui) decay, melt away
teneo, tenere, tenui, tentus hold, keep, have
terreo, terrere, terrui, territus frighten, scare, terrify
timeo, timere, timui fear, be afraid of
tolero, tolerare, toleravi, toleratus bear, endure
transeo, transire, transivi, transitus pass over, cross, desert
vaco, vacare, vacavi, vacatus be empty
veto, vetare, vetavi, vetatus forbid
vindico, vindicare, vindicavi, vindicatus defend, protect
vito, vitare, vitavi, vitatus avoid
voco, vocare, vocavi, vocatus call
volo, volare, volavi, volatus fly

vulnero, vulnerare, vulneravi, vulneratus wound, hurt

Type II—Perfect Stem Ending in –s or –x (Palatal Consonant + s)

accedo, accedere, accessi, accessurus approach, be added, to agree, support
amitto, amittere, amisi, amissus lose, send away
ardeo, ardere, arsi, arsus burn, be on fire
augeo, augere, auxi, auctus increase, enlarge
cedo, cedere, cessi, cessus go away, withdraw, yield
concedo, concedere, concessi, concessum grant, allow, withdraw
conspicio, conspicere, conspexi, conspectus observe
consumo, consumere, consumpsi, consumptus use up, consume, spend
dico, dicere, dixi, dictus say, speak
diligo, diligere, dilexi, delectus value, love
discedo, discedere, discessi, discessus withdraw, go away, leave
duco, ducere, duxi, ductus lead
educo, educere, eduxi, eductus lead out
gero, gerere, gessi, gestus carry on, wage
instruo, instruere, instruxi, instructus draw up, form, train
intelligo, intelligere, intellexi, intellectus understand
intercludo, intercludere, interclusi, interclusus shut off, stop
iubeo, iubere, iussi, iussus order, command
maneo, manere, mansi, mansus remain
mitto, mittere, misi, missus send
opprimo, opprimere, oppressi, oppressus overcome, crush
permitto, permittere, permisi, permissus allow, permit
persuadeo, persuadere, persuasi, persuasus persuade
reduco, reducere, reduxi, reductus lead back
rego, regere, rexi, rectus rule
scribo, scribere, scripsi, scriptus write
sentio, sentire, sensi, sensus feel, perceive, realize
suspicio, suspicere, suspexi, suspectus mistrust, suspect
traho, trahere, traxi, tractus drag, draw
vivo, vivere, vixi, victus live

Type III—Reduplicated Perfect Stem

addo, addere, addidi, additus put on, add
cado, cadere, cecidi, casus fall
credo, credere, credidi, creditus believe, trust
curro, currere, cucurri, cursus run

dedo, dedere, dedidi, deditus give up, surrender
desisto, desistere, destiti, destitus cease, desist, stop
disco, discere, didici learn
posco, poscere, poposci ask, beg, demand
recido, recidere, reccidi recoil, fall
reddeo, reddere, reddidi, reditus return, restore
reperio, reperire, repperi, repertus find, discover
tango, tangere, tetigi, tactus touch
trado, tradere, tradidi, traditus give up, surrender

Type IV—Perfect Stem with Vowel Lengthening

accido, accidere, accidi, accisus happen
accipio, accipere, accepi, acceptus take, receive
advenio, advenire, adveni, adventus come to, reach, arrive at
capio, capere, cepi, captus take, seize, capture
caveo, cavere, cavi, cautus beware of, guard against
cogo, cogere, coegi, coactus collect, drive, compel
comperio, comperire, comperi, compertus learn, ascertain
comprehendo, comprehendere, comprehendi, comprehensus seize, discover, apprehend
conficio, conficere, confeci, confectus finish, complete, carry out
constituo, constituere, constitui, constitutus decide, establish
contendo, contendere, contendi, contentus hold together, limit, enclose, keep, repress
convenio, convenire, conveni, conventus come together, assemble
defendo, defendere, defendi, defensus ward off, repel, defend
deligo, deligere, delegi, delectus choose, select
descendo, descendere, descendi, descensus descend, come down
effugio, effugere, effugi, effugitus flee away, escape
emo, emere, emi, emptus buy
evenio, evenire, eveni, evenitus happen, come out
exsolvo, exsolvere, exsolvi, exsolutus release, free
facio, facere, feci, factus make, do
fugio, fugere, fugi, fugitus flee, run away, escape
iacio, iacere, ieci, iactus throw
incendo, incendere, incendi, incensus set fire to, burn
interficio, interficere, interfeci, interfectus kill
invenio, invenire, inveni, inventus find, come upon
iuvo, iuvare, iuvi, iutus help, aid
lego, legere, legi, lectus read
moveo, movere, movi, motus move
offendo, offendere, offendi, offensus wound, offend
patefacio, patefacere, patefeci, patefactus throw open, bring to light

permoveo, permovere, permovi, permotus stir, move
pervenio, pervenire, perveni, perventus arrive
profugio, profugere, profugi run away, flee, escape
recipio, recipere, recepi, receptus take back, receive
relinquo, relinquere, reliqui, relictus leave, leave behind
restituo, restituere, restitui, restitutus restore, rebuild
suscipio, suscipere, suscepi, susceptus take up, undertake
venio, venire, veni, venitus come
verto, vertere, verti, versus turn
video, videre, vidi, visus see
vinco, vincere, vici, victus conquer

Type V—Irregular Verbs

abeo, abire, abii, abitus go away
absum, abesse, abfui be absent, be away from
adfero, adferre, attuli, adlatus bring
adsum, adesse, adfui be present, be here
confero, conferre, contuli, conlatus bring together, collect
defero, deferre, detuli, delatus carry off, bring away, report, offer
do, dare, dedi, datus give
effero, efferre, extuli, elatus carry forth, bring out
eo, ire, ii or **ivi, itus** go
exeo, exire, exii, exitus avoid, go away, depart
fero, ferre, tuli, latus carry, bear
malo, malle, malui prefer
nolo, nolle, nolui wish not, be unwilling
perfero, perferre, pertuli, perlatus report
possum, posse, posui be able
refero, referre, retuli, relatus report, bring back
rescisco, resciscere, rescii, rescitus learn, find out
sum, esse, fui, futurus be
volo, velle, volui wish, be willing

Type VI—Deponents and Semi-Deponents

adsequor, adsequi, adsecutus sum gain, obtain, reach
aggredior, aggredi, aggressus sum approach, attack
arbitror, arbitrari, arbitratus sum think, judge
audeo, audere, ausus sum dare
colloquor, colloqui, collocutus sum speak with
commoror, commorari, commoratus sum linger, stay, remain, abide

conor, conari, conatus sum try
consequor, consequi, consecutus sum follow, catch up with
egredior, egredi, egressus sum quit, surpass, go beyond
experior, experiri, experitus sum test, try
fido, fidere, fisus sum trust, believe, confide
fio, fieri, factus sum become, be done, be made
fungor, fungi, functus sum perform, do
gaudeo, gaudere, gavisus sum rejoice
hortor, hortari, hortatus sum urge, encourage
insequor, insequi, insecutus sum follow after, pursue
loquor, loqui, locutus sum say, speak
misereor, misereri, miseritus sum pity, feel sorry for
morior, mori, moritus sum die
nascor, nasci, natus sum be born
opinor, opinari, opinatus sum think, suppose
pascor, pasci, pastus sum feed on, eat
patior, pati, passus sum allow, grant, suffer
polliceor, polliceri, pollicitus sum promise
proficiscor, profisci, profectus sum go forth, depart
profiteor, profiteri, professus sum declare, acknowledge, say
queror, queri, questus sum complain about
revertor, reverti, reversus sum turn back, return
sequor, sequi, secutus sum follow
soleo, solere, solitus sum be accustomed to
vereor, vereri, veritus sum fear

A BRIEF INTRODUCTION
TO LATIN METER

Part of the joy of learning another language is to be able to read the best of what has been written without the medium of translation. Poetry in another language, in this case Latin, can be particularly challenging without some fundamental understanding of how the poets themselves approached their task.

The fundamental difference between the meter of English language poetry and that of Latin (and Greek) is that English meter is based on stressed and unstressed syllables, while Latin meter is based on the actual quantity of the vowel sound of each syllable, i.e., whether that syllable is long or short. Long vowels literally take a longer time to pronounce. For that reason, when we speak of Latin poetry, we speak of it as being quantitative.

These quantities are arranged in various metrical patterns based on a relatively small number of feet. (See A4.6 p. 362 for an explanation of spondees, anapests, et cetera.) However, the complexity of metrical schemes that can be obtained through combinations and variation on these basic patterns can be astounding. All of Vergil's *Aeneid* (commonly Anglicized Virgil), for example, is written in dactylic hexameters. This metrical scheme allows for lines varying between twelve and seventeen syllables, twelve if each foot is a spondee, seventeen if each foot is a dactyl (other than the final foot, which is always only two syllables long).

Generally, long syllables tend to slow a verse down and make it seem ponderous and serious. Short syllables, which dominate dactyls and anapests in particular, speed things up and make the verse lighter and more joyous. This effect should not be exaggerated unduly, but ancient poets were clearly aware of this natural tendency and utilized it to great purpose at times.

Samuel Taylor Coleridge (1772–1834) wrote a nifty little poem that gives some sense of the difference meter can make to the tempo of a poem:

Trochee trips from short to long
From long to short in solemn sort.
Slow Spondee stalks; strong foot! Yet ill able
Ever to come up with Dactyl tri-syllable.
Iambics march from short to long;
With a leap and a bound the swift Anapests throng.

When approaching a Latin poem, one must first mark out any elisions (the slurring over of vowels across word boundaries according to the rules set out in A4.1 below). Next, one should mark off vowels that are known to be long either by nature or by position. This can be difficult in a text that doesn't indicate macrons, but with practice and a good ear for the language, scanning meter can be gratifying fun. **Latin Made Simple** does not indicate macrons, since the Romans themselves did not use them.

Let's look at the famous opening line from Vergil's *Aeneid*:

Arma virumque cano, Troiae qui primus ab oris
I sing of arms and a man, who first from the shores of Troy . . .

We may note first that there are no elisions. So far so good. There are fifteen syllables to the line, so we know that three of the feet have to be dactyls. Let's mark each of the known long quantities and see where it gets us. Syllables are numbered for easier reference:

A r m a	v i r u m q u e	c a n o,	T r o i a e	q u i	p r i m u s	a b	o r i s
1 2	3 4 5	6 7	8 9	10	11 12	13	14 15

Since we have fifteen syllables to our hexameter line, we know that three of the feet must be dactyls. We know that the following syllables must be long: 1 and 3 by position, 7 and 8 by nature, since they are diphthongs, and 14 because the last foot has to be disyllabic with the first syllable long. If we also recall that 7, 10, and 11 are long by nature, that helps a lot. But let's say we don't remember that. Well, we should remember at least that neuter plurals end in a short a, therefore syllable 2 must be short, which forces 3 to be short as well. That's one of our three dactyls.

Even if we don't know any other quantities from memory, a little bit of deduction can go a long way. If syllable number 5 were long (there doesn't seem to be any reason it should be, but let's explore the possibility), then 6 couldn't be short since we know the diphthong of 7 is long, and we can't have a single short syllable by itself, except the very last syllable of the line, of course. So, if 5 is long, 4 and 5 have to form a spondaic foot (foot #2), 6 and 7 would also have to form a spondaic foot (foot #3), and the two diphthongs in a row of 8 and 9 would form yet another (foot #4). That means that our one remaining foot, between syllable 9 and syllable 14, would have to be 4 syllables long. Can't happen.

It all started from our hypothesis of syllable 5 being long—so now we know it can't be. Which means 6 has to be short and 4–5–6 form foot #2, a dactyl, the second of the three we're expecting. We could guess the one penultimate foot is our remaining dactyl (11–12–13), since the penultimate foot is dactylic more often than not, but let's push our deductive reasoning a bit further. Foot number three has to be 7–8, a spondee. That leaves two feet and five syllables, i.e., one is a spondee and the other our third dactyl. No way of resolving whether these two feet are 9–10 then 11–12–13 (spondee, dactyl) or 9–10–11 then 12–13 (dactyl, spondee) without additional information. We know that the former, with the dactyl in the penultimate position, is statistically more likely, but that can't be our determinant. So, we grab a dictionary with macrons, or suddenly get our memory back, recalling that both syllable 10 and syllable 11 are, indeed, long by nature. Spondee, dactyl, then, as we'd supposed.

It seems tedious and labor intensive at first, but within a week of doing these in my Vergil class I had students lining up volunteering to scan. It's fun, and it helps give you a real feel for the movement of the language and the poetry.

The outline that follows was originally designed as a guide for teaching dactylic hexameter to my Vergil class. Take it slowly at first and try to internalize the logic of the rules. The initial investment in effort is more than rewarded by the depth that one adds to a reading of Vergil. There are other metrical schemes besides dactylic hexameter, of course. Start with this and once you've mastered it, there are numerous resources to expand into other poets, meters, and joys.

A4.1 Quantitative Meter vis-à-vis Accentual Meter

Short Syllables (*Breva*)—indicated by ∪ above the appropriate vowel
Long Syllables (*Longa*)—indicated by ˉ above the appropriate vowel/diphthong
    By nature (all diphthongs are long: ae, ai, au, ei, eu, oe, oi, ou, ui)
    By position—vowel followed by two or more consonants (whether or not they are in the same word)
    The initial letter h cannot help to make position
Anceps—syllable may be long or short (indicated by x)
Some Exceptions:
    Diastole—short vowel lengthened to long
    Systole—long vowel shorted to short
    Synizesis—two vowels read as one (e.g., *La—vin—ja*, rather than *La—vin—i—a*)
    Mute (b, d, g, k, p, t) + liquid (l, r) USUALLY counts as one consonant
    Qu- (= qw) ALWAYS counts as one consonant
        Ch, ph, ps, rh and th CAN count as one consonant (when they are from original Greek *chi*, *phi*, *psi*, *rho*, or *theta*; this happens most often in Greek names)
    X (= gs/ks) and Z (= sd) CAN count as double consonants

A4.2 Elision—The Omission or "Slurring Over" of a Vowel

final vowel/diphthong OR vowel plus m at the end of a word
elides with initial vowel/diphthong OR (h-)
pronounced as though final vowel, etc. doesn't exist, e.g., "*Multum ille et*" (five syllables) becomes (three syllables)
"*mult'ill'et*"
Exceptions:
Hiatus—final vowel doesn't elide when expected (usually at strong caesurae)
Semi-hiatus—final long vowel becomes short rather than eliding
Synapheia—elision at line-end with the following verse (the first verse is then considered *hypermetric*)—*Synapheia* is very rare

A4.3 Caesura—
Significant Word/Sense Break in the Verse
(Indicated by Two Vertical Lines)

Masculine caesura—occurs after the arsis (the longa in a dactyl)

Feminine caesura—occurs between the two short vowels in the thesis—also misleadingly called a "trochaic foot"

Diaeresis —caesura coincident with the end of the foot

A4.4 Ictus (Stress)

Each *longa* (including both *longa* of a spondee) has its own *ictus* or stress

Arsis (rising pitch)—the *longa* of the dactyl

Thesis (falling)—the two *breva* of the dactyl

N.B. Greek meter uses these terms in the opposite way, i.e., *thesis* THEN *arsis*

A4.5 Strophic Verse vis-à-vis Stichic Verse

Strophe (Strophic)—multi-line stanza based on some sort of end-rhyme scheme

Stich (Stichic)—each line independent of end-rhyme scheme

Acrostic—first letter in each line spells a word or words

Telestic—final letter in each line spells a word or words

A4.6 Major Types of Metric Feet
(Feet Are Separated by a Vertical Line)

Dactyl ¯ ◡ ◡

Spondee ¯ ¯

Anapest (cf. Dactyl) ◡ ◡ ¯

Iamb ◡ ¯

Trochee (cf. Iamb) ¯ ◡

Cretic ¯ ◡ ¯

Tribach ◡ ◡ ◡

Pyrrhic (not a true foot) ◡ ◡

A4.7 Line Lengths

one foot per line—monometer

two feet per line—dimeter

three feet per line—trimeter

four feet per line—tetrameter

five feet per line—pentameter

six feet per line—hexameter

seven feet per line—heptameter
eight feet per line—octameter

A4.8 Some Conventions of (Greek and) Latin Epic Poetic Meter

Dactyllic hexameter; stichic pattern (each line independent of end-rhyme).
The final foot (ultima) is disyllabic (i.e., either a spondee or a trochee).
The next to last foot (penultima) is almost always a dactyl.
When the penultimate foot is a spondee, the line is considered a "spondaic" verse.
The third foot frequently contains a masculine caesura.

A4.9 Suggestions for Successful Scansion

1. Indicate all elisions first (you may discover later, however, that hiatus disrupts this).
2. Mark all syllables that are long by nature or position.
3. Sometimes starting from the end helps (you know the sixth foot is always disyllabic, and the fifth foot is normally a dactyl).
4. Dactyllic hexameter will have between 12 and 17 syllables.
5. The number of syllables over 12 is the number of dactylic feet in the line.
6. Short vowels (*breva*) are always paired (except in the final foot).
7. Every foot must begin with a *longa*.
8. An even number of consecutive *longa* (i.e., a spondee) will always be followed by another *longa* (the *arsis* of the following foot).

TIMELINE OF ROMAN HISTORY

1184 B.C.   Fall of Troy to the Greeks; Aeneas wanders to Italy

The Kingdom (753–509 B.C.)

753 B.C.   Founding of Rome by Romulus and Remus
753–509 B.C.   The Seven Kings of Rome
509 B.C.   Tarquinius Superbus expelled by Collatinus and Brutus; Republic established

The Republic (509–27 B.C.)

390 B.C.   Juno's geese warn the Romans of Gauls entering the city
280–272 B.C.   Wars with Pyrrhus in southern Italy
264–241 B.C.   The First Punic War between Rome and Carthage
218–201 B.C.   The Second Punic War (Hannibal crosses the Alps into Italy)
214–146 B.C.   Wars with Greece
201–146 B.C.   Third Punic War
146 B.C.   Destruction of Carthage and Corinth; Rome becomes a world power
146–63 B.C.   Civil Strife: the Gracchi, G. Marius, L. Sulla, G. Pompey (the Great)
73 B.C.   Spartacus' uprising (90,000 slaves); defeated by Crassus & Pompey
59–51 B.C.   Caesar's conquest of Gaul; Invasion of Britain
46 B.C.   Caesar becomes dictator for life; The Long Year (80 days added)
44 B.C.   Caesar assassinated on the Ides of March
31 B.C.   Octavian defeats Antony and Cleopatra at Actiumin Western Greece

The Empire (27 B.C.–A.D. 476)

27 B.C.   Octavian declared Augustus; beginning of Roman Empire.
9 B.C.   Arminius destroys three legions in Teutoberg Forest; End of Roman expansion into Germanic lands.
A.D. 14   Death of Augustus Caesar; Tiberius becomes second Emperor.
A.D. 69   Nero commits suicide; end of Julio-Claudian emperors. The Year of the Four Emperors.
A.D. 79   The eruption of Mt. Vesuvius, burying Pompeii and Herculaneum.
A.D. 180   The death of Marcus Aurelius, last of the Good Emperors.
A.D. 212   Universal Roman citizenship extended under Emperor Caracalla.
A.D. 286   Emperor Diocletian divides the empire to facilitate administration.
A.D. 312   Constantine victorious at Milvian Bridge (*in hoc signo*); Christianity adopted as
                official religion of the empire.

A.D. 324–337   Constantine temporarily reunites the Western and Eastern empires.

A.D. 410   Visigoths sack Rome.

A.D. 451   Pope Leo I prevents Attila the Hun from entering Rome.

A.D. 455   Rome sacked by Vandals on their way to North Africa.

A.D. 476   Romulus Augustulus, last Roman emperor, overthrown by Odoacer the Goth. End of the Western Roman Empire.

A.D. 527–565   Under the Eastern Emperor Justinian, Rome and large portions of the Western empire are (temporarily) regained.

A.D. 1453   Constantinople sacked during the Crusades. End of the Eastern Roman Empire.

Legend says in the year 753 B.C., Romulus and Remus founded Rome. The Romans figured dates from this year, which they called **anno urbis conditae,** *from the year of the founding of the city* (or **ab urbe condita,** *from the founding of the city*) abbreviated to A.U.C. Since the Romans counted inclusively, years B.C. should be subtracted from 754 to calculate the Roman year; thus, the year 20 A.U.C. is the same as the year 734 B.C., and the year 763 A.U.C. is the same as the year A.D. 10 (adding 753 works for dates *anno domino,* since there was no year zero).

As indicated in the timeline above, Roman history falls into three broad periods. The earliest period is that of the kingdom, when Rome was ruled by a succession of seven kings, i.e., Romulus, Numa Pompilius, Tullus Hostilius, Ancus Marcius, Tarquinius Priscus, Servius Tullius, and Tarquinius Superbus. When the last of these kings was driven out by Collatinus and Brutus in 509 B.C., the Roman Republic was established. Eventually, the geographical empire grew beyond the capability of a government designed to rule a city-state. Rome watched a succession of strong-men, with their own military backing and little real loyalty to Rome, run the affairs of the city, beginning with Tiberius and Gaius Gracchus, through Marius, Sulla, Pompey, and Caesar.

Caesar's assassination on the Ides of March in 44 B.C. precipitated a series of civil wars, which ended only with Octavian's defeat of Antony and Cleopatra at Actium. Proclaimed Augustus, Octavian set into motion the machinery that would run the empire for the next five centuries until Odoacer the Ostrogoth deposed Romulus Augustulus in A.D. 476, bringing the Western Roman Empire to an end. The Eastern Empire persisted in its Byzantine complexity and splendor, however, for nearly another thousand years ending only with the Christian sack of Constantinople in A.D. 1453. That same year, oddly, saw the end of the Hundred Years War, and the invention of the printing press.

The Roman Empire, then, can be said to have lasted for well over 2,200 years. Rome's legacy, in such areas as the law, architecture and, not least of all, in the continuing impact of the Latin language on our own language, persists to this day.

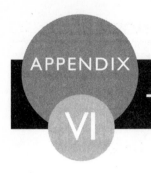
A

a, ab (prep. + abl.) from, away from; by

abeo, abire, abii, abitus (verb) go away

absum, abesse, abfui (verb) be absent, be away from

accedo, accedere, accessi, accessurus (verb) approach, be added, to agree, support

accido, accidere, accidi, accisus (verb) happen

accelero, accelerare, acceleravi, acceleratus (verb) hurry

accipio, accipere, accepi, acceptus (verb) take, receive

acer, acris, acre (adj.) sharp, active, keen

acies, aciei, f. (noun) battle line

Acco, Acconis, m. (proper noun) Acco

ad (prep. + acc.) to, towards

addo, addere, addidi, additus (verb) put on, add

adfero, adferre, attuli, adlatus (verb) bring

adfirmo, adfirmare, adfirmavi, adfirmatus (verb) strengthen, affirm, assert

administro, administrare, administravi, administratus (verb) manage, control, rule

adoro, adorare, adoravi, adoratus (verb) worship, adore

adsequor, adsequi, adsecutus sum (verb) gain, obtain, reach

adsum, adesse, adfui (verb) be present, be here

adulescens, adulescentis, m. (noun) youth (gen. pl. **adulescentium**)

advenio, advenire, adveni, adventus (verb) come to, reach, arrive at

adventus, adventus, m. (noun) arrival, approach

aedificium, aedificii or aedifici, n. (noun) building

aedifico, aedificare, aedificavi, aedificatus (verb) build

aeger, aegra, aegrum (adj.) sick, ill

aenus, aena, aenum (adj.) bronze

aequus, aequa, aequum (adj.) equal, level, fair

aestas, aestatis, f. (noun) summer

Africa, Africae, f. (proper noun) Africa

ager, agri, m. (noun) field

aggredior, aggredi, aggressus sum (verb) approach, attack

agito, agitare, agitavi, agitatus (verb) consider, discuss

agricola, agricolae, m. (noun) farmer

ala, alae, f. (noun) wing

aliquis, aliquid (pronoun) someone, something; anyone, anything

alius, alia, aliud (adj.) other, another

Allobroges, Allobrogum, m. pl. (proper noun) Allobroges

alter, altera, alterum (adj.) the one, the other

altus, alta, altum (adj.) high, deep

ambulo, ambulare, ambulavi, ambulatus (verb) walk

amicus, amica, amicum (adj.) friendly

amicus, amici, m. (noun) friend

amitto, amittere, amisi, amissus (verb) lose, send away

amo, amare, amavi, amatus (verb) like, love

amor, amoris, m. (noun) love

amphitheatrum, amphitheatri, n. (noun) amphitheater

an (conj.) or

angustus, angusta, angustum (adj.) narrow

animal, animalis, n. (noun) animal

animus, animi, m. (noun) mind, spirit

annua, annuorum, n. pl. (noun) pension, yearly pay

annus, anni, m. (noun) year

ante (prep. + acc.) before, in front of

antea (adv.) before

antequam (conj.) before

antiquus, antiqua, antiquum (adj.) ancient, old

antrum, antri, n. (noun) cave

apertus, aperta, apertum (adj.) open

Apollo, Apollonis, m. (proper noun) Apollo

appello, appellare, apellavi, appellatus (verb) address, call, name

Aprilis, Aprile (adj.) of April

apud (prep. + acc.) among, in the presence of

aqua, aquae, f. (noun) water

arbitror, arbitrari, arbitratus sum (verb) think, judge

arbor, arboris, f. (noun) tree

arca, arcae, f. (noun) chest, box

ardeo, ardere, arsi, arsus (verb) burn, be on fire

arena, arenae, f. (noun) sand, arena

Ariadne, Ariadnes, f. (proper noun) Ariadne

arma, armae, n. pl. (noun) arms, weapons

armo, armare, armavi, armatus (verb) arm

aro, arare, aravi, aratus (verb) plow

aspectus, aspectus, m. (noun) look, sight

at (conj.) but

Atalanta, Atalantae, f. (proper noun) Atalanta

Athenae, Athenarum, f. pl. (proper noun) Athens

Atlas, Atlantis, m. (proper noun) Atlas

atque, ac (conj.) and also, also

auctoritas, auctoritatis, f. (noun) power, prestige, authority

audacia, audaciae, f. (noun) boldness, daring

audax, audacis (adj.) bold

audeo, audere, ausus sum (verb) dare

augeo, augere, auxi, auctus (verb) increase, enlarge

Augustus, Augusta, Augustum (adj.) of August

Aurelius, Aurelia, Aurelium (adj.) Aurelian

aureus, aurea, aureum (adj.) golden

aurum, auri, n. (noun) gold

aut (conj.) or

aut . . . aut (conj.) either . . . or

autem (conj.) but, however

auxilium, auxilii or auxili, n. (noun) aid, help

avunculus, avunculi, m. (noun) uncle

B

Bacchus, Bacchi, m. (proper noun) Bacchus

barbarus, barbara, barbarum (adj.) savage, uncivilized, barbarian

barbarus, barbari, m. (noun) barbarian

belle (adv.) prettily, neatly, well

bellum, belli, n. (noun) war

bene (adv.) well

bis (adv.) twice

bonitas, bonitatis, f. (noun) goodness, kindness, benevolence

bonus, bona, bonum (adj.) good

brevis, breve (adj.) short, brief

Britannia, Britanniae, f. (proper noun) Britain

C

cado, cadere, cecidi, casus (verb) fall

caedes, caedis, f. (noun) slaughter, murder (gen. pl., **caedium**)

caelum, caeli, n. (noun) sky, heaven

canis, canis, m. and **f.** (noun) dog

capio, capere, cepi, captus (verb) take, seize, capture

captivus, captivi, m. (noun) captive

caput, capitis, n. (noun) head, leader

carcer, carceris, n. (noun) prison

careo, carere, carui, caritus (verb) be without, be absent from

Carnutes, Carnutum, m. pl. (proper noun) Carnutes

casa, casae, f. (noun) house, cottage

casus, casus, m. (noun) downfall, fate

castra, castrorum, n. pl. (noun) camp

causa, causae, f. (noun) cause, reason

caveo, cavere, cavi, cautus (verb) beware of, guard against

cedo, cedere, cessi, cessus (verb) go away, withdraw, yield

celer, celeris, celere (adj.) quick, swift

celeritas, celeritatis, f. (noun) speed, swiftness

cera, cerae, f. (noun) wax

Cerberus, Cerberi, m. (proper noun) Cerberus

Ceres, Cereris, f. (proper noun) Ceres

certe (adv.) surely, indeed

certus, certa, certum (adj.) certain, sure

Charon, Charontis, m. (proper noun) Charon

cibus, cibi, m. (noun) food

Cincinnatus, Cincinnati, m. (proper noun) Cincinnatus

circiter (adv.) about

circum (prep. + acc.) around, about

civis, civis, m. and **f.** (noun) citizen (gen. pl. **civium**)

civitas, civitatis, f. (noun) state

clamito, clamitare, clamitavi, clamitatus (verb) proclaim, cry aloud

clamo, clamare, clamavi, clamatus (verb) shout, cry

clandestinus, clandestina, clandestinum (adj.) secret, hidden

clarus, clara, clarum (adj.) clear, famous, bright

classis, classis, f. (noun) fleet (gen. pl. **classium**)

cogito, cogitare, cogitavi, cogatatus (verb) consider, think

cognosco, cognoscere, cognovi, cognitus (verb) learn, recognize, know

cogo, cogere, coegi, coactus (verb) collect, drive, compel

collis, collis, m. (noun) hill (gen. pl. **collium**)

colloquor, colloqui, collocutus sum (verb) speak with

Colosseum, Colossei, n. (proper noun) the Colosseum

commoror, commorari, commoratus sum (verb) linger, stay, remain, abide

communis, commune (adj.) common, public

comparo, comparare, comparavi, comparatus (verb) bring together, compare

comperio, comperire, comperi, compertus (verb) learn, ascertain

comprehendo, comprehendere, comprehendi, comprehensus (verb) seize, discover, apprehend

concedo, concedere, concessi, concessum (verb) grant, allow, withdraw

concilio, conciliare, conciliavi, conciliatus (verb) reconcile, win, win over

concilium, concilii or concili, n. (noun) council

confero, conferre, contuli, conlatus (verb) bring together, collect

conficio, conficere, confeci, confectus (verb) finish, complete, carry out

confirmo, confirmare, confirmavi, confirmatus (verb) establish, strengthen, confirm

congrego, congregare, congregavi, congregatus (verb) assemble, gather together

coniurati, coniurationis, f. (noun) conspiracy, plot

conloco, conlocare, conlocavi, conlocatus (verb) place, station

conor, conari, conatus sum (verb) try, attempt

conquiro, conquirere, conquisivi, conquisitus (verb) look for, collect

consensus, consensus, m. (noun) agreement

consequor, consequi, consecutus sum (verb) follow, catch up with

conservo, conservare, conservavi, conservatus (verb) keep safe, preserve

consilium, consilii or consili, n. (noun) plan, advice

conspectus, conspectus, m. (noun) sight, view

conspicio, conspicere, conspexi, conspectus (verb) observe

constituo, constituere, constitui, constitutus (verb) decide, establish

consumo, consumere, consumpsi, consumptus (verb) use up, consume, spend

contendo, contendere, contendi, contentus (verb) hold together, limit, enclose, keep, repress

contra (adv.; prep. + acc.) against

contumelia, contumeliae, f. (noun) mistreatment, outrage, injury

convenio, convenire, conveni, conventus (verb) come together, assemble

copia, coipiae, f. (noun) supply, abundance

copiae, copiarum, f. pl. (noun) troops

cornu, cornus, n. (noun) horn

corpus, corporis, n. (noun) body

cotidianus, cotidiana, cotidianum (adj.) daily, usual

cras (adv.) tomorrow

credo, credere, credidi, creditus (verb) believe, trust

Creta, Cretae, f. (proper noun) Crete

Creusa, Creusae, f. (proper noun) Creusa

cum (prep. + abl.) with; (conj.) when, while, since, although

cupiditas, cupiditatis, f. (noun) desire

Cupido, Cupidinis, m. (proper noun) Cupid

cupidus, cupida, cupidum (adj.) desirous, eager

cupio, cupere, cupivi, cupitus (verb) desire, wish, want

cur (adv.) why

cura, curae, f. (noun) care

curo, curare, curavi, curatus (verb) care for, cure

curro, currere, cucurri, cursus (verb) run

Cyclops, Cyclopis, m. (proper noun) Cyclops

D

Daedalus, Daedali, m. (proper noun) Dedalus

damno, damnare, damnavi, damnatus (verb) condemn, find guilty

de (prep. + abl.) about, concerning, down from

dea, deae, f. (noun) goddess

debeo, debere, debui, debitus (verb) owe, ought

decem (adj.) ten

December, Decembris, Decembre (adj.) of December

deditio, deditionis, f. (noun) surrender

dedo, dedere, dedidi, deditus (verb) give up, surrender

defendo, defendere, defendi, defensus (verb) ward off, repel, defend

defero, deferre, detuli, delatus (verb) carry off, bring away, report, offer

deinde (adv.) then, next

deleo, delere, delevi, deletus (verb) destroy, obliterate

deligo, deligere, delegi, delectus (verb) choose, select

demonstro, demonstrare, demonstravi, demonstratus (verb) point out, show

denique (adv.) finally, at last

descendo, descendere, descendi, descensus (verb) descend, come down

desero, deserere, deserui, deseritus (verb) desert, abandon

desiderium, desiderii or desideri, n. (noun) longing, loss, need

desisto, desistere, destiti, destitus (verb) cease, desist, stop

deterreo, deterrere, deterrui, deterritus (verb) frighten off, deter, prevent, hinder

deus, dei, m. (noun) god

dico, dicere, dixi, dictus (verb) say, speak

dictator, dictatoris, m. (noun) dictator

dies, diei, m. and f. (noun) day

difficilis, difficile (adj.) difficult, hard

difficultas, difficultatis, f. (noun) difficulty

diligenter (adv.) carefully

diligentia, diligentiae, f. (noun) diligence, care

diligo, diligere, dilexi, delectus (verb) value, love

discedo, discedere, discessi, discessus (verb) withdraw, go away, leave

disco, discere, didici (verb) learn

diu (adv.) long, for a long time

dives, divitis (adj.) rich

do, dare, dedi, datus (verb) give

doceo, docere, docui, doctus (verb) teach, show

doleo, dolere, dolui, dolitus (verb) grieve, be sorry

domi (adv.) at home

domina, dominae, f. (noun) mistress

dominus, domini, m. (noun) master

domus, domus, f. (noun) house, home

donec (conj.) until

donum, doni, n. (noun) gift, present

dormio, dormire, dormivi, dormitus (verb) sleep

dubito, dubitare, dubitavi, dubitatus (verb) doubt, hesitate, be uncertain

dubius, dubia, dubium (adj.) doubtful, uncertain

duco, ducere, duxi, ductus (verb) lead

dulcis, dulce (adj.) sweet

dum (conj.) while

duodecim (adj.) twelve

dux, ducis, m. (noun) leader

E

e, ex (prep. + abl.) from, out from

educo, educere, eduxi, eductus (verb) lead out

effero, efferre, extuli, elatus (verb) carry forth, bring out

effugio, effugere, effugi, effugitus (verb) flee away, escape

ego, mei (pronoun) I

egredior, egredi, egressus sum (verb) quit, surpass, go beyond

egregius, egregia, egregium (adj.) excellent, outstanding

emo, emere, emi, emptus (verb) buy

enim (conj.) for

enuntio, enuntiare, enuntiavi, enuntiatus (verb) speak out, reveal, make known

eo, ire, ii or ivi, itus (verb) go

epistola, epistolae, f. (noun) letter

eques, equitis, m. (noun) horseman, knight

equus, equi, m. (noun) horse

erro, errare, erravi, erratus (verb) be mistaken, lose one's way

et (conj.) and

et . . . et (conj.) both . . . and

etiam (conj.) even, also

etiamsi (conj.) even if

etsi (conj.) even if, although

Europa, Europae, f. (proper noun) Europe

Eurydice, Eurydices, f. (proper noun) Eurydice

Eurystheus, Eurysthei, m. (proper noun) Eurystheus

evenio, evenire, eveni, evenitus (verb) happen, come out

ex, e (prep. + abl.) out, out from

excito, excitare, excitavi, excitatus (verb) arouse, stir up

exeo, exire, exii, exitus (verb) avoid, go away, depart

exercitus, exercitus, m. (noun) army

existimo, existimare, existimavi, existimatus (verb) think, judge

experior, experiri, experitus sum (verb) test, try

expono, exponere, exposui, expositus (verb) set forth, exhibit, explain

exsolvo, exsolvere, exsolvi, exsolutus (verb) release, free

exspecto, exspectare, exspectavi, exspectatus (verb) await, expect, wait for

F

fabula, fabulae, f. (noun) story

facilis, facile (adj.) easy

facio, facere, feci, factus (verb) make, do

fama, famae, f. (noun) rumor, renown, report

familiaris, familiaris, m. or **f.** (noun) friend (gen. pl. **familiariium**)

fames, famis, f. (noun) famine, hunger (gen. pl. **famium**)

febris, febris, f. (noun) fever (gen. pl. **febrium**)

Februarius, Februaria, Februarium (adj.) of February

femina, feminae, f. (noun) woman

fero, ferre, tuli, latus (verb) carry, bear

fides, fidei, f. (noun) faith, plege

fido, fidere, fisus sum (verb) trust, believe, confide

filia, filiae, f. (noun) daughter

filius, filii or **fili, m.** (noun) son

fines, finium, m. pl. (noun) territory

finis, finis, m. (noun) end, border (gen. pl. **finium**)

finitimus, finitima, finitimum (adj.) neighboring

finitimus, finitimi, m. (noun) neighbor

fio, fieri, factus sum (verb) become, be done, be made

firmo, firmare, firmavi, firmatus (verb) strengthen, make firm

firmus, firma, firmum (adj.) firm, strong

flagito, flagitare, flagitavi, flagitatus (verb) demand

flumen, fluminis, n. (noun) river

fons, fontis, m. (noun) fountain, spring (gen. pl. **fontium**)

formica, formicae, f. (noun) ant

fortasse (adv.) perhaps

fortis, forte (adj.) brave, strong

fortuna, fortunae, f. (noun) fortune, fate, luck

forum, fori, n. (noun) forum, market place

fossa, fossae, f. (noun) ditch

frater, fratris, m. (noun) brother

frequentia, frequentiae, f. (noun) crowd

fructus, fructus, m. (noun) produce, fruit

frugaliter (adv.) temperately, frugally

frumentum, frumenti, n. (noun) grain

fuga, fugae, f. (noun) flight, escape

fugio, fugere, fugi, fugitus (verb) flee, run away, escape

fungor, fungi, functus sum (verb) perform, do

furor, furoris, m. (noun) rage, fury, passion

G

Gallia, Galliae, f. (proper noun) Gaul

Gallus, Galli, m. (proper noun) a Gaul

gaudeo, gaudere, gavisus sum (verb) rejoice

gaudium, gaudii or **gaudi, n.** (noun) joy

genus, generis, n. (noun) kind, class

Germania, Germaniae, f. (proper noun) Germany

Germanus, Germani, m. (proper noun) a German

gero, gerere, gessi, gestus (verb) carry on, wage

gladiator, gladiatoris, m. (noun) gladiator

gladius, gladii or **gladi, m.** (noun) sword

gloria, gloriae, f. (noun) glory

Graecia, Graeciae, f. (proper noun) Greece

Graecus, Graeca, Graecum (adj.) Greek

gratus, grata, gratum (adj.) pleasing

gravis, grave (adj.) heavy, severe, serious

H

habeo, habere, habui, habitus (verb) have, hold

habito, habitare, habitavi, habitatus (verb) dwell, live

haesito, haesitare, haesitavi, haesitatus (verb) hesitate, be at a loss

Hannibal, Hannibalis, m. (proper noun) Hannibal

Hellespontus, Hellesponti, m. (proper noun) the Hellespont

Helvetii, Helvetiorum, m. pl. (proper noun) the Helvetii

Hercules, Herculis, m. (proper noun) Hercules

heri (adv.) yesterday

Hero, Herus, f. (proper noun) Hero

Hesperides, Hesperidium, f. pl. (proper noun) the Hesperides

hesternus, hesterna, hesternum (adj.) yesterday

hic (adv.) here, in this place

hic, haec, hoc (adj.) this; latter; (pronoun) he, she, it

hiems, hiemis, f. (noun) winter

Hippomenes, Hippominis, m. (proper noun) Hippomenes

Hispania, Hispaniae, f. (proper noun) Spain

hodie (adv.) today

Homerus, Homeri, m. (proper noun) Homer

homo, hominis, m. (noun) man

honestus, honesta, honestum (adj.) honored, respected

hora, horae, f. (noun) hour

Horatius, Horati, m. (proper noun) Horatius

hortor, hortari, hortatus sum (verb) urge, encourage

hortus, horti, m. (noun) garden

hospes, hospitis, m. (noun) host, guest, friend

hostis, hostis, m. (noun) enemy (gen. pl. **hostium**)

huc (adv.) to this place, hither

I

iacio, iacere, ieci, iactus (verb) throw

iam (adv.) now, already

Ianuarius, Ianuaria, Ianuarium (adj.) of January

ibi (adv.) there, in that place

Icarus, Icari, m. (proper noun) Icarus

idem, eadem, idem (adj.) the same; (pronoun) he, she, it

idoneus, idonea, idoneum (adj.) fit, suitable

Idus, Iduum, f. pl. (proper noun) the Ides

ignis, ignis, m. (noun) fire (gen. pl. **ignium**)

ignoro, ignorare, ignoravi, ignoratus (verb) not know, be ignorant

ille, illa, illud (adj.) that; former; (pronoun) he, she, it

illustro, illustrare, illustravi, illustratus (verb) make clear, reveal

immortalis, immortale (adj.) immortal

impedimentum, impedimenti, n. (noun) hindrance

impedio, impedire, impedivi, impeditus (verb) hinder

imperator, imperatoris, m. (noun) commander, general, emperor

imperium, imperii or imperi, n. (noun) command

impero, imperare, imperavi, imperatus (verb) command, order

impetus, impetus, m. (noun) attack

in (prep. + abl.) in, on; (prep. + acc.) into, onto

incendo, incendere, incendi, incensus (verb) set fire to, burn

incito, incitare, incitavi, incitatus (verb) arouse, stir up, incite

incola, incolae, m. or f. (noun) inhabitant

incolo, incolere, incolui (verb) live in, reside

Inferi, Inferorum, m. pl. (noun) Those Below, the dead

infestus, infesta, infestum (adj.) threatening, dangerous, hostile

inimicus, inimica, inimicum (adj.) unfriendly

inimicus, inimici, m. (noun) personal enemy

initium, initii or initi, n. (noun) beginning, start

iniuria, iniuriae, f. (noun) injury, harm

in libertatem vindicare set free

inopia, inopiae, f. (noun) want, scarcity

insequor, insequi, insecutus sum (verb) follow after, pursue

instruo, instruere, instruxi, instructus (verb) draw up, form, train

insula, insulae, f. (noun) island

intelligo, intelligere, intellexi, intellectus (verb) understand

inter (prep. + acc.) among, between

intercludo, intercludere, interclusi, interclusus (verb) shut off, stop

interea (adv.) meanwhile

interficio, interficere, interfeci, interfectus (verb) kill

inutilis, inutile (adj.) useless, harmful

invenio, invenire, inveni, inventus (verb) find, come upon

ipse, ipsa, ipsum (adj.; pronoun) himself, herself, itself; very

is, ea, id (adj.; pronoun) he, she, it; that

iste, ista, istud (adj.; pronoun) that, that one of yours

ita (adv.) thus, so; yes

Italia, Italiae, f. (proper noun) Italy

itaque (adv.) and so, therefore

item (adv.) moreover, also

iter, intineris, n. (noun) journey, march, way

iterum (adv.) again

iubeo, iubere, iussi, iussus (verb) order, command

iudicium, iudicii, or iudici, n. (noun) judgment, sentence

iudico, iudicare, iudicavi, iudicatus (verb) judge, sentence, examine

Iulia, Iuliae, f. (proper noun) Julia

Iulius, Iulia, Iulium, m. (adj.) of Julius; Julian

Iunius, Iunia, Iunium (adj.) of June

Iuno, Iunonis, f. (proper noun) Juno

Iuppiter, Iovis, m. (proper noun) Jupiter

iureiuro, iureiurare, iureiuravi, iureiuratus (verb) swear

ius, iuris, n. (noun) right, authority

iuvo, iuvare, iuvi, iutus (verb) help, aid

K

Kalendae, Kalendarum, f. pl. (proper noun) the Kalends

L

labor, laboris, m. (noun) work, toil, labor

laboro, laborare, laboravi, laboratus (verb) work

labyrinthus, labyrinthi, m. (noun) labyrinth

laetus, laeta, laetum (adj.) happy

lana, lanae, f. (noun) wool

latinus, latina, latinum (adj.) Latin

Latinus, Latini, m. (proper noun) Latinus

Latium, Lati, n. (proper noun) Latium

Latobrigi, Latobrigorum, m. pl. (proper noun) Latobrigi

latus, lata, latum (adj.) wide

laudo, laudare, laudavi, laudatus (verb) praise

Leander, Leandri, m. (proper noun) Leander

legatus, legati, m. (noun) lieutenant, legate

legio, legionis, f. (noun) legion

lego, legere, legi, lectus (verb) read

lenitas, lenitatis, f. (noun) mercy, mildness, gentleness

lex, legis, f. (noun) law

libenter (adv.) gladly, with pleasure

liber, libera, liberum, (adj.) free

liber, libri, m. (noun) book

libero, liberare, liberavi, liberatus (verb) free, set free

lingua, linguae, f. (noun) language

littera, litterae, f. (noun) letter

loco, locare, locavi, locatus (verb) place, put

locus, loci, m. (noun) place

longus, longa, longum (adj.) long

loquor, loqui, locutus sum (verb) say, speak

ludus, ludi, m. (noun) game, school

luna, lunae, f. (noun) moon

lupa, lupae, f. or lupus, lupi, m. (noun) wolf

lux, lucis, f. (noun) light

M

magis (adv.) more

magnitudo, magnitudinis, f. (noun) greatness, vastness

magnopere (adv.) greatly

maior, maius (adj.) larger

maiores, maiorum, m. pl. (noun) ancestors, forefathers

Maius, Maia, Maium (adj.) of May

male (adv.) badly

malo, malle, malui (verb) prefer

malus, mala, malum (adj.) bad, evil

mane (adv.) in the morning

maneo, manere, mansi, mansus (verb) remain

manus, manus, f. (noun) hand; group

Marathonius, Marathonia, Marathonium (adj.) of Marathon

mare, maris, n. (noun) sea (gen. pl. marium)

maritus, mariti, m. (noun) husband

Martius, Martia, Martium (adj.) of Mars, of March

mater, matris, f. (noun) mother

matrimonium, matrimonii or matrimoni, n. (noun) marriage

maxime (adv.) most, especially

maximus, maxima, maximum (adj.) largest

medius, media, medium (adj.) middle, middle of

mehercule (interjection) by Hercules!

melior, melius (adj.) better

memoria, memoriae, f. (noun) memory

mens, mentis, f. (noun) mind (gen. pl. mentium)

Mercurius, Mercuri, m. (proper noun) Mercury

metuo, metuere, metui (verb) fear, be afraid

meus, mea, meum (adj.) my, mine

Midas, Midae, m. (proper noun) Midas

miles, militis, m. (noun) soldier

mille (adj.) thousand

mille passus (noun) mile

milia passuum (noun) miles

minime (adv.) by no means, not at all

minimus, minima, minimum (adj.) smallest

ministerium, ministerii or ministeri, n. (noun) service, work

minor, minus (adj.) smaller

Minos, Minois, m. (proper noun) Minos

Minotaurus, Minotauri, m. (proper noun) Minotaur

miser, misera, miserum (adj.) wretched, unhappy

misercordia, misercordiae, f. (noun) sympathy, pity

misereor, misereri, miseritus sum (verb) pity, feel sorry for

mitto, mittere, misi, missus (verb) send

modeste (adv.) moderately, modestly

modus, modi, m. (noun) manner, way

moneo, monere, monui, monitus (verb) warn, advise

mons, montis, m. (noun) mountain, mount (gen. pl. montium)

monstro, monstrare, monstravi, monstratus (verb) point out, show

mora, morae, f. (noun) delay

morior, mori, moritus sum (verb) die

mors, mortis, f. (noun) death (gen. pl. mortium)

mortalis, mortale (adj.) mortal

mortuus, mortua, mortuum (adj.) dead

moveo, movere, movi, motus (verb) move

mox (adv.) soon, presently

mulier, mulieris, f. (noun) woman

multitudo, multitudinis, f. (noun) great number, multitude

multo (adv.) much, by much

multus, multa, multum (adj.) much

murus, muri, m. (noun) wall

N

nam (conj.) for

narro, narrare, narravi, narratus (verb) tell, relate

nascor, nasci, natus sum (verb) be born

natio, nationis, f. (noun) nation

nato, natare, natavi, natatus (verb) swim

natura, naturae, f. (noun) nature

nauta, nautae, m. (noun) sailor

navigo, navigare, navigavi, navigatus (verb) sail, cruise

navis, navis, f. (noun) ship (gen. pl. **navium**)

-ne (enclitic particle) indicates a question

ne (adv.) that not, lest

necessaria, necessariae, f. (noun) relative, friend

necessarius, necessarii or necessari, m. (noun) relative, friend

neco, necare, necavi, necatus (verb) kill

nemo, neminis, m. (noun) no one

neque (conj.) and not

neque . . . neque (conj.) neither . . . nor

nescio, nescire, nescivi, nescitus (verb) not know, be ignorant of

Nicaea, Nicaeae, f. (proper noun) Nicaea

Nicomedia, Nicomediae, f. (proper noun) Nicomedia

nihil, nil, n. (indeclinable noun) nothing

nimis (adv.) very much, too much

nisi (conj.) if not, unless

noctu (adv.) at night

nolo, nolle, nolui (verb) wish not, be unwilling

nomen, nominis, n. (noun) name

non (adv.) not

Nonae, Nonarum, f. pl. (proper noun) the Nones

nonne (adv.) indicates a question expecting the answer "yes"

nos, nostrum (pronoun) we

noster, nostra, nostrum (adj.) our, ours

novem (adj.) nine

November, Novembris, Novembre (adj.) of November

novus, nova, novum (adj.) new

nox, noctis, f. (noun) night (gen. pl. **noctium**)

nullus, nulla, nullum (adj.) no, none

num (interrogative particle) whether; indicates a question expecting the answer "no"

numerus, numeri, m. (noun) number

numquam (adv.) never

nunc (adv.) now

nuntio, nuntiare, nuntiavi, nuntiatus (verb) announce, report

nuntius, nuntii or nunti, m. (noun) message, messenger

O

ob (prep. + acc.) on account of, because

obses, obsidis, m. (noun) hostage

obtineo, obtinere, obtinui, obtentus (verb) secure, obtain

occupo, occupare, occupavi, occupatus (verb) seize, take possession of

oceanus, oceani, m. (noun) ocean

October, Octobris, Octobre (adj.) of October

oculus, oculi, m. (noun) eye

odium, odii or odi, n. (noun) hatred

offendo, offendere, offendi, offensus (verb) wound, offend

officium, officii or offici, n. (noun) official job, official position

olim (adv.) formerly, once

omnis, omne (adj.) all, every

onus, oneris, n. (noun) weight, burden

opera, operae, f. (noun) service, pains, work

opinor, opinari, opinatus sum (verb) think, suppose

oportet, oportere, oportuit (impersonal verb) it is right, it is proper

oppidum, oppidi, n. (noun) town

opprimo, opprimere, oppressi, oppressus (verb) overcome, crush

oppugno, oppugnare, oppugnavi, oppugnatus (verb) attack

optimus, optima, optimum (adj.) best

opus, operis, n. (noun) work

oraculum, oraculi, n. (noun) oracle

ordo, ordinis, m. (noun) rank, order

oro, orare, oravi, oratus (verb) beg, pray

Orpheus, Orphei, m. (proper noun) Orpheus

otiosus, otiosa, otiosum (adj.) free, at leisure, not working

ovis, ovis, f. (noun) sheep (gen. pl. **ovium**)

P

pactum, pacti, n. (noun) way, manner

paene (adv.) almost, nearly

paeninsula, paeninsulae, f. (noun) peninsula

parens, parentis, m. or f. (noun) parent (gen. pl. **parentium**)

paro, parare, paravi, paratus (verb) prepare, get ready

parricidium, parricidii or parricidi, n. (noun) parricide, murder, treason

pars, partis, f. (noun) part (gen. pl. **partium**)

parum (adv.) too little, not enough

parvus, parva, parvum (adj.) small

pascor, pasci, pastus sum (verb) feed on, eat

passus, passus, m. (noun) pace

patefacio, patefacere, patefeci, patefactus (verb) throw open, bring to light

pater, patris, m. (noun) father

patior, pati, passus sum (verb) allow, grant, suffer

patria, patriae, f. (noun) native country

paulo (adv.) a little

pax, pacis, f. (noun) peace

pecunia, pecuniae, f. (noun) money

pedes, peditis, m. (noun) foot soldier

peior, peius (adj.) worse

per (prep. + acc.) through

perfero, perferre, pertuli, perlatus (verb) report

periculosus, periculosa, periculosum (adj.) dangerous, perilous

periculum, periculi, n. (noun) danger

permitto, permittere, permisi, permissus (verb) allow, permit

permoveo, permovere, permovi, permotus (verb) stir, move

perpetuus, perpetua, perpetuum (adj.) continuous, perpetual, uninterrupted

Persae, Persarum, m. pl. (proper noun) the Persians

persuadeo, persuadere, persuasi, persuasus (verb) persuade

pertimesco, pertimescere, pertimui (verb) fear, be alarmed at

pervenio, pervenire, perveni, perventus (verb) arrive

pes, pedis, m. (noun) foot

pessimus, pessima, pessimum (adj.) worst

peto, petere, petivi or petii, petitus (verb) seek

piscis, piscis, m. (noun) fish (gen. pl. **piscium**)

placo, placare, placavi, placatus (verb) calm, reconcile

plerusque, pleraque, plerumque (adj.) most

plurimum posse be most powerful

plurimus, plurima, plurimum (adj.) most

plus, pluris (adj.) more

plus posse be more powerful

Pluto, Plutonis, m. (proper noun) Pluto

poena, poenae, f. (noun) punishment, fine

poeta, poetae, m. (noun) poet

polliceor, polliceri, pollicitus sum (verb) promise

pollicitatio, pollicitationis, f. (noun) promise

Polyphemus, Polyphemi, m. (proper noun) Polyphemus

pomum, pomi, n. (noun) apple

pono, ponere, posui, positus (verb) put, place

pons, pontis, m. (noun) bridge (gen. pl. **pontium**)

populus, populi, m. (noun) people

porta, portae, f. (noun) gate, door, entrance

porto, portare, portavi, portatus (verb) carry

portus, portus, m. (noun) harbor, port

posco, poscere, poposci (verb) ask, beg, demand

possum, posse, posui (verb) be able

post (prep. + acc.) behind; (adv.) at the back of

postea (adv.) afterwards

posterus, postera, posterum (adj.) next, following

postquam (conj.) after, when

postremus, postrema, postremum (adj.) last, finally

postridie (adv.) on the next day

postumus, postuma, postumum (adj.) next, following

praeda, praedae, f. (noun) booty, plunder

praemium, praemii or praemi, n. (noun) reward

praesentia, praesentiae, f. (noun) presence, effect

praesidium, praesidii or praesidi, n. (noun) guard, garrison

praesto, praestare, praestavi, praestatus (verb) be better than, be superior to

pretium, pretii or preti, n. (noun) price

primum, primo (adv.) first, at first

primus, prima, primum (adj.) first

princeps, principis (adj.) chief; first, foremost

princeps, principis, m. (noun) chief, leader, emperor

pristinus, pristina, pristinum (adj.) former, earlier

prius (adv.) before, previously

priusquam (conj.) before

pro (prep. + abl.) in front of; instead of; for, on behalf of

proelium, proelii or proeli, n. (noun) battle

proficiscor, profisci, profectus sum (verb) go forth, depart

profiteor, profiteri, professus sum (verb) declare, acknowledge, say

profugio, profugere, profugi (verb) run away, flee, escape

prohibeo, prohibere, prohibui, prohibitus (verb) keep off, hinder, prohibit, prevent

propero, properare, properavi, properatus (verb) hurry, hasten

propinquus, propinqua, propinquum (adj.) near

propter (prep. + acc.) because, on account of

propterea (adv.) therefore, on that account

Proserpina, Proserpinae, f. (proper noun) Proserpina

provincia, provinciae, f. (noun) province

proximus, proxima, proximum (adj.) next, nearest, most recent

Psyche, Psyches, f. (proper noun) Psyche

publicus, publica, publicum (adj.) public, common

puella, puellae, f. (noun) girl

puer, pueri, m. (noun) boy

pugna, pugnae, f. (noun) fight

pugno, pugnare, pugnavi, pugnatus (verb) fight

pulcher, pulchra, pulchrum (adj.) pretty, beautiful

pulchritudo, pulchritudinis, f. (noun) beauty

purgo, purgare, purgavi, purgatus (verb) clean, remove, excuse

puto, putare, putavi, putatus (verb) think, believe

Pythia, Pythiae, f. (proper noun) Pythia

Q

quaero, quaerere, quaesivi, quaesitus (verb) ask, look for

quam (adv.) as possible; than

quam diu how long

quamquam (conj.) although

quamvis (conjl.) although

quantum (adj.) as much as

quantus, quanta, quantum (adj.) how much

quare (adv.) by what means, how, wherefore, therefore

-que (conj.) and

queror, queri, questus sum (verb) complain about

qui, quae, quod (pronoun) who, which, that; which, what

quia (conj.) because

quidam, quaedam, quiddam (adj.) a certain one; pl. some

quin but that

quis, quid (pronoun) who, what

quod (conj.) because

quoniam (conj.) because, now that

quoque (adv.) also

R

ratio, rationis, f. (noun) manner, fashion, reason

recido, recidere, reccidi (verb) recoil, fall

recipio, recipere, recepi, receptus (verb) take back, receive

recupero, recuperare, recuperavi, recuperatus (verb) recover, get back

recuso, recusare, recusavi, recusatus (verb) refuse, reject

reddeo, reddere, reddidi, reditus (verb) return, restore

reduco, reducere, reduxi, reductus (verb) lead back

refero, referre, retuli, relatus (verb) report, bring back

regina, reginae, f. (noun) queen

regio, regionis, f. (noun) region, boundary

regno, regnare, regnavi, regnatus (verb) rule

regnum, regni, n. (noun) kingdom

rego, regere, rexi, rectus (verb) rule

relinquo, relinquere, reliqui, relictus (verb) leave, leave behind

reliquus, reliqua, reliquum (adj.) remaining, the rest of

reperio, reperire, repperi, repertus (verb) find, discover

reporto, reportare, reportavi, reportatus (verb) carry back, bring back

res, rei, f. (noun) thing, matter, affair

res publica, rei publicae, f. (noun) republic, common good

rescisco, resciscere, rescii, rescitus (verb) learn, find out

restituo, restituere, restitui, restitutus (verb) restore, rebuild

retineo, retinere, retinui, retentus (verb) keep back, retain

revertor, reverti, reversus sum (verb) turn back, return

rex, regis, m. (noun) king

Rhenus, Rheni, m. (proper noun) the Rhine

ripa, ripae, f. (noun) river bank

robustus, robusta, robustum (adj.) strong, robust

Roma, Romae, f. (proper noun) Rome

Romanus, Romana, Romanum (adj.) Roman

Romanus, Romani, m. (proper noun) a Roman

ruri (adv.) in the country

rursus (adv.) backward, on the other hand

S

Sabini, Sabinorum, m. pl. (proper noun) the Sabines

saepe (adv.) often

sagitta, sagittae, f. (noun) arrow

sagittarius, sagittarii or sagittari, m. (noun) archer

salus, salutis, f. (noun) health, safety

saluto, salutare, salutavi, salutatus (verb) greet, welcome

salvus, salva, salvum (adj.) safe, well

sapientia, sapientiae, f. (noun) wisdom

satis (indeclinable adj.; adv.) enough

saxum, saxi, n. (noun) stone, rock

scio, scire, scivi, scitus (verb) know

scribo, scribere, scripsi, scriptus (verb) write

se (pronoun) him, her, it (reflexive)

sed (conj.) but

semper (adv.) always

senatus, senatus, m. (noun) senate

senex, senis (adj.) old, aged

sensus, sensus, m. (noun) sense, sensation, feeling

sentio, sentire, sensi, sensus (verb) see, perceive, realize

septem (adj.) seven

September, Septembris, Septembre (adj.) of September

septimus, septima, septimum (adj.) seventh

sequor, sequi, secutus sum (verb) follow

serpens, serpentis, f. (noun) snake, serpent

servo, servare, servavi, servatus (verb) save, preserve

servus, servi, m. (noun) slave, servant

severitas, severitatis, f. (noun) severity, strictness

sex (adj.) six

si (conj.) if

Sibyllinus, Sibyllina, Sibyllinum (adj.) Sibylline

sic (adv.) so, thus

signum, signi, n. (noun) signal, standard

Silenus, Sileni, m. (proper noun) Silenus

silva, silvae, f. (noun) forest, woods

similes, simile (adj.) like, similar

simulo, simulare, simulavi, simulatus (verb) pretend

sine (prep. + abl.) without

socius, socii or soci, m. (noun) comrade, ally

sol, solis, m. (noun) sun

soleo, solere, solitus sum (verb) be accustomed to

solum (adv.) alone, only

solus, sola, solum (adj.) alone, only

somnus, somni, m. (noun) sleep

soror, sororis, f. (noun) sister

Sparta, Spartae, f. (proper noun) Sparta

specto, spectare, spectavi, spectatus (verb) hope

spes, spei, f. (noun) hope

stella, stellae, f. (noun) star

sto, stare, steti, status (verb) stand

studium, studii or studi, n. (noun) zeal, eagerness

sub (prep. + abl. or acc.) under

sum, esse, fui, futurus (verb) be

summus, summa, summum (adj.) greatest, highest, top of

superbus, superba, superbum (adj.) proud, haughty

supero, superare, superavi, superatus (verb) surpass, overcome, conquer

superior, superius (adj.) higher, past, preceding

supra (adv.; prep. + acc.) over, above

suscipio, suscipere, suscepi, susceptus (verb) take up, undertake

suspicio, suspicere, suspexi, suspectus (verb) mistrust, suspect

suus, sua, suum (adj.) his, her, its, their

T

tabesco, tabescere, tabescui or tabui (verb) decay, melt away

taciturnitas, taciturnitatis, f. (noun) silence

tam (adv.) so

tamen (conj.) however, nevertheless

tametsi (conj.) even if

tandem (adv.) finally

tango, tangere, tetigi, tactus (verb) touch

tantus, tanta, tantum (adj.) so great

Tarquinius, Tarquini, m. (proper noun) Tarquinius

telum, teli, n. (noun) weapon

tempestas, tempestatis, f. (noun) storm, bad weather

templum, templi, n. (noun) temple

tempus, temporis, n. (noun) time

teneo, tenere, tenui, tentus (verb) hold, keep, have

terra, terrae, f. (noun) land, earth

terreo, terrere, terrui, territus (verb) frighten, scare, terrify

Thermopylae, Thermopylarum, f. pl. (proper noun) Thermopylae

Theseus, Thesei, m. (proper noun) Theseus

timeo, timere, timui (verb) fear, be afraid of

timidus, timida, timidum (adj.) timid

timor, timoris, m. (noun) fear, dread

tolero, tolerare, toleravi, toleratus (verb) bear, endure

tot (adj.) so many

totus, tota, totum (adj.) all, whole

trado, tradere, tradidi, traditus (verb) give up, surrender

traho, trahere, traxi, tractus (verb) drag, draw

trans (prep. + acc.) across

transeo, transire, transivi, transitus (verb) pass over, cross, desert

Troia, Troiae, f. (proper noun) Troy

tu, tui (pronoun) you

Tulingi, Tulingorum, m. pl. (proper noun) the Tulingi

tum (adv.) then, at that time

turris, turris, f. (noun) tower (gen. pl. turrium)

tuus, tua, tuum (adj.) your, yours (singular)

U

ubi (adv.) where, when

Ulixes, Ulixis, m. (proper noun) Ulysses

ultimus, ultima, ultimum (adj.) last, farthest

umerus, umeri, m. (noun) shoulder

umquam (adv.) ever

unde (adv.) from where, whence

unus, una, unum (adj.) one

urbs, urbis, f. (noun) city (gen. pl. urbium)

ut, uti (adv.) as; that, so that

uterque, utraque, utrumque (adj.) each, every

utilis, utile (adj.) useful

utinam (adv.) if only, would that

uxor, uxoris, f. (noun) wife

V

vaco, vacare, vacavi, vacatus (verb) be empty

vehementer (adv.) violently, eagerly

vel (conj.) or

vel . . . vel (conj.) either . . . or

venio, venire, veni, venitus (verb) come

ventus, venti, m. (noun) wind

Venus, Veneris, f. (proper noun) Venus

verbum, verbi, n. (noun) word

vereor, vereri, veritus sum (verb) fear

vero (adv.) truly, in truth

verto, vertere, verti, versus (verb) turn

vespera, vesperae, f. (noun) evening

vester, vestra, vestrum (adj.) your, yours (plural)

veto, vetare, vetavi, vetatus (verb) forbid

vetus, veteris (adj.) old, aged

via, viae, f. (noun) road, way, street

victoria, victoriae, f. (noun) victory

vicus, vici, m. (noun) village, street

video, videre, vidi, visus (verb) see

vinco, vincere, vici, victus (verb) conquer

vindico, vindicare, vindicavi, vindicatus (verb) defend, protect

vir, viri, m. (noun) man

virtus, virtutis, f. (noun) courage, virtue

vis, vis, f. (noun) force

vita, vitae, f. (noun) life

vito, vitare, vitavi, vitatus (verb) avoid

vivo, vivere, vixi, victus (verb) live

voco, vocare, vocavi, vocatus (verb) call

volo, velle, volui (verb) wish, be willing

volo, volare, volavi, volatus (verb) fly

vos, vestrum (pronoun) you (plural)

vox, vocis, f. (noun) voice

vulnero, vulnerare, vulneravi, vulneratus (verb) wound, hurt

vulnus, vulneris, n. (noun) wound

Z

Zephyrus, Zephyri, m. (proper noun) Zephyr, west wind

A

abandon, desert **desero, deserere, deserui, deseritus**

abide, linger, stay, remain **commoror, commorari, commoratus sum**

able, be able **possum, posse, posui**

about **circiter**

about, around **circum**

about, concerning; down from **de**

above, over **supra**

absent, be away from **absum, abesse, abfui**

absent from, lack, be without **careo, carere, carui, caritus**

abundance, supply **copia, coipiae, f.**

Acco **Acco, Acconis, m.**

accustomed to **soleo, solere, solitus sum**

acknowledge, declare, say **profiteor, profiteri, professus sum**

across **trans**

active, keen, sharp **acer, acris, acre**

add, put on **addo, addere, addidi, additus**

added, agree, approach, support **accedo, accedere, accessi, accessurus**

address, call, name **appello, apellare, apellavi, appellatus**

administer, rule, manage, control **administro, administrare, administravi, administratus**

adore, worship **adoro, adorare, adoravi, adoratus**

advice, plan **consilium, consilii or consili, n.**

advise, warn **moneo, monere, monui, monitus**

affair, thing, matter **res, rei, f.**

affirm, assert, strengthen **adfirmo, adfirmare, adfirmavi, adfirmatus**

Africa **Africa, Africae, f.**

after, when **postquam**

afterwards **postea**

again **iterum**

against **contra**

aged, old **senex, senis**

aged, old **vetus, veteris**

agree, added, approach, support **accedo, accedere, accessi, accessurus**

agreement **consensus, consensus, m.**

aid, help **auxilium, auxilii or auxili, n.**

aid, help **iuvo, iuvare, iuvi, iutus**

alarmed at, fear **pertimesco, pertimescere, pertimui**

all, every **omnis, omne**

all, whole **totus, tota, totum**

Allobroges **Allobroges, Allobrogum, m. pl.**

allow, grant, withdraw **concedo, concedere, concessi, concessum**

allow, grant, suffer **patior, pati, passus sum**

allow, permit **permitto, permittere, permisi, permissus**

ally, comrade **socius, socii or soci, m.**

almost, nearly **paene**

alone, only **solum**

alone, only **solus, sola, solum**

already, now **iam**

also **quoque**

also, and also **atque, ac**

also, even **etiam**

also, moreover **item**

although **quamquam**

although **quamvis**

although, when, while, since; with **cum**

although, even if **etsi**

always **semper**

among, in the presence of **apud**

among, between **inter**

amphitheater **amphitheatrum, amphitheatri, n.**

ancestors, forefathers **maiores, maiorum, m. pl.**

ancient, old **antiquus, antiqua, antiquum**

and also, also **atque, ac**

and **et**

and **-que**

and not **neque**

and so, therefore **itaque**

animal **animal, animalis, n.**

announce, report **nuntio, nuntiare, nuntiavi, nuntiatus**

another, other **alius, alia, aliud**

ant **formica, formicae, f.**

anyone, anything; someone, something **aliquis, aliquid**

Apollo **Apollo, Apollonis, m.**

apple **pomum, pomi, n.**

apprehend, discover, seize **comprehendo, comprehendere, comprehendi, comprehensus**

approach, added, to agree, support **accedo, accedere, accessi, accessurus** approach, arrival **adventus, adventus, m.**

approach, attack **aggredior, aggredi, aggressus sum**

April, of April **Aprilis, Aprile**

archer **sagittarius, sagittarii or sagittari, m.**

arena, sand **arena, arenae, f.**

Ariadne **Ariadne, Ariadnes, f.**

arm **armo, armare, armavi, armatus**

arms, weapons **arma, armae, n. pl.**

army **exercitus, exercitus, m.**

around, about **circum**

arouse, stir up **excito, excitare, excitavi, excitatus**

arouse, stir up, incite **incito, incitare, incitavi, incitatus**

arrival, approach **adventus, adventus, m.**

arrive **pervenio, pervenire, perveni, perventus**

arrive at, come to, reach **advenio, advenire, adveni, adventus**

arrow **sagitta, sagittae, f.**

as; that, so that **ut, uti**

as much as **quantum**

as possible; than **quam**

ascertain, learn **comperio, comperire, comperi, compertus**

ask, look for **quaero, quaerere, quaesivi, quaesitus**

assemble, gather together **congrego, congregare, congregavi, congregatus**

assemble, come together **convenio, convenire, conveni, conventus**

assert, affirm, strengthen **adfirmo, adfirmare, adfirmavi, adfirmatus**

at back of, behind **post**

at first, first **primum, primo**

at home **domi**

at last, finally **denique**

at leisure, free, not working **otiosus, otiosa, otiosum**

at night **noctu**

at that time, then **tum**

Atalanta **Atalanta, Atalantae, f.**

Athens **Athenae, Athenarum, f. pl.**

Atlas **Atlas, Atlantis, m.**

attack, approach **aggredior, aggredi, aggressus sum**

attack **impetus, impetus, m.**

attack **oppugno, oppugnare, oppugnavi, oppugnatus**

attack; seek, look for **peto, petere, petivi or petii, petitus**

attempt, try **conor, conari, conatus sum**

August, of August **Augustus, Augusta, Augustum**

Aurelian **Aurelius, Aurelia, Aurelium**

authority, power, prestige **auctoritas, auctoritatis, f.**

authority, right **ius, iuris, n.**

avoid, go away, depart **exeo, exire, exii, exitus**

avoid **vito, vitare, vitavi, vitatus**

await, expect, wait for **exspecto, exspectare, exspectavi, exspectatus**

away from, from; by **a, ab**

B

Bacchus **Bacchus, Bacchi, m.**

backward, on the other hand **rursus**

bad, evil **malus, mala, malum**

bad weather, storm **tempestas, tempestatis, f.**

badly **male**

band, group; hand **manus, manus, f.**

battle **proelium, proelii or proeli, n.**

battle line **acies, aciei, f.**

barbarian **barbarus, barbari, m.**

barbarian, savage, uncivilized **barbarus, barbara, barbarum**

be **sum, esse, fui, futurus**

be able **possum, posse, posui**

be afraid, fear **metuo, metuere, metui**

be afraid of, fear **timeo, timere, timui**

be better than, be superior to **praesto, praestare, praestavi, praestatus**

be born **nascor, nasci, natus sum**

be empty **vaco, vacare, vacavi, vacatus**

be mistaken, lose one's way, wander **erro, errare, erravi, erratus**

be more powerful **plus posse**

be most powerful **plurimum posse**

be unwilling, wish not, not want **nolo, nolle, nolui**

be willing, wish **volo, velle, volui**

bear, carry **fero, ferre, tuli, latus**

bear, endure **tolero, tolerare, toleravi, toleratus**

beautiful, pretty **pulcher, pulchra, pulchrum**

beauty **pulchritudo, pulchritudinis, f.**

because **quod**

because, now that **quoniam**

because, on account of **ob**

because, on account of **propter**

because **quia**

become, be done, be made **fio, fieri, factus sum**

before, in front of **ante**

before **antea**

before **antequam**

before, previously **prius**

before **priusquam**

beg, pray **oro, orare, oravi, oratus**

beg, demand, ask **posco, poscere, poposci**

beginning, start **initium, initii or initi, n.**

behind, at the back of **post**

believe, trust **credo, credere, credidi, creditus**

believe, confide, trust **fido, fidere, fisus sum**

believe, think **puto, putare, putavi, putatus**

Below (Those Below), the dead **Inferi, Inferorum, m. pl.**

benevolence, goodness, kindness **bonitas, bonitatis, f.**

best **optimus, optima, optimum**

better **melior, melius**

better than, be superior to **praesto, praestare, praestavi, praestatus**

between, among **inter**

beware of, guard against **caveo, cavere, cavi, cautus**

body **corpus, corporis, n.**

bold **audax, audacis**

boldness, daring **audacia, audaciae, f.**

book **liber, libri, m.**

booty, plunder **praeda, praedae, f.**

border, end **finis, finis, m.**

born, be born **nascor, nasci, natus sum**

both . . . and **et . . . et**

boundary, region **regio, regionis, f.**

box, chest **arca, arcae, f.**

boy **puer, pueri, m.**

brave, strong **fortis, forte**

bridge **pons, pontis, m. (gen. pl. pontium)**

brief, short **brevis, breve**

bright, clear, famous **clarus, clara, clarum**

bring, carry towards **adfero, adferre, attuli, adlatus**

bring away, carry off, report, offer **defero, deferre, detuli, delatus**

bring back, report **refero, referre, retuli, relatus**

bring back, carry back, **reporto, reportare, reportavi, reportatus**

bring out, carry forth **effero, efferre, extuli, elatus**

bring to light, throw open **patefacio, patefacere, patefeci, patefactus**

bring together, compare **comparo, comparare, comparavi, comparatus**

bring together, collect **confero, conferre, contuli, conlatus**

Britain **Britannia, Britanniae, f.**

bronze **aenus, aena, aenum**

brother **frater, fratris, m.**

build **aedifico, aedificare, aedificavi, aedificatus**

building **aedificium, aedificii or aedifici, n.**

burden, weight **onus, oneris, n.**

burn, be on fire **ardeo, ardere, arsi, arsus**

burn, set fire to **incendo, incendere, incendi, incensus**

but **at**

but **sed**

but, however **autem**

but that **quin**

buy **emo, emere, emi, emptus**

by; from, away from **a, ab**

by Hercules! **mehercule**

by much, much **multo**

by no means, least of all, not at all **minime**

by what means, how, wherefore, therefore **quare**

C

call, address, name **appello, appellare, apellavi, appellatus**

call **voco, vocare, vocavi, vocatus**

calm, reconcile **placo, placare, placavi, placatus**

camp **castra, castrorum, n. pl.**

captive **captivus, captivi, m.**

capture, seize, take **capio, capere, cepi, captus**

care **cura, curae, f.**

care, diligence **diligentia, diligentiae, f.**

care for, cure **curo, curare, curavi, curatus**

carefully **diligenter**

Carnutes **Carnutes, Carnutum, m. pl.**

carry, bear **fero, ferre, tuli, latus**

carry **porto, portare, portavi, portatus**

carry back, bring back **reporto, reportare, reportavi, reportatus**

carry forth, bring out **effero, efferre, extuli, elatus**

carry off, bring away, report, offer **defero, deferre, detuli, delatus**

carry on, wage **gero, gerere, gessi, gestus**

carry out, complete, finish **conficio, conficere, confeci, confectus**

carry towards, bring **adfero, adferre, attuli, adlatus**

catch sight of, observe **conspicio, conspicere, conspexi, conspectus**

catch up with, follow **consequor, consequi, consecutus sum**

cause, reason **causa, causae, f.**

cave **antrum, antri, n.**

cease, desist, stop **desisto, desistere, destiti, destitus**

Cerberus **Cerberus, Cerberi, m.**

Ceres **Ceres, Cereris, f.**

certain, sure **certus, certa, certum**

certain one; some (pl.) **quidam, quaedam, quiddam**

certainly, surely, indeed **certe**

Charon **Charon, Charontis, m.**

chest, box **arca, arcae, f.**

chief; first, foremost **princeps, principis**

chief, leader, emperor **princeps, principis, m.**

choose, select **deligo, deligere, delegi, delectus**

Cincinnatus **Cincinnatus, Cincinnati, m.**

citizen **civis, civis, m. and f.**

city **urbs, urbis, f. (gen. pl. urbium)**

class, kind **genus, generis, n.**

clean, remove, excuse **purgo, purgare, purgavi, purgatus**

clear, famous, bright **clarus, clara, clarum**

collect, drive, compel **cogo, cogere, coegi, coactus**

collect, bring together **confero, conferre, contuli, conlatus**

collect, look for **conquiro, conquirere, conquisivi, conquisitus**

Colosseum **Colosseum, Colossei, n.**

come **venio, venire, veni, venitus**

come down, descend **descendo, descendere, descendi, descensus**

come out, happen **evenio, evenire, eveni, evenitus**

come to, reach, arrive at **advenio, advenire, adveni, adventus**

come together, assemble **convenio, convenire, conveni, conventus**

come upon, find **invenio, invenire, inveni, inventus**

command **imperium, imperii or imperi, n.**

command, order **impero, imperare, imperavi, imperatus**

command, order **iubeo, iubere, iussi, iussus**

commander, general, emperor **imperator, imperatoris, m.**

common, public **communis, commune**

common, public **publicus, publica, publicum**

common good, republic **res publica, rei publicae, f.**

compare, bring together **comparo, comparare, comparavi, comparatus**

compel, collect, drive **cogo, cogere, coegi, coactus**

complain about **queror, queri, questus sum**

complete, finish, carry out **conficio, conficere, confeci, confectus**

comrade, ally **socius, socii or soci, m.**

concerning, about, down from **de**

condemn, find guilty **damno, damnare, damnavi, damnatus**

confide, believe, trust **fido, fidere, fisus sum**

confirm, establish, strengthen **confirmo, confirmare, confirmavi, confirmatus**

conquer, surpass, overcome **supero, superare, superavi, superatus**

conquer **vinco, vincere, vici, victus**

consider, discuss **agito, agitare, agitavi, agitatus**

consider, think **cogito, cogitare, cogitavi, cogatatus**

conspiracy, plot **coniurati, coniurationis, f.**

consume, spend, use up **consumo, consumere, consumpsi, consumptus**

continuous, perpetual, uninterrupted **perpetuus, perpetua, perpetuum**

control, rule, manage **administro, administrare, administravi, administratus**

cottage, house **casa, casae, f.**

council **concilium, concilii or concili, n.**

courage, virtue **virtus, virtutis, f.**

Crete **Creta, Cretae, f.**

Creusa **Creusa, Creusae, f.**

cross, pass over, desert **transeo, transire, transivi, transitus**

crowd **frequentia, frequentiae, f.**

cruise, sail **navigo, navigare, navigavi, navigatus**

crush, overcome **opprimo, opprimere, oppressi, oppressus**

cry, shout **clamo, clamare, clamavi, clamatus**

cry aloud, proclaim **clamito, clamitare, clamitavi, clamitatus**

Cupid **Cupido, Cupidinis, m.**

cure, care for **curo, curare, curavi, curatus**

Cyclops **Cyclops, Cyclopis, m.**

D

daily, usual **cotidianus, cotidiana, cotidianum**

danger **periculum, periculi, n.**

dangerous, threatening, hostile **infestus, infesta, infestum**

dangerous, perilous **periculosus, periculosa, periculosum**

dare **audeo, audere, ausus sum**

daring, boldness **audacia, audaciae, f.**

daughter **filia, filiae, f.**

day **dies, diei, m. and f.**

day following, on the next day **postridie**

dead, Those Below **Inferi, Inferorum, m. pl.**

dead **mortuus, mortua, mortuum**

death **mors, mortis, f.**

decay, melt away **tabesco, tabescere, tabescui or tabui**

December, of December **December, Decembris, Decembre**

decide, establish **constituo, constituere, constitui, constitutus**

declare, acknowledge, say **profiteor, profiteri, professus sum**

Dedalus **Daedalus, Daedali, m.**

deep, high **altus, alta, altum**

defend, ward off, repel **defendo, defendere, defendi, defensus**

defend, protect **vindico, vindicare, vindicavi, vindicatus**

delay **mora, morae, f.**

demand **flagito, flagitare, flagitavi, flagitatus**

demand, beg, ask **posco, poscere, poposci**

depart, avoid, go away **exeo, exire, exii, exitus**

depart, go forth **proficiscor, profisci, profectus sum**

descend, come down **descendo, descendere, descendi, descensus**

desert, abandon **desero, deserere, deserui, deseritus**

desert, pass over, cross **transeo, transire, transivi, transitus**

desire **cupiditas, cupiditatis, f.**

desire, wish, want **cupio, cupere, cupivi, cupitus**

desirous, eager **cupidus, cupida, cupidum**

desist, cease, stop **desisto, desistere, destiti, destitus**

destroy, obliterate **deleo, delere, delevi, deletus**

deter, prevent, hinder, frighten off **deterreo, deterrere, deterrui, deterritus**

dictator **dictator, dictatoris, m.**

die **morior, mori, moritus sum**

difficult, hard **difficilis, difficile**

difficulty **difficultas, difficultatis, f.**

diligence, care **diligentia, diligentiae, f.**

discover, apprehend, seize **comprehendo, comprehendere, comprehendi, comprehensus**

discover, find **reperio, reperire, repperi, repertus**

discuss, consider **agito, agitare, agitavi, agitatus**

ditch **fossa, fossae, f.**

do, make **facio, facere, feci, factus**

do, perform **fungor, fungi, functus sum**

dog **canis, canis, m. and f.**

door, gate, entrance **porta, portae, f.**

doubt, hesitate, be uncertain **dubito, dubitare, dubitavi, dubitatus**

doubtful, uncertain **dubius, dubia, dubium**

down from; about, concerning **de**

downfall, fate **casus, casus, m.**

drag, draw **traho, trahere, traxi, tractus**

draw up, form, train **instruo, instruere, instruxi, instructus**

dread, fear **timor, timoris, m.**

drive, collect, compel **cogo, cogere, coegi, coactus**

dwell, live **habito, habitare, habitavi, habitatus**

E

each, every **uterque, utraque, utrumque**

eager, desirous **cupidus, cupida, cupidum**

eagerly, violently **vehementer**

eagerness, zeal **studium, studii or studi, n.**

earlier, former **pristinus, pristina, pristinum**

earth, land **terra, terrae, f.**

easy **facilis, facile**

eat, feed on **pascor, pasci, pastus sum**

effect, presence **praesentia, praesentiae, f.**

either . . . or **aut . . . aut**

either . . . or **vel . . . vel**

equal, level, fair **aequus, aequa, aequum**

emperor, commander, general **imperator, imperatoris, m.**

emperor, chief, leader **princeps, principis, m.**

empty **vaco, vacare, vacavi, vacatus**

enclose, hold together, limit, keep, repress **contendo, contendere, contendi, contentus**

encourage, urge **hortor, hortari, hortatus sum**

end, border **finis, finis, m.**

endure, bear **tolero, tolerare, toleravi, toleratus**

enemy **hostis, hostis, m.** (gen. pl. **hostium**)

enemy (personal) **inimicus, inimici, m.**

enlarge, increase **augeo, augere, auxi, auctus**

enough **satis**

entrance, gate, door **porta, portae, f.**

escape, flee away **effugio, effugere, effugi, effigitus**

escape, flight **fuga, fugae, f.**

escape, flee, run away **fugio, fugere, fugi, fugitus**

escape, run away, flee **profugio, profugere, profugi**

especially, most **maxime**

establish, strengthen, confirm **confirmo, confirmare, confirmavi, confirmatus**

establish, decide **constituo, constituere, constitui, constitutus**

Europe **Europa, Europae, f.**

Eurydice **Eurydice, Eurydices, f.**

Eurystheus **Eurystheus, Eurysthei, m.**

even, also **etiam**

even if **etiamsi**

even if, although **etsi**

every, all **omnis, omne**

evil, bad **malus, mala, malum**

examine, judge, sentence **iudico, iudicare, iudicavi, iudicatus**

excellent, outstanding **egregius, egregia, egregium**

excuse, clean, remove **purgo, purgare, purgavi, purgatus**

exhibit, explain, set forth **expono, exponere, exposui, expositus**

expect, await, wait for **exspecto, exspectare, exspectavi, exspectatus** eye **oculus, oculi, m.**

even if **tametsi**

evening **vespera, vesperae, f.**

ever **umquam**

every, each **uterque, utraque, utrumque**

F

fair, equal, level **aequus, aequa, aequum**

faith, plege **fides, fidei, f.**

fall **cado, cadere, cecidi, casus**

fall, recoil **recido, recidere, reccidi**

famine, hunger **fames, famis, f.**

famous, bright. clear **clarus, clara, clarum**

farmer **agricola, agricolae, m.**

farthest, last **ultimus, ultima, ultimum**

fashion, manner, reason **ratio, rationis, f.**

fate, downfall **casus, casus, m.**

fate, fortune, luck **fortuna, fortunae, f.**

father **pater, patris, m.**

fear, be afraid **metuo, metuere, metui**

fear, be afraid of **timeo, timere, timui**

fear, be alarmed at **pertimesco, pertimescere, pertimui**

fear, dread **timor, timoris, m.**

fear **vereor, vereri, veritus sum**

February, of February **Februarius, Februaria, Februarium**

feed on, eat **pascor, pasci, pastus sum**

feel, perceive, realize **sentio, sentire, sensi, sensus**

feel sorry for, pity **misereor, misereri, miseritus sum**

feeling, sense, sensation **sensus, sensus, m.**

fever **febris, febris, f.**

field **ager, agri, m.**

fight **pugna, pugnae, f.**

fight **pugno, pugnare, pugnavi, pugnatus**

finally **tandem**

finally, at last **denique**

finally, last **postremus, postrema, postremum**

find, come upon **invenio, invenire, inveni, inventus**

find, discover **reperio, reperire, repperi, repertus**

find guilty, condemn **damno, damnare, damnavi, damnatus**

find out, learn **rescisco, resciscere, rescii, rescitus**

fine, punishment **poena, poenae, f.**

finish, complete, carry out **conficio, conficere, confeci, confectus**

fire **ignis, ignis, m.**

firm, strong **firmus, firma, firmum**

first, at first **primum, primo**

first **primus, prima, primum**

first, foremost; chief **princeps, principis**

fish **piscis, piscis, m.**

fit, suitable **idoneus, idonea, idoneum**

flee, run away, escape **fugio, fugere, fugi, fugitus**

flee, run away, escape **profugio, profugere, profugi**

flee away, escape **effugio, effugere, effugi, effugitus**

fleet **classis, classis, f.**

flight, escape **fuga, fugae, f.**

fly **volo, volare, volavi, volatus**

follow **sequor, sequi, secutus sum**

follow, catch up with **consequor, consequi, consecutus sum**

follow after, pursue **insequor, insequi, insecutus sum**

following, next **posterus, postera, posterum**

following, next **postumus, postuma, postumum**

food **cibus, cibi, m.**

foot **pes, pedis, m.**

foot soldier **pedes, peditis, m.**

for **enim**

for **nam**

for, on behalf of; in front of; instead of **pro**

for a long time, long **diu**

forbid **veto, vetare, vetavi, vetatus**

force **vis, vis, f.**

forefathers, ancestors **maiores, maiorum, m. pl.**

foremost, first; chief **princeps, principis**

forest, woods **silva, silvae, f.**

form, draw up, train **instruo, instruere, instruxi, instructus**

former, that; he, she, it **ille, illa, illud**

former, earlier **pristinus, pristina, pristinum**

formerly, once **olim**

fortune, fate, luck **fortuna, fortunae, f.**

forum, market place **forum, fori, n.**

fountain, spring **fons, fontis, m.**

free **liber, libera, liberum**

free, release **exsolvo, exsolvere, exsolvi, exsolutus**

free, set free **libero, liberare, liberavi, liberatus**

free, at leisure, not working **otiosus, otiosa, otiosum**

friend **amicus, amici, m.**

friend **familiaris, familiaris, m. or f.**

friend, host, guest **hospes, hospitis, m.**

friend, relative **necessaria, necessariae, f.**

friend, relative **necessarius, necessarii or necessari, m.**

friendly **amicus, amica, amicum**

frighten, scare, terrify **terreo, terrere, terrui, territus**

frighten off, deter, prevent, hinder **deterreo, deterrere, deterrui, deterritus**

from, away from; by **a, ab**

from, out from **e, ex**

from where, whence **unde**

frugally, temperately **frugaliter**

fruit, produce **fructus, fructus, m.**

G

gain, obtain, reach **adsequor, adsequi, adsecutus sum**

game, school **ludus, ludi, m.**

garden **hortus, horti, m.**

garrison, guard **praesidium, praesidii or praesidi, n.**

gate, door, entrance **porta, portae, f.**

gather together, assemble **congrego, congregare, congregavi, congregatus**

Gaul **Gallia, Galliae, f.**

a Gaul **Gallus, Galli, m.**

general, commander, emperor **imperator, imperatoris, m.**

gentleness, mercy, mildness **lenitas, lenitatis, f.**

German **Germanus, Germani, m.**

Germany **Germania, Germaniae, f.**

get back, recover **recupero, recuperare, recuperavi, recuperatus**

get ready, prepare **paro, parare, paravi, paratus**

gift, present **donum, doni, n.**

girl **puella, puellae, f.**

give **do, dare, dedi, datus**

give up, surrender **dedo, dedere, dedidi, deditus**

give up, surrender **trado, tradere, tradidi, traditus**

gladiator **gladiator, gladiatoris, m.**

gladly, with pleasure **libenter**

glory **gloria, gloriae, f.**

go **eo, ire, ii or ivi, itus**

go away **abeo, abire, abii, abitus**

go away, leave, withdraw **discedo, discedere, discessi, discessus**

go away, avoid, depart **exeo, exire, exii, exitus**

go beyond, quit, surpass **egredior, egredi, egressus sum**

go forth, depart **proficiscor, profisci, profectus sum**

god **deus, dei, m.**

goddess **dea, deae, f.**

go away, withdraw, yield **cedo, cedere, cessi, cessus**

gold **aurum, auri, n.**

golden **aureus, aurea, aureum**

good **bonus, bona, bonum**

goodness, kindness, benevolence **bonitas, bonitatis, f.**

grain **frumentum, frumenti, n.**

grant, allow, withdraw **concedo, concedere, concessi, concessum**

grant, allow, suffer **patior, pati, passus sum**

great number, multitude **multitudo, multitudinis, f.**

greatest, highest, top of **summus, summa, summum**

greatly **magnopere**

greatness, vastness **magnitudo, magnitudinis, f.**

Greece **Graecia, Graeciae, f.**

Greek **Graecus, Graeca, Graecum**

greet, welcome **saluto, salutare, salutavi, salutatus**

grieve, be sorry **doleo, dolere, dolui, dolitus**

group, band; hand **manus, manus, f.**

guard, garrison **praesidium, praesidii or praesidi, n.**

guard against, beware of **caveo, cavere, cavi, cautus**

guest, host, friend **hospes, hospitis, m.**

H

hand; group, band **manus, manus, f.**

Hannibal **Hannibal, Hannibalis, m.**

happen **accido, accidere, accidi, accisus**

happen, come out **evenio, evenire, eveni, evenitus**

happy **laetus, laeta, laetum**

harbor, port **portus, portus, m.**

hard, difficult **difficilis, difficile**

harm, injury **iniuria, iniuriae, f.**

harmful, useless **inutilis, inutile**

hasten, hurry **propero, properare, properavi, properatus**

hatred **odium, odii or odi, n.**

haughty, proud **superbus, superba, superbum**

have, hold **habeo, habere, habui, habitus**

have, hold, keep **teneo, tenere, tenui, tentus**

he, she, it; this **hic, haec, hoc**

he, she, it; that **is, ea, id**

head, leader **caput, capitis, n.**

health, safety **salus, salutis, f.**

heaven, sky **caelum, caeli, n.**

heavy, severe, serious **gravis, grave**

Hellespont **Hellespontus, Hellesponti, m.**

help, aid **auxilium, auxilii or auxili, n.**

help, aid **iuvo, iuvare, iuvi, iutus**

Helvetii **Helvetii, Helvetiorum, m. pl.**

her, him, it (reflexive) **se**

her, his, its, their **suus, sua, suum**

Hercules **Hercules, Herculis, m.**

here, to be present **adsum, adesse, adfui**

here, in this place **hic**

Hero **Hero, Herus, f.**

herself, himself, itself; very **ipse, ipsa, ipsum**

hesitate, doubt, be uncertain **dubito, dubitare, dubitavi, dubitatus** hesitate, be at a loss **haesito, haesitare, haesitavi, haesitatus**

Hesperides **Hesperides, Hesperidium, f. pl.**

hidden, secret **clandestinus, clandestina, clandestinum**

high, deep **altus, alta, altum**

higher, past, preceding **superior, superius**

highest, top of, greatest **summus, summa, summum**

hill **collis, collis, m.**

him, her, it (reflexive) **se**

himself, herself, itself; very **ipse, ipsa, ipsum**

hinder, prevent, frighten off, deter **deterreo, deterrere, deterrui, deterritus**

hinder **impedio, impedire, impedivi, impeditus**

hinder, keep off, prohibit, prevent **prohibeo, prohibere, prohibui, prohibitus**

hindrance **impedimentum, impedimenti, n.**

Hippomenes **Hippomenes, Hippominis, m.**

his, her, its, their **suus, sua, suum**

Hither, to this place **huc**

hold, have **habeo, habere, habui, habitus**

hold, keep, have **teneo, tenere, tenui, tentus**

hold together, limit, enclose, keep, repress **contendo, contendere, contendi, contentus**

home, house **domus, domus, f.**

Homer **Homerus, Homeri, m.**

honored, respected **honestus, honesta, honestum**

hope **specto, spectare, spectavi, spectatus**

hope **spes, spei, f.**

Horatius **Horatius, Horati, m.**

horn **cornu, cornus, n.**

horse **equus, equi, m.**

horseman, knight **eques, equitis, m.**

host, guest, friend **hospes, hospitis, m.**

hostage **obses, obsidis, m.**

hostile, threatening, dangerous **infestus, infesta, infestum**

hour **hora, horae, f.**

house, cottage **casa, casae, f.**

house, home **domus, domus, f.**

how, by what means, wherefore, therefore **quare**

how long **quam diu**

how much **quantus, quanta, quantum**

however, but **autem**

however, nevertheless **tamen**

hunger, famine **fames, famis, f.**

hurry **accelero, accelerare, acceleravi, acceleratus**

hurry, hasten **propero, properare, properavi, properatus**

hurt, wound **vulnero, vulnerare, vulneravi, vulneratus**

husband **maritus, mariti, m.**

I

I **ego, mei**

Icarus **Icarus, Icari, m.**

Ides **Idus, Iduum, f. pl.**

if **si**

if not, unless **nisi**

if only, would that **utinam**

ignorant, not know **ignoro, ignorare, ignoravi, ignoratus**

ignorant, not know **nescio, nescire, nescivi, nescitus**

ill, sick **aeger, aegra, aegrum**

immortal **immortalis, immortale**

in, on; into, onto **in**

in front of, before **ante**

in front of; instead of; for, on behalf of **pro**

in that place, there **ibi**

in the country **ruri**

in the presence of, among **apud**

in truth, truly **vero**

incite, arouse, stir up **incito, incitare, incitavi, incitatus**

increase, enlarge **augeo, augere, auxi, auctus**

indeed, certainly, surely **certe**

indicates a question **-ne**

indicates a question expecting the answer "no"; whether **num**

indicates a question expecting the answer "yes" **nonne**

inhabitant **incola, incolae, m. or f.**

injury, mistreatment, outrage **contumelia, contumeliae, f.**

injury, harm **iniuria, iniuriae, f.**

instead of; in front of; for, on behalf of **pro**

into, onto; in, on **in**

island **insula, insulae, f.**

it, he, she; that **is, ea, id**

it, him, her (reflexive) **se**

it is right, it is proper (Impersonal verb) **oportet, oportere, oportuit**

Italy **Italia, Italiae, f.**

its, his, her, their **suus, sua, suum**

itself, himself, herself; very **ipse, ipsa, ipsum**

J

January, of January **Ianuarius, Ianuaria, Ianuarium**

journey, march, way **iter, intineris, n.**

joy **gaudium, gaudii or gaudi, n.**

judge, think **arbitror, arbitrari, arbitratus sum**

judge, think **existimo, existimare, existimavi, existimatus**

judge, sentence, examine **iudico, iudicare, iudicavi, iudicatus**

judgment, sentence **iudicium, iudicii, or iudici, n.**

Julia **Iulia, Iuliae, f.**

Julian, of Julius of July **Iulius, Iulia, Iulium**

June, of June **Iunius, Iunia, Iunium**

Juno **Iuno, Iunonis, f.**
Jupiter **Iuppiter, Iovis, m.**

K

Kalends **Kalendae, Kalendarum, f. pl.**
keen, sharp, active **acer, acris, acre**
keep, have, hold **teneo, tenere, tenui, tentus**
keep, hold together, limit, enclose, repress **contendo, contendere, contendi, contentus**
keep back, retain **retineo, retinere, retinui, retentus**
keep off, hinder, prohibit, prevent **prohibeo, prohibere, prohibui, prohibitus**
keep safe, preserve **conservo, conservare, conservavi, conservatus**
kill **interficio, interficere, interfeci, interfectus**
kill **neco, necare, necavi, necatus**
kind, class **genus, generis, n.**
kindness, benevolence, goodness **bonitas, bonitatis, f.**
king **rex, regis, m.**
kingdom **regnum, regni, n.**
knight, horseman **eques, equitis, m.**
know, learn, recognize **cognosco, cognoscere, cognovi, cognitus**
know **scio, scire, scivi, scitus**

L

labor, work, toil **labor, laboris, m.**
labyrinth, maze **labyrinthus, labyrinthi, m.**
lack, be without, be absent from **careo, carere, carui, caritus**
land, earth **terra, terrae, f.**
language **lingua, linguae, f.**
larger **maior, maius**
largest **maximus, maxima, maximum**

last, finally **postremus, postrema, postremum**
last, farthest **ultimus, ultima, ultimum**
Latin **latinus, latina, latinum**
Latinus **Latinus, Latini, m.**
Latium **Latium, Lati, n.**
Latobrigi **Latobrigi, Latobrigorum, m. pl.**
latter, this; he, she, it **hic, haec, hoc**
law **lex, legis, f.**
lead **duco, ducere, duxi, ductus**
lead back **reduco, reducere, reduxi, reductus**
lead out **educo, educere, eduxi, eductus**
leader **dux, ducis, m.**
leader, head **caput, capitis, n.**
leader, chief, emperor **princeps, principis, m.**
Leander **Leander, Leandri, m.**
learn, recognize, know **cognosco, cognoscere, cognovi, cognitus**
learn, ascertain **comperio, comperire, comperi, compertus**
learn **disco, discere, didici**
learn, find out **rescisco, resciscere, rescii, rescitus**
least of all, by no means, not at all **minime**
leave, withdraw, go away **discedo, discedere, discessi, discessus**
leave, leave behind **relinquo, relinquere, reliqui, relictus**
legate, lieutenant **legatus, legati, m.**
legion **legio, legionis, f.**
lest, that not **ne**
letter **epistola, epistolae, f.**
letter **littera, litterae, f.**
level, equal, fair **aequus, aequa, aequum**
lieutenant, legate **legatus, legati, m.**
life **vita, vitae, f.**
light **lux, lucis, f.**

like, love **amo, amare, amavi, amatus**
like, similar **similis**
limit, hold together, enclose, keep, repress **contendo, contendere, contendi, contentus**
linger, stay, remain, abide **commoror, commorari, commoratus sum**
little, a little **paulo**
live, dwell **habito, habitare, habitavi, habitatus**
live **vivo, vivere, vixi, victus**
live in, reside **incolo, incolere, incolui**
long, for a long time **diu**
long **longus, longa, longum**
longing, loss, need **desiderium, desiderii or desideri, n.**
look, sight **aspectus, aspectus, m.**
look for, collect **conquiro, conquirere, conquisivi, conquisitus**
look for, seek; attack **peto, petere, petivi or petii, petitus**
look for, ask **quaero, quaerere, quaesivi, quaesitus**
lose, send away **amitto, amittere, amisi, amissus**
lose one's way, be mistaken, wander **erro, errare, erravi, erratus**
loss, longing, loss **desiderium, desiderii or desideri, n.**
love **amor, amoris, m.**
love, like **amo, amare, amavi, amatus**
love, value **diligo, diligere, dilexi, delectus**
luck, fortune, fate **fortuna, fortunae, f.**

M

make, do **facio, facere, feci, factus**
make clear, reveal **illustro, illustrare, illustravi, illustratus**
make firm, strengthen **firmo, firmare, firmavi, firmatus**

make known, speak out, reveal **enuntio, enuntiare, enuntiavi, enuntiatus**

man **homo, hominis, m.**

man **vir, viri, m.**

manage, control, rule **administro, administrare, administravi, administratus**

manner, fashion, reason **ratio, rationis, f.**

manner, way **modus, modi, m.**

manner, way **pactum, pacti, n.**

Marathon, of Marathon **Marathonius, Marathonia, Marathonium**

march, journey, way **iter, intineris, n.**

March, of March, of Mars **Martius, Martia, Martium**

market place, forum **forum, fori, n.**

marriage **matrimonium, matrimonii or matrimoni, n.**

master **dominus, domini, m.**

matter, thing, affair **res, rei, f.**

May, of May **Maius, Maia, Maium**

maze, labyrinth **labyrinthus, labyrinthi, m.**

meanwhile **interea**

melt away, decay **tabesco, tabescere, tabescui or tabui**

memory **memoria, memoriae, f.**

Mercury **Mercurius, Mercuri, m.**

mercy, mildness, gentleness **lenitas, lenitatis, f.**

message, messenger **nuntius, nuntii or nunti, m.**

Midas **Midas, Midae, m.**

middle, middle of **medius, media, medium**

mildness, mercy, gentleness **lenitas, lenitatis, f.**

mile **mille passus**

miles **milia passuum**

mind, spirit **animus, animi, m.**

mind **mens, mentis, f.**

mine, my **meus, mea, meum**

Minos **Minos, Minois, m.**

Minotaur **Minotaurus, Minotauri, m.**

mistreatment, outrage, injury **contumelia, contumeliae, f.**

mistress **domina, dominae, f.**

mistrust, suspect **suspicio, suspicere, suspexi, suspectus**

moderately, modestly **modeste**

money **pecunia, pecuniae, f.**

moon **luna, lunae, f.**

more **magis**

more **plus, pluris**

more powerful **plus posse**

moreover, also **item**

morning, in the morning **mane**

mortal **mortalis, mortale**

most, especially **maxime**

most **plerusque, pleraque, plerumque**

most **plurimus, plurima, plurimum**

most powerful **plurimum posse**

most recent, next, nearest **proximus, proxima, proximum**

mother **mater, matris, f.**

mountain, mount **mons, montis, m.**

move **moveo, movere, movi, motus**

move, stir **permoveo, permovere, permovi, permotus**

much, by much **multo**

much **multus, multa, multum**

multitude, great number **multitudo, multitudinis, f.**

murder, slaughter **caedes, caedis, f.** (gen. pl. **caedium**)

murder, parricide, treason **parricidium, parricidii or parricidi, n.**

my, mine **meus, mea, meum**

N

name, address, call **appello, appellare, apellavi, appellatus**

name **nomen, nominis, n.**

narrow **angustus, angusta, angustum**

nation **natio, nationis, f.**

native country **patria, patriae, f.**

nature **natura, naturae, f.**

near **propinquus, propinqua, propinquum**

nearest, next, most recent **proximus, proxima, proximum**

nearly, almost **paene**

neatly, neatly, well **belle**

need, longing, loss **desiderium, desiderii or desideri, n.**

neighbor **finitimus, finitimi, m.**

neighboring **finitimus, finitima, finitimum**

neither . . . nor **neque . . . neque**

never **numquam**

nevertheless, however **tamen**

new **novus, nova, novum**

next, then **deinde**

next, following **posterus, postera, posterum**

next, following **postumus, postuma, postumum**

next, nearest, most recent **proximus, proxima, proximum**

Nicaea **Nicaea, Nicaeae, f.**

Nicomedia **Nicomedia, Nicomediae, f.**

night **nox, noctis, f.**

nine **novem**

no, none **nullus, nulla, nullum**

no one **nemo, neminis, m.**

Nones **Nonae, Nonarum, f. pl.**

not **non**

not at all, by no means, least of all **minime**

not enough, too little **parum**

not know, be ignorant **ignoro, ignorare, ignoravi, ignoratus**

not know, be ignorant of **nescio, nescire, nescivi, nescitus**

not want, wish not, be unwilling **nolo, nolle, nolui**

not working, free, at leisure **otiosus, otiosa, otiosum**

nothing **nihil, nil, n.**

November, of November **November, Novembris, Novembre**

now, already **iam**

now **nunc**

now that, because **quoniam**

number **numerus, numeri, m.**

O

obliterate, destroy **deleo, delere, delevi, deletus**

observe, catch sight of **conspicio, conspicere, conspexi, conspectus**

obtain, gain, reach **adsequor, adsequi, adsecutus sum**

obtain, secure **obtineo, obtinere, obtinui, obtentus**

ocean **oceanus, oceani, m.**

October, of October **October, Octobris, Octobre**

offend, wound **offendo, offendere, offendi, offensus**

offer, carry off, bring away, report **defero, deferre, detuli, delatus**

official job, official position **officium, officii or offici, n.**

often **saepe**

old, ancient **antiquus, antiqua, antiquum**

old, aged **senex, senis**

old, aged **vetus, veteris**

on the next day, day following **postridie**

on, in; onto, into **in**

on account of, because **ob**

on account of, because **propter**

on behalf of, for; in front of; instead of **pro**

on that account, therefore **propterea**

on the other hand, backward **rursus**

once, formerly **olim**

one **unus, una, unum**

one of two, the other **alter, altera, alterum**

only, alone **solum**

only, alone **solus, sola, solum**

onto, into; on, in **in**

open **apertus, aperta, apertum**

or **an, aut**

or **vel**

oracle **oraculum, oraculi, n.**

order, command **impero, imperare, imperavi, imperatus**

order, command **iubeo, iubere, iussi, iussus**

order, rank **ordo, ordinis, m.**

Orpheus **Orpheus, Orphei, m.**

other, another **alius, alia, aliud**

ought, owe **debeo, debere, debui, debitus**

our, ours **noster, nostra, nostrum**

out from, from **e, ex**

outrage, injury, mistreatment **contumelia, contumeliae, f.**

outstanding, excellent **egregius, egregia, egregium**

over, above **supra**

overcome, crush **opprimo, opprimere, oppressi, oppressus**

overcome, surpass, conquer **supero, superare, superavi, superatus**

owe, ought **debeo, debere, debui, debitus**

P

pace **passus, passus, m.**

pains, service, work **opera, operae, f.**

parent **parens, parentis, m. or f.**

parricide, murder, treason **parricidium, parricidii or parricidi, n.**

part **pars, partis, f. (gen. pl., partium)**

pass over, cross, desert **transeo, transire, transivi, transitus**

passion, fury, rage **furor, furoris, m.**

past, preceding, higher **superior, superius**

peace **pax, pacis, f.**

peninsula **paeninsula, paeninsulae, f.**

pension, yearly pay **annua, annuorum, n. pl.**

people **populus, populi, m.**

perceive, realize, feel **sentio, sentire, sensi, sensus**

perform, do **fungor, fungi, functus sum**

perhaps **fortasse**

perilous, dangerous **periculosus, periculosa, periculosum**

permit, allow **permitto, permittere, permisi, permissus**

perpetual, continuous, uninterrupted **perpetuus, perpetua, perpetuum**

Persians **Persae, Persarum, m. pl.**

personal enemy **inimicus, inimici, m.**

persuade **persuadeo, persuadere, persuasi, persuasus**

pity, sympathy **misercordia, misercordiae, f.**

pity, feel sorry for **misereor, misereri, miseritus sum**

place, station **conloco, conlocare, conlocavi, conlocatus**

place, put **loco, locare, locavi, locatus**

place **locus, loci, m.**

place, put **pono, ponere, posui, positus**

plan, advice **consilium, consilii or consili, n.**

pleasing **gratus, grata, gratum**

plege, faith **fides, fidei, f.**

plot, conspiracy **coniurati, coniurationis, f.**

plow **aro, arare, aravi, aratus**

plunder, booty **praeda, praedae, f.**

Pluto **Pluto, Plutonis, m.**

poet **poeta, poetae, m.**

point out, show **demonstro, demonstrare, demonstravi, demonstratus**

point out, show **monstro, monstrare, monstravi, monstratus**

Polyphemus **Polyphemus, Polyphemi, m.**

port, harbor **portus, portus, m.**

power, prestige, authority **auctoritas, auctoritatis, f.**

praise **laudo, laudare, laudavi, laudatus**

pray, beg **oro, orare, oravi, oratus**

preceding, higher, past **superior, superius**

prefer **malo, malle, malui**

prepare, get ready **paro, parare, paravi, paratus**

present, be here **adsum, adesse, adfui**

presence, effect **praesentia, praesentiae, f.**

presence of, among **apud**

present, gift **donum, doni, n.**

presently, soon **mox**

preserve, keep safe **conservo, conservare, conservavi, conservatus**

preserve, save **servo, servare, servavi, servatus**

prestige, power, authority **auctoritas, auctoritatis, f.**

pretend **simulo, simulare, simulavi, simulatus**

prettily, neatly, well **belle**

pretty, beautiful **pulcher, pulchra, pulchrum**

prevent, hinder, frighten off, deter **deterreo, deterrere, deterrui, deterritus**

prevent, keep off, hinder, prohibit **prohibeo, prohibere, prohibui, prohibitus**

previously, before **prius**

price **pretium, pretii or preti, n.**

prison **carcer, carceris, n.**

proclaim, cry aloud **clamito, clamitare, clamitavi, clamitatus**

produce, fruit **fructus, fructus, m.**

prohibit, keep off, hinder, prevent **prohibeo, prohibere, prohibui, prohibitus**

promise **polliceor, polliceri, pollicitus sum**

promise **pollicitatio, pollicitationis, f.**

Proserpina **Proserpina, Proserpinae, f.**

protect, defend **vindico, vindicare, vindicavi, vindicatus**

proud, haughty **superbus, superba, superbum**

province **provincia, provinciae, f.**

Psyche **Psyche, Psyches, f.**

public, common **communis, commune**

public, common **publicus, publica, publicum**

punishment, fine **poena, poenae, f.**

pursue, follow after **insequor, insequi, insecutus sum**

put, place **loco, locare, locavi, locatus**

put, place **pono, ponere, posui, positus**

put on, add **addo, addere, addidi, additus adfero, adferre, attuli, adlatus**

Pythia **Pythia, Pythiae, f.**

Q

queen **regina, reginae, f.**

question **-ne**

question expecting the answer "no"; whether **num**

question expecting the answer "yes" **nonne**

quick, swift **celer, celeris, celere**

quit, surpass, go beyond **egredior, egredi, egressus sum**

R

rage, fury, rage **furor, furoris, m.**

rank, order **ordo, ordinis, m.**

reach, gain, obtain **adsequor, adsequi, adsecutus sum**

reach, arrive at, come to **advenio, advenire, adveni, adventus**

read **lego, legere, legi, lectus**

realize, feel, perceive **sentio, sentire, sensi, sensus**

reason, cause **causa, causae, f.**

reason, manner, fashion **ratio, rationis, f.**

rebuild, restore **restituo, restituere, restitui, restitutus**

receive, take **accipio, accipere, accepi, acceptus**

receive, take back **recipio, recipere, recepi, receptus**

recognize, know, learn **cognosco, cognoscere, cognovi, cognitus**

recoil, fall **recido, recidere, reccidi**

reconcile, win, win over **concilio, conciliare, conciliavi, conciliatus**

reconcile, calm **placo, placare, placavi, placatus**

recover, get back **recupero, recuperare, recuperavi, recuperatus**

refuse, reject **recuso, recusare, recusavi, recusatus**

region, boundary **regio, regionis, f.**

rejoice **gaudeo, gaudere, gavisus sum**

relate, tell **narro, narrare, narravi, narratus**

relative, friend **necessaria, necessariae, f.**

relative, friend **necessarius, necessarii or necessari, m.**

release, free **exsolvo, exsolvere, exsolvi, exsolutus**

remain, linger, stay, abide **commoror, commorari, commoratus sum**

remain, stay **maneo, manere, mansi, mansus**

remaining, the rest of **reliquus, reliqua, reliquum**

remove, clean, excuse **purgo, purgare, purgavi, purgatus**

renown, rumor, report **fama, famae, f.**

repel, ward off, defend **defendo, defendere, defendi, defensus**

report, announce **nuntio, nuntiare, nuntiavi, nuntiatus**

report, bring back **refero, referre, retuli, relatus**

report, carry off, bring away, offer **defero, deferre, detuli, delatus**

report, rumor, renown **fama, famae, f.**

report **perfero, perferre, pertuli, perlatus**

repress, hold together, limit, enclose, keep **contendo, contendere, contendi, contentus**

republic, common good **res publica, rei publicae, f.**

reside, live in **incolo, incolere, incolui**

respected, honored **honestus, honesta, honestum**

rest of, remaining **reliquus, reliqua, reliquum**

restore, return **reddeo, reddere, reddidi, reditus**

restore, rebuild **restituo, restituere, restitui, restitutus**

retain, keep back **retineo, retinere, retinui, retentus**

return, turn back **revertor, reverti, reversus sum**

reveal, speak out, make known **enuntio, enuntiare, enuntiavi, enuntiatus**

reveal, make clear **illustro, illustrare, illustravi, illustratus**

reward **praemium, praemii or praemi, n.**

Rhine **Rhenus, Rheni, m.**

rich **dives, divitis**

right, authority **ius, iuris, n.**

river **flumen, fluminis, n.**

river bank **ripa, ripae, f.**

road, way, street **via, viae, f.**

robust, strong **robustus, robusta, robustum**

rock, stone **saxum, saxi, n.**

Roman **Romanus, Romana, Romanum**

Roman **Romanus, Romani, m.**

Rome **Roma, Romae, f.**

rule, manage, control **administro, administrare, administravi, administratus**

rule **regno, regnare, regnavi, regnatus**

rule **rego, regere, rexi, rectus**

rumor, renown, report **fama, famae, f.**

run **curro, currere, cucurri, cursus**

run away, escape, flee **fugio, fugere, fugi, fugitus**

run away, flee, escape **profugio, profugere, profugi**

S

Sabines **Sabini, Sabinorum, m. pl.**

safe, well **salvus, salva, salvum**

safety, health **salus, salutis, f.**

sail, cruise **navigo, navigare, navigavi, navigatus**

sailor **nauta, nautae, m.**

same; he, she, it **idem, eadem, idem**

sand, arena **arena, arenae, f.**

savage, uncivilized, barbarian **barbarus, barbara, barbarum**

save, preserve **servo, servare, servavi, servatus**

say, speak **dico, dicere, dixi, dictus**

say, speak **loquor, loqui, locutus sum**

say, declare, acknowledge **profiteor, profiteri, professus sum**

scarcity, want **inopia, inopiae, f.**

scare, frighten, terrify **terreo, terrere, terrui, territus**

school, game **ludus, ludi, m.**

sea **mare, maris, n.** (gen. pl. **marium**)

secret, hidden **clandestinus, clandestina, clandestinum**

secure, obtain **obtineo, obtinere, obtinui, obtentus**

see **video, videre, vidi, visus**

seek, look for; attack **peto, petere, petivi or petii, petitus**

seize, capture, take **capio, capere, cepi, captus**

seize, discover, apprehend **comprehendo, comprehendere, comprehendi, comprehensus**

seize, take possession of **occupo, occupare, occupavi, occupatus**

select, choose **deligo, deligere, delegi, delectus**

senate **senatus, senatus, m.**

send **mitto, mittere, misi, missus**

send away, lose **amitto, amittere, amisi, amissus**

sense, sensation, feeling **sensus, sensus, m.**

sentence, judgment **iudicium, iudicii, or iudici, n.**

sentence, judge, examine **iudico, iudicare, iudicavi, iudicatus**

September, of September **September, Septembris, Septembre**

serious, heavy, severe **gravis, grave**

serpent, snake **serpens, serpentis, f.**

servant, slave **servus, servi, m.**

service, work **ministerium, ministerii or ministeri, n.**

service, work, pains **opera, operae, f.**

set fire to, burn **incendo, incendere, incendi, incensus**

set forth, exhibit, explain **expono, exponere, exposui, expositus**

set free **in libertatem vindicare**

set free, free **libero, liberare, liberavi, liberatus**

seven **septem**

seventh **septimus, septima, septimum**

severe, serious, heavy **gravis, grave**

severity, strictness **severitas, severitatis, f.**

sharp, active, keen **acer, acris, acre**

she, he, it; that **is, ea, id**

sheep **ovis, ovis, f.**

ship **navis, navis, f.**

short, brief **brevis, breve**

shoulder **umerus, umeri, m.**

shout, cry **clamo, clamare, clamavi, clamatus**

show, point out **demonstro, demonstrare, demonstravi, demonstratus**

show, point out **monstro, monstrare, monstravi, monstratus**

show, teach **doceo, docere, docui, doctus**

shut off, stop **intercludo, intercludere, interclusi, interclusus**

Sibylline **Sibyllinus, Sibyllina, Sibyllinum**

sick, ill **aeger, aegra, aegrum**

sight, look **aspectus, aspectus, m.**

sight, view **conspectus, conspectus, m.**

signal, standard **signum, signi, n.**

silence **taciturnitas, taciturnitatis, f.**

Silenus **Silenus, Sileni, m.**

similar, like **similes, simile**

since, when, while, although; with **cum**

sister **soror, sororis, f.**

six **sex**

sky, heaven **caelum, caeli, n.**

slaughter, murder **caedes, caedis, f. (gen. pl. caedium)**

slave, servant **servus, servi, m.**

sleep **dormio, dormire, dormivi, dormitus**

sleep **somnus, somni, m.**

small **parvus, parva, parvum**

smaller **minor, minus**

smallest **minimus, minima, minimum**

snake, serpent **serpens, serpentis, f.**

so, thus; yes **ita**

so, thus **sic**

so **tam**

so great **tantus, tanta, tantum**

so many **tot**

so that, that; as **ut, uti**

soldier **miles, militis, m.**

some (pl.); certain one **quidam, quaedam, quiddam**

someone, something; anyone, anything **aliquis, aliquid**

son **filius, filii or fili, m.**

soon, presently **mox**

sorry, be sorry; grieve **doleo, dolere, dolui, dolitus**

Spain **Hispania, Hispaniae, f.**

Sparta **Sparta, Spartae, f.**

speak, say **dico, dicere, dixi, dictus**

speak, say **loquor, loqui, locutus sum**

speak out, reveal, make known **enuntio, enuntiare, enuntiavi, enuntiatus**

speak with **colloquor, colloqui, collocutus sum**

speed, swiftness **celeritas, celeritatis, f.**

spend, use up, consume **consumo, consumere, consumpsi, consumptus**

spirit, mind **animus, animi, m.**

spring, fountain **fons, fontis, m.**

stand **sto, stare, steti, status**

standard, signal **signum, signi, n.**

star **stella, stellae, f.**

start, beginning **initium, initii or initi, n.**

state **civitas, civitatis, f.**

station, place **conloco, conlocare, conlocavi, conlocatus**

stay, linger, remain, abide **commoror, commorari, commoratus sum**

stay, remain **maneo, manere, mansi, mansus**

stir, move **permoveo, permovere, permovi, permotus**

stir up, arouse **excito, excitare, excitavi, excitatus**

stir up, arouse, incite **incito, incitare, incitavi, incitatus**

stone, rock **saxum, saxi, n.**

stop, cease, desist **desisto, desistere, destiti, destitus**

stop, shut off **intercludo, intercludere, interclusi, interclusus**

storm, bad weather **tempestas, tempestatis, f.**

story **fabula, fabulae, f.**

street, road, way **via, viae, f.**

street, village **vicus, vici, m.**

strengthen, affirm, assert **adfirmo, adfirmare, adfirmavi, adfirmatus**

strengthen, confirm, establish **confirmo, confirmare, confirmavi, confirmatus**

strengthen, make firm **firmo, firmare, firmavi, firmatus**

strictness, severity **severitas, severitatis, f.**

strong, firm **firmus, firma, firmum**

strong, brave **fortis, forte**

strong, robust **robustus, robusta, robustum**

suffer, allow, grant **patior, pati, passus sum**

suitable, fit **idoneus, idonea, idoneum**

summer **aestas, aestatis, f.**

sun **sol, solis, m.**

superior to, be better than **praesto, praestare, praestavi, praestatus**

supply, abundance **copia, coipiae, f.**

support, to agree, added, to approach **accedo, accedere, accessi, accessurus**

suppose, think **opinor, opinari, opinatus sum**

sure, certain **certus, certa, certum**

surely, certainly, indeed **certe**

surpass, quit, go beyond **egredior, egredi, egressus sum**

surpass, overcome, conquer **supero, superare, superavi, superatus**

surrender **deditio, deditionis, f.**

surrender, give up **dedo, dedere, dedidi, deditus**

surrender, give up **trado, tradere, tradidi, traditus**

suspect, mistrust **suspicio, suspicere, suspexi, suspectus**

swear **iureiuro, iureiurare, iureiuravi, iureiuratus**

sweet **dulcis, dulce**

swift, quick **celer, celeris, celere**

swiftness, speed **celeritas, celeritatis, f.**

swim **nato, natare, natavi, natatus**

sword **gladius, gladii or gladi, m.**

sympathy, pity **misercordia, misercordiae, f.**

T

take, capture, seize **capio, capere, cepi, captus**

take back, receive **recipio, recipere, recepi, receptus**

take possession of, seize **occupo, occupare, occupavi, occupatus**

take up, undertake **suscipio, suscipere, suscepi, susceptus**

Tarquinius **Tarquinius, Tarquini, m.**

teach, show **doceo, docere, docui, doctus**

tell, relate **narro, narrare, narravi, narratus**

temperately, frugally **frugaliter**

temple **templum, templi, n.**

ten **decem**

terrify, frighten, scare **terreo, terrere, terrui, territus**

territory **fines, finium, m. pl.**

test, try **experior, experiri, experitus sum**

than; as possible **quam**

that; the former; he, she, it **ille, illa, illud**

that; he, she, it **is, ea, id**

that, that one of yours **iste, ista, istud**

that, who, which; which, what **qui, quae, quod**

that, so that; as **ut, uti**

that not, lest **ne**

their, his, her, its **suus, sua, suum**

then, at that time **tum**

then, next **deinde**

there, in that place **ibi**

therefore, and so **itaque**

therefore, on that account **propterea**

therefore, by what means, how, wherefore **quare**

Thermopylae **Thermopylae, Thermopylarum, f. pl.**

Theseus **Theseus, Thesei, m.**

thing, matter, affair **res, rei, f.**

think, judge **arbitror, arbitrari, arbitratus sum**

think, consider **cogito, cogitare, cogitavi, cogatatus**

think, judge **existimo, existimare, existimavi, existimatus**

think, suppose **opinor, opinari, opinatus sum**

think, believe **puto, putare, putavi, putatus**

this, the latter; he, she, it **hic, haec, hoc**

thousand **mille**

threatening, dangerous, hostile **infestus, infesta, infestum**

through **per**

throw **iacio, iacere, ieci, iactus**

throw open, bring to light **patefacio, patefacere, patefeci, patefactus**

thus, so; yes **ita**

thus, so **sic**

time **tempus, temporis, n.**

timid **timidus, timida, timidum**

to, towards **ad**

to this place, hither **huc**

today **hodie**

toil, work, labor **labor, laboris, m.**

tomorrow **cras**

too little, not enough **parum**

too much, very much **nimis**

top of, greatest, highest **summus, summa, summum**

touch **tango, tangere, tetigi, tactus**

tower **turris, turris, f.**

town **oppidum, oppidi, n.**

train, draw up, form **instruo, instruere, instruxi, instructus**

treason, parricide, murder **parricidium, parricidii or parricidi, n.**

tree **arbor, arboris, f.**

troops **copiae, copiarum, f. pl.**

Troy **Troia, Troiae, f.**

truly, in truth **vero**

trust, believe **credo, credere, credidi, creditus**

trust, believe, confide **fido, fidere, fisus sum**

try, attempt **conor, conari, conatus sum**

try, test **experior, experiri, experitus sum**

Tulingi **Tulingi, Tulingorum, m. pl.**

turn **verto, vertere, verti, versus**

turn back, return **revertor, reverti, reversus sum**

twelve **duodecim**

twice **bis**

U

Ulysses **Ulixes, Ulixis, m.**

uncertain, be uncertain, doubt, hesitate **dubito, dubitare, dubitavi, dubitatus**

uncertain, doubtful **dubius, dubia, dubium**

uncivilized, barbarian, savage **barbarus, barbara, barbarum**

uncle **avunculus, avunculi, m.**

under **sub**

understand **intelligo, intelligere, intellexi, intellectus**

undertake, take up **suscipio, suscipere, suscepi, susceptus**

unfriendly **inimicus, inimica, inimicum**

unhappy, wretched **miser, misera, miserum**

uninterrupted, continuous, perpetual **perpetuus, perpetua, perpetuum**

unless, if not **nisi**

until **donec**

urge, encourage **hortor, hortari, hortatus sum**

use up, consume, spend **consumo, consumere, consumpsi, consumptus**

useful **utilis, utile**

useless, harmful **inutilis, inutile**

usual, usual **cotidianus, cotidiana, cotidianum**

V

value, love **diligo, diligere, dilexi, delectus**

vastness, greatness **magnitudo, magnitudinis, f.**

Venus **Venus, Veneris, f.**

very; himself, herself, itself **ipse, ipsa, ipsum**

very much, too much **nimis**

victory **victoria, victoriae, f.**

view, sight **conspectus, conspectus, m.**

village, street **vicus, vici, m.**

violently, eagerly **vehementer**

voice **vox, vocis, f.**

W

wage, carry on **gero, gerere, gessi, gestus**

wait for, await, expect **exspecto, exspectare, exspectavi, exspectatus**

walk **ambulo, ambulare, ambulavi, ambulatus**

wall **murus, muri, m.**

wander, be mistaken, lose one's way **erro, errare, erravi, erratus**

want, desire, wish **cupio, cupere, cupivi, cupitus**

want, scarcity **inopia, inopiae, f.**

war **bellum, belli, n.**

ward off, repel, defend **defendo, defendere, defendi, defensus**

warn, advise **moneo, monere, monui, monitus**

water **aqua, aquae, f.**

wax **cera, cerae, f.**

way, journey, march **iter, intineris, n.**

way, manner **modus, modi, m.**

way, manner **pactum, pacti, n.**

way, road, street **via, viae, f.**

we **nos, nostrum**

weapon **telum, teli, n.**

weapons, arms **arma, armae, n. pl.**

weight, burden **onus, oneris, n.**

welcome, greet **saluto, salutare, salutavi, salutatus**

well **bene**

well, neatly, prettily **belle**

well, safe **salvus, salva, salvum**

west wind, Zephyr **Zephyrus, Zephyri, m.**

what, who **quis, quid**

when, while, since, although; with **cum**

when, after **postquam**

whence, from where **unde**

where, when **ubi**

wherefore, by what means, how, therefore **quare**

whether; indicates a question expecting the answer "no" **num**

which, what; who, which, that **qui, quae, quod**

while, when, since, although; with **cum**

while **dum**

who, which, that; which, what **qui, quae, quod**

who, what **quis, quid**

whole, all **totus, tota, totum**

why **cur**

wide **latus, lata, latum**

wife **uxor, uxoris, f.**

win, win over, reconcile **concilio, conciliare, conciliavi, conciliatus**

wind **ventus, venti, m.**

wing **ala, alae, f.**

winter **hiems, hiemis, f.**

wisdom **sapientia, sapientiae, f.**

wish, desire, want **cupio, cupere, cupivi, cupitus**

wish, be willing **volo, velle, volui**

wish not, be unwilling, not want **nolo, nolle, nolui**

with; when, while, since, although **cum**

with pleasure, gladly **libenter**

withdraw, go away, yield **cedo, cedere, cessi, cessus**

withdraw, allow, grant **concedo, concedere, concessi, concessum**

withdraw, go away, leave **discedo, discedere, discessi, discessus**

without **sine**

wolf **lupa, lupae, f.** or **lupus, lupi, m.**

woman **femina, feminae, f.**

woman **mulier, mulieris, f.**

woods, forest **silva, silvae, f.**

wool **lana, lanae, f.**

word **verbum, verbi, n.**

work, toil, labor **labor, laboris, m.**

work **laboro, laborare, laboravi, laboratus**

work, service **ministerium, ministerii or ministeri, n.**

work, service, pains **opera, operae, f.**

work **opus, operis, n.**

worse **peior, peius**

worship, adore **adore, adorare, adoravi, adoratus**

worst **pessimus, pessima, pessimum**

would that, if only **utinam**

wound, offend **offendo, offendere, offendi, offensus**

wound, hurt **vulnero, vulnerare, vulneravi, vulneratus**

wound **vulnus, vulneris, n.**

wretched, unhappy **miser, misera, miserum**

write **scribo, scribere, scripsi, scriptus**

Y

year **annus, anni, m.**

yearly pay, pension **annua, annuorum, n. pl.**

yes; thus, so **ita**

yesterday **hesternus, hesterna, hesternum**

yield, go away, withdraw **cedo, cedere, cessi, cessus**

you (sing.) **tu, tui**

you (pl.) **vos, vestrum**

your, yours **tuus, tua, tuum**

your, yours **vester, vestra, vestrum**

youth **adulescens, adulescentis, m.**

Z

zeal, eagerness **studium, studii or studi, n.**

Zephyr, west wind **Zephyrus, Zephyri, m.**